PARTY WARS

THE JULIAN J. ROTHBAUM DISTINGUISHED LECTURE SERIES

PARTY WARS

Polarization and the Politics of National Policy Making

BARBARA SINCLAIR

UNIVERSITY OF OKLAHOMA PRESS : NORMAN

Also by Barbara Sinclair

The Women's Movement: Political, Socioeconomic, and Psychological Issues (New York, 1975, 1979, 1983)
Congressional Realignment, 1925–1978 (Austin, 1982)
Majority Leadership in the U.S. House (Baltimore, 1983)
The Transformation of the U.S. Senate (Baltimore, 1989)
Legislators, Leaders, and Lawmaking: The House of Representatives in the Postreform Era (Baltimore, 1995)
Unorthodox Lawmaking: New Legislative Processes in the U.S. Congress (Washington, D.C., 1997, 2000)

This book was researched and written with the generous assistance of the Marvin Hoffenberg Chair endowment.

Library of Congress Cataloging-in-Publication Data

Sinclair, Barbara, 1940–
Party wars : polarization and the politics of national policy making / Barbara Sinclair.
p. cm. — (The Julian J. Rothbaum distinguished lecture series ; v. 10)
Includes bibliographical references and index.
ISBN 0-8061-3756-8 (alk. paper) — ISBN 0-8061-3779-7 (pbk. : alk. paper)
1. Political parties—United States. 2. Party affiliation—United States. 3. United States—Politics and government. I. Title. II. Series.

JK2261.S49 2006
324.273—dc22

2005052992

Party Wars: Polarization and the Politics of National Policy Making is Volume 10 in The Julian J. Rothbaum Distinguished Lecture Series.

The paper in this book meets the guidelines for permanence and durability of the Committee on Production Guidelines for Book Longevity of the Council on Library Resources, Inc. ∞

1 2 3 4 5 6 7 8 9 10

To Lucy, Carl, and Terry

CONTENTS

TABLES

FIGURES

FOREWORD

JULIAN J. ROTHBAUM LECTURE SERIES

Among the many good things that have happened to me in my life, there is none in which I take more pride than the establishment of the Carl Albert Congressional Research and Studies Center at the University of Oklahoma, and none in which I take more satisfaction than the Center's presentation of the Julian J. Rothbaum Distinguished Lecture Series. The series is a perpetually endowed program of the University of Oklahoma, created in honor of Julian J. Rothbaum by his wife, Irene, and son, Joel Jankowsky.

Julian J. Rothbaum, my close friend since our childhood days in southeastern Oklahoma, has long been a leader in Oklahoma in civic affairs. He served as a Regent of the University of Oklahoma for two terms and as a State Regent for Higher Education. In 1974 he was awarded the University's highest honor, the Distinguished Service Citation, and in 1986 he was inducted into the Oklahoma Hall of Fame.

The Rothbaum Lecture Series is devoted to the themes of representative government, democracy and education, and citizen participation in pubic affairs, values to which Julian J. Rothbaum has been committed throughout his life. His lifelong dedication to the University of Oklahoma, the state, and his country is a tribute to the ideals to which the Rothbaum Lecture Series is dedicated. The books in the series make an enduring contribution to an understanding of American democracy.

CARL B. ALBERT

Forty-sixth Speaker of the
United States House of Representatives

PREFACE

In the summer of 2003, Congress made news not for what it did or did not pass, which is usually how it makes the front pages, but for how it was conducting its business. The story began with Bill Thomas, chairman of the powerful House Ways and Means Committee, releasing the Republican version of a long, complicated pension reform bill at about midnight on Thursday, July 17, and scheduling a vote in committee for the following morning.

When the committee met, Democrats, upset at not being given time to analyze the bill, insisted on it being read word for word. They then repaired to the committee library, where they locked themselves in, to examine the bill and plan strategy. Pete Stark, the second-ranking Democrat on the committee, was left behind in the committee room to keep the Republicans honest. Nevertheless Chairman Thomas asked unanimous consent to suspend the reading of the bill and to approve it, and though Stark claimed he objected, Thomas claimed he heard no objections. Stark then protested vehemently; Republican Scott McInnis told him to shut up; and Stark responded: "You think you are big enough to make me, you little wimp? Come on, come over here and make me, I dare you, you little fruitcake."

At some point, Thomas called the Capitol police to clear the Democrats out of the library. (When they refused his polite request that they leave, the cop sensibly decided that going further was way over his pay grade and went back to headquarters for instructions.) Republicans claimed that Thomas had called the police not to eject the Democrats from the library but because he feared that the seventy-one-year-old Stark would attack and presumably injure the fortyish McInnis, though Thomas later admitted he had asked the police to clear the Democrats out of the library.[1]

That afternoon on the House floor, Democrats tried to pass a resolution expressing House disapproval of Thomas's conduct and instructing the committee to reconsider the bill. But after some more name calling—a committee Republican, seeking to justify the calling of the police, said of Stark: "I did not know whether [he] could control either his emotions or his bodily functions"—the resolution was defeated on a straight party-line vote.[2]

Members of one party calling the cops on their partisan opponents in the House is unusual. That was why it made the front pages across the country. Both Thomas and Stark are well known on the Hill for their short fuses. Yet the partisan hostility as well as the highly partisan decision making evident in this incident are not at all extraordinary. The atmosphere in contemporary Washington is intensely partisan and highly conflictual. And this is characteristic not just of the House, which does tend to be more rambunctious than the Senate; legislative decision making on the big issues tends to be partisan in the Senate, the White House, and the interest group community as well. Even the media have been affected.

We now have highly polarized politics, with polarization along partisan and ideological lines that largely coincide. That is, congressional Republicans are more uniformly conservative and Democrats more uniformly moderate and liberal than at any time during the past half century; the result is that most important policy and political fights pit most Democrats against most Republicans.

Combine that with narrow margins of party control, and the result is highly polarized, and often highly charged and even antagonistic, politics.

In this book, I explain how partisan polarization came about and examine its impact on the politics and process of lawmaking at the national level. Although my primary focus is on Congress, of necessity I bring in other political actors, especially the president and interest groups but also voters and party activists. My aim is to understand the contemporary politics of our national policy-making process, how we got to where we are, and what the consequences are.

In the first four chapters I trace the development of partisan polarization. I examine its roots in the electorate and in the activist core of the Republican Party. I show how House members' responses to polarization have altered the way in which the House functions and have thereby amplified the effects of polarization. In Chapters 5 and 6 I ask: What have been the consequences of partisan polarization for the policy process? And how and why have the consequences differed in the House and Senate? In the remaining chapters, I ask a series of still broader questions about how and why our politics have changed: What has been the impact of partisan polarization on the relationship between president and Congress in the policy-making process? Have the president and the congressional parties responded strategically to the changed political environment, and if so, how and with what effect? How has the Washington political world of interest groups, policy experts, and news media changed as a response to the hardening of partisanship? And with what consequences? To what extent and in what ways should we worry about the consequences of partisan polarization, and is there anything we can do about them?

In addition to the sources cited, this book is based on my observations and experiences in the office of the House Majority

Leader in 1978–79 as an American Political Science Association Congressional Fellow and in the office of the Speaker in 1987–88 on an informal basis and on the hundreds of interviews I conducted with members of Congress, their staffs, and informed observers over the course of my career. Interviews were conducted on a not-for-attribution basis. All unattributed quotations are from my interviews or from meetings I witnessed.

This book began as the Julian J. Rothbaum Lectures, which I delivered at the University of Oklahoma in October 2003. My sincere thanks to the Rothbaum family for their generosity in endowing this outstanding lecture series. I would especially like to acknowledge Joel Jankowsky, Julian Rothbaum's son, for his role and for helping to make my visit to Norman such a pleasure. My thanks go to the Carl Albert Center, the Department of Political Science, and especially Gary Copeland and Ron Peters for inviting me to give the lectures and for making my stay at Oklahoma so rewarding. As anyone who has had any dealings with the Carl Albert Center knows, I also owe a debt of gratitude to LaDonna Sullivan, who makes the most complicated arrangements look simple; guests feel pampered and yet as if they are no trouble at all.

Tom Mann of the Brookings Institution and Gary Jacobson of the University of California, San Diego, read an earlier version of the manuscript and gave me many helpful suggestions for improvement. I cannot thank them enough for their willingness to do so. Such distinguished senior scholars have enormous calls on their time; giving me some of it is a considerable act of kindness for which I am grateful. Of course, any failings that remain are my own and may well stem from my not having taken all their advice.

It has been a pleasure to work with John Drayton, director of the University of Oklahoma Press; Steven Baker, manuscript editor; and Sally Antrobus, who copyedited the manuscript.

To all the colleagues from whom I have learned over the years, to all the Washington folks—members of Congress, staffers, and other knowledgeable people—whom I have interviewed, and most especially to Dick Fenno and Jim Wright, thank you. Finally, to Howard, thanks for everything.

PARTY WARS

CHAPTER 1

FROM SAM RAYBURN TO NEWT GINGRICH:

The Development of the Partisan Congress

HOW DID THE CONGRESSIONAL parties of the Rayburn-McCormack-Albert era—the 1950s, 1960s, and early 1970s—become over the course of one generation, less than three decades, the congressional parties of Newt Gingrich and Tom DeLay? In the early 1970s, congressional parties were so uncohesive that many members of Congress voted more frequently with the opposition than with their own party colleagues; parties were so weak that respected commentators—David Broder, specifically—spoke of "the party being over." Yet by the 1990s, congressional Democrats and Republicans seemed to be segregated into hostile camps with very different and often diametrically conflicting ideas of what constitutes good public policy. Decision making in committee and on the floor now typically pits Republicans against Democrats. In the House, where that is possible, the majority party largely excludes the minority party from a meaningful role in legislating. Harsh exchanges, if not exactly name calling, are far from rare. The majority calls the cops on the minority.

How did this transformation come about?

CONGRESS POLARIZES

Sam Rayburn, a long-serving and highly respected Speaker of the House, used to instruct new members on his prescription for success: to get along, go along. By the early 1970s, the placid decade of the 1950s, Rayburn's heyday, was long gone. The cocoon of good feeling that enveloped Capitol Hill into the 1960s, according to Clem Miller, a member from 1959 to 1962, had been at least punctured by the battles over civil rights and then the Vietnam War. Yet to a considerable extent, the folkways and traditional modes of doing things persisted. Civility was the norm off and on the floor of the chambers. Members addressed one another as "the distinguished gentleman" and, as Speaker John McCormack explained, if they really didn't like each other as "the *very* distinguished gentleman." The floors of the chambers were forums of great decorum with never a hostile or pejorative phrase aimed at another member.

Certainly there were policy battles, but these were as likely to split members across as along party lines. In the 91st Congress (1969–70), for example, majorities of Democrats and Republicans voted on opposing sides on less than 30 percent of recorded House votes and on 36 percent of Senate votes. And even on those votes that pitted the parties against each other, members voted with their party colleagues only about 70 percent of the time. Party members, especially members of the majority Democratic Party, disagreed with one another on a great many issues—from civil rights to labor legislation, environmental issues, and the Vietnam War.

Friendships were about as likely to form across the aisle as within the party. After all, members of a party seldom met as such; Democrats, for example, held a caucus meeting of all House Democrats only once every two years at the beginning of a new Congress. And this meeting was largely devoted to ratifying organizational decisions actually made elsewhere. Members spent most of their time in committee and might well strike up close friendships there with opposition party members. Why not? Committees seldom split along partisan lines. Even the party leaders had cordial relationships with each other. Speaker Rayburn and Minority Leader Joe Martin were close friends. As late as the speakership of Tip O'Neill, O'Neill and Republican Leader Bob Michel were regular golfing buddies.

Fast forward to the 1990s. The cocoon of good feeling had been replaced by overt partisan hostility. Republicans accused Democrats of tyranny and corruption, of having created a "corrupt legislative process," of "trampling on minority rights . . . and stifling dissent."[1] A backbench Republican brought down a Democratic Speaker with such accusations and was rewarded by his party colleagues with the second-ranking leadership position. (This was, of course, Newt Gingrich; and he would eventually be severely damaged by similar no-holds-barred attacks by Democrats.) Partisan antagonism ran so high that it spilled over onto the floor, where according to a study by the Annenberg Public Policy Center, the rate of "name calling" and "vulgarity usage" skyrocketed.[2] And such studies do not even capture much of the antagonism on the floor and in committee. Early in the Clinton Administration, Dick Armey, then Republican Conference chairman, referred to Clinton as "*your* president." What members said about the other party off the floor was a good deal more incendiary.

Policy debates and voting alignments split along rather than across party lines. In the 104th Congress (1995–96), for example, two-thirds of the recorded votes in the House and Senate were party votes pitting a majority of Republicans against a majority of Democrats, and on those votes, the average Republican voted with party colleagues more than 90 percent of the time, while the average Democrat did so about 85 percent of the time. Members spent much more of their time with fellow party members; each of the party groups met at least weekly, and in addition members often worked on single-party task forces with their party colleagues. The House party leaders were golf buddies no more; in fact, they seldom spoke. Gingrich and Dick Gephardt,

TABLE 1.1
Party Voting in Congress by Decade

Decade	House Votes (%)	Senate Votes (%)
1970s (1969–80) 91st–96th	36	42
1980s (1981–90) 97th–101st	51	45
1990s on (1991–2004) 102nd–108th	54	57

Source: Compiled by the author from data in *Congressional Quarterly Almanacs*.
Note: Figures represent the percentage of all roll calls (recorded votes) on which a majority of Democrats voted against a majority of Republicans.

the Democratic leader, reportedly spoke personally only eight times in four years.[3]

Table 1.1 and figure 1.1 provide a systematic look at how congressional voting changed. Table 1.1 shows the percentage of all recorded votes on which a majority of Democrats voted against a majority of Republicans—what Congress watchers call party votes. It was low in the 1970s; on about two-thirds of recorded votes in the House and three-fifths in the Senate, majorities of Republicans and Democrats voted on the same side—either there was little controversy or members split along regional, ideological, or constituency-interest lines rather than party lines. In the House, party voting went up significantly in the 1980s and then further in the 1990s. In the Senate most of the increase occurred in the 1990s, to a level about as high as in the House.

A problem with party votes as indicators of partisan polarization is that they classify significantly different situations together;

FIGURE 1.1

Distance between the Parties on Partisan Votes, 1955–2004

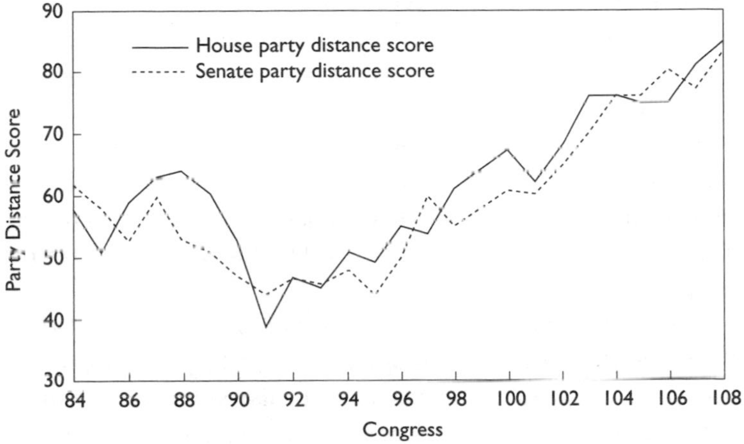

Party distance score = mean Dem Party voting score – (100 – mean Rep party voting score); party voting scores are derived from *Congressional Quarterly Almanacs*, 1955–2004.

90 percent of Democrats voting against 90 percent of Republicans constitutes a party vote, but so does 51 percent of Democrats voting against 51 percent of Republicans. Yet the level of partisanship is obviously very different in the two cases. We can calculate the frequency with which the average member of each party voted with his or her party colleagues to get a better sense of how cohesive the parties are. Since 1991, members of Congress have voted with their party colleagues between 85 and 90 percent on average. When we talk about party voting in the 1990s and beyond, we are really talking about almost all Republicans lined up in opposition to almost all Democrats.

These party voting scores can be used to construct a measure of the difference or distance between the parties. If on average 85 percent of Democrats voted against 90 percent of Republicans on party votes, then on average 10 percent of Republicans voted with the 85 percent of Democrats, and the difference between these figures (75 = 85 – 10) provides an indicator of the distance between the parties. Figure 1.1 depicts this measure for the House and the Senate over time. Clearly the distance has increased greatly in both chambers; that is, as the number of party votes increased, so did the cohesion of the parties on these votes. Note also that the House and Senate track each other closely; the increase in partisanship is not a one-chamber phenomenon. This becomes important when explanations for polarization are considered.

Still another perspective on what happened is provided by the Poole-Rosenthal DW-nominate scores.[4] These scores, which are based on all non-unanimous recorded votes, can be interpreted as locating members of Congress on a left-right dimension, and hence as a kind of ideology score. By ideology, here and throughout this book, I mean a consistent pattern of voting behavior that I assume is a function of the policy preferences of the member's constituency, of the member's personal policy preferences, and, though to a lesser extent, of other member goals, such as influence. That is, and most relevant here, ideology as measured by roll call voting is public behavior and can be seen as a reflection of members' (public) legislative preferences; it cannot be interpreted as a privately held "true" preference, though I do assume that members' true preferences, along with the other factors mentioned, influence their public behavior, their expressed preferences.

Figure 1.2 depicts the difference between the two parties' median scores and as such is a measure of the ideological distance between Democrats and Republicans. The figure clearly tells much the same story as the party voting figure; the parties in both chambers have diverged ideologically. The typical Democrat and the typical Republican are much more dissimilar now,

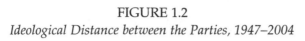

FIGURE 1.2

Ideological Distance between the Parties, 1947–2004

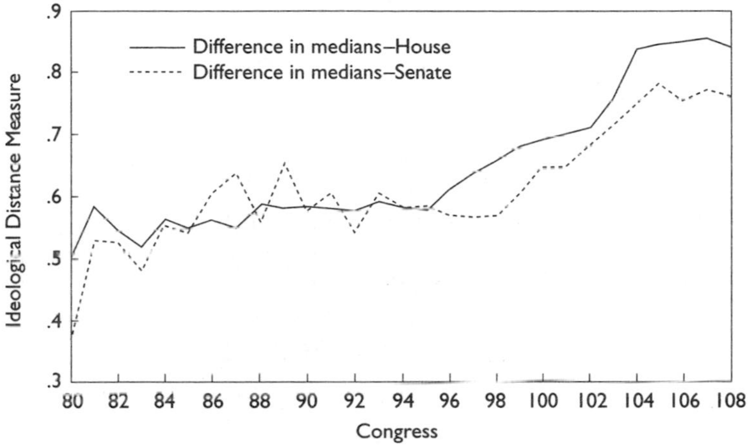

Ideological distance measure = difference between the parties' median DW-nominate scores

much further apart in their voting behavior, than they were thirty years ago.

Figure 1.3 shows the distribution of House members' and senators' DW-nominate scores in selected Congresses between the late 1960s and the early 2000s. These distributions depict the points I have already made: in the earlier Congresses, the typical Democrat and the typical Republican in both chambers were closer to each other, and each party's membership was quite spread out or heterogeneous in its voting patterns. By the 103rd Congress (1993–94) and even more so by the 107th (2001–2002), Republicans and Democrats were much further apart and each party's membership had grown considerably more similar or homogeneous.

Note especially the extent to which in the earlier Congresses, members of the two parties overlap in their voting behavior. In

FIGURE 1.3

Changing Distribution of DW-Nominate Scores over Time

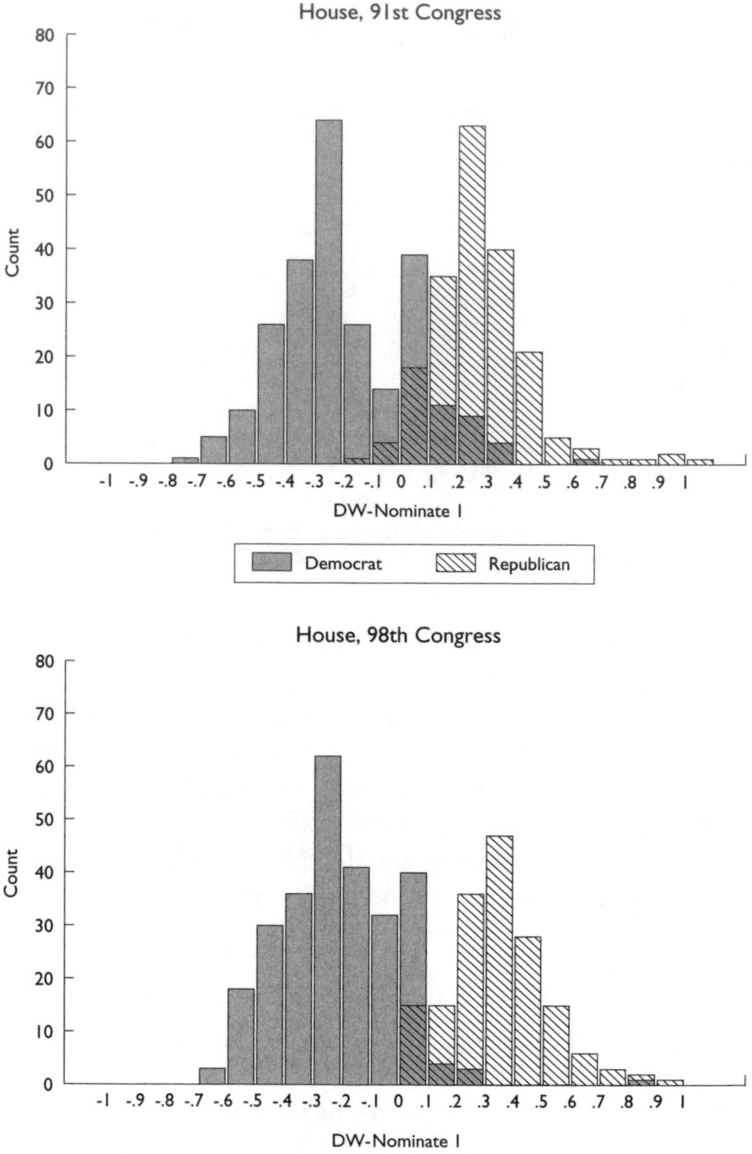

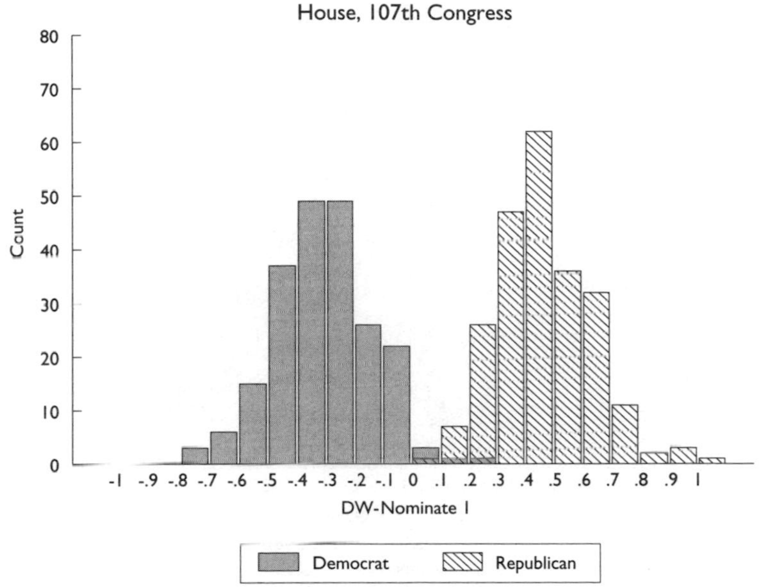
House, 107th Congress
80
70
60
50
40
30
20
10
0
Count
-1 -.9 -.8 -.7 -.6 -.5 -.4 -.3 -.2 -.1 0 .1 .2 .3 .4 .5 .6 .7 .8 .9 1
DW-Nominate 1
Democrat
Republican

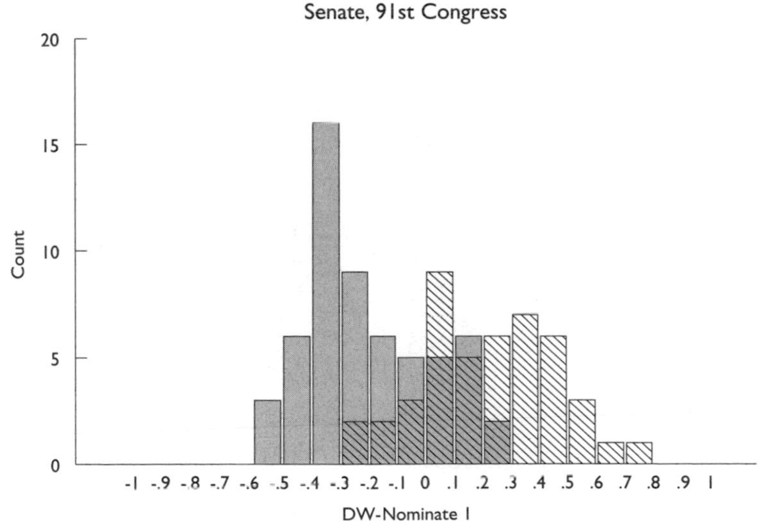
Senate, 91st Congress
20
15
10
5
0
Count
-1 -.9 -.8 -.7 -.6 -.5 -.4 -.3 -.2 -.1 0 .1 .2 .3 .4 .5 .6 .7 .8 .9 1
DW-Nominate 1

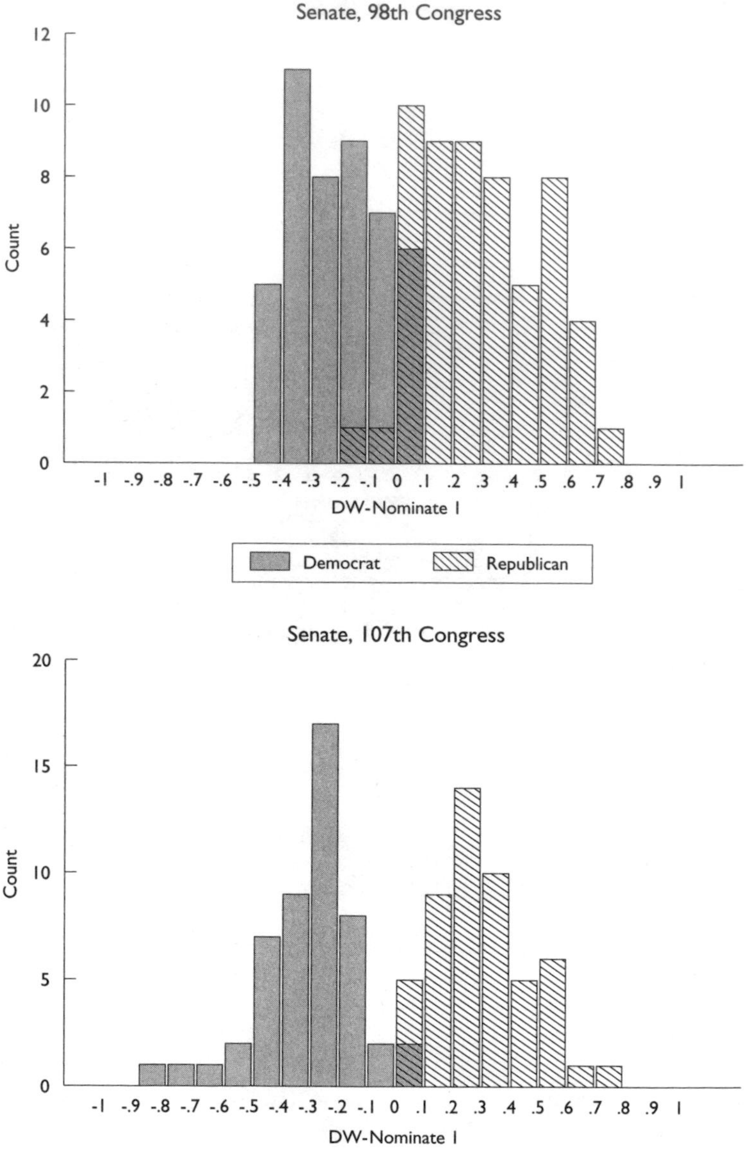
Senate, 98th Congress
Count
12
10
8
6
4
2
0
-1 -.9 -.8 -.7 -.6 -.5 -.4 -.3 -.2 -.1 0 .1 .2 .3 .4 .5 .6 .7 .8 .9 1
DW-Nominate 1
Democrat
Republican
Senate, 107th Congress
Count
20
15
10
5
0
-1 -.9 -.8 -.7 -.6 -.5 -.4 -.3 -.2 -.1 0 .1 .2 .3 .4 .5 .6 .7 .8 .9 1
DW-Nominate 1

the 91st House and Senate, a considerable number of De fell toward the conservative end of the continuum an number of Republicans toward the liberal end. Now, by trast, there is almost no overlap between the parties; the n conservative Democrat is to the left of almost all Republicans, and conversely, the most liberal Republican is to the right of almost all Democrats.[5] The one Republican to the left of the mean score for all House members in the 107th Congress, Connie Morella, who represented a liberal district in the Maryland suburbs of Washington, D.C., was defeated by a Democrat in the 2002 elections; the Democrat who was furthest to the right in the 107th—Ralph Hall of Texas—switched to the Republican Party in March 2004, in the middle of the 108th Congress. In the 108th, Hall was the only Democrat to the right of the most liberal Republican, and he was a Democrat for only about half of that Congress. In the Senate, the only Democrat to the right of any Republicans was Zell Miller of Georgia, who is no longer in the Senate; according to the DW-nominate scores, Miller was more conservative than four moderate Republicans—Olympia Snow and Susan Collins of Maine, Arlen Specter of Pennsylvania, and Lincoln Chafee of Rhode Island. Within each of the parties, then, members have become considerably more similar in their legislative preferences as measured by these ideology scores and by party voting scores; and, according to the same measures, the difference between the legislative preferences of the members of the two parties has greatly increased.

THE CONSTITUENCY CONNECTION

If the congressional parties of the 1990s and early twenty-first century are internally more homogeneous ideologically and also ideologically more distant from each other than they were thirty years ago, why did this happen? Political science does not yet have a consensus explanation, though elements of one are emerging.

The full story is seemingly fairly complicated, and in assembling it, scholars may well differ, at least in emphasis.

My explanation is a story in which voters, political activists, and politicians (including members of Congress) all play significant roles. I proceed from the assumption that members of Congress—and other elected politicians as well—respond to and try to please those in their environment who significantly affect whether they will get what they want. What do members of Congress want? Following Fenno, I argue that members have multiple goals; they want reelection, influence in their chamber and perhaps in the wider Washington political community, and good public policy.[6] Most members, I contend, do care about policy, and many also want to attain influence. However, as reelection is a prerequisite for the realization of a member's other goals, electoral considerations take priority in a member's calculus when they are seriously at issue.

In this chapter I focus on the external, mostly electoral, roots and engines of congressional partisan polarization. In chapter 3, I argue that House members' reactions have channeled and amplified the effects of changes in the electoral environment.

Realignment in the South

The best-known part of the story, and the part on which everyone largely agrees, has to do with change in the South. In the 1950s there were almost no Republicans elected to the House from what was then called the solid South—the states of the old Confederacy minus the border state of Tennessee. And there were zero senators (see figure 1.4). John Tower was the first Republican elected to the Senate from the states of the old Confederacy in the twentieth century, and his election was something of a fluke. When Lyndon B. Johnson became vice president in 1961, a special election was called to replace him in the Senate. The huge number of Democrats running split the vote and enabled

FIGURE 1.4

Southern Republicans in the House and Senate, 1947–2006

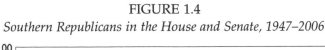

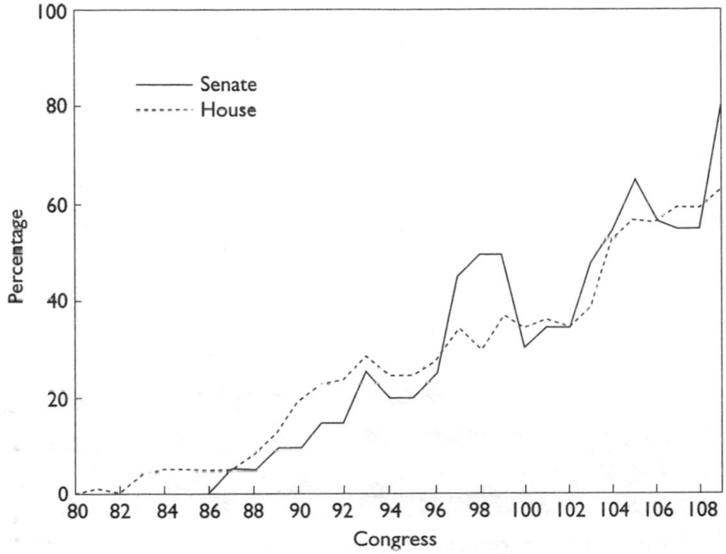

Tower, the sole Republican, to finish first in the free-for-all initial election; in the runoff, Texas liberals refused to support the extremely conservative Democrat who had finished second, and Tower won the seat.[7]

The first time the number of House Republicans broke into the double digits—and there were approximately one hundred southern representatives—was in the mid-1960s. With the passage of the Civil Rights Act in 1964 and the Republican nomination of Barry Goldwater, a staunch conservative who had voted against the act, significant numbers of southerners began to break away from their long-standing loyalty to the Democratic Party. Although Johnson won by a landslide nationally, Goldwater carried four Deep South states, and Republicans picked up seven new House seats in the South, for a net gain of five and a total of twelve seats.[8]

In 1966, Republicans won twenty seats. Yet, despite these breakthroughs, Democrats continued to predominate in Congress through the 1970s.

Contrast that with the situation now. Republicans have constituted considerably more than half of the House members and of the senators from the South since the 104th Congress elected in 1994. In the 104th, four of the ten southern states had majority Republican House delegations; in the 108th and 109th (2003–2006), seven of the ten did, and one was evenly split. Only Arkansas consistently elects more Democrats than Republicans to the House. The 2004 elections reduced the number of Democratic senators from the South to four and increased the number of Republicans to sixteen.

Since most southern Democrats were on the conservative end of their party, when a Republican replaced a southern Democrat in Congress, the result was to make the congressional Democratic Party less conservative and, as these southern Republicans were often highly conservative, to make the congressional Republican Party more conservative. Sean Theriault and Michael McDonald and Bernard Grofman in separate studies estimate that about a third of the increase in partisan polarization between the early 1970s and the late 1990s is due to the replacement of southern Democrats by Republicans.[9]

A major party realignment occurred in the South; the region went from almost totally Democratic—in voter allegiance (party identification), in voter behavior, and in congressional representation—to an increasing Republican advantage. In the 1950s and before, almost everyone in the South thought of himself or herself as a Democrat; according to the 1952 National Election Study, 79 percent of native white southerners identified themselves as Democrats and only 9 percent as Republicans.[10] Few Blacks could vote, and turnout among whites was low; most whites who did vote were conservative, and the result was the election of

FIGURE 1.5

Republican Presidential and Congressional Vote in the South, 1952–2002

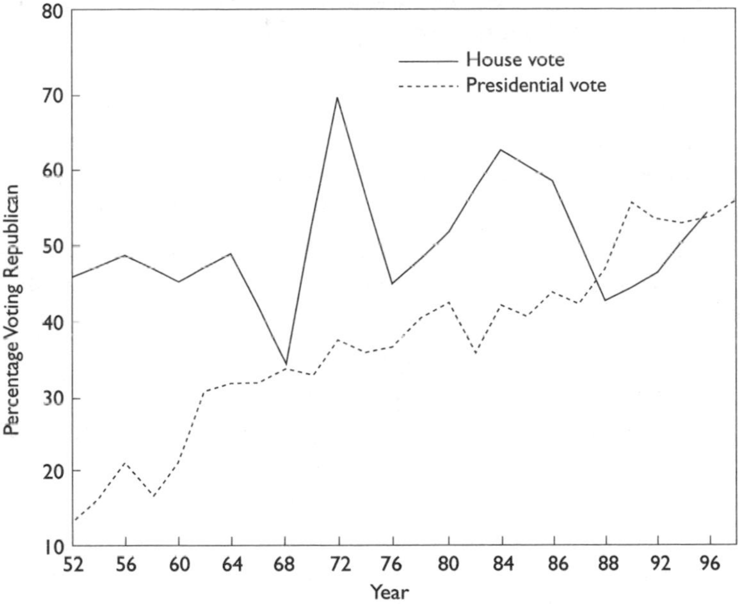

predominantly conservative Democrats to Congress. And, of course, these members—and most of their voting constituents—were especially conservative on the issue of race.

The civil rights movement and the 1965 Voting Rights Act transformed southern politics. Black southerners were now able to vote. The percentage of blacks registered to vote in the eleven states of the old Confederacy rose from 29 percent in 1960 to 62 percent in 1970.[11] More conservative southern whites began to vote Republican—first for president and later for other offices, including seats in Congress (see figure 1.5).[12] Gradually, party identification also changed. Between the mid-1970s and the early

1990s, Democratic Party identification dropped by 16 percentage points among white southerners, and more voters considered themselves Republicans than Democrats.[13] Conservative southerners brought their party identification in line with their ideological inclinations and their issue preferences.[14]

This changed the world in which southern politicians and would-be politicians functioned. First, it now made sense for an ambitious wanna-be to run as a Republican; it had not before. Trent Lott, a Republican House member and then senator from Mississippi, says that growing up in the 1940s and 1950s, he never met a Republican in the flesh. People who in Massachusetts or Nebraska would have been Republicans ran as Democrats in the South. No longer was this necessary; thus in 1972, Lott, who had served as an aide to a conservative House Democrat, ran to succeed him as a Republican—with the endorsement of his nominally Democratic boss. Since it was the more conservative southern white voters who switched to the Republican Party, candidates, to appeal to them, would also be conservative. And, of course, running as a Republican would be especially congenial to conservatives.

Incumbent southern Democrats faced a changed constituency. Blacks now voted; they were Democrats thanks to LBJ and the Civil Rights and Voting Rights acts; and they were liberals. With the Republican Party now a real threat, these black voters had to be courted. As Gary Jacobson shows, by the 1970s blacks were supplying a significant proportion (15 to 25 percent) of the votes for southern Democratic senators and representatives; by the late 1980s and 1990s that increased to about a third.[15] Furthermore, with Democratic incumbents' most conservative constituents being most likely to vote Republican, the whites who were left were on balance more moderate. By the 1980s, those white southerners who voted Democratic in congressional elections were significantly less conservative than those who voted Republican in terms of their self-placement on the liberal-conservative scale and on economic issues such as whether the government should guarantee everyone a job and a good standard of living.[16] According to recent polls, Democratic identifiers (and leaners) in the South, while culturally more conservative than their northern fellow partisans, are very similar on other issues; thus 64 percent in each region agreed that government should help needy people more, even if it increases the national debt.[17]

The impact of these constituency changes became evident in the 1970s. Southern Democrats modified their voting behavior, especially on issues such as civil rights.[18] New Democrats elected from the South were on average more moderate—and so more like their northern party colleagues—than their predecessors had been. Then, in the 1980s and 1990s, with the creation of majority minority House districts in the South, a number of minority Democrats were elected; reflecting their districts, most of these members held policy views similar to those of their northern counterparts. The proportion of southern Democrats who were minorities (blacks except in Texas, where minority representatives are both black and Latino) rose enormously from the early 1990s to the early 2000s. In the 102nd Congress (1991–92) before reapportionment and redistricting, 11 percent of southern House Democrats were minority group members; this jumped to 28 percent in the 103rd Congress after redistricting and to 37 percent after the 1994 elections, in which many southern seats formerly held by white Democrats switched to Republican. (The total number of southern Democrats decreased from 71 to 54.) In the 107th and 108th Congresses (2001–2002, 2003–2004), 42 percent of southern Democrats were minority group members.[19]

Briefly put, with the establishment of two-party competition in the South, voters and politicians sorted themselves out along the same lines that prevailed in the rest of the country: conservatives became Republicans and liberals became—or remained—

Democrats. Thus in 1972 self-described conservatives in the South were still somewhat more likely to consider themselves Democrats than Republicans, by 11 points; by 1984 conservatives were more likely to consider themselves Republicans, by 32 points, while southerners who considered themselves liberals or moderates were more likely to identify as Democrats, by 34 points.[20]

Republican and Democratic Voters Diverge

Important as the change in the South was to partisan polarization, it is far from the whole story. As figure 1.6 shows, the same pattern of partisan polarization is evident for northern House members and senators; starting in the early 1980s, northern Republicans and Democrats increasingly diverged in their legislative preferences, when measured by DW-nominate scores.

A similar sorting out of conservatives into the Republican Party and liberals into the Democratic Party has been occurring outside the South as well—among members of Congress, as figure 1.6 shows, and among voters. Survey data show that the relationship between voters' self-described ideology (where they place themselves on a liberal-conservative scale) and their party identification grew considerably stronger between 1972 and 1998 and that it did in both the North and the South.[21] The more conservative voters consider themselves, the more likely they are to think of themselves as Republicans. In the 1980s and 1990s, Republican voters became significantly more conservative by self-report, and this, of course, increases partisan polarization at the voter level.[22] The relationship between party identification and voters' positions on issues has grown stronger as well—and this is true of so-called social (though more appropriately labeled cultural) issues, such as abortion and the role of women, in addition to economic issues. In fact, the increase in convergence has been steepest on cultural issues; that is, increasingly, voters who are pro-choice and strongly in favor of women having an equal role in society are also likely to consider themselves Democrats.[23]

FIGURE 1.6
Ideological Divergence in the North,
House and Senate, 1947–2004

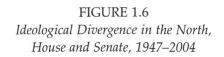

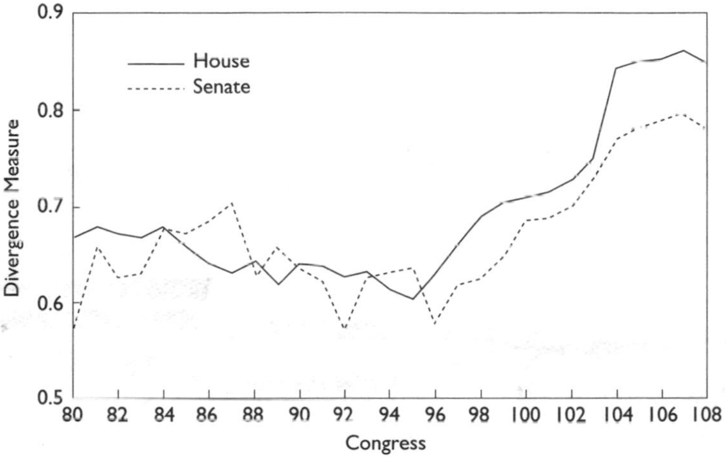

Divergence measure = difference in DW-nominate score medians between House Republicans and Democrats from the North, and between Senate Republicans and Democrats from the North

The relationship between party identification and issue preferences is stronger than it used to be for weak partisans as well as strong partisans and for both younger and older people.[24]

Voters have also become more likely to see important differences between the parties since the early 1980s; the big increase comes with Ronald Reagan—significant timing, as I argue later.[25] If voters see important differences between the parties and if voters' issue positions and ideology line up with their party identification, it is not surprising that voters are voting consistently with their party identification more than they used to or that they split their ticket less frequently.[26]

Those people who identify as Republicans and those who consider themselves Democrats differ considerably more than they formerly did on a host of issues and attitudes and in how they vote. The impact of these trends depends on the proportion of voters who are party identifiers. Conventional wisdom, certainly in the journalism community, holds that party identification has weakened and is less important than it used to be. In fact, partisanship in the electorate did weaken starting in the mid-1960s, but the weakening trend ended about 1976, and since the 1980s, a trend toward strengthening of party identification is evident.[27] The proportion of strong identifiers has rebounded and the proportion of pure independents has declined.

A differential decline in voter turnout has also contributed to increasing partisan polarization among voters. The decline in voter turnout over the last several decades has been sharper among those with weak attachments to the parties, leaving a more partisan electorate.[28] "The decline in partisanship . . . has been almost entirely reversed among voters," Larry Bartels concludes.[29]

Activists Polarize

My explanation for partisan polarization is a story in which voters, political activists, and politicians all play significant roles. Voters and, to some extent, politicians have been considered. What is the role of the political activist? A critical role, I argue. Political activists know more and care more than other voters do about politics and about what candidates espouse and what elected officials do; and activists are far more likely to act on the basis of their knowledge—by voting in primaries as well as general elections, by giving money, by working in campaigns. Consequently activists have a greater impact on whether candidates and elected officials get what they want—especially whether they get elected—and so candidates have to be more responsive to activists than to the ordinary voter.

Who are the activists? Activists are not as clearly defined a group as either voters or candidates; just how politically active we require people to be before we are willing to label them activists is a matter of scholarly judgment. But however we define activists, party activists have become significantly more polarized over time.

Many studies going back to the 1950s have shown that Republican and Democratic activists, when fairly demandingly defined, differ from each other on issues and ideology much more than Republican and Democratic voters do. Thus a survey of delegates to the 1956 national party conventions found substantial differences between these Republican and Democratic activists on a range of issues including economic policy and "egalitarian and human welfare issues," such as the minimum wage and aid to education; ordinary party identifiers surveyed by Gallup at the same time differed much less.[30] This is as we would expect, partly because it is often strong views that propel people to become politically active and also because voters who do not have much of an opinion tend to put themselves in the middle in response to surveys.[31]

In a study of national party convention delegates, Kent Jennings and Warren Miller found that from 1972 to 1976 to 1980, Republican delegates became more conservative both on issues and in terms of ideological self-identification.[32] Two different processes could account for such change: replacement, meaning that different—and in this case more conservative—people were chosen as delegates in the later years; and conversion, meaning that the people who were delegates to more than one convention changed their views toward greater conservatism. Jennings and Miller found that the change was due both to conversion, delegates to more than one convention becoming more conservative over time, and to replacement, especially with the influx of Reagan supporters in 1976 and the more so in 1980. The Reagan delegates in 1976 and 1980 who had not been delegates in 1972 moved the averages substantially to the right.[33] The researchers found little systematic change among Democratic delegates over this period. The result of the Republican move to the right was increased polarization between party activists.

Walter Stone, Ronald Rapoport, and Alan Abramowitz show that political party activists, already highly distinctive in 1980, polarized significantly more over the course of the 1980s, the Reagan period.[34] While in 1980 a substantial majority of Democrats labeled themselves liberal (60 percent) and few considered themselves conservative (18 percent), by 1988 the proportion who considered themselves liberal had increased further (68 percent) and the proportion who considered themselves conservative had decreased (13 percent).[35] Most of the Republican activists surveyed in 1980 labeled themselves conservative (80 percent); by 1988 the Republicans had become nearly monolithically conservative (92 percent). Similar polarization occurred on a series of issue questions from abortion to defense spending. On whether they favored or opposed a constitutional amendment to outlaw abortion, Democrats became even more lopsidedly opposed over the course of the 1980s. Republicans, interestingly, moved from a bare majority opposed in 1980 to about two-thirds in favor in 1988! That is, the center of gravity of these Republican activists shifted from mildly pro-choice—or at least opposed to a constitutional amendment—to strongly pro-life. The Stone study surveyed delegates to state party conventions. One of the states surveyed was Virginia; that Democratic activists showed up as so liberal is quite a strong indicator of how much the Democratic Party in the South has changed.

To understand how the polarization they found came about, Stone and his colleagues examined replacement (there labeled circulation) and conversion. Replacement had a big effect in moving the Republican Party to the right; moderates were more likely to drop out and newcomers were much more likely to be staunch conservatives. The difference between continuing delegates and newcomers was especially pronounced on abortion.[36] Stone and colleagues suggest that Reagan had the effect of recruiting into the activist strata a much more conservative group of people. Conversion contributed to polarization as well; the Democrats who were delegates in both years tended to move left over the course of the 1980s and the Republicans to move right, with the result that by 1988 they were much more polarized than they had been in 1980. The events of the 1980s, thus, left their mark on these continuing activists.

The people who get themselves elected to state and national conventions are a tiny—though politically significant—proportion of the electorate, and certainly considering these people alone as activists limits that group unduly. What has happened among activists less constrainingly defined? Jacobson defines activists as those who in a national survey reported engaging in at least two political acts in addition to voting; for example, trying to get others to vote for a candidate, attending meetings or rallies, or wearing a campaign button.[37] About 20 percent of voters are activists according to this measure. These less active but more numerous activists have also polarized along partisan lines since the early 1970s; the Democrats are more likely to place themselves toward the liberal end of the ideology scale and the Republicans toward the conservative end.[38]

Polls conducted in the summer of 2004 show continuing if not intensified polarization among activists and voters. The figures in table 1.2 are from *New York Times*/CBS News polls of delegates to the 2004 national conventions. The voters are registered voters who self-identified as Democrats or Republicans and who were also surveyed in the summer of 2004. In terms of self-described ideology and on a wide range of issues—economic, cultural, and related to foreign policy—Republican and Democratic activists are worlds apart. For example, almost 80 percent of Democratic delegates believe the government should do

TABLE 1.2

Divergence among Republican and Democratic Party Activists and Voters, 2004

Issue	Democratic Delegates	Democratic Voters	Republican Voters	Republican Delegates
Ideology self-described				
% Liberal	41	34	8	1
% Conservative	3	19	61	63
Government should do more to solve national problems or government is doing too many things better left to business and individuals				
% Do more	79	48	35	7
Which comes closest to your view about the tax cuts Congress passed since 2000?				
% All made permanent	1	10	30	61
% Most made permanent	6	23	38	34
% Most or all repeal/allow to expire	89	59	23	2
The federal government should do more/is doing enough/should do less to regulate the environmental and safety practices of business				
% Do more	85	71	45	15
% Doing enough	11	20	32	50
% Do less	2	6	15	26
Concerned more that government is enacting new anti-terrorism laws which excessively restrict the average person's civil liberties				
% Agree*	77	53	25	15

Government should do more to promote traditional values or government should not favor one set of values over another				
% Do more	15	26	61	55
What is your personal feeling about abortion?				
% Permit in all cases	64	37	13	8
% Permit with greater restrictions	14	16	12	13
% Only for rape, incest, to save a life	10	31	37	41
% Save life only or not permitted	3	14	35	29
Your view on gay couples:				
% Allowed to marry	44	36	11	3
% Allowed to form civil unions	43	28	36	41
% No legal recognition	5	33	52	49
Do you think the U.S. did the right thing in taking military action against Iraq or should the U.S. have stayed out?				
% Did right thing	7	21	78	96
How important that U.S. work through the U.N. to solve international problems?				
% Extremely	79	66	31	7
% Not so/not at all	0	6	30	46

Source: *New York Times*/CBS News polls, 2004. Delegates to the 2004 national conventions: Republicans surveyed August 3–23, N = 1,200; Democrats surveyed June 16–July 17, N = 1,085. Voters were registered voters who self-identified as Democrats or Republicans, in polls conducted July 11–15 and August 15–18. Report accessed on *New York Times* website, August, 30, 2004.

* The full question was: "Which concerns you more now—that the government is failing to enact strong anti-terrorism laws or that the government is enacting new anti-terrorism laws which excessively restrict the average person's civil liberties?"

more to solve national problems; only 7 percent of Republican activists agree. Republican activists oppose permitting abortion except in the most dire of circumstances or never (70 percent); Democrats favor permitting abortion in all cases or with minor restrictions (78 percent). Almost all Republican activists (96 percent) believe the United States did the right thing in taking military action against Iraq; only 7 percent of Democratic activists agree. In most but not all cases, Democratic and Republican voters fall between the activists, as we would expect. But by and large, voters also diverge significantly along party lines and are closer to the activists of their party than to the voters of the other party. On the Iraq war, for example, 89 percent of Republican voters but only 21 percent of Democratic voters think the United States did the right thing. Sixty-one percent of Republican voters believe the government should do more to promote traditional values, actually a little higher than the 55 percent of Republican activists who agree; only 26 percent of Democratic voters (and 15 percent of Democratic activists) agree. On abortion, 53 percent of Democratic voters take a relatively permissive position, compared to only 25 percent of Republican voters.

On tax cuts, arguably the most controversial domestic issue of President George W. Bush's first term, the party divide is enormous among both activists and voters, with 89 percent of Democratic activists and 59 percent of Democratic voters believing that most or all of the Bush tax cuts should be repealed or allowed to expire, while 68 percent of Republican voters and 94 percent of Republican activists favor making most or all of the tax cuts permanent.

THE ROOTS OF PARTISAN POLARIZATION

Since the 1970s, then, voters' party identification, their views on a wide variety of issues, and their self-described ideology have become increasingly consistent. The result is that Republican and Democratic voters now more consistently diverge in self-described ideology and in their positions on many issues, both cultural and economic. This does not mean that the typical Democrat is an extreme liberal who favors socialized medicine and supports abortion for birth control or that the typical Republican is a fanatical conservative who wants to abolish social security and deny women abortions under all circumstances. It does mean that the typical Democrat agrees considerably more often across a range of issues with other Democrats than with members of the Republican Party. Similarly, the typical Republican is likely to agree on many issues with other Republicans and to disagree on those same issues with Democrats. As Fleisher and Bond show, there is "a growing gap in the way that Democrats and Republicans understand and view the political world in which they live."[39]

As we have seen, party activists have polarized even more than ordinary voters; and, in their voting and in other behavior as well, members of the House and Senate have become highly polarized along partisan lines. Certainly these trends are related. Candidates may well want everyone in their constituencies to love them and vote for them, but if constituents are polarized, candidates have to choose a segment of voters to whom to be attentive; each candidate will choose the segment most likely to vote for him or her. Even more than in the past, this means the segment of voters who identify with the candidate's party. An individual's probable electoral constituency—those voters who are likely to vote for a given candidate and on whom that candidate must depend for election and reelection—is likely to be heavily made up of fellow partisans; and increasingly the voters are likely to think of themselves as moderates or liberals if they are Democrats or as conservatives if they are Republicans.[40]

Average voters, while more polarized than they used to be, are not grouped into two hostile and distant camps. But to a considerable extent, activists are, and activists are much more important than their numbers. They always vote, they vote in primaries, and they give money or work for candidates. To win in the primary, the candidate needs to be especially attentive and responsive to activists who are more polarized than less interested voters. The candidates who emerge from primaries are likely to be those acceptable to the activists. Furthermore, who are these candidates, anyway? Where do they come from? They are quite likely to come from the activist stratum themselves and to share the dominant views of that stratum. Hence both personal inclination and the desire to get elected and reelected are likely to produce conservative Republicans and liberal Democrats in Congress and considerably more so than was the case a generation ago.

Is the increase in partisan polarization in Congress mostly due to changes in the electorate or is it in some sense imposed on voters?

Morris Fiorina argues that the "culture war," the divide between "red" and "blue" America, is purely an elite phenomenon.[41] Ordinary voters, he contends, are not deeply split; it is elites that foist extremist candidates on an unhappy electorate that remains, by and large, moderate. "It is not voters who have polarized, but the candidates they are asked to choose between."[42] Party activists are undeniably more extreme than ordinary voters, as they have been since at least the 1950s. Fiorina is also correct in emphasizing that most voters are not at the far extremes ideologically. Still, he underemphasizes the extent to which voters have sorted themselves into opposing partisan camps that are much more homogeneous in policy preferences than they used to be. Average voters are less likely to face cross-pressures that would weaken their party identification or complicate their voting decisions. While party activists are certainly an important part of the story, so are ordinary voters.

A number of analysts have argued that partisan polarization is the result of redistricting. The redistricting argument contends that state legislatures, often with a considerable push from their House members, have created districts that are highly lopsided in their partisan inclinations and so completely safe for a member of one party or the other—generally the incumbent's. In such districts the party activists, who are more ideologically extreme than ordinary voters, can nominate an extreme candidate; they need not worry about moving too far from the median voter in the district, since any candidate of the advantaged party will win.

Determining whether redistricting or change in the electorate provides the basic explanation for partisan polarization is important because the answer affects both our evaluation of the phenomenon and any prescriptions one might propose to alleviate it. Most of us would judge partisan polarization to be a greater problem if it is imposed on voters than if it primarily reflects voter attitudes. Reforming the redistricting process is likely to have more effect if that process rather than change in the electorate is at the root of the phenomenon.

When Alan Abramowitz and Brad Alexander test for the effect of redistricting in a straightforward and convincing way, they find little impact.[43] They define potentially competitive House seats as those in which the major party division of the presidential vote was within five percentage points (plus or minus) of the national average. The presidential vote is usually considered the best surrogate for a district's underlying partisanship that is available for all districts; by using the deviation from the national average, they are attempting to factor out the impact of variables peculiar to a given presidential race that might deflect the vote from its partisan baseline—the recession in 1992, for example. Then they compare the percentage of potentially competitive House seats directly before and directly after each of the last three decennial redistrictings. Between 1980 and 1982 and between 2000 and 2002, the percentage of competitive seats dropped a little, perhaps two percentage points; between 1990 and 1992 it increased a little, perhaps one percentage point. In the period *between* each of these redistrictings, however, the percentage of competitive seats dropped much more.[44] The number of potentially competitive seats decreased from 165 in 1982, to 148 in 1992, to 114 in 2002.[45] Using a quite different methodology, McDonald and Grofman argue that possibly one sixth of the polarization between the 1970s and the 1990s is due to redistricting.[46]

The best case for a so-called bipartisan partisan redistricting—that is, a redistricting in which the parties work together with the aim of creating a maximum number of safe seats for each party and thus few competitive seats—is the 2000 redistricting. Even then there were cases of partisan advantage redistricting, in Georgia by the Democrats and, more successfully, by the Republicans in Michigan, Ohio, and Pennsylvania. Because of the one-person-one-vote requirement, partisan advantage redistricting should not create large numbers of seats that are overwhelmingly safe for one party.[47] Still, the balance of power in many states did lead to compromise plans, and that usually meant plans with many safe seats, though Abramowitz and Alexander's figures raise questions about how big the net impact was. But obviously the post-2000 redistricting cannot account for what happened in the 1980s and 1990s.

Redistricting, then, seems at most to have contributed marginally to polarization in the House. Yet the decrease in potentially competitive seats as measured by our best surrogate for district partisanship is considerable. The change in the electorate discussed earlier combined with demographic/geographical change seems the best explanation. Not only have Democratic and Republican voters diverged in their issue preferences and self-described ideology, and not only are voters more faithful to their party in how they vote, but they also seem to have become geographically more concentrated. Jeffery Stonecash and colleagues show that Democratic districts and Republican districts differ more than they used to in terms of urbanism and minority population and, to a lesser extent, income, all demographic characteristics related to party identification and policy preferences.[48] This increased differentiation in districts is not purely a result of partisan realignment in the South; it is evident in the North as well. Nolan McCarty, Keith Poole, and Howard Rosenthal find that the relationship between party identification and income has grown considerably closer since the 1950s.[49] And, of course, residential segregation on the basis of income is ubiquitous. Bruce Oppenheimer has speculated that even within groups with similar income, people may be more likely and more able now than they once were to choose to live with like-minded others.[50] A study conducted by sociologist Robert Cushing found that as of 2004, almost half of all Americans were living in what he calls landslide counties, counties in which one party received 60 percent or more of the presidential vote.[51] Comparing relatively close presidential elections, Cushing shows that about a third of Americans lived in landslide counties in 1948 and in 1960; this reached a low in 1976, when only 27 percent did; it then began to increase, hitting 38 percent in 1992, 45 percent in 2000, and 48 percent in 2004. Thus, quite apart from any impact redistricting has had, districts that are "naturally" Democratic and liberal or Republican and conservative may be more numerous than they used to be.

One obvious problem with the redistricting argument as a full explanation of partisan polarization is that it cannot apply to the Senate. The Senate is not subject to reapportionment or redistricting, yet as we saw earlier, senators have also polarized along partisan lines that coincide quite closely with ideology. (The correlation between the difference in DW-nominate medians in the House and Senate over time is 0.968).

Demographic trends may help to explain partisan polarization in the Senate, but to my knowledge, studies making the case convincingly are lacking. We do know that if the presidential vote is used as a surrogate for partisanship, more states are now lopsidedly Democratic or Republican than was the case in the past few decades. When Abramowitz and Alexander compared the three close presidential elections of 1960, 1976, and 2000, they found that the number of states won narrowly—by less than 10 percentage points—decreased from 34 in 1960 to 31 in 1976 to 22 in 2000.[52] Conversely, states won by more than 10 points increased from 16 in 1960 to 28 in 2000. According to Abramowitz's figures for 2004, the number of close states had declined to 19. Thus in the early 2000s, well over half of senators—56—came from and had to seek reelection in states that were solidly in one partisan camp or the other; more than a quarter—28—represented "blow-out" states won by over 20 percentage points. After the 2004 elections, 62 senators represented solidly Democratic or Republican states.

Changes in the orientation of voters and activists seem to provide the most convincing explanation for the external or electoral roots of polarization in the House and Senate. Redistricting, especially the most recent round, may have exacerbated the effects of voter change on the House to some extent but certainly did not cause partisan polarization. Whether activists influenced ordinary voters or both activists and voters responded to environmental factors is a question that cannot be answered definitively. It seems likely that both processes were at work but that activists led the way.[53] That is, when activists sorted themselves out into the two parties based on their ideological proclivities and then polarized further in their policy preferences, they presented voters with much clearer signals about what the two parties stand for and what differentiates them. Voters then responded to those clearer signals by sorting themselves out accordingly.

But even if activists were the drivers, ordinary voters were willing passengers. By the mechanisms of whom activists and voters chose as candidates and what those candidates needed to do for election and reelection, polarization among activists and voters translated into polarization in Congress.

Why did party activists and voters polarize? Although this really interesting question cannot be answered definitively, some of the important components of an answer can be outlined. Several that I see as most important for shaping the contemporary Republican Party are the subject of the next chapter.

• Parties homogenize and (polarization) diverge from each other
(major realignment)
Civil Rights - Changes in South
Democratic Party becomes more liberal
Republican Party becomes more conservative

• Party activists more polarized than ordinary voters => but still polarized; decline in voter turnout; replacement; conversion

• landslide counties (redistricting and "naturally")

External Factors

CHAPTER 2

THE REPUBLICAN PARTY MOVES RIGHT

Right-Wing Intellectuals and Evangelical Christians Transform the Republican Party

DURING THE 1964 PRESIDENTIAL campaign, the media depicted Goldwater as an outside-the-pale right-wing nut. Republican columnist Joseph Alsop wrote of his "itchy finger on the nuclear trigger"; the *New York Times* quoted former president Eisenhower as suggesting that Goldwater "might take this country into war"; Walter Lippman called him a "war hawk"; and Cyrus Sulzberger of the *New York Times* wrote that were Goldwater elected, "there might not be a day-after-tomorrow."[1] What was said about his domestic program was only marginally less pejorative. During the 1980 presidential campaign, Democrats attempted to depict Ronald Reagan as Goldwater redux—a trigger-happy, social security–endangering crazy. But they were unsuccessful; the media did not respond and carry that message. The press treated Reagan much like any other candidate.

Why the difference? Certainly it was not the result of a difference in the personalities of the two candidates. In terms of personality and style, Goldwater was no Newt Gingrich; by all accounts he was polite, soft-spoken, and low-key. Nor was Goldwater significantly to the right of Ronald Reagan ideologically. Both espoused a hard-line anti-Communist and anti-Soviet policy, one deeply skeptical of negotiations. Both strongly believed in the "magic" of the market and opposed most social programs at the national level as counterproductive; it was Reagan who argued that government *was* the problem. Both expressed concern about a moral crisis in America and argued for a return to traditional values. What happened between 1964 and 1980, I argue, is that conservativism became respectable; here I mean conservativism not of the relatively mild and often pragmatic Main Street variety but conservativism of the Goldwater and Reagan stripe—that is, more ideological, more hard-line and uncompromising, more far right—what later came to be called movement conservativism.

For a political philosophy, defined here simply as a more or less coherent set of political ideas, to influence public policy, it must pass the test of being "thinkable," of falling within "the outer limits of 'responsible' opinion."[2] Goldwater conservativism was beyond the pale in 1964; when Reagan espoused very similar ideas in 1980, that form of conservativism had moved into the realm of the thinkable. How did that happen? How it came about is an important part of the story of how the Republican Party and American politics have changed since the early 1970s.

A political philosophy may be respectable without being widely popular. For it to become dominant in one of the two major parties, either masses of current party adherents must adopt the political philosophy, or masses of those holding the philosophy must flood into the party.

In this chapter I argue that the neoconservatives played a major role in making the early forms of movement conservativism respectable. (These neoconservatives are not to be confused with the later group so labeled—Vice President Dick Cheney and former deputy secretary of defense Paul Wolfowitz, for example—who were never *new* conservatives; there is considerable continuity of ideas, however.) Evangelical Christians flooding into the Republican Party provided a significant proportion of the foot soldiers of the movement. Of course, conducive environmental conditions were essential, and other discontented groups were important as well, but they can be discussed only briefly here.

NEOCONSERVATIVES AND SUPPLY-SIDERS

How did ideas considered "loony" in the mid-1960s become respectable? A group of intellectuals who in the 1970s became known as neoconservatives played a key role. As Peter Steinfels, a student of neoconservativism, points out: "Intellectuals are legitimators." They powerfully influence the answer to a basic question shaping politics in any society: *"Where will one set the outer limits of 'responsible' opinion to which busy decision-makers should attend?"*[3]

These original neoconservatives were actually new conservatives. Leftists as students in the 1930s (Irving Kristol had been a Trotskyist), mainstream liberals in the 1950s, they were well-regarded public intellectuals, mostly connected to prestigious universities in the East. The neoconservatives—people like Kristol, Norman Podhoretz, Nathan Glazer, Daniel Bell, James Q. Wilson, and, for a time, Daniel P. Moynihan—turned away from liberalism in reaction to the 1960s. The activities of student protesters, black militants, and antiwar activists horrified them and led them to see heretofore unperceived virtues in social stability and order. The "counterculture" deeply disturbed them and led them to perceive previously unnoticed merit in traditional bourgeois values and mores. The abandonment of what they saw as "meritocracy" with programs like affirmative action offended their sense of what America was all about. Supporters of a muscular anti-Communism throughout the postwar period, they believed the anti–Vietnam War stance of increasing numbers of Democrats was disastrously wrongheaded; they perceived the reassessment of the Cold War consensus by many liberals as "the blame America first" syndrome. And they found in the Great Society programs proof that government cannot solve major societal problems.[4]

They became conservatives and in the process went a long way toward making conservativism intellectually respectable again. These were not, after all, "John Birch paranoids" or "undereducated businessmen from the intellectual wasteland of middle America." They were bona fide intellectuals with—not incidentally—close connections to elite reporters and columnists as well as to the editors of prestige magazines: the *Atlantic Monthly*, *Harpers*, and the *New York Times Sunday Magazine*. Of course, the unease that many in the intellectual elite felt with aspects of the 1960s upheavals made them receptive to at least some strands of the neoconservative arguments.

The neoconservatives collectively were largely responsible for promulgating the notion that the Great Society programs were an unalloyed failure, showing the folly of social engineering, a notion that came to have the status of unquestioned truth.[5] Their "law of unintended consequences" held that well-meaning social reform often made the situation at issue worse rather than better; through a series of articles, neoconservatives analyzed one Great Society program after another and argued that each had failed. The fact that some of the most prominent Great Society programs—especially the War on Poverty—had been wildly oversold increased the credibility of these critiques. Neo- and just plain conservatives increasingly followed the logic of this line of argument to its clear implication: that social reform through government is neither possible nor desirable. Sometimes they proceeded to its obvious corollary: that those who promote such reform have ulterior, self-serving motives for so doing and thus do not deserve the higher moral standing that American culture customarily confers on reformers.

As Godfrey Hodgson writes, the neoconservatives were "immensely influential. . . . They enabled conservatives to say that liberal ideas were no longer endorsed *even* by the very people—New York intellectuals, professors, and contributors to the upscale monthlies and quarterlies—who had been assumed since the New Deal . . . to legitimate liberal orthodoxy."[6]

Neoconservatives spread their ideas through their own publications, especially *The Public Interest* and *Commentary*. Founded in 1965, *The Public Interest* was coedited from its inception to 2002 by Kristol, who was also one of the cofounders; Kristol's coeditors were, first, Daniel Bell and then, from 1973 to 2002, Nathan Glazer. Kristol was a major proponent of the law of unintended consequences in its direst version, and the failures of Great Society programs and other attempts at social reforms were the theme of article after article in the magazine.[7] *Commentary*, a highly regarded intellectual journal of politics and literary criticism published by the American Jewish Committee, began on the left and remained there in the early years of Norman Podhoretz's editorship, which began in 1960.[8] By the late 1960s, however, Podhoretz was moving right, and in the winter of 1970–71 *Commentary* published a series of articles castigating just about every aspect of the liberal left in America, including prominently the New Left, the counterculture, the women's movement, and the environmental movement.[9]

Because of the neoconservatives' intellectual credentials and connections, they had access to mainstream magazines as well; their articles and ideas appeared in highbrow journals such as *Harper's* and the *American Scholar*, the middlebrow newsweeklies *Time* and *Newsweek*, and occasionally in such mass-market publications as *Reader's Digest* and *TV Guide*.[10] Even the *New York Times*, that venerable hothouse of liberalism, added a sprinkling of neoconservatives among its editors and editorial page writers. Neoconservatives also had direct links to political decision makers—Senator Henry Jackson and Richard Nixon, among others. (Moynihan worked for Nixon when he was president.) In 1966 Kristol began writing a column called "Books and Ideas" for *Fortune*, and in 1972 he joined the Board of Contributors of the *Wall Street Journal*.[11]

In disseminating their ideas, the neoconservatives benefited greatly from the patronage of wealthy businessmen and conservative foundations. Distressed by what they interpreted as the ascendancy of the left and its threat to the free enterprise system, they became generous financial supporters of the neoconservatives and their ideas, as I discuss more fully later.

The *Wall Street Journal* plays an important role in a related part of this story. The neoconservatives were not economists, and through the late 1960s, Keynesianism was the dominant paradigm in academic economics. This was not a radical form of Keynesianism, but with its reliance on government action, it was certainly not conservative. A few holdouts did exist, most notably the University of Chicago, and there the leading light of a more conservative, free market economics was Milton Friedman. In the late 1960s and early 1970s the development of "stagflation," the combination of inflation and recession, discredited Keynesian economic theory; that combination is not supposed to be possible within the Keynesian paradigm. For political discourse, the most important lesson drawn from the seeming failure of Keynesianism was that government policy was incapable of engineering good economic outcomes, and this was increasingly stretched to mean that government interference with the market inevitably did much more harm than good. Previously a fringe figure, Friedman prospered as the stock of Keynesianism declined. His receiving the Nobel Prize for Economics in 1976 marked a major shift in respectable economic theory. This change in mainstream economic theory was almost certainly necessary for the rise of supply-side economics.

Supply-side economics was incubated and disseminated by the *Wall Street Journal* editorial page, not by papers presented at economics meetings and published in learned journals. Jude Wanniski, a literal neoconservative though not one of the group usually so identified (he had been on the left as a student in the

1950s), was working for the *National Observer*, a weekly paper published by the *Journal*'s parent corporation Dow Jones, when he first met Arthur Laffer in 1971. Laffer was a young economist of no particular distinction who was then working for the Office of Management and Budget. Wanniski realized he needed to learn something about economics, and Laffer became, in effect, Wanniski's economics tutor. Laffer quickly made an enthusiastic convert to what would come to be called supply-side economics, a set of notions that he and a more established economist, Robert Mundell, were promoting in response to stagflation.

In February 1972 Wanniski was hired by Robert Bartley, the editorial page editor of the *Wall Street Journal*, after George Will, then an aide to a conservative senator, had turned down an offer from the *Journal*. Bartley himself had become editor only in 1970 and at a relatively young age. He wanted to make the traditionally conservative and stodgy editorial page interesting, exciting, and influential. As he later explained, "The time was coming to make conservativism respectable. I could see hooking up conservative ideas with erudition to capture some of the intellectual appeal traditionally associated with liberalism. . . . I was gratified to run across Irving Kristol's magazine [*The Public Interest*]. Here were some people talking sense."[12] It was Bartley who asked Kristol to join the *Journal*'s Board of Editors and write a monthly column.

Nevertheless Bartley was initially dubious about the prescriptions of supply-side economics. "Jude is trying to sell me a policy of enormous tax cuts accompanied by tight money. It seemed crazy," Bartley explained.[13] However, Wanniski's enthusiasm carried the day, and he was given the go-ahead to write an article. In that article, published in December 1974, Wanniski wrote: "The level of U.S. taxes has become a drag on economic growth in the United States. The national economy is being choked by taxes. . . . A tax cut not only increases demand, but increases the incentive to produce. . . . With lower taxes, it is more attractive to invest and more attractive to work; demand is increased, but so is supply."[14] This piece came to be considered the supply-side manifesto. Bartley was convinced, and the *Wall Street Journal* editorial page became a fervent and influential promoter of supply-side economics.

At Kristol's behest, Wanniski wrote a longer piece, entitled "The Mundell-Laffer Hypothesis: A New View of the World Economy," which appeared in the spring 1975 issue of *The Public Interest*.[15] In 1978 Wanniski's book, modestly entitled *The Way the World Works*, was published.

In 1976, after much fruitless effort, Wanniski finally found a politician who would take supply-side economics seriously and run with it. This was Republican congressman Jack Kemp of Buffalo, who had come to Washington in 1971 as a traditional conservative, "a balance-the-budget, root-canal, austere Republican," as he himself put it.[16] Buffalo, however, was a declining blue-collar town with high unemployment. A former quarterback for the Buffalo Bills, as Kemp was, might win election, but a "root-canal" Republican was going to find it difficult to maintain support. "I . . . realized that my career was going to be ended very quickly if I couldn't come up with something more hopeful," he explained.[17] In the supply-side doctrine Kemp found a solution to his problem. Kemp, in turn, helped introduce supply-side economics to a number of his junior colleagues, including David Stockman.[18]

Kemp and Wanniski became close friends, and Kemp met Kristol and other neoconservatives and supply-siders through Wanniski. Wanniski made Kemp into a national figure, and Kemp gave Wanniski the access he so badly wanted to the policy process. In 1977, Kemp and Delaware Republican senator William Roth introduced a bill to reduce income tax rates by 30 percent over three years, justifying the proposal by supply-side arguments.

The "tax revolt" of 1978 enormously amplified the attention focused on tax policy. An extraordinary run-up in home values, which translated into huge increases in property taxes, and the legislature's slowness in responding led Californians to approve overwhelmingly Proposition 13, reducing property taxes. Misinterpreting a problem largely confined to Southern California and a quite focused public response as a tsunami of populist outrage against taxes in general, the media greatly raised the visibility of taxes as a political issue and provided incentives for politicians to exploit it. In August 1978, House Republicans supported the Kemp-Roth plan by 140 to 3 on a recorded vote.[19] While the tax revolt may have been overhyped, economic problems that seriously concerned citizens were rampant. The 1970s had been a decade of stagflation and energy crises; incomes had stagnated, especially for those without a college education. In 1979 oil prices increased at a "staggering rate," and they continued to increase in 1980 even as economic growth slowed. In January 1980, the consumer price index increased at a frightening 18 percent annual rate.

Clearly these were favorable conditions for a presidential challenger. Yet a challenger needs more than widespread dissatisfaction with the status quo; a prescription for change is also required. Ronald Reagan was, of course, a strong conservative. By 1980 he had a long record in the public sphere. He was the heir to Barry Goldwater, whom he had supported with an eloquent speech that had first made Reagan a national figure. Reagan clearly favored lower taxes and a smaller government. But even in the late 1970s, supply-side economics was not yet Republican Party orthodoxy; during the 1980 Republican presidential primary campaign, George Bush would label it "voodoo" economics. Exactly how, when, and why Reagan was converted—or whether he had been a supply-sider all along, as Laffer claims—is unclear.[20] Certainly its optimistic, "no pain" approach must have appealed to Reagan both personally and politically. Kemp's not running and supporting Reagan instead seems to have depended on Reagan's adopting the supply-side approach. In any case, by the 1980 primaries, Reagan was airing explicitly supply-side television ads:

> *Announcer*: Ronald Reagan believes that when you tax something, you get less of it. We're taxing work, savings, and investment like never before. As a result, we have less work, less savings and less investment.
>
> *Reagan*: I didn't always agree with President Kennedy. But when his 30 percent federal tax cut became law, the economy did so well that every group in the country came out ahead. Even the government raised $54 billion in unexpected revenues. If I become president, we're going to try that again.[21]

In June of 1980, on the steps of the Capitol, House and Senate Republicans unanimously endorsed a revised version of the Kemp-Roth bill, and Reagan simultaneously backed a similar tax cut.[22] After Reagan became president, Kemp-Roth became Reaganomics.

Reagan did not win the presidency *because* he adopted supply-side economics; polls show that the 1980 election outcome was the result of severe dissatisfaction with conditions and a repudiation of President Jimmy Carter, not an endorsement of specific policies. Nevertheless, without a set of policy proposals that had some plausibility and appeal, Reagan could not have won. He also could not have won if he had been portrayed by the media as loony, as Goldwater had been in 1964—if his policy positions and proposals had been depicted as completely outside the range of the thinkable. For shattering the elite consensus that had prevailed when Goldwater ran in 1964 and that strongly affects media coverage, Reagan had the neoconservatives to thank. It is perhaps indicative that whereas most of the future neoconservatives had strongly opposed Goldwater in 1964, many were avid Reagan supporters in 1980.

Reagan's victory, in turn, made conservativism, neo- and otherwise, more respectable. In the United States, nothing succeeds like success. Reagan could and did lend the prestige of the presidency to conservatives' ideas, causes, and organizations.

THE MOBILIZATION OF THE CHRISTIAN RIGHT

Another key chapter in the story is the political mobilization of the Christian Right. After the battles over prohibition and evolution in the teens and 1920s, white evangelical Protestants withdrew from politics.[23] As late as 1965 Jerry Falwell, a fundamentalist preacher who in the late 1970s would found the explicitly political Moral Majority, was arguing that pastors should attend to winning souls, not to "fighting communism" or "reform[ing] the externals."[24] Specific events as well as broader trends in the 1960s and early 1970s changed Falwell's mind and the minds of many other fundamentalists and evangelicals. The Supreme Court's decisions on prayer in the schools in the early 1960s and on abortion in the early 1970s; the social movements of the 1960s, perhaps especially the women's movement with its anti-traditionalist implications; the "new permissiveness" of popular culture; and, in the late 1970s, the threat to the charitable status and so tax deductions for independent Christian schools—all these factors served to shake evangelicals' assumption that they could somehow live apart.[25]

Since evangelicals were especially numerous in the South, one might suspect that race figured prominently in their political activation. Certainly conservative attitudes on race were prevalent among white southern evangelicals and fundamentalists, and the national government's "intrusion" into the South's traditional arrangements stirred great resentment.[26] Some of Falwell's comments about pastors staying out of politics were prompted by Martin Luther King, Jr. Southern evangelicals continue to score much higher than other regional religious groups—including nonsouthern evangelicals—on questions intended to measure racism, while on issues such as abortion and homosexuality, evangelicals from the South and the North are equally conservative.[27] Yet race was only one of a series of issues that deeply disturbed evangelicals, persuading them that they could no longer simply "withdraw from what they regarded as a corrupt and hostile society, pursue their own salvation, and bring up their children in righteousness."[28]

Secular New Right leaders such as Richard Viguerie and Paul Weyrich worked assiduously to convince evangelical religious leaders to become involved in politics.[29] "Social" issues broadly defined had become prominent in the late 1960s in response to the counterculture, antiwar protestors, crime in the streets, urban rioters, and the whole panoply of social and political developments that disturbed many Americans, not just evangelicals. "The seeds of the . . . New Right [may have been] sown by the Goldwater campaign," as Weyrich argues; many of its leaders had some sort of connection to that campaign.[30] The issues that propelled these leaders to prominence, however, were the social issues (more properly labeled cultural issues); their focus was on "preserving *values* we know are revered by other middle class Americans."[31]

Despite enormous media attention and some successes, the New Right lacked an organized mass constituency. If their brand of conservativism was to prevail, whether within the Republican Party or in a new party, the movement needed a constituency large enough to affect at least primary elections and organized enough to do so, and evangelicals offered a obvious and tempting target. The fit was a good one, because although the New Right leaders were secular in the sense of not being politically affiliated with a religious group, most were in fact religious and were certainly not opposed to mixing religion and politics. Weyrich wrote: "It is my basic philosophy that God's truth ought to be manifest politically."[32] As "battle-tested generals in search of an army," in Ralph Reed's words, New Right leaders such as Viguerie, Weyrich, and Howard Phillips focused on prominent evangelical pastors.[33] "[Weyrich] and Howard Phillips spent countless hours with electronic ministers like Jerry Falwell, James Robinson and Pat Robertson, urging them to become involved in conservative politics," Viguerie reported in his 1980 book.[34] At a meeting in May 1979 at Falwell's headquarters, Weyrich, Phillips, and other conservative strategists urged Falwell to form an organization to mobilize fundamentalists. A month later Falwell founded the Moral Majority, a nationwide network of fundamentalist protestant ministers.[35] Yet whatever encouragement and help the New Right strategists may have provided, many evangelical leaders—and their followers—were primed to be convinced.

The evangelicals of the 1970s were significantly different from their predecessors of earlier in the century in some important ways. They were considerably better educated and more affluent; they were growing in numbers, having gained at the expense of mainline Protestants; and they had a potent communication network that extended beyond the local church pulpit with a coterie of well-known television preachers.[36]

Considerably more numerous in the South than the North, evangelical Protestants had tended to be Democrats.[37] The 1960s had certainly weakened their allegiance to the Democratic Party and, not surprisingly, 1972 Democratic presidential candidate George McGovern (the candidate of "acid, amnesty and abortion," according to the Republican slogan) was hardly popular with that group in any region. Yet in 1976 a sizable proportion of conservative Protestants did vote for Jimmy Carter, a born-again Christian and a southerner. But Carter was a disappointment to evangelicals; his administration did not reverse any of the permissive policies of the recent past and it threatened the tax exemption for their private schools on the basis of racial discrimination.[38]

Furthermore, Republicans were beginning to reach out to cultural conservatives. In 1976, despite some opposition from President Jerry Ford, the Republican platform endorsed a constitutional amendment banning abortion, though it did so rather cautiously, acknowledging differences of opinion among Republicans and favoring "a continuance of the public dialogue." (The Democratic platform took an even more cautious position that was pro-choice only by default: "We fully recognize the religious and ethical nature of the concerns which many Americans have on the subject of abortion. We feel however that it is undesirable to attempt to amend the U.S. Constitution to overturn the Supreme Court decision in this area.")[39]

Ronald Reagan had taken conservative positions on cultural issues that appealed to evangelicals. His supporters had fought to drop support for the Equal Rights Amendment from the 1976 Republican platform, a battle that they lost. The 1980 Republican platform took much more conservative stances on cultural issues than the 1976 platform had. Support for an amendment barring abortion was strengthened; prayer in the public schools and tuition tax credits were endorsed; support for the ERA was dropped.[40] (The 1980 Democratic platform took a clear pro-choice stance and added "sexual orientation" to its anti-discrimination plank.)

During the campaign, Reagan appealed directly to religious conservatives, attending rallies and other events sponsored by their organizations.[41] In August 1980, Reagan spoke to twenty thousand evangelicals at the "National Affairs Briefing," a meeting of the Religious Roundtable, an umbrella organization formed to encourage cooperation among Christian Right groups. With a bevy of major leaders of the religious right behind him, Reagan declared: "I know you can't endorse me, but I want you to know that I endorse you and what you are doing."[42] He also questioned the theory of evolution. Ralph Reed of the Christian Coalition called that gathering "the wedding ceremony of evangelicals and the Republican party."[43]

Soon after its founding in June of 1979, Falwell's Moral Majority had undertaken a massive voter registration drive. Evangelical Protestants were much more prominent among Republican National Convention delegates in 1980 than they had been in 1976 and, in both years, tended strongly to be Reagan supporters.[44] "Throughout the summer and fall of 1980, the word went out through these religious Paul Reveres (Jerry Falwell, Ed McAteer, Bob Billings, Adrian Rogers, Charles Stanley, Jim Kennedy, James Robinson, and many others) that America was in danger and only Ronald Reagan could cure her," wrote Richard Viguerie.[45] Observant evangelical Protestants—those who attend church frequently—responded by voting heavily for Reagan.[46] They also helped elect enough new Republican senators to switch control of the Senate from Democratic to Republican; two of the most surprising Republican winners—Don Nickles in Oklahoma and Jeremiah Denton of Alabama—had assiduously courted the religious right.[47]

Over the course of the 1980s and 1990s, those evangelicals who are regular church attendees—who also tend to be the most conservative on cultural issues—became increasingly Republican in party identification. Through the 1960s and 1970s, such observant evangelicals had become less and less likely to call themselves Democrats and increasingly inclined to label themselves independents. Into the 1980s, however, less than 30 percent of observant evangelicals called themselves Republicans. But throughout the 1980s and 1990s, Republican identification increased and Democratic identification decreased, and starting in the late 1980s, the proportion of observant evangelicals calling themselves independents also decreased. By the mid-1990s, about half of observant evangelicals labeled themselves as Republican, while less than a quarter called themselves Democrats. Observant evangelicals make up about a quarter of all Republican identifiers, more than any other single group.[48] In a 2004 poll, 48 percent of registered voters who identified as Republicans considered themselves evangelical or born-again Christians.[49]

Observant evangelicals became even more Republican in their presidential voting during this period; at least 60 percent voted Republican in every presidential election from 1980 through 2000, and at least 65 percent did so from 1984 through 2000.[50] In 2000, 74 percent of evangelicals—and 89 percent of evangelicals holding traditionalist beliefs—voted for George W. Bush for president, and similar percentages voted Republican in House races.[51] In 2004, again, Bush got 74 percent of the evangelicals' vote.[52]

In 1994, when Republicans won control of the House for the first time in forty years, white evangelicals contributed greatly to the Republican victory; they cast about a third of all the votes cast for House Republican candidates.[53]

Evangelicals also became increasingly prominent among Republican activists. In 1996, 31 percent of Republican convention delegates considered themselves to be "Evangelical or Born-Again Christians"; in 2004, 33 percent did, and 39 percent said that religion was extremely important in their daily life.[54] According to an informed 1994 estimate, conservative Christians dominated the Republican party organization in eighteen states and exerted considerable influence in thirteen more.[55] A similar study carried out after the 2000 elections estimated that conservative Christians were strong in eighteen state Republican party organizations and moderately influential in twenty-six; they were judged weak in only six northeastern states and the District of Columbia.[56] The religious right, then, has become a core Republican constituency, an important part of the base that no national candidate and few other candidates can afford to alienate.

Since the partisan realignment in the South discussed in chapter 1 and the realignment of evangelicals occurred more or less during the same period, and since evangelicals are much more numerous in the South than in the North, one might suspect that these are the same phenomenon. Layman convincingly shows that the increase in Republican identification in the South over the period 1964 to 1996 (and primarily in the 1980s and 1990s) is much greater among observant evangelicals than among other whites and that there is also an increase among observant evangelicals outside the South. Furthermore, among other whites, only young southerners show a trend toward greater Republican identification, and that trend is modest compared to the trend among observant evangelicals.[57] "In fact," Layman concludes, "the argument that partisan change among evangelicals has been driven by the realignment of the South can, to some extent, be turned on its head. It appears that the partisan transformation of committed evangelicals has played a large role in driving the pro-Republican trends in the former Confederacy."[58]

The movement of observant evangelicals into the Republican Party has led to the parties becoming increasingly polarized in terms of both religious orthodoxy and cultural conservativism. Slowly from the mid-1960s through the mid-1980s and then much more steeply in the 1990s, Republicans and Democrats diverged on measures of religious orthodoxy and on issues such as abortion, homosexual rights, women's role in society, and prayer in the schools.[59]

THE DEVELOPMENT OF CONSERVATIVE INFRASTRUCTURES

By 1980 a substantial conservative infrastructure had developed. Ronald Reagan's victory strengthened existing conservative institutions and led to further proliferation. Although this risks oversimplifying matters, one can divide these developments into two relatively independent streams—the Christian Right and the "intellectual right."

Institutions and Organizations of the Religious Right

Evangelicals have always had the bases of organization in their churches, but each church tended to be quite independent. Evangelicals' increasing affluence made possible the megachurches that sprang up in the 1960s and especially in the 1970s; by the late 1960s, Falwell's thousand-seat church built in 1964 was already too small.[60] That growing affluence also made it possible for evangelicals to build separatist institutions of all kinds. Motivated by their abhorrence of developments in the greater society, evangelicals had by the 1970s established Christian summer camps and retirement homes; universities such as Oral Roberts University, Bob Jones University in South Carolina, and Pat Robertson's Regents University in Norfolk; and thousands of independent Christian schools.[61] The number of such schools grew enormously during the 1970s. By the mid-1980s they numbered more than seventeen thousand with an enrollment of 2.5 million students.[62] According to a number of participants and scholars, the Carter Administration's threat to these schools' tax exemption, more than any other single event, spurred evangelicals to become politically active.[63] When the IRS promulgated guidelines in the late 1970s that seemed to threaten Christian academies' charitable status on the basis of racial discrimination, it received 120,000 protest letters, more than it had ever received before, and Congress blocked the change.[64]

Christian publishing flourished, and the electronic church flourished even more. Nonmainstream churches had made more extensive use of radio from early in the medium's history and also made the switch from radio to television more successfully than did mainline denominations. With their fervent espousal of conservative Christian tenets and values, which made their equally fervent appeals for financial support from their audience successful, the evangelical TV preachers could afford to pay for TV time. Jerry Falwell, through his *Old-Time Gospel Hour*, was just one of a bevy of televangelists who became well-known to conservative Christians around the country. By the late 1970s there were five religious broadcast networks and more than sixty syndicated television programs. By 1979 Pat Robertson's *700 Club* was being shown on 150 TV stations and 1,800 cable TV systems and was generating $54 million in income, Robertson claimed.[65]

In 1979, as mentioned earlier, Falwell formed the Moral Majority. Falwell, who had argued fifteen years earlier that preachers should stay out of politics, had completely changed his tune. "The day of the silent church is passed," he declaimed in 1980. "We're here to stay. . . . Preachers, you need as never before to preach on the issues, no matter what they say or what they write about you. Get involved, registered, informed, and voting."[66] The Moral Majority's board of directors included the pastors of some of the nation's largest evangelical churches; in 1979 and 1980, Falwell "held rallies and parades and packed halls and churches from coast to coast, always passing the hat among the faithful as a choir belted out 'God Bless America.'"[67] Although Falwell's estimate of a membership of seven million families is considered wildly inflated, the Moral Majority did succeed in registering several million evangelicals for the 1980 elections.[68]

The Moral Majority, however, relied heavily on the rally strategy and on direct mail fund-raising, rather than on grassroots organizing; "strong state organizations were not built, few neighborhood coordinators were appointed, chapter growth was scattered, and training programs were sparse."[69] Its recruits were political neophytes and fervent evangelicals, and without the necessary training, many found it impossible to function effectively in mainstream politics; thus, one chapter leader publicly stated his belief in the death penalty for homosexuals. Falwell himself was prone to inflammatory comments, arguing, for example, that AIDS is God's judgment on society.[70] Such outlandish comments discredited the group, making all but the most far-right candidates leery of any association with it. In combination, this and its organizational weakness, led to the Moral Majority's demise. In 1989 Falwell shut it down.

The Moral Majority was almost immediately succeeded by the Christian Coalition, which came out of Pat Robertson's 1988 run for the Republican presidential nomination.[71] Urged on by operatives in the campaign, Robertson decided in the fall of 1989 to form a political organization to harness the energy of those his campaign had brought into politics. Under the operational leadership of the talented Ralph Reed, the Christian Coalition emphasized grassroots organizing and action. Starting from mailing lists of financial supporters and activists in the Robertson presidential campaign, Reed, the organization's first employee, began raising money and organizing. He soon hired four regional field directors who traveled the country, setting up local chapters and holding training sessions. By the mid-1990s, the Christian Coalition had seventeen hundred local chapters and 1.7 million members spread across all fifty states.[72]

For leadership, the Christian Coalition organizers looked not to pastors but to lay people, especially small-business people well connected in their communities. Reed believed the Moral Majority had made a mistake in relying so heavily on pastors, who could seldom devote enough time to the enterprise.[73] Nevertheless, Reed explained: "Pastors are still critically important. They teach, exhort their members to be good citizens, facilitate the distribution of nonpartisan voter education information."[74]

The distribution of voter guides became the signature strategy of the Christian Coalition. From its first major effort in the 1991 elections for the Virginia state legislature, the coalition's capacity grew quickly. In the 1994 elections, the Christian Coalition distributed 40 million voter guides to evangelicals and other religious conservatives. In 2000, almost half of the congregations in the Southern Baptist Convention and more than two-thirds of the congregations in the Assemblies of God used voter guides, mostly from conservative groups.[75]

Christian Coalition activists distribute information through traditional door-to-door canvassing, phone calls, and now e-mail, but also through the church liaison program. Church liaisons are lay people charged with "[conducting] regular voter registration drives to achieve registration of all eligible voters in the church, . . . [distributing] non-partisan voter guides, legislative scorecards and special inserts through the church bulletin, . . . [and disseminating] legislative updates and issue alerts throughout the year."[76] Such grassroots activity has an effect. Studies have shown that evangelicals who are subject to such religious contacts are considerably more likely to vote than those who are not contacted, and although all evangelicals tend to vote heavily Republican, those contacted are even more likely to vote Republican than those not contacted.[77]

Under Reed's savvy leadership, the Christian Coalition also sought to make itself a respected political player in the mainstream of politics. Reed was aware that the language of the Christian Right often alienated outsiders, and he sought to tone it down. He even commissioned surveys to "to help us find effective language that motivated our supporters without turning off voters sitting on the fence."[78] His insistence on labeling the religious right as the pro-family movement may well stem from this concern about language. He reached out to other conservative Christians and sought to build alliances, with conservative Catholics for example.[79]

The Christian Coalition began holding training seminars for local as well as state activists and candidates. Coalition members got involved in school board and city council races across the country. In 1991, the coalition participated in the fight over the confirmation of Clarence Thomas to the Supreme Court. It broadcast radio and TV ads in Georgia, Louisiana, and Pennsylvania to put pressure on swing senators and delivered to Capitol Hill fifty thousand petitions and letters supporting Thomas. In 1993, Reed opened a fully staffed lobbying office in Washington.

Other groups formed or became more prominent during this period as well. Focus on the Family began in 1977 "in response to Dr. James Dobson's increasing concern for the American family"; its mission, the organization states, is "to cooperate with the Holy Spirit in disseminating the Gospel of Jesus Christ to as many people as possible, and, specifically, to accomplish that objective by helping to preserve traditional values and the institution of the family."[80] Among its many activities, the organization produces the widely heard radio programs that have made Dobson a major star of the religious right. The Reverend Lou Sheldon's Traditional Values Coalition was founded in 1980 as "a non-denominational grass roots church lobby" with a motto of "empowering people of faith with truth." It claims to have a membership of forty-three thousand churches.[81] Concerned Women for America, founded in 1979 by Beverly LaHaye, bills itself as "the nation's largest public policy women's organization with a rich 25-year history of helping our members across the country bring Biblical principles into all levels of public policy." According to its self-description, "CWA is a unique blend of policy experts and an activist network of people in small towns and big cities across the country working to address mutually held goals and concerns."[82] And these are only some of the more prominent groups.

The Christian Right, thus, developed an infrastructure of groups and communication networks that allowed its members to play a major role in Republican politics both at the grass roots and in Washington.

Constructing the Idea Factory

Development of the infrastructure of the "intellectual right" followed a rather different path. The intellectual right had ideas, not bodies, to offer and as such required preeminently structures for the nurturing, exchange, and dissemination of ideas. At first the neoconservative periodicals such as *The Public Interest* and *Commentary* served that purpose; the early conversion of the *Wall Street Journal* editorial page was extraordinarily important to the dissemination of neoconservative and supply-side ideas; after all, the *Journal*'s readers included the business elite—and, increasingly, many policy makers.

Foundations on the right, some new and some revitalized, became important as nurturers and disseminators of conservative ideas. The American Enterprise Institute was transformed from a stodgy, hard-line, and little-known free enterprise foundation to an influential think tank peopled by cutting-edge neoconservatives as well as respectable free marketeers, such as Milton Friedman. Well-known neoconservative academics were added to AEI's Council of Academic Advisors, and Irving Kristol became a resident scholar.[83] Kristol joined the advisory council of AEI's newly formed Center for the Study of Government Regulation. *Regulation*, the journal published by the center, became a primary advocate of government deregulation. Increasingly well funded by business, AEI attracted numerous scholars and journalists, both well-known and young and obscure, for special projects. By 1985 AEI had a staff of 176, 90 adjunct scholars, and a budget of $12.6 million.[84] AEI spent as much effort disseminating positions to the media as generating them. "I make no bones about marketing," explained William Baroody, a former AEI president. "We pay as much attention to the dissemination of the product as we do to content. We're probably the first major think tank to get into the electronic media. We hire ghost writers for scholars to produce op-ed articles that are sent to the one hundred and one cooperating newspapers—three pieces every two weeks."[85]

The Heritage Foundation has taken that approach one step further. "Our targets are the policy-makers and the opinion-making elite. Not the public. The public gets it from them," explained Burt Pines, then a foundation vice president.[86] Heritage was founded by Paul Weyrich and Edwin Feulner in 1973 with a quarter-million-dollar grant from Joseph Coors, the ultraconservative beer magnate. Weyrich, a former congressional aide, had already founded the Committee for the Survival of a Free Congress, one of the first right-wing PACs. Feulner was a former staffer for the House Republican Conference and had founded the Republican Study Committee to generate ideas and research for conservative House members.

Heritage from its inception focused on feeding ideas into the policy-making process, both directly and through the media. Its staff policy analysts have always been expected to develop contacts with key committee and personal staffers on the Hill, to track issues, and to be prepared to provide research papers at the most opportune time. Heritage also keeps a register of conservative scholars around the country and works to get them invited to testify before congressional committees. It seeks to amplify the effect of such scholars' testimony by arranging media interviews and giving press luncheons for them. Heritage maintains a computer list of thousands of journalists. When a Heritage study is released, it and an executive summary are sent to any journalist thought to be potentially interested. Often the studies are turned into op-ed pieces.[87] When Reagan was elected, Heritage worked with some success to get conservatives placed in administration posts. Reagan acknowledged the status of the foundation by attending and speaking at its tenth anniversary celebration.

These Washington think tanks thus developed excellent channels of communication to the mass media. Their scholars often became the "experts" to whom reporters went for comments. Some became regulars on the op-ed pages, both in the prestige national papers and, through syndication, in newspapers around the country.[88]

AEI and Heritage are just the best known of the conservative think tanks that were established or revitalized during the 1970s and that continue to be influential today. The Cato Institute founded in 1977, the Manhattan Institute (1979), and the National Center for Public Policy Research (1982) are only a few among many others; see chapter 9 for additional discussion.[89]

These think tanks were able to achieve prominence because of the generous financial support they received from conservative businesspeople. The successes of the environmental and consumer movements led to a countermobilization by business in the early 1970s; shocked by a succession of losses in policy battles, business became much more active in Washington lobbying.[90] Some business leaders believed that more was required—that business was losing the war of ideas and needed a counteroffensive on that front. Thus Lewis Powell, later a Nixon Supreme Court appointee, published a memo in a U.S. Chamber of Commerce periodical in 1971, arguing that the universities, the media, the political establishment, and the courts were attacking the American free enterprise system with devastating effect and that business needed to "stop suffering in impotent silence and launch a counter-attack."[91] Instead of giving money to foundations, which he claimed often funded the enemies of free enterprise, business should fund "scholars, writers and thinkers" who would spread the pro-business message and thereby "inform and enlighten the American people."[92] Wealthy men on the far right, such as Coors and Richard Mellon Scaife, and conservative foundations, such as the John M. Olin Foundation and the Smith-Richardson Foundation, did just that. The Olin Foundation had assets of $61.3 million in 1983 and gave about $5 million to conservative institutions that year.[93] The Smith-Richardson Foundation financed *The Public Interest*'s annual operating deficit and, under a chief program officer recommended by Kristol, became a strong supporter of supply-side economics.[94] "I raise money for conservative think tanks," Kristol explained. "I am a liaison to some degree between intellectuals and the business community."[95]

Conservative foundations and think tanks nurtured many of the right's rising stars, funding them, publishing their work in many publications, and sometimes supporting them with fellowships to give them time to develop their ideas into book-length manuscripts. Thus AEI provided a resident fellowship for Jude Wanniski to write his book on supply side economics. The fellowship was funded by the Smith-Richardson Foundation on the recommendation of Irvin Kristol.[96] The same foundation funded the writing of two other influential books that were published in the early 1980s: George Gilder's *Wealth and Poverty*, published in 1981, and Michael Novak's *The Spirit of Democratic Capitalism*, published in 1982. Gilder contended that the rich—"a large class of risk-taking men"—not only create wealth but do so for the benefit of the lower orders. The function of the rich is "fostering opportunities for the classes below them in the continuing drama of the creation of wealth and progress."[97] Novak's treatise is a theological defense of capitalism. Charles Murray's argument that welfare fosters poverty first appeared in a Heritage Foundation pamphlet. He was supported by the Manhattan Institute in writing his influential book *Losing Ground* (1984), with some of the money coming from the Olin Foundation, again at the recommendation of Irvin Kristol.[98] Through an elaborate marketing campaign, the Manhattan Institute turned *Losing Ground* into a best seller, a feat conservative organizations would accomplish regularly for other favored works.[99]

One can argue that these entities were essential to the incubation of ideas that would greatly influence the conservative movement and the larger political debate. Attentive publics outside Washington and New York became aware of conservative ideas through op-ed pieces and books generated by the writers cultivated by these foundations and think tanks. The think tanks housed in Washington linked the idea people with elected politicians, thus getting the ideas to those who could bring them into actual policy debates. These conservative entities almost all sponsor internships, many have visiting scholar positions, and some give grants. Movement conservativism established a solid campus presence early on. The Collegiate Network, founded in 1979, funds conservative college journalism and as of 2005 consists of "89 independent student newspapers on 81 college campuses."[100] Young America's Foundation (YAF), also founded in the 1970s, bills itself as America's largest campus outreach organization, annually sponsoring conservative speakers on campuses around the country and organizing conferences and seminars for young conservatives, including high school students.[101] Such programs assure a continued supply of young conservatives and of conservative ideas and arguments. Starting with the Reagan Administration, both policy ideas and people nurtured in the movement moved into government when Republicans were in power.

COMING TOGETHER AND SPREADING THE MESSAGE

Over time, the two strands of movement conservativism that I have emphasized here became less distinct from each other and from other strands one can identify as having at least somewhat, if not completely, independent origins—the western-based property rights movement, the gun rights advocates organized in the National Rifle Association and some more extreme groups, and small-business owners organized in the highly ideological National Federation of Independent Business.[102]

In part, the blurring of lines between components was due to overlapping memberships. For example, almost half of small-business owners consider themselves born-again Christians.[103] Certain bridging ideas and figures also played a role. Neoconservatives and many others in the intellectual right had little in common culturally with the typical member of the Christian Right. Yet from the beginning, neoconservatives had emphasized the importance for social stability of traditional values and structures, including especially religious values and organizations. William Bennett, a neoconservative who served as chair of the National Endowment for the Humanities and then as secretary of the Department of Education in the Reagan Administration, appealed to conservative Christians and other traditionalists with his emphasis on teaching children the basics and instilling in them old-fashioned values without nuance or apology. The Founding Fathers had "envisioned a Federal government neutral between religions in particular, but sympathetic to religion in general," Bennett insisted.[104]

Perhaps most important in bridging various strains of conservativism and keeping them firmly linked to the Republican Party was Ralph Reed. Before he took on the position of organizing and then directing Pat Robertson's Christian Coalition, Reed had been a Republican operative, working in the early 1980s in a low-level job at the Republican National Committee and then as executive director of the College Republicans. In his autobiography, Reed writes of wanting "to unite social conservatives and economic conservatives by supporting traditional issues like welfare reform, a balance budget, and tax cuts for families."[105] Reed expanded the policy agenda of the religious right, tempered its public statements, engineered a sophisticated media strategy to soften its image, and always kept it firmly in the Republican fold.[106]

In popularizing movement conservativism, however, it is hard to overestimate the role of talk radio. Call-in talk radio grew enormously in the 1980s, and most of the hosts with a political bent espoused the conservative position.[107] Conservative listeners found in talk radio a validation of their views. "Conservatives felt isolated," explained New Right strategist Paul Weyrich. "What talk radio has done. . . is taught them there are a lot of people who feel like they do."[108] Rush Limbaugh became the leader of the pack and a highly influential figure in movement conservativism in his own right. Beginning with his own show in 1984 and becoming nationally syndicated in 1988, Limbaugh commanded an enormous audience, estimated to number 20 million a week at one point.[109] Limbaugh, says conservative writer John Fund of the *Wall Street Journal*, "took the ideals that had been current in the conservative movement for decades, popularized them, made them entertaining, and brought an entire non-policy audience the benefits of that work."[110] Although Limbaugh was certainly the king of conservative talk radio, a horde of right-wing talk show hosts came to dominate the air.

When cable television took off in the 1990s, it too became a forum for the dissemination of movement conservative ideas. Many younger movement conservatives who had been trained as idea disseminators via journalism or the think tanks easily moved into the multiple "talking heads" slots that cable TV provided. The conservative magazine the *Weekly Standard*, begun in 1995 by Bill Kristol, son of Irving, contributed Kristol himself, David Brooks, David Frum, and Tucker Carlson, among others.[111] Shows in which commentators and pundits talked—or yelled—politics were cheap to produce, attracted intense though small audiences, and thus proliferated on cable networks such as CNN, MSNBC, and Fox. With the advent of the Fox News channel in 1996, a clearly conservative network appeared, and it developed a number of now famous conservative commentators.

Collectively these people, their institutions, and their efforts have moved the political center to the right. Notions that were completely beyond the pale thirty years ago—that welfare breeds poverty, that privatizing social security makes sense—no longer seem wild and extreme. These people and entities have profoundly changed the debate in this country; they have altered the fundamental assumptions from which much policy analysis begins (especially in terms of what government can and cannot do well) and have thereby had a major effect on the policy process.

American political parties are extraordinarily permeable; these various strands of conservativism found a home in the Republican Party and so transformed the party. Neoconservatives claimed they were driven out of the Democratic Party by its embrace of leftist notions and tendencies in the 1960s—the counterculture, the antiwar movement—and conservative evangelical Christians could make the same claim with rather more justification. Once feminism became a dominant tenet in the Democratic Party and feminist women a core constituency, the party would no longer seem welcoming to conservative evangelical Christians, and at least for some, much the same was true of the Democratic Party's embrace of civil rights and black Americans.[112] For other strains of what became movement conservativism—supply-siders, small-business owners, property rights crusaders—the Republican Party was the obvious choice of partisan vehicle and, for many, already their partisan home. By strongly advocating more conservative positions within the party, they too participated in transforming the party's ideological center of gravity. The surveys of convention delegates discussed in chapter 1 demonstrate how extremely conservative the typical Republican activist is.

It is thus the Republican Party's move to the right that accounts for much of the ideological polarization of the parties since the 1970s. To be sure, the Democratic Party moved left in the 1960s and early 1970s on race and on some cultural issues such as women's rights; one can argue that on some other cultural issues—particularly gay rights—the Democratic Party has continued to move left. But on many major issues, particularly economic and social welfare issues, the Democratic Party position did not shift left. The Republican Party, in contrast, moved right on the entire spectrum of issues that animate political activists and a considerable number of ordinary voters as well.

• Republican Party moves to the right
External factor ~ mobilization of Evangelical Christians who were not involved in politics

CHAPTER 3

THE INTERNAL ENGINES OF PARTISAN POLARIZATION

The House in the Democratic Era

IS THE EXTREME PARTISAN polarization and the hostility between Democrats and Republicans that we see in Congress entirely a result of external factors—that is, of changes in voters and activists? These external factors, I argue, made possible and were a necessary condition for some of the internal changes discussed in this chapter. But I also contend that internal changes have shaped and amplified the effect of external factors and have had consequences of their own for how Congress makes law.[1]

One might expect this to be a story of the Republican Party in Congress, of Gingrich and DeLay. These Republican figures have received more media attention than most congressional Democrats ever did. The press has hailed—and sometimes maligned—Gingrich and DeLay as strong—and sometimes strong-armed—party leaders; in the last thirty years, a congressional Democrat has seldom if ever been so described by the media. Republicans, especially Gingrich, are important actors in the drama, but they moved to center stage quite late in the process. Much of this is a story of the Democratic Party, which was after all the majority party in the House almost continuously from 1930 to 1994; and in the House, the majority party tends to be the protagonist—if not necessarily the hero—when it comes to important internal developments.[2] I tell the Democratic story in this chapter.

LAYING THE FOUNDATIONS FOR A MORE PARTISAN HOUSE

We can rarely get at true—first—origins of this kind of complex political and institutional change; but one good place to start is with the events of January 1975.

The elections of 1974 were fought in the wake of Watergate and President Ford's pardon of Nixon and also in the midst of a recession. Democrats, who before the election had had a comfortable House majority—242 of 435—picked up a net of forty-nine seats. When House Democrats met to organize, three venerable committee chairmen, men who had collectively served twenty-four years as committee chairs and 116 years in the House, were stripped of their chairmanships. The seventy-five freshmen, it was clear, had made the difference, and the headlines were all about how these "Watergate babies," as they were dubbed, had come into this hidebound institution and produced a revolution, suddenly and completely upending the old power structure.

The three senior members deposed were F. Edward Hebert of Louisiana, chairman of Armed Services; W. R. (Bob) Poage of Texas, chairman of Agriculture; and Wright Patman of Texas, chairman of Banking and Currency. Patman, although a liberal of the populist stripe, was considered erratic by many members. Hebert and Poage were very conservative. Hebert, in addition, was known as an autocrat in his committee. When Pat Schroeder and Ron Dellums, a woman and a black man and both liberals, were assigned to the Armed Services Committee over his objections in 1973, Hebert purposely provided only one chair for them at the committee's first meeting; as Pat Schroeder tells the story, she and Dellums, unwilling to give Hebert the satisfaction of complaining, sat "cheek to cheek" in that chair. Hebert also made the mistake of condescendingly addressing the class of 1974 as "boys and girls" when he spoke to the group. The freshmen had asked all the chairs to appear and explain why class members should vote for them! When the chairman of one of the most powerful committees indicated he was too busy, the freshmen sent back word that they would not vote for anyone who had not appeared. Miraculously, chairmen's schedules suddenly opened up and all spoke to the freshmen.

If, in fact, this group of seventy-five freshmen had managed on their own to engineer this coup within two months of being elected and after far less time in Washington, that would indeed have been miraculous. But while this made a great story, it was oversimplified to the point of being wrong. We need to go back briefly to the 1950s for clarification.

Committee Government and Liberal Discontent

The 1950s can be labeled an era of "committee government" in the House.[3] Legislation was produced by a number of autonomous committees headed by powerful chairmen who derived their positions solely from their seniority on the committee. The chairmen's great organizational and procedural powers—over subcommittee structure and membership, staff, and agenda—enabled them to shape decision making in their committees. The chairs usually worked with the Republican ranking member and other senior members and they collectively dominated the committee. Mutual deference among committees protected most legislation from serious challenge on the floor.

Within this system, the role of the majority party and its leadership was limited. Both the meager institutional resources of the party leaders and, especially for Democrats, party factionalism limited the scope of the party leadership's involvement and its influence. Democrats were in the majority for most of the period after 1930 and continuously from 1955 to 1994, yet from the late 1930 through the early 1980s, the party was split into a generally conservative southern wing and a more liberal northern wing (see fig. 3.1).

FIGURE 3.1
The North-South Split in the House Democratic Party, 1947–2004

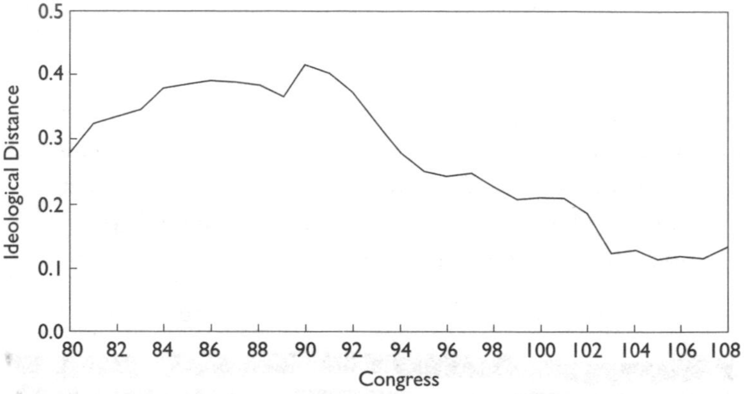

Ideological distance measure = difference between northern Democrats' and southern Democrats' DW-nominate score medians (absolute value)

The role of the party leadership in the policy process was largely limited to facilitating the passage on the floor of legislation written by autonomous committees. Party leaders seldom interceded in committees to shape legislation. Lacking any mechanism for holding the committees and their chairs accountable to the party, leaders coordinated and cajoled but played little policy role. Thus the leadership of Speaker Sam Rayburn (1940–46, 1949–52, 1955–61), the most highly regarded speaker of the committee-government era, was permissive, informal, and highly personalized. In his relations with the powerful committee chairs and in building floor coalitions, he relied on personal persuasion and made few demands. As Congressman Dick Bolling wrote in the mid-1960s, "A modern Democratic Speaker is something like a feudal king—he is first in the land; he receives elaborate homage and respect; but he is dependent on the powerful lords, usually committee chairmen, who are basically hostile to the objectives of the national Democratic Party and the Speaker. . . . Rayburn was frequently at odds with the committee oligarchs, who rule their own committees with the assured arrogance of absolute monarchs."[4] Members were seldom pressured to vote a given way; rather Rayburn, who obtained some leverage from the myriad small favors he performed for members, such as speaking to a committee chair on behalf of a project in a member's district, relied upon personal persuasion and members' sense of obligation.

The independence of the Rules Committee during this period even limited the party leadership's control over the scheduling of legislation for floor consideration. The Rules Committee reports out the special rules by which controversial legislation is brought to the floor and governs its consideration on the floor. In the late 1930s, the Rules Committee had come under the control of a bipartisan conservative coalition, and thereafter Democratic Speakers often had to bargain with the committee to get legislation supported by a majority of the majority party to the floor.

Intercommittee reciprocity meant that most committees could expect to pass most of their legislation on the floor without great difficulty. Consequently committees and their chairs did not often require help from the leadership. On the other hand, on those highly controversial issues that were fought out on the floor, bills involving race or labor relations, for example, party leaders often confronted a deep North-South split and had great difficulty in successfully building winning coalitions.

In the 1950s, conservative southern Democrats dominated Congress. They disproportionately held committee chairmanships and positions on the most desirable committees. In 1957, for example, nine of the nineteen committee chairmanships were held by Democrats from the southern states and four more by border state Democrats. Coming from the one-party South, they accumulated the necessary seniority more easily than their northern colleagues, many of whom represented more competitive constituencies. Thus the system, which allocated key positions on the basis of seniority, produced an ideologically biased distribution of influence that benefited conservative southern Democrats and disadvantaged liberal northern Democrats.

Some conservative southerners blatantly used their positions of influence to thwart northern liberals' policy goals. For example, Graham Barden, a very conservative North Carolinian, chaired the Education and Labor Committee, which had jurisdiction over much of the social welfare legislation that liberals advocated during the 1950s. His aim was to prevent the committee from reporting out progressive legislation, and he used all his powers as chair to accomplish that goal. He kept the committee staff small and, reportedly, incompetent; he refused to call committee meetings, and when committee members attempted to do so, he used the chairman's procedural powers to prevent the committee from making decisions. For a time he refused to set up permanent subcommittees, and later he denied liberal Adam Clayton Powell of Harlem a subcommittee chairmanship to which Powell should have been entitled by seniority.

Many House members found the committee government system well suited to advancing their goals. It enabled them to vote their districts and pay little or no penalty if that dictated voting against party majorities. It gave them the opportunity to ascend the seniority ladder to committee power, secure in the knowledge that no leader or faction could block them. For those from safe districts, the wait was not a major problem. And for those members who favored spending for constituency projects but opposed most broader social and economic legislation, the system produced the particularistic, constituency-benefit legislation they needed for reelection and not a great deal else. This group included the typical southern Democrat but a considerable number of other members as well.

For programmatic liberal Democrats, however, the calculus was different. Throughout the 1950s, liberal Democrats were discontented with the distribution of influence. They complained that no attempt was ever made to ascertain whether a party position could be reached on policy; instead policy making was left solely to the committees. They contended that senior committee leaders and the memberships of the most important committees were unrepresentatively conservative. They objected that even when liberal legislation was reported from a committee in the House, it was likely to be blocked or watered down by the very conservative Rules Committee. Liberals, many of whom were junior, were also unhappy with the limited opportunities afforded to junior members to participate meaningfully in the legislative process. Lack of sufficient staff, maldistribution of desirable committee positions, and autocratic committee chairs were sources of grievance.

Reforming the House

Until 1959 liberal Democrats lacked the numbers to do much more than complain. When conservative southern Democrats combined with Republicans in committee or on the chamber floor, this conservative coalition was more than large enough to dominate outcomes. The 1958 elections, however, brought in significant reinforcements, since most of the sixty-three new Democrats were liberals from competitive northern states and districts.

The class of 1958 swelled the ranks of the Democratic Study Group (DSG), a recently formed organization dedicated to mobilizing votes for liberal legislation and ultimately to reforming the House.[5] The class, however, had little other immediate effect. The Rules Committee, chaired by wily veteran "Judge" Howard Smith, a deeply conservative Virginian, continued to block liberal legislation from floor consideration or to extract substantive concessions in return for a rule. In a particularly notorious instance,

Smith and the bipartisan conservative coalition that controlled the committee refused a rule for a federal aid to education bill that had passed both chambers in 1960. Smith thus stopped the bill from going to a conference committee to work out House-Senate differences. His action killed legislation that liberals had spent years bringing to that point.

The 1960 election of John Kennedy as president confronted House Democrats with a potential embarrassment if not a full-fledged crisis. Kennedy's program might well be blocked by the Rules Committee in a chamber formally controlled by his own party. The DSG and the administration persuaded Speaker Sam Rayburn that something had to be done. He chose the least disruptive option—the least painful, in his words—of "packing" the committee. After a tough fight in early 1961, the House agreed by a 217–212 vote to increase the size of the Rules Committee, enabling the majority party to add to it two usually loyal Democrats. Even so, the Rules Committee was not always responsive to the party leadership or the administration.[6]

Although the enormous policy successes of the Great Society overshadowed reform efforts in the news and may have reduced liberal pressure for reform temporarily, the reform effort continued. Richard Nixon's election as president in 1968 again strengthened the reform impetus in the House. Liberals feared for the future of the Great Society programs and became increasingly concerned about the Vietnam War. The Democratic Party, in which the reform thrust was centered, had changed greatly in composition over the course of the 1960s and was now much more heavily northern and liberal than the Democratic Party of the 1950s. The proportion of House Democrats from the South (not including the border states), had decreased from 40 percent in the 1953–58 period to 33 percent during 1959–64 and 30 percent during 1965–74.[7] Yet southern Democrats still held a highly disproportionate share of the committee leadership positions;

in 1969, southern Democrats chaired eight of the twenty standing committees, including all three of the power committees—Appropriations, Ways and Means, and Rules—and a border state Democrat chaired one more. Of the thirteen powerful subcommittee chairmanships on the Appropriations Committee, five were held by southerners and three more by border state Democrats.

In 1969, reformers persuaded Speaker John McCormack to accept a party rule requiring monthly meetings of the House Democratic Caucus and thereby established that party body as a forum for further reform efforts.[8] Many of the issues reformers wanted to address were controlled by party rather than chamber rules and customs. In addition, though little noticed at the time, Caucus ratification of committee lists was instituted; previously the Committee on Committees had sent these lists directly to the floor.[9]

The first visible fruit of reform in the House was the 1970 Legislative Reorganization Act, which changed House rules. The act was the product of the Joint Committee on the Reorganization of Congress set up in 1965 under pressure from reformers in both chambers. In mid-1970, the House Rules Committee finally reported out a reform measure—but one that was considerably weaker than the Joint Committee's bill, itself far from radical, that had been referred to Rules. An informal bipartisan group composed of DSG leaders and junior, reform-minded Republicans (known as "Rumsfeld's Raiders" after their leader, Donald Rumsfeld of Illinois) decided to try to strengthen the bill by offering floor amendments aimed at opening up the legislative process to greater public scrutiny. In a brilliant tactical move, DSG leaders persuaded Thomas P. (Tip) O'Neill, Jr. (D-Mass.), a popular House insider not known as a reformer, to sponsor their most important amendment. Their successful proposal allowed twenty members to demand a recorded vote in the Committee of the Whole, where bills are amended. Previously such votes were not recorded, which greatly advantaged both the committee that had reported the bill and the committee chair. If a House member proposed or just voted for an amendment that the committee chair opposed, the chair, being on the floor, would know, but constituents and interest groups who supported the amendment would not. Hence the course politically safest for House members was to support the committee and its chair. Among other significant provisions in the act were several aimed at safeguarding the rights of committee minorities; for example, the act formalized the minority's right to call witnesses at hearings.[10]

By and large, however, the rules changes included in the 1970 act were the easiest reforms to pass. The Joint Committee had been specifically prohibited from making any recommendations about the rules, parliamentary procedure, practices, and precedents of the Senate or House, thus barring a consideration of seniority, House floor procedures, or the Senate filibuster.[11]

Reforms that changed the distribution of power in the House more significantly were made over the next five years. In 1970 the DSG persuaded the party leadership and then the Caucus to set up a committee to study seniority and recommend changes. Dubbed the Hansen Committee after its chair Julia Hansen (D-Wash.), a moderate with close ties to party leaders, the committee recommended many of the reforms eventually approved by the Democratic Caucus. The DSG, a number of whose leaders served on the Hansen Committee, remained the primary source of reform ideas and the chief internal proponent. Cooperating with outside reform groups such as Common Cause and the National Committee for an Effective Congress, the DSG also worked to arouse media interest and put external pressure on the House to change.

Two competing visions of a reformed House can be identified. One was associated with Representative Richard Bolling (D-Mo.), a cerebral student of the House as an institution, who had written several well-received books critiquing the House of the committee-government era. A protégé of Speaker Sam Rayburn and intimately familiar with the problems Rayburn had experienced with recalcitrant conservative committee chairs, Bolling advocated a House in which responsible parties governed. Long a loyalist member of the Rules Committee, Bolling saw the problem as one of autonomous committees with powerful chairs that the majority party had no means of holding accountable. Bolling's solution was strengthening the elected party leadership and making committees and their leaders responsive and accountable to the party as a whole.

The other was espoused by Phillip Burton (D-Calif.). A hard-charging DSG activist and a key member of the Hansen Committee, he put more emphasis on a House that gave its members maximum opportunity to participate in the legislative process. To be sure, Burton was a strong programmatic liberal dedicated to policy results, so presumably he did not favor participation at the expense of policy. But whether because he saw no conflict or because of the institutional positions he held (chair of the Democratic Study Group and then of the Democratic Caucus but not a member of the core elected party leadership), he usually stressed reforms such as the "Subcommittee Bill of Rights" that, as he himself expressed it, "spread the action."[12]

From the perspective of the ordinary rank-and-file reformer, both policy and participation were key problems that reforms needed to address, and at the heart of both problems were the overly powerful and independent committee chairmen. The rank and file perceived no conflict between increasing the opportunities for all members to participate in the legislative process and making the process more capable of producing legislation responsive to the policy preferences of the party majority.

These multiple perspectives driving reformers account for the seemingly contradictory thrusts of the early 1970s reforms. While some rules changes displayed a clearly centralizing thrust, others tended just as clearly toward decentralization. Centralizing reforms included granting the Speaker the power to nominate all Democratic members and the chairman of the Rules Committee, subject only to ratification by the Caucus, a Bolling proposal passed in early 1975. It was intended to give the party leadership true control over the scheduling of legislation for the floor and, in fact, made the committee an arm of the central leadership. Also in 1975, the power to make committee assignments was moved from the Ways and Means Committee Democrats, a fairly conservative group and one that did not include the Speaker as a member, to a new Steering and Policy Committee. This new party committee, which had been created in 1973, was chaired by the Speaker and included among its members the other elected leaders and a number of Speaker appointees. Thus the party leadership gained more influence over the composition of the committees as well as more resources for influencing members' behavior.

The new party rules that required committee chairs and the chairs of Appropriations subcommittees to win majority approval on a secret ballot in the Democratic Caucus were intended to make them responsive to the party majority and thus also had centralizing implications. The rules on choosing committee chairs were changed in a series of steps in 1971, 1973, and 1975; in 1975, Appropriations subcommittee chairs, who were considered to have as much policy-making power as many full committee chairs, were made subject to the same procedure.

In 1974, in response to Richard Nixon's assertion of what Congress considered unwarranted power over money matters, Congress passed the Budget and Impoundment Control Act, which instituted a new budget process. Every year, Congress is required to pass a budget resolution that provides guidelines for other legislative decisions about spending and taxing; the resolution may instruct committees to make changes in law to conform with the guidelines. If so, the Congress is mandated to pass a reconciliation bill, which is a package of changes in law in accordance with the budget resolution; that is, the bill reconciles law with the budget resolution. The new budget process would prove to have powerful centralizing implications.

Another set of reforms implemented at the same time was aimed at "spreading the action" and, as such, had decentralizing implications. In 1971 members were limited to chairing only one subcommittee, thus forcing some senior members to relinquish multiple chairmanships and distributing chairmanships more broadly among the membership. In addition, each subcommittee chair was authorized to hire one professional staff member. The 1973 "Subcommittee Bill of Rights" took the power to select subcommittee chairs from committee chairs and gave it to the Democratic caucus of the committee. It also guaranteed subcommittees automatic referral of legislation and adequate budget and staff. These reforms, all strongly advocated by Burton, reduced the control of the full committee chair and of other senior committee leaders over the committee's legislative activities.

The climax of the reform movement came in early 1975 with the deposing of the three committee chairs. The Watergate babies provided the votes, but they were the foot soldiers, not the generals. The DSG had fought a long series of battles before these freshmen were elected and had prepared the ground for this final climatic fight. Certainly the deposing of these chairs put even the least perceptive committee chairs on notice that they had to be responsive to the party membership if they wished to retain their positions.

During this period, in addition, both committee and personal staffs were expanded and distributed much more broadly among members. The number of employees of House committees increased from 702 in 1970 to 1,909 in 1979. In 1967, personal staff totaled

4,055, and few House members had even one full-time legislative assistant on their personal staff. By 1979, the total number of personal staff had risen to 7,067.[13] By the early 1980s, every House member was entitled to hire a personal staff of eighteen full-time and four part-time aides. Even junior members thus gained the resources to exploit their new opportunities for participation.

"Sunshine" reforms to open up the legislative process to public scrutiny, another important part of the reform thrust, were also successfully instituted in the first half of the 1970s. With most committee markups and conference committee meetings now open to the media and the public, members were encouraged to use those forums for policy entrepreneurship but also for grandstanding.[14]

By the mid-1970s, the committee-government system was dead and a very different House was emerging. The powers of committee chairs and their control over scarce resources had been severely curtailed; the bases of committee autonomy had been undermined. Committee action shifted from the full committee to the subcommittee level, with most hearings and many markups now taking place in subcommittee. The reforms significantly enhanced the powers and resources available to the party leadership for facilitating the passage of legislation. Most notably, the Speaker now controlled the Rules Committee, which sets the ground rules for the debate and amending of legislation on the floor. At the same time, however, rank-and-file members' incentives and capacity for participating in the legislative process had also expanded.

From Anarchy toward Party Government

In the immediate aftermath of the 1970s congressional reforms, the decentralizing thrust predominated in the House. By the mid-1970s, participation by the rank and file at the committee and the floor stage had increased enormously, and as a result, the number of significant participants in the legislative process on any particular bill multiplied. In the prereform era most legislation was brought to the House floor under a simple open rule that allowed all germane amendments; but since no recorded votes were possible in the Committee of the Whole (where bills are amended), the incentives to offer amendments were limited. Tax bills and often other legislation from the Ways and Means Committee were considered under a closed rule that allowed no amendments (except those offered by the committee itself); such legislation was regarded as too complex and too politically tempting a target to allow floor amendments. The reforms provided a procedure whereby members could offer floor amendments to such bills.

With rank-and-file members having greater incentives and resources for offering amendments on the floor, the number of floor votes and the number of amendments offered and pushed to a roll call vote shot up. The House took 433 recorded votes during the 91st Congress (1969–70), the last before the institution of the recorded teller vote; the number had more than tripled by the 95th Congress (1977–78), when 1,540 recorded votes were taken. Many more amendments were offered and pushed to a vote. In the 91st Congress, 107 amendments were offered and decided on a teller vote, the most transparent procedure then allowed in the Committee of the Whole. During the 92nd Congress, the first in which recorded votes were allowed in the Committee of the Whole, the number of amendments offered and pushed to a recorded vote rose to 195. Electronic voting on the House floor was instituted for the 93rd Congress, and the number of recorded votes on amendments jumped to 351. By the 95th, the number stood at 439.[15]

The large numbers of inexperienced subcommittee chairs combined with high participation radically increased uncertainty in the legislative process; predicting who would be involved, what amendments would be offered, and how members would vote became much harder. For example, in 1977 John Ashbrook, a conservative and clever Republican gadfly, offered an amendment that on the surface looked innocuous and attractive but in actuality would have placed severe restrictions on the political activities of labor unions—not the sort of policy that Democrats would knowingly embrace. But the floor manager—the subcommittee chair—was new, there were a lot of junior Democrats who had not learned to be suspicious of anything Ashbrook offered, and no system was in place to analyze the amendment immediately and inform Democrats. So the amendment passed. The committee staff figured out the amendment's real effect quite quickly and informed the party leadership, which pulled the bill off the floor. An internal information campaign was mounted: "It's a legislative lemon. It looks sweet on the outside but tastes bitter on the inside."[16] The results were reversed, but the party and many individual Democrats had been embarrassed.

The Democratic leaders of the mid-1970s believed—probably correctly—that their members were unwilling to accept significant constraints on their newly acquired opportunities to participate and thus made little use of their own new powers. As a senior leadership staffer observed at the time, "People . . . want leadership for the other guys, the guys who don't agree with them. They want the leadership to get those who defect from the positions they desire, but they don't want to be told what to do."[17]

By the end of the 1970s, however, many Democrats had become concerned about unexpected consequences of the reforms. The Ashbrook example shows why. Floor sessions regularly stretched late into the night, legislation crafted by now more representative committees was picked apart on the floor, and Democrats were repeatedly forced to go on the record on controversial amendments—on busing and abortion, for example. Democrats were having great difficulty passing legislation that they and their supporters badly wanted. For example, despite a Democratic president, Jimmy Carter, and big margins in both chambers in the late 1970s, Democrats failed to enact labor law reform or to establish a consumer protection agency, both high priorities. And yet, as figure 3.1 illustrates, Democratic ideological heterogeneity had steadily decreased as the North-South split declined.

House Democrats began to look to their party leadership for assistance. In the late 1970s, for example, some Democrats began to pressure their leaders to use special rules to bring floor proceedings under control. Forty Democrats wrote to Speaker Tip O'Neill in 1979 asking that he make more use of restrictive rules in order to curtail frequent late-night sessions.[18] With the election of Republican Ronald Reagan as president in 1980, members' need for leadership assistance became even more acute.

In an attempt to restore some control, House Democratic leaders began making more aggressive use of the powers and resources the reforms had bestowed on them. They began to employ special rules to bring order to floor proceedings and, over the course of the 1980s, developed them into powerful and flexible tools for managing floor time, focusing debate, and sometimes advantaging party-preferred outcomes. With committees and their chairs weakened, party leaders were more often drawn into what had previously been committee business; when committee leaders were unable to do so, it fell to party leaders to see that legislation the party membership wanted was moved to the floor—and in a form that could command a floor majority and was satisfactory to most Democrats. Over time, leaders became more and more deeply involved in the shaping of the most controversial legislation, which was also frequently the most important. Leaders often worked out postcommittee compromises to engineer passage; they occasionally set up extra-committee task forces to draft legislation. The new budget process demanded party leadership oversight, especially once it began to be used for enacting comprehensive policy change. When the president and Congress began to resort to summits—high-level, fairly formal direct negotiations—to come to agreement on seemingly intractable policy disputes, congressional party leaders, not committee leaders, most often represented their party and chamber.

ORGANIZATIONAL ELABORATION, CHANGING INCENTIVES, AND THE AMPLIFICATION OF PARTY COHESION

During the 1970s and 1980s, the Democratic Party revitalized and elaborated its organization in the House; both the leadership's need for assistance in putting together legislative majorities and members' desire to participate in the legislative process drove this development. The changing expectations of a more ideologically homogeneous party membership influenced how the various party entities functioned. A consequence of these developments was an alteration in members' incentives.

During the committee-government era, the party organization was skeletal by later standards, and the entities that existed were seldom used. Under Rayburn, the Caucus met only at the beginning of a Congress and primarily to ratify decisions made elsewhere. In Rayburn's view, meetings would provide a forum for the factions in the party to confront each other directly and would thereby only worsen the intraparty split. A Steering Committee existed on paper but never met. A Democratic whip system consisting of a whip and a number of regional assistant whips first arose in the early 1930s. By Rayburn's speakership, it was composed of the whip, a deputy whip, and approximately eighteen regionally elected zone whips, but it was not very active. The whip operation infrequently gathered systematic information on Democrats' voting intentions and seldom engaged in organized persuasion efforts. Because the zone whips were chosen by the members of their regional zones, the leadership could not depend on their being loyal to the party position.

The development of Democratic party organization from the early 1970s through the early 1990s illustrates how external and internal factors interacted to heighten party cohesion. Briefly stated, party leaders—responding to demands from members who were increasingly homogeneous ideologically—revitalized, elaborated, and aggressively used party organs and the resources they gave the leaders and, in the process, significantly increased members' incentives to act as team players.

The Committee Assignment Process: Changing Criteria and Changing Behavior

In 1973 House Democratic reformers succeeded in creating a Steering and Policy Committee, replacing a long-inactive Steering Committee, and in late 1974 they made it the Democratic committee on committees, thus assuring it a role of real significance. The reformers intended the Steering and Policy Committee to be a centralizing entity that would increase the party leadership's clout; they also intended it to be accessible and accountable to the membership.

For members of the House, committee assignment decisions have been and continue to be among the most crucial of their House lives. The committees on which they serve determine the issues on which they spend most of their time and shape the strategies they have available for advancing their reelection, policy, and power goals.[19] The membership composition of a committee strongly influences the character of its policy outputs and, consequently, is important to all those members whose policy or reelection goals are thereby affected. Thus members—and leaders—care not only about their own committee assignments but also, though to a widely varying extent, about the makeup of other committees.

Throughout the committee-government era, the Democrats on the Ways and Means Committee served as the party's committee on committees. The party leaders, thus, were not members of the party organ that assigned members to the standing committees, and the influence they exercised over such assignments was informal and indirect. Moving the assignment function to a committee chaired by the Speaker and one with a heavy leadership presence was therefore a major augmentation of leadership resources, at least potentially.

Initially, the committee consisted of twenty-four members: the Speaker, the Majority Leader, and two other elected party leaders were ex officio members; twelve members were elected from geographical zones; and eight members were appointed by the Speaker. Through a mix of regionally elected, appointed, and ex officio members, reformers hoped to strike a balance among a number of not necessarily congruent concerns. The regional members were expected to represent the subsets that elected them: to provide access for and be accountable to those members. The Speaker was expected to use his appointments in part to assure the representativeness of the committee by appointing members from subgroups not otherwise included. Thus the Speaker's appointees usually included a woman, an African American, and a freshman. Making the Speaker chair, including other top leaders as ex officio members, and giving the Speaker appointive powers were clearly intended to give the leadership—and the kind of party-based criteria the leadership was expected to emphasize—significant influence on the committee's decisions.

In fact, from the 1970s to the 1990s, party loyalty did become an increasingly important criterion for assignment, especially to the power committees—Appropriations, Ways and Means, and Budget. The decisions of these committees with their jurisdiction over spending and revenue were of great interest to all party members and were considered vital to the party's reputation. As early as the late 1970s, Steering and Policy had available during its deliberations explicit indicators of party loyalty. Thus, in 1979, several party leaders brought in indexes of party loyalty, and at the request of other members of Steering and Policy the scores were written on the blackboard next to the nominees' names. Data on House Democrats' committee requests indicate that loyalty did make a difference. In 1979, for example, nineteen incumbent members requested the Budget Committee; the mean party unity score of those assigned was 81.8 percent; of those passed over, 72.8 percent.[20] The four Steering and Policy Committee choices of incumbent members for the Appropriations Committee had a mean party unity score of 65.9 percent, while the mean score of the five requestors not assigned was 54.4 percent.

Steering and Policy's Ways and Means assignments were the exception in the 96th Congress—with revealing results. The three incumbents selected by the Steering and Policy Committee as a group scored slightly lower than six not selected (65 percent versus 68.9 percent). A conflict among leadership goals accounts for this deviation from the pattern. Two of the nominees had high party support scores (84 percent mean); the third, Ralph Hall of Texas, had a very low score (26.8 percent). The Texas Democratic delegation, traditionally ideologically heterogeneous, had long followed a seniority rule in deciding whom among its members to support for committee positions. When a "Texas" seat on Ways and Means opened up and Ralph Hall was the senior delegation member expressing interest, Majority Leader Jim Wright believed he had to support his state colleague, despite opposition from some in the inner leadership circle. Wright prevailed in the Steering and Policy Committee. In the Democratic Caucus, however, Hall was defeated by a much more supportive southerner. Clearly the use of party loyalty as a criterion was not leadership-imposed.

By the late 1980s and early 1990s, the importance of party loyalty had increased significantly, my interviews indicate. The party leaders computed party support scores for members based upon their own selection of key votes. In nominating speeches for exclusive committees, the party loyalty of nominees in voting and their efforts on behalf of party causes were prominently mentioned. One nomination began: "'A' voted 97 percent with the leadership." This nominee to Appropriations had "taken some tough votes," had helped the Democratic Congressional Campaign Committee with fund-raising despite still having a campaign debt, and "was a team player." Another candidate was presented as having "over 90 percent support for the leadership. He has been very active on [whip] task forces, he represents a good Democratic district and is a team player." About a third candidate, the nominator said: "He comes from a conservative district but votes with the leadership a good part of the time. He's shown himself to be courageous." Even for committees below the top ranks of the exclusive committees, party loyalty was increasingly mentioned.

Although data on committee requests for these Congresses are not available, other evidence does support the increased importance of party loyalty. The mean party unity score in the Congress before appointment of the sixteen nonfreshmen members who received Appropriations slots during the 98th through 102nd Congresses (1983–92) was 87 percent, and only two of the sixteen scored more than two points below the mean for all Democrats in the Congress. Ways and Means appointees averaged 86 percent party unity, and only three of eleven scored below the Democratic mean. For Budget, the mean score was 85 percent, and ten of thirty-nine appointees scored more than a point below the mean for all Democrats.

Because of the unusually large number of vacancies, assignments to the key committees in the 103rd Congress provide a particularly good test of the importance of party loyalty. The eleven continuing members newly assigned to Appropriations had a mean party unity score in the previous Congress of 92; the lowest scorer who received an assignment, a southerner, had voted with his party 83 percent of the time. The nine continuing members who received Ways and Means assignments had averaged 89 percent on the party unity index; the two who had scored below the party mean of 86—both southerners—had scores in the mid-70s. On Budget with its rotating membership, Steering and Policy relaxed the standard, but only a little; five of the twelve newly assigned members had scored below the party average in the previous Congress, though only one—Bill Orton of Utah—was among the party's least reliable supporters with a score of 59, and the mean of all the new members was 85. Thus most of the members who landed spots on these desirable committees were loyalists.

The party leadership's increasing clout on the Steering and Policy Committee likely contributed to this growing emphasis on party loyalty. As leadership positions proliferated in the 1980s and early 1990s, the number of ex officio leadership members on Steering and Policy increased—to thirteen of thirty-five in the mid-1990s—giving the Speaker "operating control" of the committee, as a leadership staffer phrased it. The leaders increasingly put together leadership slates for the most desirable slots, and leaders could and did promise members good committee assignments as future rewards.

The emphasis on loyalty, however, was by no means imposed by a heavy-handed leadership on a reluctant membership. Especially in the early years, members pushed the leadership in that direction. In 1979, it was nonleadership members of Steering and Policy who insisted that leadership loyalty indices be publicly displayed during the selection process. When Steering and Policy chose the ultraconservative Ralph Hall for Ways and Means, the party membership revolted and defeated him by a Caucus vote. Early in Tom Foley's speakership, when two choice positions went to members who, though generally loyal, had defected on an important leadership vote, "there was a lot of grumbling by members." As members' party unity scores increased, selecting loyal members for the choice assignments became easier, of course; but, in addition, most members came to believe that party support should make a difference and to expect that the committee contingents, especially on the most important committees, would reflect the party mainstream.

To be sure, party loyalty has never been nor is it now the only criterion of concern to either members or leaders. Giving Democratic Party members committee assignments that will aid them in reelection has always been a major goal, as has producing a slate that the membership outside Steering and Policy considers fair. In a body where representation is geographically based, fairness is largely though not exclusively defined in terms of region. Southern Democrats were, of course, more conservative than northern Democrats and, even now, are on average somewhat less liberal than their northern party colleagues; but their region is nevertheless considered entitled to its share of the good committee assignments. However, as overall party loyalty increased, it became easier and more accepted to choose more rather than less loyal southern Democrats for the most desirable positions.

Because committee assignments are so important to members' House careers, members are highly attentive to the criteria the selection committee employs. As early as the late 1970s, members became aware that loyalty was being given more emphasis. One participant, discussing the process in 1979, said: "Generally, loyalty to the leadership and to the principles of the Democratic Party was stressed much more than in the past—certainly more than four years ago. Members seem to have realized that this would be the case. The letters sent to the leadership asking for support for committee positions tended to stress loyalty explicitly." And the increased attention to loyalty does seem to affect members' behavior. "[The leadership] was watching and so we who were interested in Appropriations did watch our votes at the end of the 101st, feeling that might make a difference, that we could screw things up if we didn't watch out," a member explained. In sum, the change in the criteria for choice committee assignments, made possible by decreasing ideological heterogeneity, seems also to have had some amplifying effect on party voting and other sorts of party-regarding behavior.

Choosing Committee Chairs

The alteration in the rules for choosing committee chairs had an immediate and dramatic effect. Even after the reforms weakening the power of committee chairs, committee chairmanships remained highly valued positions, and the dumping of sitting chairs in early 1975 made it clear that the positions were "the gift of the Caucus." My interviews in the late 1970s suggested that party leaders then expected the chairs qua chairs to be responsive to strongly held sentiments in the party Caucus and, in a general way, to leaders' judgments on issues of central concern to the party and its reputation; they did not necessarily expect chairs to toe the line tightly in their own floor voting behavior. Yet, in fact, there was a change in chairs' and other senior committee members' voting behavior. John Hibbing found a sharp increase in the party support scores of chairs and second- and third-ranked Democrats from the early 1970s to the early 1980s (92nd to 97th Congresses); and this was true for southern and northern Democrats considered separately.[21] Jamie Whitten's journey from southern conservative to mainstream Democrat illustrates this nicely. Whitten, a Mississippi Democrat first elected in 1941, became a subcommittee chair on the Appropriations Committee in the heyday of committee government. But when the rules on picking Appropriations subcommittee chairs and full committee chairs changed and he got close to and then

FIGURE 3.2
Whitten Joins the Fold

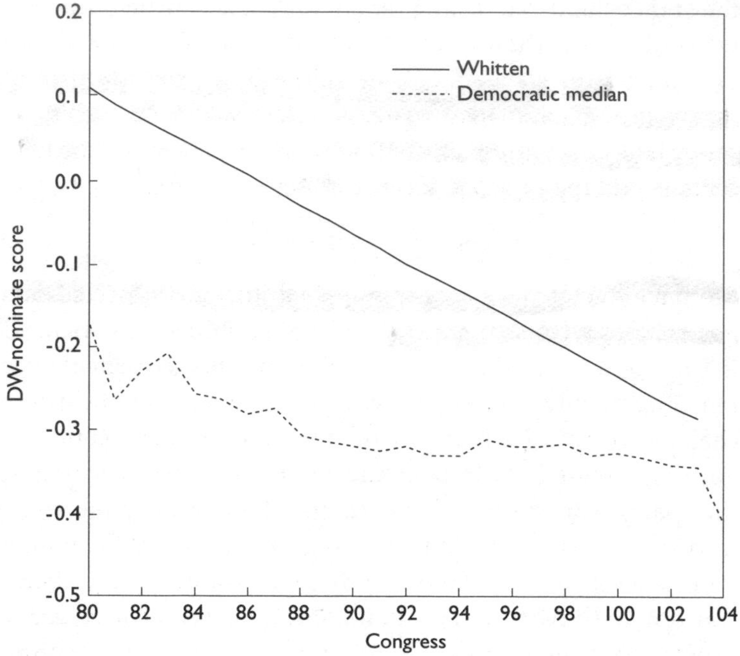

became chair of the full committee, Whitten's voting behavior also changed (see fig. 3.2).

Because committee chairs by and large got the message and realized that they had to be attentive to strongly held caucus sentiment, the Caucus seldom had to enforce responsiveness by voting out chairs. In the 1980s and early 1990s, there were a few other instances of the most senior member being passed over or of a chair being dumped, but in most cases, ideological deviance and recalcitrance were not the primary problems.

In Les Aspin's close call in 1987, arguments that he had acted as an unfaithful agent of the Democratic Caucus in policy terms did play a major role. Aspin, who in 1985 succeeded Mel Price as chair of Armed Services even though he was less senior than six other committee Democrats, was rejected by the Caucus on the initial ratification vote in January of 1987. A considerable proportion of Democrats believed he had reneged on policy promises he had made two years earlier. In the end, Aspin won the chairmanship again in a four-person contest. He certainly interpreted the experience as a warning and promised to be more responsive, "more open [and] more up front."[22]

In the remaining cases, however, policy responsiveness seems to have played a secondary role. Mel Price lost the chairmanship of Armed Services in 1985; in late 1990 Glen Anderson was voted out of the Public Works chairmanship and Frank Annunzio lost his position as chair of House Administration. All three were perceived by many members as incompetent committee leaders due in large part to advanced age. In the first and last cases, policy position and party image also motivated the revolts. Price was seen as too unquestioning a supporter of the military and as not capable of representing the Democratic position in debates with the administration on the questions of arms control, weapons systems, and military spending that were so prominent during the 1980s. Many Democrats opposed Annunzio because they did not want a member tainted by the savings and loan scandal representing them in the battle over campaign reform legislation, which was within the jurisdiction of the House Administration Committee. Commenting on the events of 1990, senior Democrat and activist David Obey remarked: "It sends a message to all chairmen that they have to be more responsive. What this demonstrates is that people don't want to have to work around chairmen. They want to be able to work through them."[23]

When the chairman of the Appropriations Committee died in 1994, the Steering and Policy Committee by a strong vote chose as his successor David Obey rather than Neal Smith (D-Iowa), who was next in line, and the Caucus ratified the nomination handily. Both Smith and Obey were liberals, but most Democrats decided that Obey's aggressive leadership style and his skill at promoting party priorities outweighed the dictates of seniority.

These cases show how Democrats' expectations of their committee leaders changed. In the mid-1970s, Democrats expected committee chairs to be fair, to allow participation within their committees, and to refrain from blocking legislation on which the Democratic membership wanted to vote. By the mid-1980s, they increasingly expected the committee chairs to act as party leaders, promoting the party agenda and the party image through legislation and in public debate.

It was Democratic members, not their party leaders, who spearheaded these efforts against chairs. In fact, in some of these cases, the leadership opposed violating seniority. During the 1985 fight over the Armed Services Committee chairmanship, Speaker Tip O'Neill first tried to get Mel Price to take the title of "chairman emeritus" and step aside but, when Price refused, strongly supported him.[24] From the leaders' perspective, the existence of the rules requiring Steering and Policy and Caucus approval of committee chairs was highly beneficial because they put chairs on notice. Leaders sometimes used the existence of the rules to pressure committee leaders. In the late 1970s, leaders would occasionally suggest that a chair who refused to show responsiveness might have trouble with Caucus ratification. When a committee chair voted against upholding a ruling of the chair (that is, of the presiding officer of the House), Speaker O'Neill upbraided him publicly, pointing out that such votes were crucial to the majority party's control of the floor and threatening him with loss of his chairmanship were he ever to do it again. But the leaders preferred the rules to serve as a "gun in the closet"; they feared the divisiveness actual use might engender. Still, by the mid-1990s, when Steering and Policy passed over

Neal Smith for David Obey, the leadership was carefully neutral, at least in public. Given the overwhelming vote for Obey in Steering and Policy (18 to 7 when the vote count was stopped because Obey had a majority of the total vote) and the leadership's influence in that panel, the top leaders may well have voted for Obey and certainly did not lobby against him.

Subcommittee chairs and aspirants have also been challenged in the Democratic caucus of the committee, which chooses subcommittee chairs. Committee Democrats bid for chair positions in order of committee seniority and required a majority in a secret-ballot ratification vote by their fellow committee Democrats. In 1979, in perhaps the earliest case, Henry Waxman (D-Calif.), a member of the 1974 class, won the chairmanship of the prestigious Health and Environment Subcommittee of the powerful Interstate and Foreign Commerce Committee over the more senior Richardson Preyer (D-N.C.). As Preyer was a moderate and a respected member, ambition seems to have played a greater role than concern about a too-conservative and unresponsive chair. At the same time, however, the very conservative David Satterfield (D-Va.) did not even bid for a subcommittee on the Commerce Committee despite his seniority; according to the contemporary consensus, he knew he had absolutely no chance of being ratified. Both ambition and concern about subcommittee chairs who were either out of step ideologically or simply not active enough continued to motivate occasional challenges. When in 1989 Judiciary Committee Democrats voted Romano Mazzoli (D-Ky.) out of the Immigration Subcommittee chairmanship he had held for eight years, Mazzoli's tendency to deviate from the party position on selected important votes and his leadership style were at issue.[25] Certainly the selection procedure that the reforms had instituted and how it has been used have changed the incentives for sitting or aspiring subcommittee chairs; responsiveness in both policy and leadership style are encouraged.

At the height of the reform period, liberals attempted to use the Democratic Caucus as an instrument for enforcing responsiveness by committee leaders. The Caucus in the early 1970s passed a series of resolutions urging or ordering committees to act on anti–Vietnam War measures that had been bottled up. In 1972, for example, the Caucus directed the Foreign Affairs Committee to report out legislation ending U.S. military involvement in Southeast Asia. The committee complied, but the resolution failed in the House. The Caucus also several times used its new authority to instruct the Rules Committee to allow floor votes on specific amendments to tax bills, which had previously been considered under closed rules. The repeal of the oil depletion allowance resulted from that procedure. Greater committee responsiveness and concerns about undermining the committee system led to a decline in Caucus legislative activity by the late 1970s, and the frequency of Caucus meetings declined. When the Caucus became more active again in the 1980s, it performed somewhat different functions.

The Whip System

The development of the whip system also significantly increased members' incentives to act as team players, if in a less direct way. As noted, in the late 1960s the Democratic whip system consisted of the whip, a deputy whip, and approximately eighteen regionally elected zone whips.[26] In the 1970s and 1980s the whip system expanded as the number of whips appointed by the leadership increased. The deputy whip position was divided into two positions in 1970. In 1972 the position of chief deputy whip was created, and the number of deputy whips grew to three. Three new appointive positions, called at-large whips, were added in 1975. Women, blacks, and freshmen were demanding inclusion in the whip system, and these new positions were created in response. When Tip O'Neill became Speaker in 1977, he increased the number of at-large whips to ten. In 1981 a fourth deputy whip position was created, and the number of at-large whips rose to fifteen. The title "task force chairman" was created for Richard Gephardt in the mid-1980s. During the 1980s and early 1990s, the number of deputy and at-large whips continued to grow, and in 1991 and 1992, the chief deputy whip position was split into three and then four positions to accommodate women, African Americans, southerners, and Latinos, who were all clamoring for inclusion in the top ranks of the leadership.

In summary, a whip system that consisted of twenty-one members in the 91st Congress (1969–70) expanded to forty-four by the 97th (1981–82), to eighty-one by the 100th Congress (1987–88), and to ninety-four in the 103rd Congress (1993–94). In 1993, the whip system consisted of the whip, four chief deputy whips, eleven deputy whips, a floor whip, an ex officio whip, two task force chairs, fifty-six at-large whips, and eighteen zone whips. "The next step is to rent RFK Stadium for the whip meetings," a long-time deputy whip joked. Except for the whip, who like the Speaker and the Majority Leader is elected by the full Democratic Caucus, and the zone whips, who are elected by regional groups of members, the whips are appointed by the top leaders.

The expanded whip system has always been highly diverse, including members from all segments of the party. Northerners and southerners, conservatives and moderates as well as liberals, women, African Americans, and Latinos are all represented. Junior members—including, in the 103rd Congress, eight freshmen—were a part of the system but so were very senior members; in the 103rd, seven committee chairs served as appointed whips.

The leadership's need for help in a changing environment fueled the whip system's early expansion.[27] The initial impetus came from the Democratic loss of the White House in 1968, which deprived the House leadership of services previously provided by the administration liaison staffs. The unpredictability of the immediate postreform House environment and the adverse political climate of the 1980s increased the demands members placed on their leaders for legislative assistance and made meeting those expectations difficult for the leadership. In the 1960s the zone whips were charged with both obtaining vote counts and persuading their colleagues to support the leadership position.[28] Yet because they are chosen by the members of their zones, their loyalty to party and to the leadership was sometimes minimal. A few southern whips even refused to provide the leadership with names in their polling results, supplying only total "yeses" and "nos." The leadership needed a loyal group of assistants to aid in persuasion efforts and appointed whips to get that help.

Members' desire for inclusion contributed to the expansion as well. The size and workload of the House makes it difficult for an ordinary member to obtain an overview of what is going on. Most members' participation was limited to their often rather narrow committee turf. Party leaders did have the overview, and the whip system offered one of the few routes to broader participation. Jim Wright described the whip meetings of the early 1970s when he served as a deputy whip as the most interesting, stimulating meetings he attended, saying he looked forward all week to those get-togethers. And he at the time was a senior member of the Public Works Committee.

As the leadership became more active and more central in the legislative process, members became increasingly eager for access to the leadership and for inclusion in its orbit. More and more Democrats sought to become part of the whip system, and since the number of regionally elected whips is fixed, they asked to be appointed by the leadership. Democrats who had served the maximum of two consecutive zone whip terms that Caucus rules allow often requested an appointed slot.

The expanded whip system performed two primary functions: it served as a central conduit for information between leaders and members, and it played a key role in the vote mobilization process. Weekly whip meetings provided an important forum for the exchange of information. Leaders announced the legislative schedule, discussed strategy, alerted members to late-breaking developments, and urged them to work and vote for the party position. At the leaders' behest or on their own initiative, whips informed their fellow members of progress on legislation of general interest, explained floor strategy, and asked for support. The whip meetings gave members the opportunity to convey their concerns to their leaders on the whole spectrum of issues, to question and confront leaders, and to require them to justify their decisions. Thus the meetings gave members a shot at influencing their leaders and a basis for assessing whether the leadership was, in fact, acting as a faithful agent. This was valued by members and was considered a major payoff of being a whip. As one whip explained, "It is clearly of some value in terms of the access to the leadership and being in the network of activities so that you know what is happening earlier. . . . There have been a number of instances where I have learned of things in time to have an influence that I may not have learned about quite so promptly [otherwise] and where the time frame would have been too short to have influenced events." For leaders, the meetings provided information on the wishes and moods of their members and an opportunity to explain their decisions to a cross section of the membership.

The core functions of whip system are conducting whip counts and mobilizing votes. Whip counts are conducted to determine the voting intentions of House Democrats on major legislation. The initial count provides the information necessary for an effectively targeted persuasion effort. "A whip count is never really completed," a participant explained. "It's a rolling process of turning names over, of counting and persuading. A process, not an event."

By the 1980s, Democrats had divided that process into two distinct phases: the initial count conducted by the zone whips, and the process of refining the count and of persuasion carried out by a whip task force. The division arose out of the problem created by the uncertain loyalty of some of the zone whips. The heavy workload contributed to its continuation. The uncertainty of the 1970s House environment with its large number of floor votes made it necessary to conduct whip polls more frequently.

By the mid-1970s, appointed whips and then other interested members were being drawn into vote mobilization efforts on a fairly frequent basis. Then, in 1977, Speaker O'Neill began using especially appointed task forces to carry out vote mobilization on legislation considered centrally important and difficult. According to a senior O'Neill aide, the new leadership had narrowly lost an important bill early in 1977, a loss O'Neill attributed to lack of organization. The Speaker's response was the task force, an ad hoc group charged with passage of a specific bill.

In the early 1980s, new whip Tom Foley brought task forces into the whip system. In 1987, when Tony Coelho became whip, he instituted a streamlined procedure that then became institutionalized. All leadership vote mobilization efforts became task force efforts. With rare exceptions, the decision to conduct a whip count was also a decision to have a task force. A chair was chosen first, or often two or more cochairs; almost always one was from the committee that reported the bill; the other was often but not always from the whip system. Then, in most cases, an invitation to participate was sent to all the whips and to the Democrats on the committee or committees of origin. The notice informed them of the time and place of the first task force meeting and invited them to attend. Whoever showed up constituted the task force. Occasionally, on legislation of extreme political delicacy—a congressional pay raise, for example—task force members were selected and invited individually, but the great majority were general-invitation task forces. The task force usually worked from the zone whip count; it was responsible both for refining the count and for persuasion.

The task force device developed and persisted because it benefited both leaders and members. Task forces gave leaders badly needed help; they made it possible for the leadership to involve itself in a large number of legislative battles. Conducting several full-scale vote mobilization efforts simultaneously—as often occurred during the busiest periods—became feasible.

Task forces provided members, especially junior members, with opportunities to participate meaningfully in the legislative process on issues that interested them. One of the reformers' complaints had been that the committee-government system severely restricted opportunities to participate for junior members in particular. While reforms had opened up committee processes to greater involvement by all committee members, senior and midlevel members continued to have advantages of expertise and experience and so to take the lead. Effective task force work required time and political savvy rather than deep substantive expertise, and it allowed members to get involved in issues outside their committees' jurisdiction.

Serving on task forces "has been useful in at least three ways," explained David Price, an unusually reflective junior member, in the early 1990s:

> First, it has let me help mobilize support for measures that I thought were important. . . . Second, it has made me a partner, albeit a junior one, in leadership undertakings. This can be intrinsically satisfying and it can also bring other rewards. Those of us [seeking assignment to Appropriations] joked about what a coincidence it was that we so often found ourselves on the whip's task forces. Finally, it has brought me into discussions of floor strategy and the last-minute alterations needed to maximize votes on various bills.[29]

Speaker Tip O'Neill believed that giving a large number and a wide variety of Democrats "a piece of the action," but under the aegis of the leadership, and thus giving them a stake in the leadership's success, would make those members more responsive to the leadership generally. Work on a task force was thought to be especially likely to influence junior members, to teach them the value of joint action under the aegis of the party. Studies indicate that he was correct; working on a task force did seem to lead to an increase in party voting in the late 1970s and early 1980s.[30] Even as the Democratic membership became progressively less heterogeneous ideologically, the leadership still benefited from members' understanding the problems of coalition building and the payoffs of joint action. Junior members, with their lesser committee responsibilities, continued to serve on task forces disproportionately, and the experience likely continued to heighten their perception of having collective interests with their fellow party members and so to socialize them to partisanship.

Forums for Participation

Other partisan forums for participation also developed in the wake of the reforms. The Democratic Caucus itself could potentially serve as the most inclusive forum. Caucus rules specify that the Caucus meets monthly and upon petition of fifty members. The frequency of meetings had declined in the late 1970s, as noted. But after the 1980 elections, with the loss of the White House and the blow to Democratic morale these elections brought, Caucus meetings again became much more frequent as a forum for the discussion of legislative and political strategy—and the venting of dissatisfaction. Since the early 1980s, the level of Caucus activity has remained fairly high, though it continues to vary with members' felt need for the sort of inclusive forum the Caucus provides. During the 102nd Congress (1991–92), for example, the Caucus met forty-four times; thirty-two of the meetings were primarily devoted to policy discussions, most of the rest to organizational matters.[31]

The Caucus also spawned a variety of committees and task forces, providing still more opportunities for members to participate. Since 1981, the Caucus has always established issue task forces. In recent years, these task forces have usually consisted of a mix of senior members, often from the committee or committees with jurisdiction, and of issue activists, who often did not serve on the committee or were more junior. These task forces produced issue papers and positions on a variety of the issues of concern to Democrats. Again, the membership of each task force was as diverse as the Caucus leadership could make it, and any Democrat who wanted to participate was welcome. The activity level of these task forces varied greatly; some seem to have been mere paper entities; others did serious substantive and sometimes public relations work. As I discuss later, they became somewhat more important when Democrats lost their majority.

To allow members to reflect upon issues in some depth and with a longer-range time horizon and to provide them with opportunities to discuss with colleagues political and policy problems in a broad context, the Caucus has since 1981 sponsored yearly issue conferences or retreats. A three-day event, the annual retreat is often held in a resort setting; members bring their families and spend the time getting to know one another better and discussing issues in a way that the normal jam-packed congressional schedule does not allow. As with the other forums for participation, the retreat sessions provide members with an opportunity to communicate their views to the leadership and give them a shot at influencing both their leaders and their colleagues.

The various forums for participation grew in importance as the Democratic Party leadership escalated its use of restrictive rules in the 1980s. Offering floor amendments had become a pervasive means of participation in the wake of the reforms, one used by Democrats as well as Republicans and, of course, one favored especially by energetic activists. As I discuss in chapter 5, the leadership's response to the uncertainty and sometimes chaos that large numbers of floor amendments created was to use special rules to restrict the amendments that could be offered; and this affected Democrats as well as Republicans. To be sure, the leadership could not have restricted the amending process as it did if the Democratic membership had not become considerably more ideologically homogeneous by that time. These special rules require majority support on the floor, and because Republicans increasingly voted against such rules, passing the rules necessitated much more than a bare majority of Democrats. That is, if Democrats had not seen restrictive rules as being in their collective interest, the rules would not have been approved; and that perception of collective interest depended on a considerable coincidence of legislative preferences. Nevertheless, no American party is ever perfectly homogeneous ideologically, and offering floor amendments was a valued means of participation in the legislative process, even beyond any policy effect it might have. The partisan forums for participation thus provided an alternative and a safety valve.

Asserting Control over House Rules

Because the House is not a continuing body, it must adopt its rules anew in each Congress. Most of the rules in the resolution offered, usually as the first order of business after the election of the Speaker, are identical to the rules from the previous Congress, but the resolution does provide an opportunity to make alterations. Although offered by the majority party, the resolution before the mid-1970s reforms nevertheless frequently split majority Democrats; those who voted against their leadership and the majority of their party colleagues faced no retribution, even when the rules package had been endorsed by a formal vote in the Democratic Caucus.

At the beginning of nine of the thirteen Democratic-controlled Congresses from 1949 through 1976 (81st through 94th Congresses), rules fights occurred that resulted in a recorded vote. The twenty-one-day rule for circumventing the Rules Committee when it refused to report a rule for legislation before it for twenty-one days was the bone of contention in the 81st Congress, when such a rule was adopted, and in the 82nd, when it was repealed. In the 87th Congress, Speaker Rayburn's proposal to pack the Rules Committee provoked an epic battle. In the 88th Congress, the Rules Committee was permanently enlarged. The heavily Democratic 89th Congress again adopted the twenty-one-day rule and a rule that made it easier to send bills to conference. In the next Congress, the twenty-one-day rule was once more repealed. In the 92nd Congress, an attempt to reinstate a thirty-one-day version of the same rule failed. Thus, from 1949 through 1971, when there were fights over rules, they centered on the power of the Rules Committee. On the most indicative roll call in each of these Congresses, an average of sixty-four Democrats defected from the party majority, and almost all of these were southerners. In fact, in three of these seven Congresses, the majority party leadership and the majority of the majority party lost (82nd, 90th, 92nd).

At the beginning of the 93rd and 94th Congresses (1973, 1975), the rules resolutions, now aimed at a variety of problems, elicited far fewer defections, an average of twenty-five, again almost all southerners.[32] After the 94th Congress, when the reforms were fully in place, Democratic defections almost disappeared; the mean for the 95th through the 108th Congresses is less than four. By far the highest number was twenty-seven in 1993, when the Democratic package included an extremely controversial provision giving nonvoting delegates and commissioners a vote in the Committee of the Whole. Even in this case, the defections were on adoption of the resolution, not on the previous question, on which only three Democrats defected. If the previous question is defeated, the opposition gains the right to offer an amendment. After the mid-1970s and the reforms, expectations changed, and the vote on the party rules package became a test of party loyalty almost as much as the speakership vote; voting with the party was especially expected on the previous question vote, the loss of which would turn control of the floor over to the minority party.

Republican voting on these rule package votes suggests that their expectations underwent a similar change. In the 1950s and into the 1960s, members seem to have considered the votes ideological tests not really related to one's partisan standing. On the 81st and 82nd Congress votes, an average of forty-three Republicans voted against the majority of their party and with the bulk of northern Democrats; in the 87th through 89th Congresses, Republican defections still averaged fifteen; but thereafter Republican defections almost completely vanished, averaging 0.3 over the nineteen Congresses from 1967 through 2004.

The growing ideological homogeneity, the perception of collective interest heightened by members' participation in party activities, and the more concrete preferments the leadership commanded made possible changes in House rules that then further promoted partisan cohesion. An early such rules change was won in September 1979. Richard Gephardt, at Speaker Tip O'Neill's behest, inserted into a bill to raise the debt ceiling a rules change that would in the future automatically—without a vote—raise the debt limit the necessary amount when the House approved its budget resolution. The provision was upheld on the floor with only twenty Democrats voting against it.[33] The periodic vote to raise the debt ceiling had bedeviled House majority party leaders for years. Were the Congress to refuse, the United States would go into default on its debt, an unthinkable catastrophe. Yet, especially when the same party controlled both the presidency and the Congress, the debt limit vote offered the minority party an irresistible opportunity for posturing and putting majority members on the spot. Some Democrats wilted under the pressure, and others succumbed to the temptation to posture as well. Consequently passing the debt limit increase absorbed a great deal of leadership time and energy, and frequently the first vote failed. The new procedure under what was dubbed the Gephardt rule thus saved the leadership resources it could use elsewhere and saved Democrats from having to take a hard vote.[34]

In 1983, Democrats instituted a new procedure making it much harder for members to offer and get votes on limitation amendments to appropriation bills.[35] House rules bar legislating on appropriations (that is, money) bills but, as interpreted, allow amendments that bar the spending of any money for a specific purpose—paying for abortions for women on Medicaid, for example. These amendments became a favorite way for minority members to get their issues considered on the floor and to put majority members on the record on hot-button issues. The leadership-sponsored rules change effectively nullified this strategy. (Democrat John Breaux of Louisiana called the new rule a "gag rule" and threatened to fight it, but he backed down after the leadership reminded him that were he to do so, he would have trouble even getting nominated for the Budget Committee slot he coveted.)[36] During the 102nd Congress (1991–92), Republicans frequently used a House rule—the rule giving immediate floor access for motions involving the privileges of the House—to disrupt the schedule and embarrass Democrats. The rules package brought to the floor and adopted at the beginning of the 103rd Congress gave the Speaker new powers over the floor consideration of such motions. Rules changes such as these facilitated party cohesion by making it easier for Democrats to vote with their party.

During the 1980s and early 1990s, majority Democrats put together their House rules package—and their proposals for changes in Caucus rules as well—through a process that combined member participation and leadership influence over the product. The Caucus Committee on Organization, Study and Review (OSR), the same committee that the reformers had used to formulate and implement the revolutionary caucus rules changes in the early and mid-1970s, considered proposed changes in Caucus and House rules and made recommendations on them to the Caucus during the organizational period. Although the chair of OSR was appointed by the chair of the Democratic Caucus, it was understood that he had the Speaker's imprimatur.

OSR held a series of meetings in the months before the organizational caucuses. Any Democrat could bring a proposal to the committee. Thus OSR provided members with an official yet easily accessible and quite informal forum where they could bring their ideas and get a hearing. OSR served the leadership as an instrument for promoting desired rules changes and for discouraging those it opposed. The chair of OSR and its other members could bear the brunt of arguing against and voting down proposals the leadership believed unwise. When the leaders wanted a particular change, especially a potentially controversial one, OSR could begin the process of educating members. And, of course, the leadership could use OSR to launch trial balloons; should substantial opposition arise, a proposal could be quietly withdrawn without ever having been formally labeled as deriving from the leadership.

OSR recommendations, both positive and negative, usually prevailed in the Caucus. The committee's success reflected its own and the leadership's sensitivity to member sentiment as well as members' willingness, in many cases, to defer to the leadership's greater interest in and knowledge of party and especially chamber rules. With those House rules changes approved by the Caucus included in the House rules resolution, the leadership's strong influence on OSR recommendations and Caucus decisions translated into a significant impact on House rules during the period of Democratic control; however, the process also gave rank-and-file members a say. Thus well before the Republicans took control of the House, the rules package had clearly become a party product.

CHAPTER 4

THE INTERNAL ENGINES OF PARTISAN POLARIZATION

The Republican House

REPUBLICANS WON A HOUSE majority in the elections of 1994, but the House Republican Party became important to the story of increasing partisan polarization well before that. Although the minority party is less consequential to how the House functions than the majority party, the minority party can affect majority party behavior and cohesion. The minority party can become the majority, as happened to the Republicans, and then their experiences in the minority influence their behavior in the majority.

THE EVOLUTION OF A CONFRONTATIONIST OPPOSITION

From at least the early 1980s forward, minority Republicans' increasing conservativism and their much more aggressive opposition behavior affected majority Democrats' behavior, just as Democrats' increasing ideological homogeneity and greater legislative discipline affected Republicans. As Republicans became more conservative and the distance between the centers of gravity of the two parties grew, legislative compromise across party lines became more difficult and more painful. Feeling increasingly impotent, Republicans began to harass Democrats at every turn; that created hostility and provoked retaliation by Democrats, which in turn elicited more hostility from Republicans.

From Collaboration to Confrontation

By the 1970s, most astute political observers had come to think of the congressional Republican Party as a permanent minority. After all, Republicans had not controlled either chamber since 1955 and had averaged less than 40 percent of the seats in the House and in the Senate in the Congresses elected from 1958 to 1978.

Not surprisingly, congressional Republicans themselves largely subscribed to this view and acted accordingly. Most chose career strategies that allowed them to make the best of a bad situation. They cooperated and compromised with Democrats, which enabled them to play a meaningful, if secondary, role in the legislative process, especially in committee. To be sure, many found minority status frustrating; and as Democrats reined in conservative committee chairs in the 1970s, that frustration grew. Nevertheless, many committees did much of their work on a bipartisan basis, and under those circumstances committee Republicans, especially senior members who had established good relations with senior Democrats over years of working together, could wield significant influence. Barber Conable, a Republican member of the tax-writing Ways and Means Committee from 1967 through 1984, explained: "Early in my committee career, I had to decide—as all of us had to decide—whether I would be an absolute purist and decline to participate in the give and take of compromise, thus remaining immaculately unproductive, or whether I would become a willing participant and work hard to get the very best results I could. For me the choice was easy."[1]

In the later 1970s a new breed of Republicans began to enter the House. The 1976 class, for example, included Bob Walker (Pa.) and David Stockman (Mich.); the 1978 class, Richard Cheney (Wyo.), Newt Gingrich (Ga.), and Dan Lundgren (Calif.). Not only were the members first elected in the late 1970s conservative, but a number had been influenced by new conservative intellectual currents—supply-side economics and the neoconservative critique of liberalism—and so were more sharply ideological. Many had run conservative, issue-based campaigns.[2] Furthermore a number were also much more aggressive politically, arguing from early in their tenure that Republicans should confront rather than go along with the Democratic majority.

The startling 1980 election results strengthened this nascent group, bringing in reinforcements. The 1980 class included Vin Weber (Minn.), Duncan Hunter (Calif.), Bill McCollum (Fla.), and Dan Coates (Ind.).[3] Ronald Reagan, an unambiguous conservative and a convert to supply-side economics, was elected president. Perhaps most important, Republicans won control of the Senate and made big gains in the House; achieving control of the House no longer seemed like an impossible dream.

Newt Gingrich, the exemplar of the new House Republican, was never willing to concede that House Republicans were a permanent minority. An erstwhile college professor who had begun his political life as a Rockefeller Republican, he had been much influenced by the new conservative thought. *Politics in America*, the influential reference to members of Congress, said of him in 1981: "This history professor managed to set a few precedents during a tempestuous first term in which he regularly offered strategy advice to his party's leadership and plotted out scenarios for Republican political dominance. . . . Gingrich brought a new supply of intellectual vitality to a House GOP bloc that had been accused of lacking it in the past. . . . [His] initial argument centered on the need for confrontation in the House between the Republicans and the Democratic majority."[4]

The thirty-five-member-strong Republican class of 1978, of which Gingrich served as secretary, was an activist group who met frequently during their freshman Congress. They made a noisy attempt to expel Charles Diggs (D-Ill.) for ethics infractions and involved themselves in the budget fight by offering their own alternative—a "budget of hope"—to contrast with the Democratic proposal that was labeled "a budget of despair." In 1980, Jack Kemp, the most prominent congressional proponent of supply-side economics and something of a guru to the activist junior conservatives, proposed and Gingrich ran "Governing Team Day," an event involving Ronald Reagan and Republican congressional candidates on the Capitol steps pledging themselves to work together. Kemp and Gingrich had hoped to have candidates endorse specific policy stands, but the Reagan campaign insisted on only vague campaign-style pledges.

After being involved in several precursor groups, Gingrich in 1983 formed the Conservative Opportunity Society (COS), the ultimate goal of which was to elect a Republican majority to the House; the group aggressively used floor amendments and other procedural tactics and, importantly, C-SPAN. In the past, individual Republicans had employed such tactics to harass majority Democrats on the floor; during the 1970s after recorded votes in the Committee of the Whole were allowed, conservatives John Ashbrook and Bob Bauman became notorious on Capitol Hill for their adept use of amendments to put Democrats on the political spot.[5] COS was the first group organized for that purpose.

The televising of House sessions that began in 1979 gave COS a way to reach beyond the chamber. The House is a majority-rule institution; the most confrontational and clever of oppositions might cause the majority some annoyance and even some pain, but a reasonably cohesive majority party could always defeat them. The most effective strategy, as Gingrich saw it, was to "use the chamber as a political forum to express opposition and build electoral support."[6] The aim was to frame issues and shape the debate beyond the House in the broader political world. Specifically, Gingrich and COS sought to promulgate an image of the Democratic Congress as completely divorced from the American people, arrogantly indifferent to their wants and needs while catering to special interests and wallowing in pork, perks, and worse.

With C-SPAN televising House proceedings from gavel to gavel, the one-minute speeches at the beginning of the session and especially the special orders at the end of the day provided opportunities for the "guerrilla theatre on the floor" that Gingrich advocated.[7] During special orders, members can talk as long as they like on the topic of their choice. If getting as much publicity as possible is the aim, being as outrageous as possible is an effective strategy. On January 23, 1984, COS members asked unanimous consent to call up bills on school prayer, abortion, a line-item veto, and a balanced budget amendment, all issues Democrats wanted to keep off the floor. Of course Democrats objected, as COS knew they would. Then the National Republican Congressional Committee (NRCC) sent press releases to the home districts of those objecting Democrats considered likely to be hurt electorally. To preempt that tactic in the future, Speaker O'Neill required that all future unanimous consent requests be cleared with the leadership on both sides of the aisle. The presiding officer was instructed to refuse recognition if that had not been done.

COS's first big breakthrough into the national media spotlight occurred in May 1984. It began with COS special order speeches slamming Democrats, as they had done all year. Gingrich and Walker read into the *Congressional Record* a Republican staffer's report that accused congressional Democrats of a "radical worldview" in which "there is no crime by a Communist army or government that can't either be trivialized or blamed on America."[8] The report specifically named fifty House Democrats; and Gingrich and Walker, it was later charged, acted as if those members were in the chamber but did not even attempt to defend themselves from the accusation.[9] Incensed by what he saw as an underhanded trick and responding to complaints from some of the members named and to a growing unease among Democrats about the barrage of attacks on them, O'Neill retaliated. Without informing COS, he instructed the TV camera operators to show the full chamber during special order speeches. Until then, the camera had stayed on the speaker so that the TV audience never knew that the chamber was nearly empty. Walker was the first victim; he spoke to what he intimated was a rapt crowd, and all the while and unbeknownst to him, the wide-angle lens showed an empty chamber.

O'Neill's actions outraged Republicans well beyond COS. Still angry himself, the Speaker in a floor speech justified his actions and called the COS speechmaking a "sham." The next day Gingrich took to the floor to defend the report. A furious O'Neill then made a major strategic mistake. He responded to what he saw as Gingrich's questioning the "Americanism" of the Democrats named by calling it "the lowest thing I have ever seen in my 32 years in Congress."[10] Republican Whip Trent Lott demanded that "the Speaker's words be taken down" and ruled out of order. On the recommendation of the parliamentarian, the presiding Democrat—a close friend of O'Neill's—ruled that the words did violate the House's rule against personal insults. O'Neill became the first Speaker since 1797 to have his words taken down.

This proved to be an irresistible news story; as a result of O'Neill's mistake, Gingrich and his colleagues received much more coverage than they could ever have commanded by their own actions. Then, to sour the atmosphere further, the NRCC ran TV ads accusing O'Neill of breaking House rules and falsifying congressional records. By the mid-1980s, *Politics in America* spoke of COS as "an organization of junior House Republicans that attracts regular national media attention" and reported that many of its members "are heroes to conservatives who regularly watch C-SPAN." At the Republican National Convention a few weeks after the O'Neill-Gingrich confrontation, Gingrich "was mobbed by reporters, tourists and conservative admirers virtually everywhere he went."[11]

Initially many House Republicans were leery about the "bomb throwers," as COS members were frequently called. Many wanted to maintain reasonable relationships with majority Democrats, at least with those on their committees. Over the course of the 1980s, however, sentiment within the party changed. External and internal forces and processes interacted to bring about this change.

The key external factor was the changing character of the new members elected on both sides of the aisle. As discussed earlier, due in large part to the change in the activist base of the party, Republicans first elected to the House in the late 1970s and the 1980s were much more likely to be ideological or movement conservatives rather than the more pragmatic Main Street moderates and conservatives prevalent before. With the change in southern politics, newly elected Democrats, even those from the South, were unlikely to be conservatives. As a consequence, the overlap of policy views between Democrats and Republicans shrank; members of the two parties were less and less likely to agree on what constituted good public policy.

During the early 1980s, in the wake of Ronald Reagan's election as president and his early legislative success, House Democrats felt under attack. Reagan seemed to threaten both their electoral and their policy goals. COS's harassment, while perceived as less serious, was nevertheless annoying. As the memberships became more ideologically homogeneous, Democrats increasingly expected their leaders to use the resources at their command to respond to these problems. Leaders did so, especially by increasing their use of restrictive rules that barred many Republican floor amendments—amendments that majority Democrats saw as harassment but Republicans saw as their only way of promoting their policy preferences.

Crafting major legislation that will pass the House always requires compromises. As the Democratic Party leadership became more involved in the substance of legislation at the prefloor stage and as Republicans moved right, the process of reaching those compromises increasingly took place within the majority party. The Republicans were excluded from the process, often even at the committee level.

The Spiral of Hostility

A number of notable showdowns exacerbated partisan hostilities. An extremely narrow House election outcome in Indiana in 1984 blew up into a bitter partisan confrontation. Although Indiana's Republican secretary of state had certified Republican Richard McIntyre as winner over incumbent Democrat Frank McCloskey, the narrow margin of victory—34 votes—led the House Democrats to refuse to seat McIntyre pending an investigation. Indignant Republicans forced several floor votes while the House Administration Committee task force worked, but lost them all on highly partisan divisions. On March 4, on which only a pro forma session was scheduled and so many members were still home in their districts, Republicans forced a surprise roll call on seating McIntyre and, with many Democrats absent, lost by only one vote, 168–167. Democrats pulled out the victory only by delaying the vote and calling members back to Washington post haste. Speaker O'Neill accused the Republicans of breaching House norms by the lack of notice, and Republican Leader Bob Michel justified the move by the "very shoddy, shoot-from-the-hip, partisan manner" in which the dispute had been handled.[12] The task force's and then the full House Administration Committee's deciding by partisan votes that Democrat McCloskey had won the election further inflamed Republicans. They kept the House in session an entire night and then blocked legislative business with what *Congressional Quarterly* (CQ) called "parliamentary guerrilla tactics."[13] After Democrats prevailed on the floor vote to seat McCloskey, Republicans walked out of the chamber en masse. The four-month-long battle left Republicans convinced they had been cheated out of a House seat.

In late 1987 a floor battle over a reconciliation bill left Republicans convinced that they had been cheated out of a legislative victory. The Democratic leadership considered passing the reconciliation bill quickly to be essential in the party's policy battles with President Reagan. Thus when the rule for floor consideration was defeated, the leaders believed extraordinary measures were justified.[14] A procedural maneuver was employed to get around the usual twenty-four-hour layover requirement for a new rule: the House was formally adjourned and then immediately reconvened, thus creating for parliamentary purposes a new legislative day.[15] The first rule had been voted down at a little after noon; at 2:40, the Majority Leader took the floor to begin the procedural maneuvering leading to a vote on the second rule, which excluded the provisions that had led to the defeat of the first. At 4:45, the House voted 238 to 182 to approve the second rule, with only one Republican voting in favor and thirteen Democrats opposed. Still the vote on the bill itself was a cliff-hanger; when the fifteen-minute minimum time for a roll call ran out, the vote stood at 205 to 206. As the Speaker held the vote open, proponents scurried around seeking a Democrat willing to switch. Finally, after the vote had stretched to about double its usual fifteen minutes, the whip and a senior speaker's aide prevailed upon a junior Texan for whom the Speaker had done many favors to switch his vote, and the bill passed by one vote. Already chafing under what they considered Wright's too- aggressive leadership and frustrated by the string of defeats House Democrats had handed Reagan, Republicans went ballistic; an infuriated Dick Cheney, Republican Conference chair, called Wright "a heavy handed son of a bitch."[16] Black Thursday, as Republicans thereafter referred to the event, became a prime exhibit in Republicans' long list of grievances.[17]

As a result of this episode, Newt Gingrich's attack on Speaker Jim Wright gained overt as well as tacit support among many angry House Republicans. In keeping with his campaign to paint the Democratic House as corrupt, Gingrich aggressively went after Speaker Wright from close to the beginning of Wright's tenure, charging him with a variety of ethics infractions. Through a confluence of factors, importantly the media's interest in the story, Wright was forced to resign after a long and tortuous battle. He was followed quickly by Majority Whip Tony Coelho, who decided not to fight an ethics charge. Democrats were incensed. The atmosphere in the House had become truly poisonous. Nevertheless, although these dramatic episodes caught the media's attention and did exacerbate the partisan division, they were not root causes but largely symptoms. The changing character of the two parties' memberships and the parties' strategic responses to the changes were what drove the process.

Confrontationists Take Over the House GOP

This dynamic made possible Newt Gingrich's election to the second-ranking position in the House Republican party leadership in March of 1989. When Dick Cheney left the House to become secretary of defense, the whip position opened up. By a vote of 87 to 85 Gingrich, who had never held an official party leadership post, defeated Ed Madigan, chief deputy whip and a close ally of Republican Leader Bob Michel. The race explicitly pitted two distinct conceptions of the appropriate minority party strategy against each other. Madigan contended that the job was "coalition building" and helping with "getting things done."[18] Gingrich argued that the party needed to abandon its "timid" manner of dealing with Democrats and adopt his aggressive style; it was a race about "what kind of party" the Republicans would be, he said.[19] And that does seem to be how House Republicans interpreted the choice. According to conventional vote-based measures, supporters of the two candidates did not differ significantly in ideology, and in fact a considerable number of moderates supported Gingrich. Rhode Island's Claudine Schneider, one of the most liberal House Republicans, explained the vote: "We were sending a signal. Basically there is an abuse of power by Democrats in the House. . . . Newt will fight for changes."[20] Gingrich himself concluded: "I regard my election as a coalition victory for activists of all the ideological views of the Republican Party."[21]

Gingrich was not the first COS member to win election to a leadership post, nor would he be the last. After a close loss for the Policy Committee chairmanship in 1987, Duncan Hunter won the Research Committee chairmanship in late 1988, and Bob McCollum and Vin Weber won election as vice chair and secretary of the Republican Conference. At the organizing conference after the 1992 elections, Dick Armey (Tex.) defeated incumbent Conference chair Jerry Lewis (Calif.), whom he accused of being "too cozy with the Democrats."[22] Tom DeLay also entered the leadership, winning the Conference secretary position easily.[23] The entire elected Republican leadership now consisted of conservatives and, with the sole exception of Leader Bob Michel, of confrontationists. Michel believed that the minority party had "an obligation to the American people to be participants in the process, responsible participants in the process"; that was now a minority view.[24]

Almost certainly necessary for Armey's victory was the class of 1992.[25] Forty-seven strong, the class made up more than a quarter of the Republican House membership in the 103rd Congress (1993–94), and its members were by and large movement conservatives who believed in confrontation, not conciliation. Bob Michel himself labeled the House Republican membership of the 103rd Congress as "the most conservative and antagonistic to the other side" that he had ever seen and said of the freshman class "seven are thoughtful moderates and the other forty are pretty darn hard-liners, some of them real hard line."[26]

The changing composition of the activist base of the Republican Party drove this change in the character of the Republican members, but Gingrich's activities contributed as well. In 1986 Gingrich had become chairman of GOPAC, a political action committee founded by former House member and governor of Delaware Pierre duPont to recruit and assist candidates for state and local offices with the aim of strengthening the Republican "farm team." Gingrich shifted GOPAC's emphasis from supplying money to supplying ideas, rationales, and motivation. He sent prospective candidates audio- and videotapes on tactics, strategy, ideas, and issues; many Republican candidates listened to those tapes and were influenced in their view of issues, and some were inspired to run for federal office.[27] Some began winning election to the House as Gingrich hoped. By the late 1980s, most Republican House freshmen had been helped and influenced by Gingrich.[28] Many of the big 103rd Congress Republican class had received direct help from GOPAC.

Partisan confrontation intensified in the early 1990s. In the 102nd Congress (1991–92), House Republicans exploited the bank "scandal" to embarrass deeply the Democrats, their leaders, and the House. Encouraged by Gingrich, a group of freshmen who became known as the "Gang of Seven" repeatedly took to the House floor to demand the release of the names of all those members with overdrafts. Jim Nussle, one of the seven, became momentarily famous for appearing on the House floor with a brown paper bag over his head and demanding: "It is time to take the mask off this institution. It is time to expose the check writing scandal."[29] The political pressure thus generated eventually forced Democrats to capitulate. Members with large numbers of overdrafts decided to retire in droves, and of those who did not, a number were defeated. Republicans as well as Democrats were caught in the probe, but because Republicans exploited the situation for political purposes, Democrats felt victimized.

Unified government returned with the election of Bill Clinton as president in 1992. Not since Carter's presidency had one party controlled the House, the Senate, and the White House. As I have demonstrated, both congressional parties were radically different in the early 1990s from the parties of Carter's time. With the much more conservative and aggressive Republican Party now completely without governing responsibilities and the more ideologically homogeneous Democratic Party commanding a substantial House majority, Democrats largely excluded the Republicans from meaningful participation in the legislative process, and Republicans harassed Democrats within the House when they could and mounted a media-oriented campaign to discredit them with the public. With crucial help from talk show host Rush Limbaugh, the Republican firebrands successfully fueled Americans' normal disdain for Congress and disseminated a portrait of a corrupt and arrogant Democratic Congress.[30] By mid-1993 Gingrich had made himself the de facto Republican leader in the House, leaving Bob Michel (R-Ill.), the titular leader, little choice but to announce his retirement.

THE REPUBLICAN REVOLUTION AND ITS AFTERMATH

To the astonishment of almost everyone, the 1994 elections saw Republicans win control of the House of Representatives for the first time in forty years. Gingrich, in the eyes of most Republicans and the media, was the miracle maker; he was seen as responsible for the unexpected Republican victory. Gingrich had worked to build a majority for years; he had recruited many of the challengers who won and had helped them with fund-raising and campaign advice; the Contract with America on which House Republican candidates had run was Gingrich's idea, and he had orchestrated its realization.

Consequently the election results gave Gingrich enormous prestige. They also provided him with a membership that was both unusually homogeneous ideologically and determined to enact major policy change. The huge freshman class—seventy-three strong—consisted largely of true believers, deeply committed to cutting the size and scope of government and to balancing the budget; with the sophomores, who were very similar in outlook, they made up over half of the Republican House membership. More senior conservatives had waited for years for such an opportunity. The junior members and a considerable number of more senior Republicans believed themselves to be mandated to make dramatic policy change. Even moderate Republicans strongly agreed that for the party to maintain its majority, Republicans had to deliver on their promises.[31]

By the end of the 104th Congress's first one hundred days, Speaker Newt Gingrich (R-Ga.) was being hailed by the national media and the Washington political community as a combination of Czar Reed, the president of the United States, and Lenin: a powerful legislative leader, the nation's premier political figure and agenda setter, and the leader of a successful revolutionary movement. In fact, the combination of an extraordinarily ambitious agenda, a new majority united behind the agenda, and a leader with enormous prestige made the exercise of strong leadership both necessary and possible. Without strong central direction, passing the agenda would have been impossible. Without a membership united in its commitment to swift and dramatic policy change, no Speaker could have exercised such strong central direction of the legislative process.

Republican Conference rules changes made well before the 104th Congress had significantly augmented the resources of the Republican leadership. During the 1980s and early 1990s, House Republicans had adopted rules that decreased the autonomy of their committee leaders and strengthened their party leadership. Republican committee leaders (ranking minority members when the party was in the minority, committee chairs when Republicans became the majority) were made subject to a secret-ballot ratification vote in the Republican Conference; the Republican Party leader was given the power to nominate Republican members of Rules and given more say on the party committee that makes committee assignments. The Conference adopted a rule that reads: "The Republican Leader may designate certain issues as 'Leadership Issues.' Those issues will require early and ongoing cooperation between the relevant committees and the Leadership as the issue evolves." And ranking committee Republicans were "obligat[ed] to ensure that the managerial responsibilities on the Floor of the House of Representatives for each measure on which the Republican Conference has taken a position are managed in accordance with such position."[32] Both the felt need to respond to the Democrats' strengthening of their leadership and the confrontationists' desire to hold accountable committee leaders whom they perceived as too willing to collaborate with Democrats motivated these new rules.

At the beginning of the 104th Congress, Republicans made further changes in party and House rules, but although significant, they were far from revolutionary—with one exception. The committee on committees, renamed the Steering Committee, was reconstituted so as to give the leadership a considerably greater voice. Modest committee jurisdiction reform was accomplished by shifting some of the Energy and Commerce Committee's immense jurisdiction to other committees; three minor committees (all with primarily Democratic constituencies) were eliminated; and committee staffs were cut by a third. Proxy votes, which absent committee members could give to any other committee member to cast for them but most often gave to the chair, were banned; and sunshine rules were modestly strengthened, making it harder to close a committee meeting.

The Speaker augmented his budget and staff. The Republican whip system, which had grown during the 1980s and early 1990s, expanded further; in the 104th Congress it consisted of the whip, a chief deputy whip, thirteen deputy whips, and thirty-nine assistant whips—still not as big as the Democratic whip system but more similar than before. Junior representation in the leadership was expanded; one sophomore and two freshmen elected by their class were made part of the designated leadership.

Because Republican party rules pertained and Republicans had never adopted the subcommittee bill of rights, the new Republican committee chairs were in some ways stronger than their Democratic predecessors. They controlled the entire majority staff of the committee and had more control over the choice of subcommittee chairs and over the assignment of members to subcommittees.

In the most significant of the rules changes, committee and subcommittee chairs, by House rule, were subjected to a limit of three terms. However, the effects of this new rule would not become evident until a number of years later.

Political circumstances, not rules changes, made Newt Gingrich an unusually powerful Speaker. The new rules had not given Gingrich any formal powers his Democratic predecessors lacked. Rather, relying on his immense prestige with House Republicans in the days after the 1994 elections, Gingrich exercised power well beyond that specified in Republican Conference rules. He designated Republicans to serve as committee chairs, bypassing seniority in several instances. Thus the conservative but unaggressive Carlos Moorhead was bypassed for the chairmanships of both the Judiciary and Commerce committees in favor of more energetic and articulate second-ranking Republicans. On Appropriations, Gingrich reached further down the seniority ladder to pick the hard-charging Bob Livingston as chair. According to the rules, the party committee on committees nominates chairs and the Conference approves them. Gingrich preempted that process, assuming correctly that his stature would prevent anyone from challenging his choices. He used his influence to reward junior Republicans, his strongest supporters, with choice committee assignments. Six freshmen received Appropriations slots; six, Budget Committee slots; eight, Commerce; three, Ways and Means; and one, Rules. By his early actions, Gingrich augmented his own resources, but it was his prestige and the membership's belief in its mandate that made his actions possible and that constituted his greatest resource.

The 104th Congress saw enormous party leadership involvement and oversight on major legislation; committee leaders were clearly subordinate to party leaders on Contract with America bills and on much of the major legislation that went into the Republicans' attempt to balance the budget. To bring every item in the Contract to a vote within the first hundred days as promised, Gingrich set strict time limits for the committees and refused to brook significant changes in the Contract items. Because most senior Republicans had signed the Contract, Gingrich had a strong tool for persuading committee leaders to report legislation without making major changes and to do so quickly. He could and did remind them: "We promised to do it in 100 days; we must deliver." In early 1995, and later when balancing the budget was at issue, the chairs knew that the leadership was backed up by the freshmen's strong support.

When a committee was incapable of mustering a majority for legislation that the party leadership and the membership wanted, the leadership stepped in and bypassed the committee; for example, when the Agriculture Committee refused to report the "Freedom to Farm" bill, which made cuts in farm programs as required by the budget resolution, the leadership simply inserted the language into the reconciliation bill. When the legislation a committee reported was unacceptable to a majority of the Republican membership, as on the term limits constitutional amendment, the leadership altered the language substantially after it had been reported and before it went to the floor. On Medicare, one of the most politically sensitive issues the Republicans took on, Gingrich himself headed the "design group" that made the major substantive decisions; the group did include the Republican leaders of the committees and subcommittees with jurisdiction.

The 104th House passed every item in the Contract but one within the first hundred days; only a constitutional amendment imposing term limits on members of Congress failed, and that required a two-thirds vote. House Republicans' voting cohesion was remarkable; on thirty-three final passage votes on the Contract items, only 4.7 members on average defected from the party position.[33] House Republicans then proceeded to pass a massive bill balancing the budget in seven years and revamping popular entitlement programs such as Medicare and Medicaid. (Hardly any of these bills became law, but that is another story; see chapter 7.)

An unusual confluence of factors made these extraordinary events possible. A new majority after so many years, the sense of mandate, and Gingrich's role in the events leading up to the elections were unique to the 104th Congress. A membership that was increasingly homogeneous ideologically and a more activist, assertive party leadership, also key factors, predated the elections and, as I have shown, were not unique to Republicans. The 104th Congress, I contend, does not represent a sharp discontinuity as the media and even some scholars have claimed. It represents rather the amplification of a preexisting trend.

Majority party leadership strategies in the 104th show considerable continuity as well. Like the Democratic leaders before him, Gingrich knew that leading the postreform House requires a strategy of inclusion; the activists that make up a substantial proportion of each party's membership expect to participate meaningfully in the legislative process; by providing that opportunity, the leadership gets help that it badly needs. Furthermore, those members involved in leadership efforts develop a stake in their success.

Gingrich sought to involve others in his majority-building efforts, to get them to "buy in," long before he moved into the leadership. As whip he continued that effort, reaching out to members with whom he had little in common ideologically. Thus, for example, the Contract was put together through a process that involved as many members as Gingrich could inveigle into participating; even Republican challengers were surveyed about what should be included.[34]

Once in the majority, Gingrich and the Republican leadership team continued the buy-in strategy. Gingrich established numerous task forces to carry out a great variety of tasks; at one point there were so many and they had been set up so quickly that no one had a list. Some were charged with expediting action on Contract legislation, some with developing broad-based compromises on divisive issues, others with outreach beyond Congress, and still others had an electoral purpose.[35] Inclusion—especially of junior members—was clearly an important goal.[36] "Newt uses task forces to get people involved who have a common interest on something. To get them together. Newt's very open to new ideas," a moderate Republican explained. "He wants to let everybody do their own thing, pursue their own interests."[37]

The Conference met weekly, as did a large leadership group of about twenty, which included a cross section of the party membership. Gingrich also made it a point to consult and stay in regular contact with the various party subgroups. "He meets once a month with all the groups, the California delegation, the freshmen group, the sophomore group, the Tuesday lunch bunch, the Wednesday group, CATS [Conservative Action Team], all these groups," a member explained. "Newt has constant meetings. Anybody can see him. After he opens the session, or is there for the opening of the session, he stays on the floor and circulates, and this is a time when people can come up and talk to him."

Gingrich's effort to include members in the process and give them a stake in its success was especially intense with respect to the freshmen. Not only did they constitute about 30 percent of the party's membership; they had made the party a majority, and significant losses among them would make it the minority again. Thus freshmen were heavily represented on task forces, and as noted, two were included in the large leadership group that met weekly. Gingrich had made sure they received good committee assignments and at Gingrich's behest, two even chaired subcommittees.

Inclusion, however, cannot substitute for legislative and political success, especially when member expectations are high. The budget debacle, in which President Clinton pummeled the Republicans, sticking them with the blame for irresponsibly shutting down the government, burst the bubble of Gingrich's reputation as a world-class political strategist who never miscalculated. As long as Republicans were convinced that Gingrich was infallible as a strategist, they were more than willing to let him exercise great power in order to assure that legislation was passed and in a form that would accomplish the party's objectives. Once they lost that faith, they were less willing to follow. After the government shutdown over Christmas 1995 and the public opprobrium Republicans suffered as a result, Gingrich never again exercised as much power as he had through most of 1995.

But the underlying conditions fostering active and assertive party leadership remained in place. Gingrich during the rest of his speakership exercised leadership that, although not as great as during that heady first year, was nevertheless extraordinarily strong by mid-twentieth-century standards. When House Republicans lost seats in the 1998 elections, Gingrich, battered by ethics investigations and by member disillusionment, chose to resign rather than face a challenge for the speakership. In the sixth year of a presidency, the opposition party historically gains significant numbers of seats, so the loss was a nasty surprise. After more turmoil when Gingrich's challenger, Bob Livingston, was forced to resign, the little-known Dennis Hastert (R-Ill.), who had been deputy whip, was chosen as Speaker. Yet those who expected a weakened leadership and a return to any semblance of committee government were quickly proven wrong.

POLITICAL PARTIES IN THE HOUSE TODAY

The parties in the House today are ideologically polarized. They are highly organized both for joint action and for member participation because that is what members want; House members want an active party and a strong leadership because these things are prerequisites for members to advance their goals in the current political environment. "All of us want a strong leadership because we want to get things done," summed up moderate Republican Chris Shays.[38]

Members of the House, I have argued, desire reelection, good public policy, and influence in the chamber. When members' reelection needs and personal policy preferences are similar within the party and differ substantially between the parties, as is the case today, it makes sense for members to organize their party and endow their leaders with the resources necessary to facilitate the achievement of members' goals. The contemporary parties are elaborately organized in the House so as to facilitate joint action toward collective goals while also providing members with much-prized opportunities to participate in the legislative process; rank-and-file members' participation is thus channeled largely through their party and takes forms that benefit rather than endanger the party effort.

With many opportunities to participate through the party and bipartisan participation opportunities fewer and often fraught with difficulty, members' House lives now take place mostly within their party. Advancement within the chamber depends on a member's reputation with party peers and the party leadership, thus increasing the incentives to be a team player. Members expect their party leaders to use aggressively the resources they have given the leaders to further the membership's common goals, and that, of course, includes encouraging members to act as team players. Given the narrow margins of control, members are all the more willing to allow their leaders to employ resources in ways that amplify party cohesion even beyond that which the extent of constituency-based ideological homogeneity would dictate.

The advantages of collective action to the members of an ideologically homogeneous majority party in the House are major. By working and voting together, majority party members can pass legislation that furthers their individual reelection chances and embodies their notions of good public policy; to the extent that their record of achievement enhances the party's reputation, they may be able to increase their majority and certainly should increase their chances of maintaining control.

For members of the minority party, the calculus may be more complicated. In the House, if the majority party maintains cohesion, the minority can seldom win. Those minority party members closest ideologically to the majority thus have an incentive to defect and deal with the majority. But an ideologically homogeneous majority party may be unwilling to compromise enough to make it worthwhile for such members, especially when the ideological gulf between the parties is great. Furthermore, control of the chamber is the great prize on which majority and minority party members' goals are in direct and irreconcilable conflict; the majority wants to keep it, the minority wants to take it. When control actually seems in play, members of the minority, like members of the majority, have a strong incentive toward within-party teamwork that favorably affects their probability of taking control. Both conditions currently hold; the ideological gulf between the parties is substantial, and narrow margins mean chamber control is within reach of the minority. Consequently minority members also have much to gain from an active party organization and strong leadership. Still, as I show in later chapters, minority party leaders do confront somewhat different problems in holding their members together than do majority party leaders with their greater resources.

Republican leaders at the time of writing are Dennis Hastert (Ill.), genial but strongly conservative, as Speaker since 1999; Tom DeLay (Tex.), an extreme conservative whom even his best friends would not call genial and who moved up from whip to Majority Leader at the beginning of the 108th Congress (2003–2004); and Roy Blunt (Mo.), an affable conservative who was elected whip after serving as deputy whip under DeLay. Republicans also elect a Conference chair, vice chair, and secretary, a chair of the Policy Committee, and a chair of the National Republican Congressional Committee, all of whom are considered part of the leadership. The chief deputy whip, who is chosen by the whip, is not officially a member of the leadership according to Conference rules but is so treated in fact. The freshman, sophomore, and junior classes each elect a representative to the official leadership, and the chairs of the top five committees are also designated part of the official leadership.

Democrats elected new leaders for the 108th Congress after longtime Democratic Leader Dick Gephardt (Mo.) decided to step down, and those leaders were reelected at the beginning of the 109th Congress. Nancy Pelosi, a "San Francisco liberal," as Republicans like to call her, became the first woman to serve as the top-ranked leader of either party in the House, and Steny Hoyer (Md.), a moderate to liberal member, was elected whip. Democrats elect a chair and vice chair of the Caucus, who rank third and fourth in the leadership hierarchy. The Democratic Leader selects a member who is officially designated assistant to the Democratic Leader, John Spratt (S.C.), at the time of writing; cochairs of the Steering Committee, Rosa DeLauro (Conn.) and George Miller (Calif.); and a chair of the Democratic Congressional Campaign Committee. The whip appoints a number of chief deputy whips, currently seven, plus one senior chief deputy. The members holding these posts are all considered part of the Democratic leadership.

The large number of party leadership positions on both sides of the aisle reflects to some extent the growth of leadership responsibilities; members expect their party and their leadership to do more than they used to, and that requires more people. It also reflects members' desires for opportunities to participate. Thus much of the proliferation in Republican leadership posts predates the party's gaining of House control and can be attributed to the desires of minority party members to find arenas for participation and influence in what was becoming a less congenial chamber for the minority. In addition and in both parties, as the leadership and party activity became more central to the legislative process—as that became "where the action is"—more members, and especially the more energetic and politically savvy members, wanted to take part. The top leaders benefit from such members' becoming a part of the leadership in a number of ways; they bring their efforts and skills to the leadership enterprise, they often provide links to important party subgroups, and they are less likely to cause problems when they are inside the tent.

For all these reasons, leaders draw in members even beyond the officially designated leadership. Republicans, for example, have an informal post entitled "chairman of the leadership" to chair the leadership meetings. Selected by the Speaker, the incumbent until his appointment to an administration post was Rob Portman (Ohio). Hastert also designated Portman as the leadership's conduit to President Bush, a position for which

Portman was well suited by virtue of his service in the first Bush White House.[39] Democrats have a Democratic Leadership Council that meets with and advises the top leaders. It consists of the chairs of six Democratic member caucuses—the Black Caucus, Hispanic Caucus, Women's Caucus, the left-leaning Progressive Caucus, the moderate New Democratic Coalition, and the more conservative Blue Dog Coalition.

The House parties' elaborate organization makes a high level of party activity possible and provides members with opportunities to participate. The whip systems include a substantial proportion of each party's membership. The Republican whip system, which is headed by an elected whip, consists of sixty to seventy members, including an appointed chief deputy whip, approximately twenty regional assistant whips, and a number of appointed deputy whips. The Democratic whip system is even bigger, generally numbering almost a hundred members; twenty or so are regionally elected, and the rest are leadership-appointed whips. The whip operations provide rank-and-file members with opportunities to participate in legislative efforts and with regular, direct contact with the top leadership, both of which are especially prized by junior members. The weekly whip meetings give the whips a chance to communicate regularly with the top leaders face-to-face.

The Republican Conference and the Democratic Caucus are also important forums for communication among party members and between the leaders and the rank and file. Both meet at least weekly. Believing that intensive contact between leaders and members is especially vital for the minority party, Pelosi also holds a weekly luncheon to which all members of the Democratic Caucus are invited. Both the Republican Conference and the Democratic Caucus sponsor annual issue conferences away from the Hill. As noted, these are often in resort settings where members can bring family and socialize informally in addition to holding in-depth discussions of issues.

The Democratic Caucus has eighteen issue task forces, which are charged with "developing and communicating legislative priorities and party policy for House Democrats."[40] For minority party members, having an opportunity to develop policy and to participate on issues of special interest to the district or to them personally is especially important, and large numbers—more than half the Democratic membership—sign up for one or more tasks forces.

The Republican Policy Committee, with a diverse and representative membership of forty-eight, is charged with the "enunciation of official Republican policies."[41] In 2001–2002, for example, the committee issued fourteen policy statements on issues ranging from tax policy to the exclusion of Taiwan from the World Health Organization. The committee also hears guests, often Republican cabinet secretaries but also a variety of nongovernmental speakers—economist Arthur Laffer, former secretary of state Henry Kissinger, and chess champion Gary Kasparov have been guests. Subcommittees of the Policy Committee perform much the same function that the Democratic Caucus task forces do; as the committee's website states, they offer "a unique opportunity for participation by members whose legislative ideas do not in every case coincide with their committee assignments."[42]

With so much of a House member's Washington life and work now spent in exclusively partisan settings, within-party peer pressure works to accentuate party loyalty. Republican Conference meetings tend to take on a "locker room" atmosphere, especially before a big vote, according to Amo Houghton (R-N.Y.). A member on the outs with party colleagues in the contemporary House is going to be pretty lonely. A member's reputation with fellow partisans, of course, is important for reasons beyond sentiment. Getting ahead in the contemporary House now largely depends on one's standing in the party and with the party leadership. Party loyalty, defined as a willingness to behave in a party-regarding fashion whenever possible, pays off in the contemporary House.

Party leaders' influence over committee assignments, which had increased so substantially since the committee-government era, as I described earlier, has continued to grow. Backed up by member expectations, leaders are willing to use that influence to reward the loyal and to disadvantage—if not punish—the disloyal. When Republican leaders made committee assignments for the 108th Congress, three junior members—Rob Simmons (Conn.), Todd Platts (Pa.), and Charlie Bass (N.H.)—who asked for better committees were denied because they had signed a discharge petition on the campaign finance reform bill.[43] "My hope of ever serving on the Ways and Means Committee is probably closed off," said Adam Putnam (R-Fla.) after he voted against the trade promotion authority (fast track) bill.[44] Mark Foley, another Florida Republican who voted against the bill, already served on Ways and Means. "Some people are thinking he shouldn't be on Ways and Means anymore," a senior leadership aide said. "People make promises that they will support free trade when they get on Ways and Means and when they vote 'no' on fast track, they've broken a pledge."[45]

The incentives to show responsiveness to the party and its leadership have become even stronger for committee chairs and those aspiring to committee chairmanships, especially on the Republican side of the aisle. The Gingrich "time bomb," as the three-term limit for committee chairs has been labeled, went off in 2000. With thirteen chairmanships vacant, mostly because of term limits, the Republican party leadership instituted a new procedure for the selection of committee chairs: chair aspirants were required to appear before the Steering Committee, which nominates chairs to the Conference. There they were put through rigorous interviews about their legislative and communication strategies and their proposed agendas.

Twenty-nine members interviewed for the thirteen vacant chairmanships; Gingrich's violations of seniority and term limits themselves seem to have decreased the sense that seniority should be followed unless there was a strong reason for not doing so. And, in fact, in choosing the new chairs for six of the thirteen vacant positions, the Steering Committee did not follow seniority. Most of the aspirants, like most House Republicans, were conservatives. However, on two important committees, a fairly moderate member—Marge Roukema (N.J.) at Banking and Tom Petri (Wis.) at Education—was passed over for a less senior conservative; in two other cases the senior moderate receive the chairmanship, but these were on lesser committees.[46]

In filling four vacant chairmanships at the beginning of the 108th Congress, Republicans passed over Chris Shays (Conn.), a moderate and the chief sponsor of the detested campaign finance reform bill. For the Resources Committee, they passed over Jim Saxton of New Jersey, a moderate on environmental issues, and reached down four more seniority slots to pick Richard Pombo, a hard-line ally of Tom DeLay.[47] Interviews for sitting chairs are usually a formality, but Chris Smith, who had first been chosen to head the Veterans Affairs Committee in 2000, was warned during his interview that he needed to be more of a team player. Against the wishes of the leadership, Smith had fought for greater funding for veterans' programs.[48] He seems not to have heeded the warning to the satisfaction of the leadership or the membership. At the beginning of the 109th Congress, the Steering Committee took away his chairmanship and removed him from the committee altogether.

"There will definitely be a perception out there that you need to be a team player if you want to succeed," said a leadership aide. "You don't need to be beholden to the leadership so much as to the Conference at large."[49] The contest for the highly coveted chairmanship of the Appropriations Committee in 2005 illustrates the extent to which that has become the case. The three senior members vying for the post campaigned actively by raising campaign money for their colleagues; by pledging to dedicate themselves to the task of deficit reduction, as the leadership and the Conference membership demanded; and by committing themselves to reforming the committee internally as Majority Leader Tom DeLay had proposed.

As Harold Rogers (Ky.) wrote to the Speaker in a letter asking for his support on December 10, 2004: "*Our Republican Majority is on the line in the 2006 elections* and who you select to lead the Appropriations Committee will be crucial to neutralizing our biggest vulnerability—*the soaring, historically high deficit. . . . We need a disciplined, take charge leader* who won't hesitate to say 'no' over and over again, and who can and will boldly retool, reorganize and re-energize the Committee. We need someone who can work *with* the Budget Committee, Leadership and our Members—not *against* them."[50] Steering and Policy chose Jerry Lewis (Calif.), the second-ranking Republican on the committee, over Ralph Regula (Ohio), the senior member. Regula was considered the least conservative of the candidates. As soon as he was confirmed by the Conference, Lewis announced that he was replacing Appropriations staff director Jim Dyer. Many Republicans distrusted Dyer, a longtime Appropriations aide, believing him not sufficiently dedicated to budget cutting.

In late 2002 the Republican Conference altered its rules so as to give the leadership-dominated Steering Committee the right to vote on the "Cardinals," the chairs of the Appropriations subcommittees. Previously, under the Republicans, the full committee chair picked the subcommittee chairs.[51] However, during the period of Republican control of the House, the committee most frequently in conflict with the leadership and the Conference has been the Appropriations Committee. With the Speaker's backing, the Conference agreed to the new rule proposed by a group of conservatives. "The goal," said a GOP aide, "is to make these folks accountable."[52]

In spring of 2004, the Democratic Caucus at the behest of Leader Nancy Pelosi altered its rules to give its Steering Committee a vote on who serves as subcommittee chairs or ranking members on the Appropriations, Energy and Commerce, and Ways and Means committees. In November 2003, sixteen Democrats had voted for the Republican proposal to add a prescription drug benefit to Medicare, which most House Democrats strongly opposed. The new rule, according to a Democratic leadership aide, "is not about trying to punish anyone, it's about having accountability."[53] Although some of the more conservative Democrats had opposed the rules change when Pelosi first broached the idea, the Caucus approved it on a voice vote.

When Democrats selected ranking members for the 109th Congress, the Steering and Policy Committee for the first time interviewed candidates as the Republicans do.[54] Collin Peterson (Minn.), a relatively conservative Democrat and one not known as a team player, was given the ranking position on Agriculture only after he had made strong and explicit pledges about future team play.[55] Pelosi chose Sander Levin as ranking minority member on the Ways and Means subcommittee on social security. Since social security was expected to be the biggest domestic issue of the 109th Congress, the Democratic leadership wanted to be sure that they had a staunch and effective advocate of the Democratic position in that key slot.

So long as they are backed by their membership, House party leaders have available many other inducements to promote party-regarding behavior. Majority leaders can and do aid their members with projects for their districts, sometimes by simply speaking with committee leaders on a member's behalf but increasingly by insisting that vulnerable members be well treated in appropriations bills, transportation bills, and other legislation in which earmarks are common. Majority Leader Tom DeLay, formerly a member of the Appropriations Committee, is well-known for helping his colleagues win money for pet projects.[56]

With the prevalent use of special rules that bar most floor amendments, the suspension procedure has taken on increasing importance as a way for members to pursue their individual legislative projects.[57] Leadership aides, in fact, call suspensions "pacifiers." The Speaker's control over what gets considered under suspension of the rules has thus become a more valuable resource. Because passage under the suspension procedure requires a two-thirds vote, the minority party insists on its share of bills, and consequently, the minority party leadership also benefits from members' increased demand.

Party leaders now play a major role in raising campaign funds for their members. The top party leaders are very much engaged in the campaign committees' operations. They choose or strongly influence the choice of chairs of the campaign committees. They are almost always the committees' top draws at fund-raising events; extensive travel to raise money has become expected of party leaders. Thus, Speaker of the House Dennis Hastert reportedly raised $6 million dollars in the first half of 1999. By the beginning of December 2003, Minority Leader Nancy Pelosi (D-Calif.) had raised $12 million for the Democratic Congressional Campaign Committee. Pelosi planned a busy December fund-raising for the DCCC with events in Silicon Valley, Los Angeles, Seattle, New Jersey, New York, Minneapolis, and New Orleans.[58] In addition to the money leaders raise for the campaign committees and for individual members, many have established leadership PACs. Tom DeLay's Americans for a Republican Majority PAC was the single biggest donor during the 2003–2004 election cycle, giving almost $1 million to Republican candidates; Speaker Dennis Hastert's Keep Our Majority PAC was second, with donations of over $800,000. Democratic Whip Steny Hoyer's PAC gave $752,5000 to Democratic candidates, and Pelosi's PAC $574,500.59

Leaders' fund-raising activities are important on two levels. Certainly those members who benefit directly can be expected to be grateful; and at least as important, leaders are meeting their membership's expectations that they do what they can to retain or gain chamber control. Because in recent years the margins have been so narrow and control has appeared to be in doubt in each election, leaders have been more heavy-handed in inducing the kind of party-regarding behavior from members, especially senior members, that might make a difference. On both sides of the aisle, leaders pressure their members to give money to the congressional campaign committee and to individual candidates. The best predictor of who received chairmanships in 2000 was how much money they raised for fellow House Republican candidates.[60] Ever since, chairmanship aspirants have worked to outdo one another in raising money. Vying for the Appropriations Committee chairmanship in 2004, Ralph Regula, the senior member, raised almost $1 million for Republican candidates; supporters of Jerry Lewis, his primary competitor, charged Regula with being a laggard; "Jerry's been a team player, not just this last couple of years," a Lewis supporter said pointedly. Lewis had, in fact, recently chaired a $7 million fund-raiser for the National Republican Congressional Committee.[61] In the 2003–2004 election cycle, the three candidates for chair all ranked in the top fifteen overall donors to other House candidates.[62] In his letter to Speaker Hastert already cited, Rogers pledged that "on my watch, Members of the [Appropriations] Committee will raise, at minimum, $15 million dollars per cycle."

Similarly, Democratic leaders pressure and cajole their members to contribute. The Democratic Congressional Campaign Committee sets "dues" that for the 2003–2004 cycle ranged from a low of $70,000 for vulnerable members who have their own reelection to worry about to a high of $300,000 for leaders, with the dues for ranking members, chief deputy whips, and lawmakers on the top three exclusive committees topping out at $150,000. Democrats support this approach. "There is a member culture that this is a team sport and everyone has to be on the field," said Rahm Emanuel (Ill.), a junior member. "No one can sit out." To encourage members to a pay their dues, the leaders use peer pressure: they recognize and lavish praise on the biggest givers; members who have given more than $100,000 are labeled "Hall of Famers." Leaders also offer more concrete incentives, ranging from a package of perks at the Democratic convention to special consideration for the best committee assignments.[63] Peterson, who had been a laggard in paying his dues, paid up when the Agriculture ranking position opened. In response to sharp criticism, he promised to pay his dues consistently in the future. The most generous donors in the 2003–2004 cycle did well when the most desirable positions were handed out by the Steering Committee in 2005.

Pelosi has pressured senior members to share resources with their junior colleagues in other ways as well. Because parties with a small House majority insist on a disproportionate share of committee positions, especially of positions on the most desirable committees, the demand for committee posts on the minority side is always high, and this is especially frustrating for junior members. When Pelosi became leader she insisted that those senior members who had received waivers of Caucus rules limiting committee assignments—a considerable number over time—give up their extra assignments. The better assignments thus made available to a number of junior members aided them with reelection and made them more satisfied with their House career; Pelosi's move was intended to contribute to the party's chances of retaking control, and it was perceived as such by the Democratic membership.

It is because—and only to the extent that—members do perceive their leaders' aggressive use of resources as contributing to furthering the membership's goals that members condone and, in fact, frequently demand such action. The parties in the House are highly active and strongly led because their members want them to be.

• Republican rule changes
• Gingrich
• sense of mandate: 1994 elections

Strong party leadership continues to exist because it serves members' interests
pg 130

• expect leaders now to use rules more forcefully
pg 116

- compromise is more costly
pg 110

CHAPTER 5

UNORTHODOX LAWMAKING IN THE HYPERPARTISAN HOUSE

A QUICK LOOK AT THE legislative process on the prescription drugs/Medicare bill (HR1) passed in June 2003 provides a good introduction to the legislative process in the contemporary House. Instead of a bill being introduced and then referred to one committee, the two committees with major jurisdiction over health care—Ways and Means, and Energy and Commerce—reached an "agreement in principle" on a proposal; that is, the top Republican leaders on these committees and the party leadership reached an agreement—with no input from minority Democrats, on the committees or off.[1] A bill reflecting the agreement in principle was introduced on June 16 and referred to the two committees the same day. Ways and Means approved their version the next day; Energy and Commerce took a little longer, reporting their version on June 25. In both committees, the markup sessions to consider and amend the legislation were contentious and highly partisan. Ways and Means Republicans were completely united in voting down the four key Democratic amendments and approving the bill. Every Democrat supported three of the four amendments and, on the other and on passage, one Democrat broke off to join the Republicans. In Energy and Commerce, the party contingents maintained unity almost as high. Democrats offered twenty-six amendments, all of which failed; eighteen were voted down on straight party-line votes; on seven others, an average of 1.4 Democrats and 0.7 Republicans crossed party lines. The only Democratic amendment that received a bipartisan—negative—vote was one to adopt the Senate bill; on that, fourteen of the twenty-three Democrats voting joined all Republicans in opposition. Energy and Commerce approved its bill on a 29 to 20 vote, with one Democrat and no Republicans crossing party lines.[2]

Instead of the bills going directly to the Rules Committee and then to the floor, the committee chairmen got together with Speaker Hastert and other Republican party leaders to work out a final bill to take to the floor.[3] Their aim was not just to meld the two committees' bills into one but also to make changes that would pick up the support of various groups of disgruntled Republicans. Over the course of several days, the party leaders met with small groups of members, attempting to persuade them to vote for the bill and, when necessary, negotiating changes to get their votes. At the same time, the Republican whip system was in high gear, "educating" and persuading Republicans and reaching out to more conservative "blue dog" Democrats. President Bush too got into the act, inviting groups of members to the White House to urge them to support the bill; the bill is a top White House priority and would be a huge GOP win if passed, the president emphasized.[4]

Speaker Hastert, the sponsor of the legislation, formally introduced the bill as HR1 on Wednesday, June 25; he had been saving that symbolically important number. The Rules Committee met just after midnight, and at 6:20 A.M. reported the special rule to govern floor consideration of the bill. The rule allowed only one amendment—an amendment in the nature of a substitute if offered by Charles Rangel and John Dingell, the ranking Democrats on the Ways and Means and Commerce committees respectively. The rule included a provision bringing up a bill expanding private medical savings accounts right before HR1 and specifying that, if both it and HR1 passed, the medical savings account bill would be added to HR1 and they would be sent to the Senate as a package. The medical savings account bill had not been considered and reported by a committee. Hastert agreed to bring it up and include it in the rule in return for the votes of a number of conservatives unhappy with a new entitlement.

Floor consideration began at 6:55 P.M. on the 26th. The rule was approved over fierce Democratic opposition; 99 percent of Democrats voted against the rule; 98 percent of Republicans voted for it. Democrats had wanted opportunities to offer a number of amendments, not just one. Democrats had developed their own Medicare/prescription drugs bill and offered it as their substitute; 174 Democrats supported it, but all 226 Republicans and 29 Democrats voted against it, so it was defeated.

Not long after that the vote on passage began. When the fifteen minutes allotted for a recorded vote ran out, the bill was losing by two votes. Holding the vote open, Hastert and other Republican leaders descended en mass on Republicans who had voted against the party position. Eventually they managed to persuade just enough Republicans to switch their votes to pass the bill on a 216–215 tally.[5] The fifteen-minute vote had stretched to almost an hour, but at 2:32 A.M., the bill was declared passed. Despite serious misgivings by many conservatives, only nineteen Republicans voted against the bill. Democrats had whipped the vote intensively as well, and only nine Democrats voted for the bill.

A striking feature of this case is how partisan the process was; at every stage—in the committees and on the floor—Republicans and Democrats opposed each other. The high partisan polarization documented in the previous chapters certainly seems to have affected lawmaking in the House on this controversial and salient bill.

Quite independent of the high partisanship in evidence, the legislative process on this bill is not much like the bill-becomes-a-law story of the typical college textbook. Indeed, the legislative process generally is quite different from what it was thirty years ago, and different in ways that affect the content of legislation. A variety of factors account for the changes, but the increase in partisan polarization is an important one, both as a root cause and as a shaper of the form that changes with other origins have taken, and here I concentrate on that.[6]

How the legislative process has changed and how partisan polarization affects the politics and the process of lawmaking in the House is best grasped by examining the stages in the process in sequence.

THE COMMITTEE PROCESS IN THE HOUSE

According to the textbook story, the legislative process starts in a congressional committee. That is still usually true—though less often than it used to be. But even when it is the case, what happens in committee often differs significantly from what was common in the past. The classic literature on congressional committees, which dates from the 1950s and 1960s, depicts committees as trying hard to avoid partisanship and, in fact, striving for unity. Within committee, civility was emphasized; deal cutting across party lines was standard operating procedure; if anything, members on the extremes of the ideological spectrum were the ones excluded. Ways and Means, the House tax-writing committee, was portrayed as the epitome of the committee that restrained partisanship and strove to get all committee members on board so as to enhance the prospects of success in passing the committee's legislation.[7]

In contrast, House committees now usually proceed in a highly partisan fashion when they consider the most important legislation of the session. Take, for example, Ways and Means. On the most important bills considered in 2003–2004, all were approved on highly partisan votes. Medical savings accounts and the big

2003 tax bill were approved on straight party-line votes (that is, all the Republicans voted for and all the Democrats voted against). On the Medicare/prescription drugs bill and on the energy bill, one Democrat voted with all the Republicans. The first version of the corporate tax bill was reported on a straight party-line vote in October 2003; the second version, approved in summer 2004 and so closer to the elections, saw three Democrats defecting to vote with all the Republicans for a generous bill containing many targeted benefits.

To be sure, there are still committees that try for unity and bipartisanship, though they are by and large the committees that deal with nonideological, constituency-benefit legislation—Transportation, for example. Furthermore, most committees consider a fair amount of reasonably important but largely noncontroversial legislation. For example, Ways and Means in 2003 approved consensually a bill cracking down on Medicare fraud and another giving tax benefits to members of the armed services.

Occasionally, unusual circumstances lead an ordinarily highly partisan committee to act in a bipartisan manner, as the Education Committee did on Bush's education bill in 2001. President Bush insisted that the bill included testing and accountability provisions, both of which Democrats were willing to accept in return for increased funding, but to get a bill, Bush was willing to trade away vouchers and other provisions that were anathema to Democrats. Republicans wanted to see their new president succeed, and hence although a bipartisan deal in committee required jettisoning much that conservatives most intensely wanted, a majority of committee Republicans was willing to pay the price. Thus, while not all committees operate in a highly partisan fashion and even partisan committees sometimes reach bipartisan or consensual deals, when the biggest and most consequential bills are involved, committees tend to split along partisan lines. Table 5.1 shows how much change there has been over time.

TABLE 5.1

Change in the Character of the House Committee Process

Years	Congresses	% Committee Processes Partisan
1961–82	87th–97th selected	23
1987–90	100th, 101st	27
1993–98, 2001–2004	103rd–105th, 107th–108th	51

Source: Author's calculations based on major legislation only, where "major" is defined as the legislation the *Congressional Quarterly* contemporaneously lists as major legislation under consideration by Congress and bills on which a key vote occurred, again according to CQ's contemporaneous judgment. My coding of the character of the committee process is based on the *Congressional Quarterly* account, the committee report, and/or newspaper stories when the CQ account was incomplete, and for the 106th Congress forward, Markup Reports, nationaljournal.com.

Note: When a bill bypassed committee, the drafting entity (e.g., the party leadership, a task force) was coded.

Committee markups now are often not true decision-making sessions; the real decisions have been made in behind-the-scenes bargaining among majority party members of the committee, sometimes with party leadership involvement, or in majority party committee caucuses. The public markup with minority party members present is simply a formality. In actuality, the minority has been excluded from the decision-making process.

THE PARTY LEADERSHIP IN THE PREFLOOR LEGISLATIVE PROCESS

Before the reforms of the 1970s, committees were relatively independent and insulated decision makers. Certainly, if the committee wanted the House to pass their legislation, they had to write a bill that could command a majority. But how they went about this, including what sort of majority they put together—big bipartisan, ideological, partisan—was largely left to the committee. Now committees are much less independent and not at all insulated from party conference/caucus and party leadership pressure. And the more important the committee, the less independent it is. Majority party members of the House expect committee majorities to produce legislation acceptable to most majority party members, and they expect their party leadership to see that this happens.

The result is a greater role for the majority party leadership early in the legislative process and in shaping the substance of legislation. The changes in how committee members and chairs are chosen have increased the party leaders' clout and so facilitated the highly active role they now play in the legislative process. It is important to remember, however, that it is the ideological homogeneity of the membership that made these changes as well as the assertive leadership role possible. When the leaders act aggressively, they are acting as agents of their members; that is, they are acting on their members' behalf, furthering their members' legislative preferences, not just their own. As Speaker Hastert phrased it, his job is to "please the majority of the majority."[8]

Modes of Leadership Involvement

On major legislation of importance to the party, the House majority party leadership now oversees the legislative process from the beginning; the leaders play an important role in determining the agenda, and they often set out rough timetables for when legislation should be reported out of committee. Through staff, they monitor committee proceedings and frequently confer with the chair on substance and politics. Majority Leader Tom DeLay meets weekly with the committee chairs.[9]

The objective of the majority party leadership is to assure that before it takes major legislation to the floor, the bill meets three criteria: it is acceptable to most of the party membership, it will pass the House, and preferably it will benefit and certainly not damage the party's reputation. By and large, the majority party members of most committees and especially of the most important committees have legislative preferences similar to those of the leadership and the Conference. Because of their similar legislative preferences and because they owe their positions to the party, committee chairs are usually responsive to their party leaders' informal advice and counsel. Most leadership involvement in committee thus goes on under the radar. However, if the committee process is not producing legislation that the leadership believes meets these objectives, leadership involvement becomes more overt. "On each piece of legislation, I actively seek to bring our party together," Speaker Hastert explained. "I do not feel comfortable scheduling any controversial legislation unless I know we have the votes on our side first."[10]

Changes in the legislative process and in the political environment have contributed to a more active and more visible role for the leadership. The institution of multiple referral significantly altered the legislative process and, in effect, forced the party leadership to take on enhanced legislative responsibilities. The 1975 rule permitted the referral of legislation to more than one committee. The prominent issues had changed, many had become more complex, and they no longer fit neatly into the jurisdiction of a single committee. Multiple referral became increasingly common, especially on major legislation; for the Congresses from the late 1980s to the late 1990s for which I have data, about a third of major legislation was referred to more than one committee in the House.[11]

When several committees are involved on the same piece of legislation, they may not be capable of working out their differences by themselves, and a coordinator may be needed. The party leaders are the only central leaders in the House, and from the inception of multiple referral, the tasks of coordination and mediation often fell to them. In 1990, for example, the Ways and Means Committee and the Education and Labor Committee preferred distinctly different approaches to child care legislation; during months of negotiation, neither side was willing to budge. An agreement was finally reached only after the Speaker intervened, and that intervention involved making substantive adjustments to the legislation. In 1995 the House Republican leadership produced the party's welfare reform bill by combining bills passed by three committees, in the process altering some controversial provisions.[12] The party leaders' involvement on bills referred to more than one committee may take the form of neutral coordinator, in which case the actual work is delegated to staff, but on major legislation, leaders are more often engaged in making sure the resulting bill meets the criteria of being acceptable to most majority party members, being passable, and if possible enhancing but certainly not damaging the party reputation.

Whether referred to multiple committees or just to one, legislation may require postcommittee adjustments to meet these criteria. The political environment may have changed after a bill has been reported from committee, or the committee may simply have been unwilling or unable to write legislation meeting one or more of the criteria. When Democrats controlled the House, the Education and Labor Committee typically was well to the left of the Democratic membership's center of gravity. Salient legislation needs to be substantively acceptable to the bulk of the party membership and also defensible in the public arena. The civil rights bill that the liberal Judiciary and Education and Labor committees reported in March 1991 was too easy a target for President George H. W. Bush, who had vocally and repeatedly labeled similar legislation a quota bill, thus putting Democrats on the defensive. Speaker Foley asked Whip Bill Gray to oversee the effort to draft a leadership substitute. Consulting with committee Democrats, with other members—especially southerners—concerned about supporting legislation that could be labeled a quota bill, and with interest groups on both sides of the issue,

Gray worked out a compromise. Among its provisions was an explicit ban on quotas. The resulting legislation satisfied, at least minimally, both the strongest civil rights supporters and the Democratic membership as a whole, and it passed easily.

In the 104th Congress, when the constitutional amendment imposing term limits on members of Congress emerged from the Judiciary Committee in a form that the majority of the Republican Party found unacceptable, the Rules Committee, at the direction of the leadership, dropped the committee draft and substituted another version.[13] Similarly, in 2001, the House Judiciary Committee unanimously reported a consensus anti-terrorism bill that the Bush Administration considered too weak. Speaker Hastert substituted a bill closer to the White House–supported Senate legislation and brought that to the floor.[14]

Despite a strong bipartisan consensus on the Transportation Committee for the highway reauthorization bill negotiated by its chair, the Republican leadership in 2004 forced the committee to report a bill that was much less costly and that did not assume an increase in the gas tax. President Bush had threatened to veto a "budget busting" bill, and a big public battle between a Republican Congress and a Republican president in an election year would give the party a major black eye, the leadership believed; with deficits soaring, the leaders wanted to avoid any appearance of the Republican House being fiscally irresponsible; and any tax increase was anathema to most Republicans.

Sometimes the leadership simply bypasses committee all together. The desire to move swiftly may precipitate such action. In early 1987, at the beginning of the 100th Congress, for example, the Democratic party leadership brought a clean water bill and a highway–mass transit bill directly to the floor because it wanted to score some quick victories. Both bills had gone through the full committee process and had passed by large margins in the preceding Congress. In 1988 the Democratic Party leadership took the Senate's version of the Civil Rights Restoration Act directly to the floor because time for action was getting short, and they wanted to pass the bill without change to avoid a conference. The leadership feared delay in the Senate were further Senate action required.

In 2002, the Republican leadership brought to the floor without committee action a bill raising the debt limit. Even though it is essential to maintaining the good credit of the United States, House members hate voting for raising the debt limit because it can easily be misrepresented as a vote for budget busting and to no good cause. Republicans who for years harassed the majority Democrats about their debt-ceiling votes especially detest casting such a vote. Figuring that their best chance of passing the bill was to keep the visibility of the vote as low as possible, Republican leaders with almost no warning offered an amendment to the rule for another bill that would permit the House to consider the Senate debt limit bill and would allow only an hour of debate. The bill passed 215–214.[15]

Sometimes the political sensitivity of an issue motivates the party leadership to bypass committee. In 1988 the Speaker entrusted the drafting of the House Democrats' alternative to Reagan's plan for aiding the Nicaraguan contras to a task force headed by the deputy whip; no committee was involved. The political risks inherent in strongly opposing the president on a highly charged and highly visible foreign policy issue, as House Democrats were doing, were too great to leave the decision making to a committee. When the Democratic leadership decided to take on the politically fraught issue of a congressional pay raise combined with ethics reform, it again turned to a special task force, in this case a bipartisan one.

The substantive, procedural, and political complexity of the issue of managed care reform led Speaker Gingrich to set up a task force headed by Chief Deputy Whip Dennis Hastert (R-Ill.)

to draft legislation in the 105th Congress. This was an issue that confronted Republicans with a conundrum. Most Republicans opposed allowing patients to sue their HMOs, because they thought it bad public policy and because important supportive groups opposed it. Yet the proposal was immensely popular with the public, and Democrats were scoring political points by advocating tough "patients' bill of rights" legislation. The Hastert task force drafted legislation that did not allow suits but did allow Republicans to argue that they too supported patients' rights. Gingrich brought that legislation directly to the floor, bypassing the committees of jurisdiction.

When Hastert became Speaker in the next Congress, he promised to follow regular order and not bypass committees. Yet the same constellation of problems eventually forced Hastert to turn to unorthodox processes in drafting managed care legislation, and he too effectively bypassed the committees.[16]

Again, in the 107th Congress, the leadership bypassed the committees on the issue. As CQ reported, "The bill was written largely in Hastert's office by White House domestic policy advisor Joshua Bolton; a top Bush health care aide, Anne Phelps; two Department of Labor attorneys; Shadegg [a conservative Republican member of the House long active on the issue]; Norwood [a Republican who had previously supported a bill that Democrats liked and most Republicans opposed]; and a few GOP aides."[17]

When President Bush requested that Congress quickly establish a Department of Homeland Security in spring of 2002, the House Republican leadership could anticipate some significant problems. A large number of committees would have to be involved because they had jurisdiction over programs that Bush wanted moved into the new department, and some of them would likely resist giving up any of their jurisdiction. Yet if the House did not move expeditiously, the reputation of the chamber and the party would be damaged. To handle the political problems as well as the major coordination task of melding the work of a dozen or so committees into a coherent whole, Hastert proposed and the House approved a select committee of nine members. Hastert choose Majority Leader Dick Armey to chair the select committee and appointed members of the leadership to the remaining Republican slots.[18] On June 24 the legislation was referred to twelve standing committees under a deadline; on July 16 and 17, ten of the committees presented their recommendations to the select committee. Floor consideration on the combined bill began on July 25, and the bill passed on July 26.

The homeland security bill is an example of omnibus legislation, legislation that involves a large number of issues and often many committees. Congress legislates through omnibus bills much more than it used to do; I did not find any in the Congresses I examined from before the mid-1970s; now they tend to make up somewhere between 10 and 20 percent of major bills.[19]

During the 1980s, the Democratic majority party leadership sometimes packaged legislation into omnibus measures as part of a strategy to counter ideologically hostile Republican presidents, especially Ronald Reagan, who was so skillful at using the media to his advantage. Thus, in early May 1988, Speaker Wright decided that the House should pass an omnibus drug bill. The issue had risen in the polls to be the public's top concern during an election year. The Speaker called together the chairs of eleven committees with relevant jurisdiction, discussed with them the reasons for such a bill and its possible contents, and then said he wanted a bipartisan effort and designated Majority Leader Tom Foley to coordinate the effort. Foley's tasks and those of leadership staff aides working with him were to monitor the work of all the committees involved, to spot problems and try to work them out, and to push the participants to move quickly and settle their disputes expeditiously. Those issues on which the committees were unable to reach a substantially bipartisan agreement were pushed up to Foley and Minority Leader Bob Michel; which of those would be presented to the membership to decide on the floor was determined in negotiations between them. By the August recess, the bill was ready for floor consideration, and the bill passed in September.

By packaging disparate and individually modest provisions on salient issues such as trade, drugs, or crime into an omnibus bill, Democrats sought to compete with the White House for media attention and public credit. Measures the president very much wanted could sometimes be packaged with others that congressional Democrats favored but the president opposed, thus forcing the president to accept legislative provisions that he would veto if they were sent to him in free-standing form.

Budget resolutions, reconciliation bills, massive continuing (appropriations) resolutions and, recently, omnibus appropriations bills have constituted the preponderance of omnibus measures since the passage of the Budget Act in 1974. Reconciliation bills, which enjoy some special procedural protections in the Senate, as I discuss in the next chapter, allow the packaging of a large number of major changes in law into one legislative vehicle. All of the big economic and tax packages since President Reagan's in 1981 have been brought up as reconciliation bills—the read-my-lips budget deal of George Bush, Sr., Bill Clinton's economic program in 1993, the Republicans' huge tax cut and spending cut bill in 1995, and all of George W. Bush's tax bills, to mention just the most prominent.

The majority party leadership is always deeply involved in the crafting and passing of such legislation. These bills are complex and a coordinator is required. But more crucial in dictating leadership involvement, these bills are immensely consequential both substantively and politically; members care about their provisions, often both as broad public policy and in terms of impact on their districts, and the majority party's reputation is at stake.

The House Republican Party versus the Appropriators

The House party leaders, thus, are much more actively involved in the prefloor legislative process than they used to be, but they are involved as agents of their membership. It is when there is conflict between the party leadership and a committee that the leaders' clout and its ultimate source become most evident. During the period of Republican control of the House, the committee most frequently in conflict with the leadership and the Conference has been the Appropriations Committee. The Appropriations Committee funds—that is, it appropriates money for—federal government operations and programs; each year, it is responsible for writing and then passing a number of general appropriations bills, each of which funds a number of government programs and agencies. The committee is organized into subcommittees, each of which is responsible for one bill. Thus, for example, the Labor, Health and Human Services and Education Subcommittee annually reports a bill that specifies how much money may be spent by each of the myriad programs and agencies in those three cabinet departments.[20] The Appropriations Committee's traditional thirteen subcommittees were reduced to eleven in a 2005 reorganization.

Appropriations Committee members must make a large number of decisions in a relatively short period; appropriations bills are supposed to be enacted by the beginning of the fiscal year, October 1, and that means having them ready for floor consideration in the House by June or July. Many of the decisions are ones about which executive-branch personnel, interest groups, and members themselves care, sometimes deeply; yet by and large, the realities of the situation dictate that most of the decisions be incremental. Most programs and agencies cannot absorb huge increases efficiently, and in most cases, huge cuts really mean destroying the program. The large workload and the character of the decisions to be made led the Appropriations Committee and its subcommittees long ago to a bipartisan and pragmatic mode of operation, and that, to a considerable extent, had been maintained even as the parties polarized.[21] The Appropriations Committee did become more partisan, but not nearly partisan enough for the Republican majority.

House Republicans—many of whom saw their purpose as shrinking the size of the federal government, if not dismantling it—regarded their pragmatic Appropriations Committee colleagues with distrust and even hostility. The Republican appropriators are too willing to work with Democrats and too eager to spend money and thus, in effect, are not representing their Conference, more conservative Republicans claimed. From the appropriators' point of view, conservative Republicans were being unrealistic; if the committee reported bills with as little money for popular domestic programs as conservatives wanted, the bills would never pass muster in the Senate and might well fail in the House, where the appetite for fiscal restraint is always greater in the abstract than for specific programs.

The tension dated back to well before Republicans took control of the House. At the beginning of the 104th Congress, Gingrich required each of the thirteen Appropriations subcommittee chairs—the "Cardinals"—to pledge commitment in writing to the tough budget cutting that the Republican revolution required.[22] The conflict simmered through the remainder of the Clinton presidency; as many House Republicans saw it, appropriators continued to be too accommodating, but because Republicans had learned they could not shut down the government and Clinton insisted on more spending, there was little that Republicans could do. In 2002, now with a Republican president, the conflict boiled up again. House appropriators, backed by the small group of Republican moderates, complained that the spending levels the party and the president advocated were unrealistic; the Republican Study Committee (RSC), a group of approximately seventy House Republican movement conservatives, vowed to vote against any appropriations bill that exceeded those limits. When leadership mediation failed to break the impasse, the Speaker decided to provide temporary funding through a continuing resolution, thus essentially siding with the conservatives.

At the organization sessions after the 2002 elections, the Republican Conference adopted a Speaker-backed and RSC-sponsored rule changing the way Cardinals are chosen. The new rule gave the leadership-dominated Steering Committee a vote on them, whereas they had previously been selected by the committee chair and, in practice, on the basis of seniority. The Omnibus Appropriations bill passed in early 2003 largely adhered to the tough spending limits.[23] Again in 2004, the appropriators toed the line and did not exceed the tight spending caps on domestic programs.[24]

The "case of the Cardinals" illustrates several important points. First and most obviously, ideological homogeneity does not mean identical legislative preferences and a complete lack of conflict within the party. There will always be some variation in policy preferences and some differences stemming from institutional responsibilities, as is the case with the appropriators. Thus, even when leading a quite homogeneous party, leaders benefit from having resources such as influence over committee assignments and committee leadership positions as a backup. However, only a quite homogeneous party will give its leaders such resources and allow the leaders to use them aggressively. And, as in this case, both in pressuring the Appropriations Committee Republicans and in making the rules change to rein them in, when the party leader does act aggressively, that leader is likely to be responding to the wishes of a sizable segment of the membership.

SPECIAL RULES AND NEW FLOOR PROCEDURES

How legislation is considered on the floor of the House has also changed in a way that gives the majority party leadership more control to engineer the outcomes the membership wants. Most major legislation is brought to the House floor by a special rule that allows the measure to be taken up out of order. The Rules Committee reports such rules, which take the form of House resolutions. The rule sets the terms for a measure's floor consideration. A rule always specifies the amount of time allowed for general debate and who is to control that time. A rule may also restrict amendments, waive points of order (against what would otherwise be violations of House rules in the legislation or in how it is brought up), and include other special provisions to govern floor consideration. The extent to which a rule restricts amendments and the manner in which it does so also may vary. An *open rule* allows all germane—relevant—amendments, while a *closed rule* prohibits all amendments other than those offered by the reporting committee. Between the two extremes are rules that allow some but not all germane amendments to be offered; they are often labeled *modified open* or *modified closed*, depending on just how restrictive the rule is. According to the terminology used by the contemporary Republican Rules Committee, modified open rules are those that allow any germane amendment subject only to an overall time limit on the amending process and/or a requirement that amendments be printed in the *Congressional Record* by a specific time. Modified closed or structured rules permit only those specific amendments enumerated in the Rules Committee report. Some modified closed rules allow only one amendment—a substitute by the minority party.[25]

As table 5.2 shows, as late as 1977–78, most special rules were still open rules; only 15 percent restricted amendments in some way. As Democratic members began to comprehend the costs of the wide-open amending process fostered by the reforms and to demand that their leaders do something about it, the frequency of restrictive rules increased. In the hostile and increasingly partisan climate of the 1980s and early 1990s, restrictive rules were used more and more often. Holding together compromises

TABLE 5.2
Change in the Character of House Special Rules

Congress	Years	% Restrictive
95th	1977–78	15
96th	1979–80	25
97th	1981–82	25
98th	1983–84	32
99th	1985–86	43
100th	1987–88	46
101st	1989–90	55
102nd	1991–92	66
103rd	1993–94	70
104th	1995–96	54
105th	1997–98	60

Source: Compiled by Donald Wolfensberger, former Minority Counsel, Committee on Rules, from *Rules Committee Calendars* and *Surveys of Activities*, available from the author.

Note: Rules included are all those for initial consideration of legislation, except rules on appropriations bills that only waive points of order. Restrictive rules are those limiting the germane amendments that can be offered and include modified open, modified closed, and closed rules and rules providing for consideration in the House as opposed to the Committee of the Whole.

and protecting members from political heat became both more difficult and more essential; and leaders, in response to their members' demands, developed special rules into powerful devices for shaping the choices members face on the floor. By 1993–94, 70 percent of special rules restricted amendments to some extent.[26]

The new Republican majority in the 104th Congress had promised to pass an ambitious agenda, much of it in the first hundred days. Before the election, however, House Republicans, prominently including their leadership, had vehemently denounced restrictive rules and had promised not to use them. The proportion

TABLE 5.3
Substantially Restrictive Rules on Major Legislation

Congress	Years	% Modified Closed or Closed
89th	1965–66	12
91st	1969–70	
94th	1975–76	
95th	1979–80	21
97th	1981–82	18
100th	1987–88	42
101st	1989–90	42
103rd	1993–94	60
104th	1995–96	63
105th	1997–98	72
107th	2001–2002	73

Source: Author's calculations based on categorization by Donald Wolfensberger, former Minority Counsel, Committee on Rules.

of all rules that were restrictive did go down in the 104th, though Democrats claimed Republicans manipulated the figures by considering under open rules some noncontroversial legislation that should have been considered under the suspension procedure. Major legislation was mostly considered under complex and usually restrictive rules; the usefulness of such rules for promoting the Republicans' legislative objectives outweighed any damage from the inevitable charges of hypocrisy that their use provoked. In fact, the likelihood of major legislation being considered under substantially restrictive rules has continued to go up (see table 5.3). In 2001–2002, 44 percent of all rules allowed only one Democratic substitute.[27]

Special rules, as they have evolved over the past two decades, are so useful because they can be tailored to the particular problem a specific bill faces; that is, they are strategic tools. Is the problem a bill faces on the floor uncertainty? No one knows what possibly appealing but destructive amendments might come out of the woodwork when the bill hits the floor. A special rule can require that all the amendments be submitted several days before floor consideration so that opponents lose the element of surprise. Is the problem that opponents might try to "filibuster" by amendment—that is, delay action by offering oodles of amendments? Solution: by special rule, a time limit can be put on the amendment process. Is the problem that, if allowed to offer enough amendments, opponents can target the compromises reached in the drafting process and split the majority coalition? By rule, opponents can be allowed to offer only one comprehensive substitute.

A highly restrictive rule allowing a small number of comprehensive substitutes and sometimes only one is routine for budget resolutions and reconciliation bills; there are always unpopular components to budget bills, and the majority does not want to allow the minority to target just those elements. Restrictive rules have made the budget process a valuable majority party tool in the House. Many and often significant changes in law can be made, yet because they are rolled into one bill, the reconciliation bill, the number of separate roll calls that have to be won is limited, and if there are unpopular parts of the package, the number of tough votes the leaders have to ask their members to cast is also limited.

Is the problem that the bill needs to be passed, but it is one for which members do not want to vote? Raising the debt ceiling would be an example. Package the unpopular provision with some sweeteners—provisions with strong appeal to members—and, by rule, force a vote on the package as a whole. In 1996, for example, the Republican leadership added the line-item veto as a sweetener to the debt limit–increase bill to induce their members to vote for the legislation.

Are there amendments that would put your members in a serious bind? Amendments that they believe are bad public policy but that they would find it politically hard to vote against? (For Democrats, amendments on hot-button issues such as homosexual rights or flag burning are often problematical; for Republicans, amendments increasing spending or benefits under popular domestic programs are.) By rule, one can bar that amendment from being offered at all. In 2004, for example, the Workforce Investment Act, the country's main job training legislation, included a provision that would allow religious groups running federally funded job training and literacy programs to hire and fire employees based on their religious beliefs. Republicans had failed to enact Bush's faith-based initiative as a separate bill and were attempting to enacted it piecemeal. This provision, which in effect allowed discrimination, was politically tricky for some Republicans. So the rule for the bill simply barred the Democratic amendment that would have knocked out that provision.[28]

If barring a vote altogether is not politically feasible, its proponents can be forced to offer it in a parliamentary guise that makes the vote as obscure as possible. For example, rather than allowing the minority party to offer a substitute for the majority's bill, the minority can be forced to offer their alternative through a motion to recommit with instructions. Let them try to use that against your incumbents in thirty-second advertisements! When House Republicans brought their prescription drugs bill to the floor in the summer of 2002, they forced Democrats to offer their alternative, which provided more generous drug benefits, through the motion to recommit with instructions.

Is the problem that some of your members are going to have trouble explaining to their constituents their votes for the party's bill? By what is called a self-executing rule, set up a parliamentary situation that spares them a vote at all. (Self-executing rules are rules that provide for the automatic adoption of an amendment or other matter upon the adoption of the rule, thus eliminating the need for a separate vote on the substance of the matter.) Or arrange for a vote on an amendment that provides "cover"—that is, something members can use to explain their vote to their constituents. For example, one of the three amendments made in order by the modified closed rule for the 1990 civil rights bill stated that "nothing in the act shall be construed to require an employer to adopt hiring or promotion quotas."[29]

Should the majority be in the unusual position of trying to kill legislation, specially tailored rules can be useful as well. Under intense pressure to bring the campaign finance reform bill to the floor in 2002, Speaker Hastert did so but under a rule that campaign reform supporters claimed doomed them to failure. To build support, proponents of the Shays-Meehan bill had made a number of changes in their bill after they introduced it. Instead of allowing the compromise bill to be brought to the floor, which would be the normal procedure if the Republican leaders wanted to pass the bill, the rule brought the original bill to the floor and specified that each of the compromises would have to be offered separately as an amendment. To succeed, proponents would have to win twenty-two votes in a row on amendments. Bill supporters themselves voted down the rule and thus seemed to kill the bill.

This example makes an important point. Because the majority party leadership appoints the majority members of the Rules Committee and the committee is thus an arm of the leadership, the Speaker can get essentially any rule he wants out of the committee. As Rules Committee chairman David Dreier has often said, his job is to move the majority party's agenda. However, a majority of the full House membership must approve each rule. So the leadership must be sensitive to its members' needs and wants. If members believe a rule coerces them in a manner they find unacceptable, they can vote against it. Occasionally that happens. In late 2002 the bankruptcy reform bill fell victim to such an instance. In conference, the Senate insisted on keeping language preventing anti-abortion groups from using the bill to avoid paying court judgments. When the rule for the conference report came to the House floor, a group of vehemently anti-abortion Republicans voted against it because it would have forced them to take that language along with the rest of the bill. Defeat of the rule sank the bill for the 107th Congress.

As the parties became increasingly polarized and majority party leaders increasingly used restrictive rules to their party's advantage, voting on rules has become highly partisan. Votes on restrictive rules are now regularly straight party-line votes or close to it.

Since majority party leaders can no longer expect to get an appreciable number of votes from the minority party, high cohesion by the majority is essential to pass most restrictive rules. Since the Republicans became the majority, they have had to get the votes of almost all their members on rule votes because their margins of control have been narrow. In both parties, members are now expected to vote the party line on procedural votes, such as rule votes. Freshmen members are instructed in this expectation at the parties' orientation sessions. During the organization sessions for the 108th Congress, Hastert and DeLay reiterated that whips are expected to hew to the party line on such votes and explicitly stated that not doing so would lead to a member being dropped from the whip system.[30] Nor was this a bluff. After Charlie Bass of New Hampshire voted "no" on a rule governing debate for the reauthorization of the Individuals with Disabilities Education Act because he was not allowed to offer an amendment, he resigned from the whip team.[31] And again it is not just the leadership that enforces this norm; peer pressure is also at work. The leadership has usually put together a rule that speaks to the needs of the party collectively and of most party members as individuals; if a few members bring down such a rule, their party colleagues will let them know that they do not appreciate this. Their reputations as team players, so important for many benefits, will suffer.

These expectations and the implied rewards and punishments accompanying them do make a difference. Certainly the voting behavior on procedural questions of the small group of Republican moderates appears to be affected. And occasionally, evidence of a broader effect comes to light. The Republican tax bill in the 104th Congress is one such case. Almost half of the Republican membership—102—had signed a letter to Speaker Gingrich supporting a reduction to $95,000 in the income limit of families eligible for the $500 per child tax credit. Most Democrats were on the record as supporting the reduction. If an amendment reducing the cap in the bill had been offered on the floor, it would have passed. Yet because the rule did not allow that amendment, the bill passed with its $200,000 cap intact.[32] Of the 102 Republicans who publicly declared their support for reducing the cap, only one voted against the previous question on the rule—a motion that, if successful, would have allowed the rule to be altered so as to make that amendment in order—and only eleven voted against the rule. More generally, there is a strong tendency for members of the majority party to vote for rules even on legislation they then vote against.[33]

Thus the rewards and punishments the leadership commands, and peer pressure as well, contribute to high voting cohesion on procedural votes, but intraparty ideological homogeneity and the leadership's sensitivity to its members' needs and wants are more basic determinants. What the leadership is trying to do is make it easy for members to vote in such a way that the party-preferred policy is the outcome, and given the current intraparty ideological homogeneity, that is what most of their members want—even if sometimes, without a cleverly crafted rule, it would be hard for them to vote that way.

BUILDING MAJORITIES

Before major legislation is brought to the floor, the majority party whip system has gathered information on its members' voting intentions and, if necessary, has worked to persuade enough members to pass the legislation. Republican whip system standard operating procedure calls for a first count to ascertain where the party position stands. Deputy whips canvass their assigned members, often making their contacts on the floor of the House during a recorded vote since almost all members are present.[34] When necessary, the majority party leadership can call a vote so as to facilitate counting. The whips report their results to senior staffers in the offices of the whip and the chief deputy whip who oversee the process. If deemed necessary, deputy whips then conduct another round of the count, refining it and beginning the serious persuasion process. As the scheduled vote draws nearer, if the outcome is still uncertain, higher-ranked leaders become more deeply involved—first the whip and the deputy whip, then the Majority Leader, and finally the Speaker.

Persuasion and Bargaining

Effective majority building requires leadership sensitivity to members' concerns. The whip conducts "listening" sessions with members, often well before major legislation is taken to the floor. "The best way to avoid needless conflict is to pay attention early," Whip Roy Blunt explained.[35] He discusses the initiative with small groups of members, aiming to build support through inclusion. "I think the way you move legislation with the narrow margins we've had, and still have, is a constant effort to create a sense of team responsibility, a constant effort to be inclusive, a constant effort to listen," Blunt said.[36]

The most common arguments used in persuasion efforts are policy and party based: the legislation at issue is good public policy; victory is crucial to the party. Both arguments tend to be more effective now than they use to be. High intraparty ideological homogeneity means that crafting legislation most party members consider good public policy is easier than it was when the majority party was more diverse. As a Republican insider explained, "90 percent of your caucus is with you before you call them on the phone."[37] With the majority party's House margin narrow enough that control of the chamber always seems on the line, and with members' House lives now taking place mostly within the party and advancement in both the party and committee hierarchy dependent on a member's reputation with his or her party colleagues, party-based arguments are also more persuasive.

To the extent that the ideological homogeneity is constituency based, voting the party position is also voting the district. Nevertheless House members, who must run for reelection every two years, are notoriously risk-averse when it comes to casting a vote that might hurt them back home. The traveling that party leaders do to members' districts, usually for fund-raisers, can pay off in persuasion efforts beyond engendering gratitude. As Whip Roy Blunt said, "Often you [are] able to say 'I've been to your district, and this is not a vote that's a problem for you in your district.'"[38] Still, no party is so homogeneous that district concerns never dictate a vote against the party position. Members who would prefer to vote contrary to the party position, almost always for constituency-based reasons, may nevertheless be willing to commit to providing a vote if it is needed. The whip keeps track of such "if needed" votes so that they can be called in should they be required. In one of the most famous instances, Democrats had to call in Marjorie Margolies-Mizvinsky's pocket vote to save President Clinton's economic program in 1993. Margolies-Mizvinsky (D-Pa.) had promised her constituents she would not vote to raise taxes, but she believed that personally bringing down the economic program would be irresponsible, and so, when her vote proved decisive, she cast a "yea" vote.

Even within an ideologically homogeneous party, differences on public policy do exist. Persuading members to vote against their own strongly held policy views may not be possible. The Republican leaders failed to talk a number of fervently anti-abortion members into voting for the rule for the bankruptcy bill conference report. For those members, the vote was a matter of conscience. Sometimes, however, circumstances do allow leaders to prevail even in such circumstances. Moderate Republicans have repeatedly been convinced to vote for legislation considerably to the right of their preferred position by the argument that the Senate would in any case moderate the bill before enactment. By casting a party vote, they would be protecting their reputation within the party without actually being responsible for a policy outcome they disliked. Conservative members who opposed the prescription drugs/Medicare bill because it established a new entitlement program were persuaded to vote for the conference report by the argument that if it went down, the Democrats might well prevail with a version that conservatives would like much less. The message, according to Commerce Committee Chairman Billy Tauzen, was "a not too subtle message: this is the best you are ever going to get."[39]

If ordinary persuasion fails, the leaders can bargain to get the votes they need. Of course, the substantive changes leaders are often instrumental in making in legislation after it is reported from committee and before it comes to the floor are frequently made to pick up votes. The leaders also can resort to quid pro quos of various sorts. To get the votes to pass the budget resolution in 2004, Whip Roy Blunt promised several members votes on legislation helpful to their districts.[40]

In putting together the majorities needed to pass major legislation, party leaders regularly work with supportive interest groups and, if he is a fellow partisan, with the president. Interest groups closely allied with the party are included in the planning of strategy and are expected to work on those members with whom they have a close relationship. Interest groups without close ties to the party may be included on specific efforts. The coalition that the Republican whip system put together to work the energy bill in the 108th Congress included among its core members Bob Powers of the AFL-CIO's Building and Construction Trades Department, not a usual Republican ally.[41] Powers supported the legislation because he believed it meant jobs for union workers.

The president's liaison staff work closely with the House leaders of their party on measures important to the president. When the bill is a presidential priority and the outcome is in doubt, the president gets involved personally, calling members and sometimes inviting them to the White House or for a ride in *Air Force One*. Members now believe their own fate is closely tied to that of their president; even if they perceive themselves to be electorally safe, attaining their policy goals and retaining control of the House depend to a considerable extent on the president's success. Consequently, members are more receptive to presidential persuasion.

The majority party's control over floor scheduling in the House allows the party leadership to determine unilaterally when to bring major legislation to the floor. Ordinarily, the leaders do not bring a bill to the floor unless and until they have the votes to pass it. Sometimes, however, that rule must be broken, and then aspects of the majority-building process that usually take place behind closed doors become more visible. Passage of trade promotion authority in 2001 and of the prescription drugs/Medicare conference report in late 2003 illustrate the process.

When the Republican House leaders brought up the trade promotion authority legislation (aka fast track) in December 2001, they lacked the votes to pass the bill. They had already scheduled it several times over the previous six months but had to pull the bill off the schedule each time for lack of votes. The leaders made deals with Republicans reluctant for constituency reasons to vote for the legislation; for example, language protecting the citrus and sugar industries was added to the bill to assuage the concerns of worried Florida Republicans. President George W. Bush used rides on *Air Force One* and promises of projects to persuade members. Speaker Hastert made a rare floor speech, urging members to support their president in a time of crisis: "This Congress will either support our president, who is fighting a courageous war on terrorism and redefining American world leadership, or it will undercut the president at the worst possible time."[42]

As time expired, the bill was nevertheless several votes short, and as the leaders held the vote open, furious efforts to change the few necessary votes ensued. Robin Hayes of textile-producing North Carolina was promised a number of policy concessions as well as maximum help in his tough reelection campaign. He voted for the bill, reportedly with tears in his eyes.[43] In one case at least, the party leaders overrode the committee chair, who was furious over the concessions party leaders made. "Chairman Thomas had said he would not agree to this," Jim DeMint (R-S.C.) explained. "But the leader of the House said [the leadership] would. . . . I changed my vote."[44] Thomas actually threatened to vote against the bill, but of course he did not. The trade promotion authority bill passed 215 to 214.

Passing the Medicare/Prescription Drugs Bill

The campaign to pass the Medicare/prescription drugs conference report illustrates even more clearly the combination of member ideological homogeneity, party loyalty, and leadership clout that make possible the majority Republicans' legislative success despite their narrow margins. Once a conference agreement between the House and Senate had been reached, the Republican party apparatus went to work to pass it. The agreement was largely the work of Speaker Hastert and Senate Majority Leader Bill Frist; House Democrats were completely excluded from the negotiations, and Hastert knew he could not count on many Democratic votes. The agreement went some distance toward bringing private insurance companies and thus presumably competition into Medicare, as conservatives advocated, but not to the extent that many wanted. Both the White House and the Republican congressional leadership believed the prescription drugs benefit would be a major electoral coup for the party, but the more conservative members opposed any new entitlement.

The leaders brought Newt Gingrich in to speak to a Republican Conference meeting and vigorously defend the bill from a conservative perspective. The House Republican whip system went into overdrive to produce an accurate count of Republicans' voting intentions. At a whip meeting, the chairmen of Ways and Means and of Energy and Commerce explained the complex bill's provisions and countered the arguments against it. They emphasized, as the party leaders would also do, that the addition of a prescription drug benefit to Medicare was inevitable and that if this bill failed, Democrats would eventually do it in a way conservatives found a great deal more distasteful. The whips fanned out to do their count. Whip Roy Blunt met with his whips and with the leaders of the coalition of interest groups supporting the bill to coordinate strategy. That the lobbying efforts of the coalition of several hundred groups was headed by Susan B. Hirschmann, a former chief of staff to Tom DeLay, facilitated cooperation between the Republican leadership and the groups. The GOP had scored a major coup when the leaders persuaded the American Association of Retired Persons, the largest seniors organization, to endorse the bill, and the AARP played an important role in the lobbying effort.

When a whip found a Republican who was either opposed or undecided, that member was asked for a list of specific objections to the bill. Blunt and the chief deputy whip then met with small groups of members with similar complaints, attempting to address their problems. From *Air Force One* Bush telephoned a number of holdouts as he returned from Britain. At a Republican Conference meeting the evening of floor consideration, Republican leaders picked up several votes by promising concerned members that payment rates for oncologists would be revisited in six months if the doctors were unhappy with the provision.

Consideration began on the evening of November 21, 2003. When the normal fifteen minutes allotted to a recorded vote expired at 3:15 A.M., the bill was losing, with 219 votes cast against the conference report. The problem was opposition from a group of conservatives who believed the bill did not do enough to reform Medicare and who opposed a new entitlement program. Speaker Hastert held the vote open; House Republican leaders and Health and Human Services Secretary Tommy Thompson, who had been working on members all evening, redoubled their efforts. "Knots of senior House Republicans and Health and Human Services Secretary Tommy G. Thompson huddled repeatedly around several of the two dozen skeptical members who had initially voted against the bill," reported the *Washington Post*.[45] Ernest Istook (Okla.), chair of an Appropriations Committee subcommittee, a position now subject to a Steering Committee vote, changed his vote from nay to yea. Nick Smith (Mich.), a conservative who was retiring, refused to switch, though he later said he was offered inducements to do so. Bush called recalcitrant conservatives on their cell phones to argue for a yes vote. The vote stretched on and on with no change in the tally. The party leaders met off the House floor with a group of seven conservatives. The conservatives were told, they would later say, that if the Republican bill failed, House Democrats intended bring to the floor through a discharge petition the Senate version of the Medicare prescription drugs bill, a version the conservatives found even more objectionable. Although the success of such a strategy was far from assured, the argument allowed a few of the conservatives to switch their votes. Just before 6:00 A.M., C. L. "Butch" Otter (Idaho) and Trent Franks (Ariz.) changed their votes, then a few other members followed suit. The count stood at 220–215 when the presiding officer, after almost three hours, gaveled the vote to a close. The conference report had passed. "It's nicer if you can win easy, but this was an absolute have-to," remarked House Republican Conference Chair Deborah Pryce (Ohio).[46]

MINORITY PARTY STRATEGY

The reason Republicans came so close to losing one of their own and President Bush's top priorities was that Democrats maintained remarkable cohesion. The final tally recorded sixteen Democrats as voting for the conference report (8 percent of the Democrats voting), but at the end of the initial fifteen minutes not a single Democrat had voted in favor.[47] The considerable party cohesion Democrats have maintained on most major legislation in recent years rests on a combination of member ideological homogeneity, party loyalty, and leadership clout.

Like its Republican counterpart though arguably not to the same extent, the House Democratic Party is considerably more homogeneous ideologically that it was several decades ago. That homogeneity provided the basis for the powers and resources members gave to their leadership, and it continues to provide the basis for members' willingness to allow their leaders to use these tools aggressively. The leadership's control over resources such as desirable committee assignments and campaign cash gives members direct incentives to behave in a party-regarding way. Yet minority party leaders' resources are considerably less than those of the majority. Not only can minority leaders offer their members fewer legislative inducements—projects, for example—but majority leaders can use their inducements to entice minority party members to defect on key votes. Minority party leaders lack the control over procedure and the legislative agenda that is such a powerful tool for the majority. The majority party leadership can schedule votes that present minority party members with no-win choices; if minority members would rather have something than nothing legislatively, the majority determines what that something is.

Thus the minority party in the House cannot expect to win often, and to maintain cohesion, it must depend even more than the majority on fostering a sense of within-party loyalty, a willingness of members to act in party-regarding ways. Members and leaders believe that working and voting together as a party are necessary conditions for Democrats taking back control of the House. "From the day she took office, she has made it very clear that we're not going to be able to take back the House if Democrats run around as independent contractors," said George Miller (D-Calif.) of Minority Leader Nancy Pelosi, a close friend.[48] The Democratic leaders and most members concur that a unified Democratic position on the most salient issues is essential to conveying to the public that the party is presenting a clear alternative to the Republican Party.

Democrats' desire to take back the House gives them the incentive to act as team players. But leaders and the party as an entity need to foster team effort in the face of other incentives that might induce members to defect. The Republican Party's unwillingness to include Democrats in the legislative process is perhaps the most potent factor working toward high Democratic cohesion. Additionally, however, Democratic leaders work assiduously to include all their members in party efforts and so to promote a sense of team membership. Whip Steny Hoyer talks about building "the psychology of consensus."[49] "It's a question of including and convincing," Hoyer explains.[50]

Norms and expectations about member behavior have changed. Like Republicans, Democrats have been expected to vote the party position on procedural votes for a number of years. Democratic cohesion on such procedural votes is about as high as Republican cohesion. When eleven Democrats voted for a corporate tax bill rule that barred "consideration of any Democratic amendments or substitutes," Whip Steny Hoyer wrote to all members of his caucus saying that he and Pelosi were "greatly concerned" about the vote because it threatened "to undermine the unity" of the party. "Undemocratic rules that are deliberately designed to silence our Caucus should always elicit strong, unified Democratic opposition," Hoyer wrote. "The failure to oppose such rules will only foment future procedural transgressions by our opponents. And we must not stand for it. We must fight such undemocratic rules as one."[51]

Norms concerning more substantive decisions are beginning to change. "To get Democrats unified you must raise the expectation that unless you have a very good reason to object to a piece of legislation that you will be with us on many of these issues," one of the chief deputy whips explained.[52] Pelosi has persuaded Democrats who wanted to offer their own alternatives to pull back so that party was united on one alternative.

The Democratic whip system is both large and active, consisting of about thirty senior whips, about forty assistant whips, and twenty-four regional whips.[53] At a weekly meeting of senior whips, decisions about what issues to work are made. Key members, especially those from the committees, are brought into the effort. The senior whips also meet with small groups of members early in the legislative process, attempting to build consensus against the Republican position and for a Democratic alternative.[54] If members are consulted early and have a hand in shaping

Democratic proposals, they are more likely to feel a sense of ownership that then leads to support. Before the legislation is considered on the floor, a whip count is taken, with the regional whips doing the initial count and then the other whips following up to refine the count and to persuade.

House Democrats meet weekly in a regular Wednesday-morning Caucus and at the leader's lunch. The entire whip system, about one hundred strong, also meets once a week, and subgroups meet more often. All these intraparty forums and a number of less inclusive ones as well allow leaders and other members to inform and persuade undecided Democrats. Members determined to vote against the party position can, of course, avoid those meetings the week of the vote, but they are aware that there is a cost to defecting. Furthermore the cost is in their relations not just with their leaders but also with their party colleagues.

The vote on the Medicare/prescription drugs bill conference report posed a major test for House Democrats. If significant numbers of Democrats voted for the final bill, the party's argument that the bill represented a bad deal for seniors would ring hollow. Yet, especially considering the AARP's backing, voting against the bill struck some Democrats as electorally risky. The House Democratic party leaders believed a maximum effort to hold down defections was essential. At her leader's lunch the week of the vote, Democratic Leader Nancy Pelosi told members "there will be no passes" on this issue; "this is a party vote." Other members backed her up; Marion Berry (Ark.), one of the more conservative Democrats, said: "We must not give them a single vote. . . . If you go with this, you do not belong in this party." Emphasizing the legislation's flaws, Whip Steny Hoyer argued: "This is not about party, but about policy."[55]

Outraged by what they saw as the AARP selling out and aware that they needed to counter the effects of the AARP endorsement,

Democrats publicly resigned from the organization and blasted its position. Pelosi and Senate Minority Leader Thomas A. Daschle (S.D.) sent a letter to AARP chief executive William Novelli expressing "our profound concern" and demanding an explanation for the decision.[56] Eighty-five House Democrats sent Novelli a letter canceling their memberships or, if younger, vowing not to join. The leadership worked to activate other senior groups and labor unions, urging them to express their opposition to the bill vocally.[57]

As the vote approached, Pelosi and Hoyer met continuously with members in groups and individually, trying to persuade them to vote "no." Hoyer held more than a dozen whip meetings. Because the bill was more than a thousand pages long and Democrats were given little time to study the final version, providing information and clearing up confusion were important functions of the meetings. The Democratic message was: this is a bad bill that does little for seniors in terms of prescription drug coverage but does endanger Medicare. Despite the AARP, you can sell that message to your constituents.

The effort continued on the floor; when the fifteen minutes normally allotted to a recorded vote ran out, no Democrat had voted for the bill and it was losing—a temporary victory. David Wu (Ore.), the only member who had not cast a vote, was surrounded by Pelosi and many of the whips. Wu wanted to vote for the bill, but out of party loyalty, did not want to be the one who pushed the measure over the top.[58] Only after the two Republicans switched their votes and changed the outcome did Wu cast his vote for the bill.

As a minority in a highly partisan House, the Democratic Party can seldom expect to win floor votes. The Democratic leaders' lack many of the tangible legislative inducements their majority party counterparts control. For example, at the last minute, Republicans inserted in the Medicare bill a provision benefiting a specific hospital in Tennessee; the aim was to pick up the vote of Memphis Democrat Harold E. Ford, Jr.; in the end it did not succeed.[59] The minority leaders, of course, lack the procedural powers of the majority: when the majority decides to schedule a bill quickly, so that opposition does not have time to mobilize, or decides to pull a bill because more time is needed to find the necessary votes, or when the majority holds open a vote long beyond the usual fifteen minutes, the minority has no procedural counter.

But while the minority party can seldom win floor victories, it can sometimes, by sticking together, make the majority party pay a stiff price for victory. House Republicans received considerable bad press for their nearly three-hour-long vote; their leaders were depicted as heavy-handed and less than fair. The coverage resulted in substantial publicity for the Democrats' claims against the bill and probably raised more doubts among voters. For the House minority party, that constitutes success. In addition, the Republican leaders' floor tactics infuriated Democrats, who believed they had been "robbed," and almost certainly made harder the attracting of Democratic votes for the Republican position in the future.

THE POSTPASSAGE LEGISLATIVE PROCESS

Partisanship now plays a major role at the crucial postpassage stage of the legislative process. To become law, legislation has to pass both chambers in identical form and, since the House and Senate seldom pass major legislation in identical form initially, the two chambers' versions must be reconciled. The process of doing so offers strategic opportunities, as is illustrated by Majority Leader Tom DeLay's remarks after the Senate had passed a budget resolution House Republicans disliked. "The Senate passed a budget. Who cares what it looks like?" DeLay said. "You have to get to conference. That's where the bill is going to be written."[60]

To ensure that the legislation that emerges from the reconciliation process satisfies its members as individuals and enhances the party's reputation, the party leaders now often take a central role in the postpassage process. The Speaker regularly appoints the Majority Leader or whip to conference committees on legislation of major significance to the party. Thus, in 2002, Tom DeLay, then majority whip, served on the energy bill conference; the next year, DeLay, now Majority Leader, served on the on Medicare/prescription drugs bill conference. Leadership involvement is not a Republican innovation; it developed as partisanship intensified in the 1980s. In 1987, for example, House and Senate were preparing to go to conference on a debt limit bill; the issue provoking controversy was a revision of the Gramm-Rudman deficit reduction act necessitated by a Supreme Court decision declaring a part of the original law unconstitutional. Speaker Jim Wright not only appointed Majority Leader Tom Foley as a conferee but, before officially designating the conferees, he extracted certain promises from the other Democrats: that the agreement not amend the rules of the House; that there be no provision denying a congressional pay raise (a political ploy being discussed); and that under the automatic spending cut provision, the administration be granted no flexibility in which accounts to cut.

When top priority legislation is at issue and negotiations seem stalemated, the House and Senate party leaders may even take over the negotiations altogether. In November 2003, the conference committee on the prescription drugs/Medicare bill appeared to be stymied. President Bush and the congressional Republican Party had staked their reputation on enacting a prescription drug benefit for seniors, but were the process to go into an election year, the chances of success were slim. Speaker Hastert and Senate Majority Leader Bill Frist took over from the official top negotiators—Ways and Means Chair Bill Thomas and Senate Finance Committee Chair Charles E. Grassley (Iowa). Frist and

Hastert overrode Thomas and diluted the provisions forcing Medicare to compete with private insurers. That agreement induced the AARP to support the bill. "We would have opposed the bill instead of supporting it" had the compromise failed, said John C. Rother, policy director at AARP.[61]

At the final stage in the legislative process, as at all those that come before, the party leaders' involvement is predicated on their acting as faithful agents of their membership and of the party collectively. Conference reports, after all, require majority approval in both chambers. Hastert has been willing to pressure small groups of his members to support legislation they found philosophically objectionable, such as the Medicare/drugs bill, when he believed that passing the legislation was essential to the party's reputation and future. At no stage in the process has he ever been willing to leave a big group of Republicans in opposition and rely on a significant number of Democrats to make up the majority. Thus, in late 2004, House Armed Services Committee Chair Duncan Hunter, Judiciary Committee Chair James Sensenbrenner, and, less vocally, many of their Republican committee colleagues opposed the deal the Senate was offering in conference on the intelligence overhaul bill. This was high-visibility legislation carrying out the recommendations of the 9/11 Commission, and Bush wanted it passed quickly. Hastert had the votes to pass the bill if he relied on Democrats, but he refused to bring it to the floor. Instead he waited until the Senate agreed to more changes that gave most of the opposing House Republicans at least a fig leaf and allowed them to vote for the bill. "You don't want all these guys feeling resentment toward the leadership because they got rolled on this thing. You don't want them feeling they were forced to vote on something that could have made them look bad back home," a Republican staffer explained.[62] Hastert was again following his expressed maxim that "the job of the Speaker is not to expedite legislation that runs counter to the wishes of the majority of his majority" but rather "to please the majority of the majority."[63]

During the latter years of Democratic control of Congress, when the party had become more homogeneous ideologically, the actual compromises between House and Senate, like those within the chambers, were most often made within the Democratic Party. Recently, Republicans with much narrower margins of control have taken to excluding most Democrats from conference negotiations altogether. In 2003, no House Democrats were allowed to participate in the energy bill conference or the negotiations on the Medicare/prescription drugs bill. The conference reports on both bills tilted strongly toward the more conservative House versions.

PARTY POLARIZATION AND THE POLITICS OF EXCLUSION

The ideological gulf between the parties encourages congressional Republicans to make deals among themselves and to attempt to enact legislation without Democratic support. Partisanship in the contemporary legislative processes is no mere partisan "bickering," nor does it simply reflect maneuvering for electoral advantage. Serious policy differences underlie the partisan splits on issue after issue. Democrats believe "privatizing" Medicare and Social Security will destroy those programs, and all but the most affluent will suffer severely as a result. Republicans believe their policy prescriptions will save those programs by making them more efficient. On energy policy, the size and distribution of the tax burden, tort reform, and cultural issues such as abortion rights, and increasingly on foreign policy, the parties are similarly divided. Compromising across such a wide gulf is clearly an extremely difficult process that entails high costs in terms of policy concessions.

Yet minority party exclusion fuels the partisan hostility so evident in the contemporary Congress. The most moderate and mild-mannered of Democrats perceive Republican rule as not just heavy-handed but dictatorial and fundamentally undemocratic.[64] In fact, the perspectives and interests of minority party members and those of the people they represent do not get a real hearing in the House. Trust between the parties seems to be at an all-time low. Surely this atmosphere forecloses principled compromises that might otherwise be possible.

CHAPTER 6

PARTISAN POLARIZATION, INDIVIDUALISM, AND LAWMAKING IN THE SENATE

THE SENATE, LIKE THE House, has become much more polarized along partisan lines; as I show in chapter 1, the Senate and House trend lines look very similar (see figures 1.1 and 1.2). Are consequences in terms of the legislative process the same? Those who know anything at all about the Senate know of the filibuster. Cutting off debate and getting to the point of making a decision in the Senate requires a supermajority—currently sixty of one hundred votes for most matters. This suggests that the results of high partisan polarization, when combined with a narrow margin of control as in the House, are likely to be quite different.

Understanding the effects of high partisan polarization on the legislative process in the Senate first requires a look at the internal development of the Senate in the second half of the twentieth century. The external political environment of the Senate is essentially the same as that of the House; but those external forces impinge on a body with very different basic rules. The changes in the political environment that led in the House to the 1970s reforms with their centralizing as well as decentralizing thrusts produced, I show, the individualist Senate, a body in which senators aggressively exploited the great prerogatives the rules gave them to further their own individual ends. I then examine how partisan polarization affects the politics and the process of lawmaking in a chamber with nonmajoritarian rules and with members accustomed to exploiting those rules fully.

TRANSFORMATION OF THE SENATE SINCE THE 1950s

The U.S. Senate has the most permissive rules of any legislature in the world.[1] In holding the floor and in proposing amendments, senators face fewer constraints than the members of any other legislature. Extended debate allows any senator to hold the floor as long as he or she wishes unless cloture is invoked, which requires a supermajority of sixty votes. The Senate's amending rules enable senators to offer any and as many amendments as they please to almost any bill, and those amendments need not even be germane (that is, relevant). For example, a senator can offer a civil right amendment to an agriculture bill or vice versa.

The Senate has always operated under rules that vest enormous power in each individual senator. Yet senators have not always exploited the possibilities inherent in the rules to the same extent or in the same way. How and why has that changed?

The Senate of the 1950s was a clubby, inward-looking body governed by constraining norms; influence was centered in strong committees and their senior leaders, who were most often conservatives, frequently southern Democrats.[2] The typical senator of the 1950s was a specialist who concentrated on the issues that came before his committees. His legislative activities were largely confined to the committee room; he was seldom active on the Senate floor, was highly restrained in his exercise of the prerogatives the Senate rules gave him, and made little use of the media.

The Senate's institutional structure and the political environment rewarded such behavior.[3] The lack of staff, for example, made it harder for new senators to participate intelligently right away; serving an apprenticeship prevented new members from making fools of themselves early in their careers. It also made specialization the only really feasible course for attaining influence. Restraint in exploiting extended debate was encouraged by the absence of the kind of time pressures that would later make extended debate such a formidable weapon; when floor time is plentiful, the leverage senators derive from extended debate is much less.[4] Furthermore, the dominant southern Democrats had an enormous constituency-based interest in limiting the use of and thus protecting the filibuster for their one big issue—opposition to civil rights.

The majority of senators, especially the southern Democrats, faced no imminent reelection peril so long as they were free to reflect their constituents' views in their votes and capable of providing the projects their constituents desired. The system of reciprocity, which dictated that senators do constituency-related favors for one another whenever possible, served them well. The seniority system bolstered by norms of apprenticeship, specialization, and intercommittee reciprocity assured members of considerable independent influence in their area of jurisdiction if they stayed in the Senate long enough and did not make that dependent on their voting behavior. For the generally moderate-to-conservative Senate membership, the parochial and limited legislation such a system produced was quite satisfactory. The Senate of the 1950s was an institution well designed for its generally conservative members to further their goals. Junior liberals were unhappy and chafed under the Senate's restrictive norms, but they were too few in number and, being junior, they were not influential enough to do much about the system.

Membership turnover and a transformation of the political environment altered the costs and benefits of such behavior and induced members to change the institution; over time norms, practices, and rules were altered.[5] The 1958 elections brought into the Senate a large class of new senators with different policy goals and reelection needs. Mostly northern Democrats, they were activist liberals, and most had been elected in highly competitive contests, in many cases having defeated incumbents. Both their policy goals and their reelection needs dictated a more activist style; these senators simply could not afford to wait to make their mark, nor could they confine themselves as narrowly in their issue involvements. Subsequent elections through the mid-1960s brought in more and more such members.

Then, in the 1960s, the political environment began a transformation. A host of new issues rose to prominence—first civil rights, then environmental issues and consumer rights (via Ralph Nader); the war in Vietnam and the questions about American foreign and defense policy that it raised; women's rights and women's liberation; the rights of other ethnic groups, especially Latinos and Native Americans, of the poor and the disabled, and by the late 1960s and early 1970s, gay rights. These were issues that engaged many ordinary citizens, often intensely, and politics became more highly charged. The interest group community exploded in size and became much more diverse; many of the social movements of the 1960s already had or now spawned interest groups. A horde of environmental groups, consumer groups, women's groups, and Latino groups joined the Washington political community. In response to the policy successes of some of these groups, on environmental legislation, for example, the business community mobilized; in the 1970s, many more businesses established a permanent presence in Washington, and specialized trade associations proliferated.[6]

The media—especially television—became a much bigger player in politics during this period. The 1950s saw the lightning spread of television into almost every American home. TV with its predilection for dramatic pictures had the potential to change ordinary citizens' experience of the world, including via the news. Dramatic events could be brought right into their living rooms, and people who otherwise might not attend to an issue could be caught up in it and even develop intense views. A number of scholars have suggested that the civil rights struggles of the late 1950s and early 1960s would not have had the same impact on public opinion without television coverage. By 1960 all three TV networks had created Sunday interview shows. In 1963 the evening TV news programs expanded from fifteen to thirty minutes, just in time to cover the highly dramatic events of the 1960s.[7] The TV network news, unlike local newspapers, perforce covered primarily national news and, in the 1960s and 1970s, primarily national political news.

This new environment offered enticing new opportunities to senators—and not just to liberal northern Democrats. The myriad interest groups needed champions and spokespersons, and the media needed credible sources to represent issue positions and for commentary. Because of the small size and prestige of the Senate, senators fit the bill. Thus the new environment presented senators with the chance to become significant players on a broader stage with possible policy, power, reelection, or higher office payoffs; but to take advantage of the opportunity, senators needed to change their behavior and their institution.

From the mid-1960s through the mid-1970s, senators did just that. They expanded the number of positions on good committees and the number of subcommittee leadership positions and distributed these much more broadly. Every senator ended up with several choice committee assignments and almost every majority party senator with at least one subcommittee chairmanship. Thus, in the 1950s, only twenty senators on average had more than two committee assignments; by the mid-1970s through mid-1980s period, fifty-three did. From 1953 through 1972, thirty-eight senators had no position on a top-four committee while twelve had two such positions; by 1979–86, eighty senators had top-four committee positions and only two had more than one. In 1955–70, twenty-four senators had no leadership position (chair or ranking minority member) on a good subcommittee; by 1979–86, only four lacked such a position.[8] Staff too was greatly expanded and was made available to junior as well as senior senators. By 1980, Senate staff totaled 3,746, up from 1,115 in 1957.[9]

Senators involved themselves in a much broader range of issues. They became a great deal more active on the Senate floor, offering more amendments and to a wider range of bills. In the 1950s few bills were subject to more than ten amending roll calls on the floor: less than 2 percent in the 84th Congress (1955–56), for example; the figure increased to just under 10 percent by the early 1970s and averaged about 15 percent in the early to mid-1980s.[10]

Senators exploited extended debate to a much greater extent and the frequency of filibusters shot up; the number of filibusters averaged less than one per Congress over the period 1955–60; by the 1970s the average was 11.4 filibusters per Congress (see table 6.1).[11] As filibusters became more frequent, their targets broadened; no longer were filibusters aimed only at civil right bills; legislation of all sorts, momentous and parochial, was targeted. Furthermore, the filibuster was no longer a tool only of conservatives; members of every ideological stripe came to use it to further their aims.

The media became an increasingly important arena for participation and a significant resource for senators in the pursuit of their policy, power, and reelection goals. Senators became increasingly outward-directed, focusing on their links with interest groups, policy communities, and the media more than on their ties to one another. By the mid-1970s, a Senate of individualists had taken shape. No longer constrained by the Senate folkways, senators fully exploited the great powers the Senate rules gave them to further their own ends.

Then, during the later 1980s and the 1990s, the Senate polarized along partisan and ideological lines. The external, constituency-related forces driving polarization were the same as those for

TABLE 6.1
The Increase in Filibusters and Cloture Votes, 1951–2004

Years	Congress	Filibusters per Congress	Cloture Votes per Congress	Successful Cloture Votes per Congress
1951–60	82nd–86th	1.0	0.4	0
1961–70	87th–91st	4.6	5.2	0.8
1971–80	92nd–96th	11	22	9
1981–86	97th–99th	17	23	10
1987–92	100th–102nd	27	39	15
1993–98	103rd–105th	28	48	14
1999–2002	106th–107th	32	59	31
2003–2004	108th	27	49	12

Sources: Data for 82nd–102nd Congresses: Congressional Research Service, comp., "A Look at the Senate Filibuster," in Democratic Studies Group Special Report, June 13, 1994, appendix B; Norman Ornstein, Thomas Mann, and Michael Malbin, *Vital Statistics on Congress, 1993–1994* (Washington, D.C.: CQ Press, 1994), 162. Data for 103rd Congress: Richard S. Beth, "Cloture in the Senate, 103d Congress," memorandum, Congressional Research Service, June 23, 1995. Data for 104th–108th Congresses: *Congressional Quarterly Almanac* for the years 1995–2004 (Washington, D.C.: Congressional Quarterly).

the House, as I discuss in chapter 1—realignment in the South and the polarization of voters, especially activists, throughout the country. To be sure, Senate constituencies are often much bigger than House districts and so likely to be more heterogeneous, and we would expect that to affect how senators behave. Still, the polarization of activists should have similar effects on senators as on House members and indeed appears to do so.

The big difference between the House and the Senate is in members' internal institutional responses to partisan polarization. Briefly stated, House members gave their party leaders significant new powers and resources and came to expect the leaders to use these aggressively to further members' policy and electoral goals. House members thereby amplified the effects of constituency-based partisan polarization. Senators, in contrast, have given their leaders few new resources and no new parliamentary powers. Why? My answer is that senators consider the prerogatives that Senate rules give them enormously valuable and consequently have been unwilling to constrain themselves by empowering leaders, especially since doing so would require major changes in Senate rules. Nevertheless, majority party senators do now expect their leader to exploit majority status for partisan advantage.

POLITICAL PARTIES IN THE SENATE TODAY

Although formal party leadership positions and party organization developed relatively late in the Senate, both existed well before the mid-twentieth century.[12] The more recent period of high polarization has seen some elaboration. The Senate Republican leadership consists of a floor leader, who according to Conference rules "shall perform the customary duties of the Majority or Minority Leader, as the case may be, on the floor of the Senate and shall have full authority to deal with all questions of procedure after consulting the Republican Senators who are concerned"; an assistant floor leader, usually called the whip; the chair and secretary of the Conference; the chair of the Policy Committee; and the chair of the National Republican Senatorial Committee. All are elected. The Policy Committee includes all the elected leaders and all Republican committee chairs or ranking members as ex officio members and other members appointed by the leader, subject to Conference approval. A chief deputy whip and, currently, ten deputy whips are appointed.

The Democratic leadership consists of the Democratic leader, who is also Conference chair; the assistant leader (aka the whip); the Conference secretary, chief deputy whip, and assistant floor leader; the chairs of the Policy, Steering and Outreach, and Campaign committees; chair and vice chair of the Ranking Member

Outreach Team; chair of the Rural Outreach Team; and three deputy whips. A number of these positions are quite recently established—among them the assistant floor leader, the Steering and Outreach Committee, and the chair of Rural Outreach—and are appointed. Democrats had traditionally concentrated the chairmanships of their various party organs in their Leader but devolved some of these positions—such as chair of the Policy Committee—so that more senators would hold party leadership positions. Currently seventeen senators who are not otherwise a part of the leadership serve on the Policy Committee.

In both Senate parties, then, a large proportion of the membership holds some sort of party position. And the various party entities are more active than they used to be. Partisan polarization has made participation through their parties more attractive to senators than it was when the parties were more heterogeneous and the ideological distance between them was smaller. Recent Senate party leaders have sought to provide more channels for members to participate in and through the party, hence the greater number of positions and the greater activity.[13] Democrats and Republicans each meet in closed session for lunch every Tuesday under the aegis of their Policy Committees. Other meetings abound. "In my Caucus, we meet regularly—regular Caucus lunches, regular leader lunches, regular ranking members lunches, regular Policy Committee luncheons," Democratic Leader Tom Daschle explained in 2001. "All are meant to give a pattern, a sort of predictability to an otherwise unpredictable climate."[14]

The whip systems are more active than they used to be. New committees have been established or have taken on new functions. Thus, in the 1980s, the Republican Conference began providing television, radio, and graphics services for Republican senators; the Policy Committee provides those services on the Democratic side. Beyond its traditional committee assignment function, the Democratic Steering and Outreach Committee (formerly the

Steering Committee and then the Steering and Coordination Committee) is charged with acting as a liaison with outside groups in order to build support for key Democratic legislative proposals. Both Senate parties use temporary task forces of senators to perform a variety of policy and public relations functions.

Over the course of the past several decades both Senate parties have made some changes in their rules to increase responsiveness among their committee and party leaders. In the 1970s both provided for Conference ratification votes of their committee chairs or ranking members. Republicans allow the Republican members of a committee to select from their ranks their committee leader, "who need not be the member with the longest consecutive service on such committee," the rules specify. He or she is then subject to a vote in the Conference.

Junior Senate Republicans forced a number of party rules changes in the mid-1990s. The defection of a moderate Republican on a key vote precipitated the change. After the House had approved it in 1995, the constitutional amendment requiring a balanced budget failed in the Senate by one vote, with Mark Hatfield, chair of the Appropriations Committee, casting the only Republican vote against it. The amendment was part of the Senate Republicans' agenda and the ideologically driven junior Republicans, many of whom were Gingrich admirers and allies, believed that on such a crucial vote, a senior committee chair should not be allowed with impunity to vote against the party to which he owed his chairmanship. They proposed stripping Hatfield of his chairmanship but were placated with a reform task force to which three freshmen were appointed.

The task force's proposals that the Senate Republican Conference adopted required a secret ballot vote on committee chairs, both in committee and in the Conference. They provided for the adoption of a Senate GOP agenda in the Conference by a three-quarters vote. Committee chairs and party leaders (except the top leader) were limited to three terms. The new rules went into effect at the beginning of 1997 and were intended by the junior conservatives to make their senior and often more moderate party colleagues more responsive to the predominantly conservative party membership as a whole.

When moderate Jim Jeffords (R-Vt.) was in line to become chair of the Senate Labor and Human Resources Committee in 1997, conservatives seriously explored mounting a challenge to him. He got Republican Majority Leader Trent Lott's support and received the position only after he promised the Majority Leader he would not use his position to hold up legislation the Republican membership supported.

Arlen Specter's ascent to the chairmanship of the Judiciary Committee for the 109th Congress provides an even clearer illustration of Senate Republican expectations. Specter (Pa.) was in line for the chairmanship by virtue of his seniority, but he is a moderate and an abortion rights supporter. Furthermore, shortly after the 2004 elections, in response to a TV interviewer's question about Supreme Court nominees, he said: "When you talk about judges who would change the right of a woman to choose, overturn Roe versus Wade, I think that is unlikely."[15] Conservatives in and outside the Senate, already concerned about Specter chairing the committee that would pass on Bush's judicial nominees as well as handling numerous other hot-button issues, reacted with outrage. Conservative groups including the Family Research Council, the Traditional Values Coalition, and Concerned Women for America mounted a campaign to defeat him. Social Conservative James Dobson, head of the "multimedia empire" Focus on the Family and an increasingly influential figure in Republican politics, encouraged the listeners to his popular radio program to call Congress and block Specter. Hill phone lines were jammed.[16] Specter tried to damp down the furor by explaining and reexplaining his remarks, but Majority Leader

Bill Frist pointedly said in a TV interview that Specter still needed to convince his fellow Republican senators that he deserved the chairmanship.[17] In specially called meetings first with the party leaders and then with the other Republican members of the Judiciary Committee, Specter was grilled about how he would handle Bush's judicial nominees. The next day, he addressed the entire Senate Republican Conference. The day after that, he issued a public statement pledging to move all Bush's nominees through the committee quickly.[18] Specter was confirmed as chair of Judiciary, but he is clearly on a short leash. To drive home that point, two fervently anti-abortion Republicans were added to the Judiciary Committee roster.

The Republican leader has had limited influence over his members' committee assignments. Seniority governed on the Republican side; when a vacancy occurred, the most senior Republican in the chamber had the right to claim it. If the leader wanted to bar a party colleague from a particular committee, he might be able to induce another more senior senator to take the vacancy. Thus Bob Dole, averse to having his presumed presidential nomination rival Phil Gramm on the powerful Finance Committee, talked a more senior colleague into claiming the position. However, when another vacancy occurred, Gramm got the position. The mid-1990s task force proposed giving the leader more influence, but the Republican Conference balked. Republicans did adopt a new rule for the 108th Congress stating that "all Republican Conference members shall be offered two 'A' committee slots in order of seniority. Following such process, any remaining A committee assignments shall be made by the Floor Leader unless otherwise specified by law."[19] This rule, however, enhanced the Leader's clout only minimally; although the A committees are the most sought after, the assignments left over after all members have chosen two are not likely to provide much leverage.

In the summer of 2004, efforts to make further changes surfaced again. Four moderate Republican senators had blocked approval of a Republican budget resolution lacking a provision the Senate had supported but that had been dropped in conference. Three of the recalcitrants were committee chairs. "There are a lot of Members who have voiced concerns about the fact that our leader has less levers to be able to accomplish what he wants to accomplish than any other leader here in the four caucuses," explained Republican Conference Chairman Rick Santorum (Pa.). "They believe giving the leader some more options is something we need to consider."[20] When the Conference met after the 2004 elections to adopt rules for the 109th Congress, a proposal to allow the Leader to fill half of the vacancies on the A committees passed by a 27–26 secret ballot vote.[21]

The Democratic Leader has long had considerably more influence over committee assignments than has his Republican counterpart. Democrats do not use a strict seniority rule. The Democratic leader serves on and chooses the chair and the members of the Steering Committee (now the Steering and Outreach Committee), which makes assignments, subject in both cases to ratification by the Democratic Conference. Still, every senator is considered entitled to several good committee assignments, and in any case, a senator's power is much less dependent on committee positions than a House member's is; the leverage that influence on assignments gives the leader, while important, is limited.

The Senate Republican Party in the 109th Congress was led by Bill Frist, a heart surgeon from Tennessee, who was chosen as Leader when Trent Lott was forced to resign in January 2003. Lott had made questionable remarks at a retirement party for Strom Thurmond (R-S.C.), remarks that could be interpreted as supporting racial segregation and so were deeply offensive to many. Despite his limited political experience, Republicans turned to Frist, who, while conservative, has a polished, mediagenic demeanor; he could give the party the modern, nonthreatening, and competent public face it wanted to project. Mitch McConnell of Kentucky, also a conservative, took over as the party's new whip in 2003 as well, replacing Don Nickles, who had been forced out by term limits. McConnell, however, is an experienced senator, first elected in 1984. Unlike his predecessor, he has embraced the floor-guarding function of the whip position. "I'll be on the floor a lot, trying to make the trains run on time, which is always difficult in the Senate, as well as the traditional role of the whip, which is trying to win votes," he explained.[22] Nickles had focused more on policy and was often criticized for not spending enough time on the floor. The difference in the two approaches to the same office illustrates that leadership offices and functions are less institutionalized in the Senate than in the House.

Until his defeat in the 2004 elections, the Democratic team was led by Tom Daschle (S.D.), a moderate liberal, who had served in the Senate since 1987 and as Democratic leader since 1995. During the eighteen months between Jeffords's defection from the Republican Party in June 2001 and the start of the 108th Congress, Daschle was Majority Leader. Harry Reid (Nev.) was first elected to the Senate in 1986 and became whip in 1999. Like Daschle, he is moderately liberal. As whip, Reid spent much of his time on the Senate floor. Protecting its prerogatives on the floor is essential for the minority party, and Reid won praise for his skill at doing so. "I felt that if there were a continuous presence on the floor, so someone knew what was going on at all times, things would work better," Reid explained. "And that has proven to be so."[23] When Daschle lost his reelection bid, Senate Democrats quickly chose Reid as their new leader. Dick Durbin (Ill.), a strong liberal, became whip.

These are the leaders who are charged with making the Senate legislative process function.

THE LEGISLATIVE PROCESS IN THE INDVIDUALIST, PARTISAN SENATE

How the Senate legislative process works and how partisan polarization affects the politics and the process of lawmaking in the Senate is best grasped by examining the stages in the process in sequence.

Senate Committees in the Legislative Process

In the Senate, in contrast to the House, partisan ratios on even the most powerful committees closely reflect chamber ratios, and in recent years the Senate has been narrowly split. The 2000 elections, in fact, returned a 50–50 Senate, and as long as that lasted, committees also had equal numbers of Democrats and Republicans. Most Senate committees are relatively small, so when the chamber margin is narrow, the majority party may have only one more member on each committee than the minority, as was the case during most of the early 2000s. Under those circumstances, excluding the minority party from committee decision making and relying on a purely partisan coalition in committee is problematical. Furthermore and more important, because Senate rules give individual senators so much power, any senator, whether a committee member or not, can cause problems for the legislation later in the legislative process. Consequently, a bill's supporters have a strong incentive to put together a broad supportive coalition at the committee stage, accommodating senators who are not committee members as well as those who are, and that means a bipartisan coalition.

One would thus expect committee decision making in the Senate to be less partisan than it is in the House. And as table 6.2 shows, that is in fact the case. Senate committees often explicitly put off conflict, including partisan conflict, until the floor stage; that is, major divisive amendments are held to be decided on the floor. Why have a time-consuming fight in committee when the battle will have to be refought on the floor? Nevertheless, the difference in House and Senate committee decision making is too large to be explained by this alone. Yet as table 6.2 also shows, from the mid-1990s Senate committee decision making

TABLE 6.2
Partisanship in the Committee Process in the Senate, 1961–2004

Congress	Years	% Partisan
87th	1961–62	6
89th	1965–66	
91st	1969–70	
94th	1975–76	14
95th	1977–78	
97th	1981–82	
100th	1987–88	
101st	1989–90	
103rd	1993–94	
104th	1995–96	43
105th	1997–98	32
107th	2001–2002	37
108th	2003–2004	44

Source: Author's calculations based on major legislation only, where "major" is defined as the legislation that *Congressional Quarterly* contemporaneously lists as major legislation under consideration by Congress, and bills on which a key vote occurred, again according to CQ's contemporaneous judgment. My coding of the character of the committee process is based on the *Congressional Quarterly* account, the committee report, and/or newspaper stories when the CQ account was incomplete, and for the 106th Congress forward, Markup Reports, nationaljournal.com.

Note: When a bill bypassed committee, the drafting entity (e.g., the party leadership, a task force) was coded.

has become considerably more frequently partisan than it was before. Despite incentives in Senate procedures to avoid narrow supportive majorities, partisan polarization has made it much more problematical to find compromises acceptable to both political parties.

The contrasting committee processes in the two chambers on President Bush's tax cut proposal in 2001 illustrate the differences between Senate and House. The House story is quickly told. The House Ways and Means Committee operated in a strictly partisan fashion and approved HR3 on a 23–15 party-line vote. Since the budget resolution called for tax cuts, the Senate Finance Committee could proceed to write a tax bill, assured that it would be protected by budget rules from a filibuster. Nevertheless Chairman Charles Grassley (R-Iowa) decided to write a bipartisan bill if at all possible. Both Grassley and ranking Democrat Max Baucus (D-Mont.) very much wanted the committee to take the lead role in drafting the tax legislation. As the tax issue had become a party-difference-defining issue during the 1990s, party leaders had increasingly usurped the committee's role. Grassley and Baucus could maintain control over the legislation only if they worked together and crafted a plan with bipartisan support in the committee.

Grassley and Baucus managed to put together a compromise measure and steered it through Finance, getting approval on a fourteen to six vote, with all Republicans and four of the ten Democrats voting for it. A majority of both Republicans and Democrats, including the leaders on both sides, remained dissatisfied with the bill; their committee leaders had given away too much in the negotiations, they believed. Daschle worked and voted against it in committee. Yet, despite a barrage of amendments on the floor, the bill passed largely intact. Grassley and Baucus had put together a package that could pass; neither liberal Democrats nor conservative Republicans had the votes to move the bill significantly in their preferred direction. On May 23, 2001, twelve Senate Democrats joined all fifty Republicans to pass the legislation.

As this case illustrates, Senate committees are often less strictly partisan than their House counterparts, even when working on highly salient legislation that splits the parties ideologically. In addition, Senate committee chairs do have somewhat more leeway than their House counterparts do; Grassley compromised more than his party leaders or the bulk of his party colleagues wanted. That leeway, however, is much more circumscribed than it was in the committee-government days. And on legislation of importance to the party, chairs are under considerable pressure to satisfy the party leadership and membership.

When they consider legislation important to the parties, all committees confront a similar conundrum: whether to enhance their chances for success on the floor by making a bipartisan deal or to write legislation more to the liking of the party membership, often including the committee majority itself.

The Senate Appropriations Committee, like its House counterpart, has traditionally operated in a thoroughly bipartisan fashion. It almost always reports bills out by unanimous vote. The ranking members on the Republican and Democratic sides have worked together for years. In 2002, when the Senate failed to pass a budget resolution to guide spending decisions, Robert Byrd (D-W.V.), then chair of Appropriations, and Ted Stevens (R-Alaska), then ranking Republican, agreed to oppose jointly any floor amendments exceeding majority appropriations ceilings.[24]

The Senate Appropriations Committee has come under increasing partisan pressure. In late 2003, appropriators made a series of bipartisan agreements on spending bills that Republican leaders and the White House then forced them to reverse.[25] Democrats, understandably angered, have since been less willing to cooperate in committee and in passing bills on the floor. The tight spending ceilings Republicans adopted in their budget resolution in 2004 made passing appropriations bills difficult in any case, and Republican committee and party leaders signaled that they might bring the bills to the floor in one large omnibus package or several rather than as thirteen separate bills. Democrats made clear that if Republicans pursued this strategy, they would start introducing their controversial amendments in committee rather than holding them for the floor, as is common on Appropriations, thus complicating committee markups.[26] In fact, in 2004, the Senate never considered seven of thirteen appropriations bills. Rather, an omnibus appropriations bill was again used, and again much that members had won in committee or on the floor was stripped away in conference negotiations.[27] Appropriations Committee deliberations are likely to become more contentious and more partisan as a result.

Committees with less of a tradition of bipartisanship have offered less resistance to the pressures toward partisan splits. Judiciary, which handles a number of hot-button issues, has become highly and sometimes bitterly partisan. The long-running partisan battle over judicial nominees has grown increasingly acrimonious and is spilling over to other committee business. (Judicial nominations battles are discussed later in this chapter and in chapter 8). Angry exchanges between Orrin Hatch (R-Utah), chair until 2005, and both Ted Kennedy (D-Mass.) and ranking minority member Patrick Leahy (D-Vt.) became routine, even though Hatch and Kennedy had been friends for years. Democrats complained that Hatch and committee Republicans used unfair procedures and even mislead them sometimes, hence their retaliation with obstructionist tactics.[28] During the 108th Congress, the Judiciary Committee reported out a number of major measures on partisan votes, including class action lawsuit reform, asbestos compensation legislation, and a victims' rights constitutional amendment.

Senate party leaders have less leverage vis-à-vis committee leaders and members than their House counterparts do. Still, the difficulty of passing legislation on the Senate floor in and of itself provides them with influence in that bill supporters need their leaders' help. As long as they have most of their members behind them, party leaders can and do affect legislation at the prefloor stage. The Senate leaders, unlike their House counterparts, serve on committees, and most of the recent top leaders—Mitchell and Daschle on the Democratic side; Dole, Lott, and Frist on the Republican side—have held positions on the crucial Finance Committee.

It is not uncommon for leaders to take legislation to the floor, bypassing committee, when attaining party objectives requires it. In 2001, the evenly split Senate Budget Committee was unable to agree on a budget resolution, so Majority Leader Trent Lott bypassed the committee and brought a Republican resolution directly to the floor. Tom Daschle, as Majority Leader in late 2001, canceled further energy legislation markups in the Energy and Natural Resources Committee when it appeared that the committee might approve drilling in the Arctic National Wildlife Refuge, a position opposed by most Senate Democrats. He asked Committee Chair Jeff Bingaman (D-N.M.) to put together a Democratic bill and took that directly to the floor.[29]

Getting Legislation to the Senate Floor

The Senate Majority Leader is charged with the scheduling of legislation for floor consideration. Although not the Senate's presiding officer and lacking many of the powers the House Speaker commands, the Senate Majority Leader is as close to a central leader as the chamber has. To bring legislation to the floor, the Majority Leader uses the right of first recognition, a prerogative the Leader has had under Senate precedents since the 1930s. The Majority Leader can move that a bill be taken off the calendar and considered, but the motion to proceed is a debatable—and thus filibusterable—motion. Or the Leader can ask unanimous consent that the bill be taken off the calendar and considered, a request that can be blocked by any senator's objection. Clearly any senator can cause problems for the Majority Leader. It is for that reason that the Majority Leader seeks to negotiate unanimous consent agreements before bringing legislation to the floor.

Since the 1950s, the Senate has done most of its work through unanimous consent agreements (UCAs). By unanimous consent, senators agree to bring a bill to the floor; they may also agree to place some limits on the amendments that may be offered or on the length of debate on specific amendments, and then perhaps to set a time for the final vote.

The Majority Leader's job has become more complex as senators have more fully exploited their prerogatives under Senate rules. Not only can any senator cause problems; if not consulted on something they care about, they are likely to do so. To avoid such problems, an elaborate consultation process takes place before the Majority Leader stands up on the floor and asks for unanimous consent to proceed to consideration of a bill.

The majority and minority party leaders oversee the negotiation of unanimous consent agreements and are deeply involved in the more contentious cases. The Majority Leader consults with the relevant committee chair before deciding to try to schedule a bill and throughout the process of negotiating a UCA. The majority and the minority party secretaries of the Senate now are the most important staffers involved; they serve as clearinghouses and as a point of continuous contact between the parties and often do much of the negotiating. The majority party secretary keeps the list of those majority party senators who have requested that they be consulted before the bill is scheduled. If a fellow party member has expressed opposition to the bill being brought to the floor, negotiations may be necessary to take care of his or her concerns. When the majority has an agreement it can support, the majority party's secretary conveys this to the minority party's secretary in writing, who gives it to the Minority Leader and the relevant ranking minority member. The minority secretary also calls any senators on the minority side who have asked to be notified and finds out their concerns. Eventually the minority responds with a written counteroffer and conveys it to the majority through the secretaries. This process may go through several rounds. If and when the leaders reach a tentative agreement, both parties put out a recorded message on their "hot line" to all Senate offices. The message lays out the terms of the agreement and asks senators who have objections to call their leader within a specified period of time. If there are objections, they have to be addressed. When every senator is prepared to assent to the unanimous consent agreement, the Majority Leader takes it to the floor and makes the request. As former Majority Leader Trent Lott explained, "As leader, I could not establish a rational and timely agenda for the institution to perform its business without having to first consult with, effectively, every other member of the Senate."[30]

When senators inform the Leader directly or through the party secretary that they wish to be consulted before a measure is scheduled, the senators may just want to be sure they are not otherwise committed; that they are prepared for floor debate or ready to offer an amendment. Often, however, such a notification is a "hold." A hold, as a knowledgeable participant explained, "is a letter to your leader telling him which of the many powers that you have as a senator you intend to use on a given issue." A typical such letter, addressed to then Majority Leader Trent Lott and copied to the majority secretary, reads: "Dear Trent: I will object to any time agreement or unanimous consent request with respect to consideration of any legislation or amendment that involves ———, as I wish to be accorded my full rights as a Member of the Senate to offer amendments, debate and consider such legislation or amendment. Many thanks and kindest personal regards." Most holds, then, are threats to object to a unanimous consent agreement, and as a leadership staffer said, in a body that conducts most of its business through UCAs, this is in effect "a threat to filibuster." Certainly that is how Senate leaders interpret them; then Democratic leader Daschle rather matter-of-factly called a hold a "one-person filibuster."[31]

The party secretaries confer every morning and inform each other about any new holds on legislation or nominations. They do not, however, reveal the names of the senators who have placed the holds. Holds can thus be secret, even from the bill's sponsor. But holds are often invitations to negotiate, and in those cases the senator placing the hold, of course, needs to make the hold known to the sponsor.

Holds are frequent; placing them has become standard operating procedure in the Senate. This little story appeared deep in *CongressDaily*'s roundup of Hill news on July 2, 2003; it was reported almost with a yawn, and there was not much competition since Congress was home for the Fourth of July recess:

> Senate Majority Leader Frist and Finance Chairman Grassley are continuing to negotiate with Alabama Republican Sens. Richard Shelby and Jeff Sessions over a hold they have placed on a bill that benefits hundreds of U.S. businesses by cutting tariffs on products they import, according to a Senate leadership aide. Sixty-six senators wrote Frist late last week urging him to bring the bill to the floor "without further amendments" to force a cloture vote to beat the holds. While the letter gives Frist more leverage in negotiating with the Alabamians, he "wouldn't bring it up until he has exhausted his ability to work things out amicably," the aide said. Shelby and Sessions want provisions added to the bill that would require country-of-origin labeling on packages of socks, among other demands.[32]

Getting exact figures on holds is impossible, but bits of information are available. In 1996, for example, Energy Committee Chairman Frank Murkowski complained that all seventy-two bills reported by his committee were being barred from floor consideration by holds.[33] The only firsthand data that political scientists have obtained show that in 1977–78, Senator Frank McClure, who chaired an informal group of conservative Republicans, placed ninety holds; presumably he placed the holds for the entire membership of his group.[34] The average Republican senator placed 9.8 holds. Senator James Inhofe in February 2000 announced holds on every judicial nomination that might come up during the year.[35] In 2003, Senator Larry Craig had holds on every Air Force promotion; these are normally approved as a matter of routine.

The very real possibility that legislation might be subject to a hold or an actual filibuster affects the legislative process well before the floor stage. Committee decision making must be sensitive to the policy preferences of interested senators who are not members of the committee. Because any senator can cause problems for the legislation on the floor and may in fact be able to block it from ever getting to the floor, committee proponents of the legislation have a considerable incentive to try to anticipate other senators' views and to bargain with those who harbor intense feelings before the committee reports the bill. Committee leaders especially have an incentive to put together a broad coalition, because such a coalition gives the committee's bill the best chance to survive, and if a committee cannot pass its bills, it loses influence. For all supporters, however, the incentive disappears when the necessary compromises produce an unacceptable bill, and partisan polarization has made finding compromises acceptable to both political parties more difficult.

The greater difficulty of passing legislation has also drawn party leaders into the legislative process at an earlier stage. Trying to make sure that legislation is in a form that will pass the Senate, the Majority Leader is more likely than before to become involved at the committee stage, and postcommittee adjustments negotiated by the leaders are frequently required. In fact, the process of negotiating UCAs often entails making substantive changes in the committee's bill.

Filibusters and holds are used for a variety of purposes. Their aim may be to kill legislation, as in the anti–civil rights filibusters of the 1960s and before. Holds intended to kill a bill are most likely to be kept secret. Often, however, the purpose of a hold is to extract concessions on the legislation at issue. That was the case with the Alabama senators on the trade bill and the socks-labeling issue.

Even the greatest care in accommodating senators with an interest in a bill does not always protect it from problems later in the process. An increasingly frequent use of holds is to extract concessions on an unrelated issue. As Senator Lott explained: "It has become increasingly common for holds to be placed on nominees and bills for reasons that have nothing to do with the nominee or the bill. Instead, bills and nominations are held hostage because a Senator is trying to leverage something from the Administration or from another Senator. These so-called leverage holds are routinely used by members from both parties."[36]

Senator Craig did not have anything against all those Air Force personnel up for promotion; he wanted to press the Air Force to deliver on a promise he claimed it had made to station several planes at a base in Idaho. Nor did senators oppose all the bills from the Energy Committee; rather, according to Murkowski, the holds "were based on a problem with some other bill."[37]

Sometimes a hold triggers a retaliatory hold. In October 2001, a frustrated Senator Paul Wellstone declared on the floor: "There is a Senator who has put a hold on [my bill] and I cannot find out who he or she is. These anonymous holds drive me up the wall. I have never put an anonymous hold on a bill—never. I am putting a hold on just about every single piece of legislation that any Senator on the other side of the aisle wants to put through here until this piece of legislation goes through. . . . I would love to debate a Senator about why he or she opposes this homeless veterans bill."[38]

To determine a sensible floor schedule that makes efficient use of floor time, the Majority Leader needs information. It is this need for information that explains why Majority Leaders go along with the hold system and, in fact, maintain it. Holds are nowhere specified in Senate rules, they are simply an informal practice. But as a knowledgeable observer explained, "It's to the Majority Leader's advantage to have holds because it gives him information. He's always trying to negotiate unanimous consent agreements, and he needs to know if there are pockets of problems, and holds do that."

Since holds are simply an informal practice, the Leader can and must decide whether to honor specific holds. All recent Leaders have strongly argued that holds entitle a senator only to notification; they are not automatic vetoes. A hold cannot kill appropriations bills or other must-pass legislation. The Majority Leader will not allow a hold to block bills key to the party's program. And in deciding how seriously to take a hold on less vital legislation, the Leader weighs the reputation of the senator placing the hold; "some people are taken more seriously because it's just assumed they're willing to back it up," a leadership aide explained. However, in making a choice of which bills to bring to the floor, the Majority Leader must consider how much time the bill will take and what the likelihood of successful passage is. And that gives holds considerable bite. As a staffer explained, "Holds are effective because the Majority Leader has a finite amount of time. If there are going to be cloture votes and the like, it can take days to ram something through this place. You can't do it on every bill. You can only do it on a selected few bills."

Thus visible filibusters are now just the tip of the iceberg. The Senate's permissive rules have much more effect on the legislative process through holds and other filibuster threats than through actual filibusters.

In floor scheduling, the Majority Leader must work with the Minority Leader. If an individual senator can wreck the schedule, the minority party can wreak havoc. The party leaders consult on a daily basis. "The two Leaders talk extensively to each other during the day," a knowledgeable participant explained. "You see it during votes. We'll have two or three votes a day at least, usually, and that's one of the times when they confer. But they have to talk to each other; if they don't, that's when things break down." A telephone hot line connects the Leaders' offices directly to facilitate quick communication.[39] UCAs often specify that some action will occur "at a time determined by the Majority Leader, after consultation with the Democratic Leader."[40]

Partisan polarization has complicated the working relationship between the leaders. The leaders have criticized each other publicly. In mid-2002, then Minority Leader Trent Lott was accusing then Majority Leader Tom Daschle of "either inability or incompetence."[41] In late 2003, Democratic Whip Harry Reid called Majority Leader Frist "amateurish" and Democratic Leader Tom Daschle accused him of "excessive mismanagement."[42] Frist campaigned against Daschle in his home state during his reelection race, an unprecedented step. Frist's presidential ambitions probably played a role in his decision, but so did his members' (and likely his own) frustrations with minority power in a highly partisan era. Daschle's defeat and early attempts by Republicans to demonize Reid are likely only to exacerbate the difficulties of cross-party leadership cooperation. Daschle was the target of a two-year campaign by national Republicans to tar him as a nay-saying obstructionist unwilling to work with the president and an extreme liberal who dishonestly portrays himself to his constituents as moderate. In early February 2005, the Republican National Committee sent roughly one million copies of a "research document" to journalists, donors, and grassroots activists branding Reid the "Chief Democratic obstructionist," attacking him for votes he had cast in the past and for having relatives who were lobbyists.[43]

Politics and Procedure on the Senate Floor

With the growth in partisan polarization, Republicans and Democrats now frequently use the Senate's permissive rules for partisan purposes. The Senate parties' substantial size and preexisting organization makes those rules formidable weapons. With sixty votes needed to cut off debate on most measures over any senator's objections, the minority party in the Senate has a great deal more power than its House counterpart does.

The minority party in the Senate now regularly uses extended debate to kill legislation outright or to extract concessions on legislation. In the 103rd Congress, the first in which extended debate was employed as a comprehensive strategy by a party, the minority Republicans used actual and threatened filibusters to deprive President Bill Clinton and the majority Democrats of numerous policy successes. Among the casualties were Clinton's economic stimulus package, campaign finance and lobbying reform bills, and bills revamping the Superfund program, revising clean drinking water regulations, overhauling outdated telecommunications law, and applying federal labor laws to Congress. In the 104th and 105th Congresses, the Democrats, now in the minority, returned the favor and used extended debate to kill many Republican priorities, including ambitious regulatory overhaul legislation and far-reaching property rights bills. In the 103rd Congress, Republicans extracted concessions on many major Democratic bills—voter registration legislation ("motor voter") and the national service program, for example. Then, in the 104th Congress, Democrats used the same strategy to force concessions on product liability legislation, the Freedom to Farm bill, and telecommunications legislation, among others. At the end of the first session of the 108th Congress in 2003, minority Democrats refused Republicans an up-or-down vote on the conference report for the massive energy bill that Bush and most Republicans very much wanted to enact and that many Democrats strongly opposed. Democrats also blocked medical malpractice legislation.

Extended debate is also used to score political points, even on legislation a party supports. In 2002, for example, Republicans, then in the minority in the Senate, refused to allow a vote before

TABLE 6.3
The Increasing Frequency of Extended Debate–Related Problems

Congress	Years	% of Major Measures with a Filibuster Problem
87th	1961–62	8
89th	1965–66	7
91st	1969–70	10
94th	1975–76	31
95th	1977–78	24
97th	1981–82	22
100th	1987–88	28
101st	1989–90	30
103rd	1993–94	51
104th	1995–96	50
105th	1997–98	55
107th	2001–2002	55
108th	2003–2004	43

Note: Major measures that are subject to a filibuster—that is, those that are not protected by statute from extended debate—are included. The existence of a filibuster problem, which includes a hold being placed on the bill or there being a threat to filibuster, was ascertained by the author from the public record, primarily *Congressional Quarterly* and newspaper accounts.

the elections on the Democrats' version of the bill setting up the new Homeland Security department; Democrats had the votes to pass a bill Bush disliked, and Republicans wanted to use the fact that a bill had not passed as a campaign issue.

Some sort of extended-debate-related problem is now a routine part of the legislative process on major legislation (see table 6.3).[44] In the 103rd, 104th, and 105th Congresses (1993–98), about half of the major legislation that was vulnerable to a filibuster actually encountered some sort of filibuster-related problem, and the rate was about the same in the 107th, the Bush Administration's first Congress, and only a little lower in the 108th. If measures protected by rules from filibusters (budget resolution and reconciliation bills) are included, the proportion decreases only marginally.

During the 108th Congress, several versions of medical malpractice legislation, the asbestos claims compensation bill, and legislation to overhaul class action lawsuits were stopped when the motion to proceed to consider the legislation was filibustered and the majority could not invoke cloture. Frist had not been able to work out UCAs; what Republicans were willing to offer, Democrats were unwilling to accept. Frist pulled the welfare reform authorization from the floor when Republicans failed in their attempts to invoke cloture. The big energy bill died when cloture failed on the conference report. "The status in the Senate right now is total gridlock," complained Majority Whip Mitch McConnell in the spring of 2004.[45]

Senate Democrats in 2004 even used their prerogatives to help out their House colleagues. House Republican leaders had hoped to use the defense appropriations bill as a vehicle for passing a debt limit increase without a vote in the House. Republican House members, as usual, did not want a recorded vote on that easily demagogued measure. However, Senate Democrats refused to assent to consideration of the defense appropriations bill so long as inclusion of the debt limit increase was a possibility. In order to move ahead with the bill in the Senate, Frist and Senate Appropriations Committee Chair Ted Stevens agreed, as Stevens announced on the floor, that "we will not bring back a bill that contains the provisions that were in the House-passed bill pertaining to debt ceiling issues."[46]

Nominations are also subject to extended debate, and some of the most intense partisan battles in recent years have focused on judicial nominations. The Senate Republican majority after

1995 blocked a number of President Clinton's judicial nominees in the Judiciary Committee. Altogether the Republican Senate failed to confirm thirty-six of Clinton's seventy-nine appellate court nominees—46 percent.[47] When Bush became president in 2001, Democrats were unwilling to give him great deference and warned him not to nominate highly conservative, "outside the mainstream" judges. By the time Bush sent up his first nominees, the Senate was under Democratic control. The Judiciary Committee promptly held hearings on and approved uncontroversial nominees, even some who were quite conservative. Those appellate court nominees that Democrats perceived as ideologues, however, fared less well; confirmation hearings were delayed and two were voted down in committee on straight party-line votes.

When Republicans took back control of the Senate, they were able to report the controversial nominees out of committee. But if Democrats were willing to filibuster the nominations and able to stick together, Republicans could not muster the sixty votes necessary to cut off debate and bring the nominations to a vote. With Democrats refusing to agree to an up-or-down vote on a number of nominees, Majority Leader Frist decided to bring the appellate court nomination of Miguel Estrada to the floor in early 2003. Republicans were testing whether Democrats would be willing to block a Hispanic nominee in a highly public forum. The nomination was debated for almost one hundred hours over the course of a month before the Majority Leader filed a cloture petition, and during that period the Senate did little else.[48] Democrats beat back cloture by a vote of 55–45 and, over the course of several months, won six more cloture votes on Estrada. After the seventh failure, Estrada withdrew his name from consideration. Democrats blocked nine other controversial appellate nominees during the 108th Congress, winning thirteen cloture votes.[49]

The floor debate on the Estrada nomination was as close as the modern Senate gets to conducting a filibuster that conforms to the popular image. "Classic" filibusters with the Senate in session all night, senators sleeping on cots off the Senate floor, and filibusterers making interminable speeches on the floor no longer occur. Even the Estrada filibuster saw no all-night and only two late-night sessions; the President's Day recess was not canceled, as the Majority Leader had threatened at one point; and once the first cloture vote failed, Majority Leader Frist went on to other business, though there were more cloture votes.

Frist could let the Estrada nomination dominate floor business in February 2003, because it was early in the first year of a Congress and not much legislation was ready for floor consideration. By March that situation had changed; if Republicans had forced Democrats to continue, it would have been at the expense of President Bush's initiatives. Filibusters and filibuster threats get their bite from Senate floor time being scarce (though, of course, one reason it *is* scarce is because of the Senate's permissive debate rules). Senators want floor time used productively—most have legislation they want considered on the floor as well as many other demands on their time—and the Majority Leader needs to use the time efficiently to pass as much of the party agenda as possible. Seldom will an actual filibuster of extended duration be considered a reasonable use of floor time, and so the Majority Leader tries to reach at least a partial agreement before bringing legislation to the floor. The Majority Leader may bring a bill to the floor without a UCA, either hoping that visibility will make blocking less attractive or hoping to invoke cloture, but if cloture fails, he will usually pull the bill off the floor.

With extended debate and cloture now so frequently used as partisan weapons, cloture votes are less and less likely to be successful. In the early to mid-1980s, 43 percent of cloture votes got the requisite sixty votes to cut off debate; in the late 1980s and early 1990s, 39 percent did; in the period 1993–98, only 28 percent did. The likelihood of a cloture vote being successful did increase in the 106th and 107th Congresses to a little more than half but only because more were taken after an agreement had been reached. Almost all of the successful cloture votes were very one-sided. When the parties opposed each other on a cloture vote, cloture was seldom successful. In the 108th Congress, only twelve of forty-nine cloture votes (24 percent) were successful.

Extended debate and how it is used in the Senate has made the legislative process in the House and Senate increasingly different; so too have amendment marathons. Since the nineteenth century, House rules have severely limited members' debate time. Modern special rules now frequently limit the number of amendments that can be offered. Senate rules impose no such restrictions, and in the 1960s and 1970s, customs that had imposed some restraints gave way under contrary incentives. Floor amendments, like extended debate, can be used to publicize an issue or problem, to cater to an interest group or constituency, or to attempt to shape policy. Considering just major measures, the average number of amendments offered and pushed to a roll-call vote more than doubled from the prereform to the postreform period—from 4.1 to 8.6.[50] Many major bills now routinely attract dozens of amendments. Typically more than forty amendments are offered and pushed to a recorded vote on budget resolutions; in 1999, juvenile justice legislation considered in the aftermath of the Columbine High School shootings was subject to thirty-one amendments that were pushed to a roll call. On the energy bill the Senate considered in July 2003, more than four hundred amendments were filed. And when the defense authorization bill was considered in June 2004, 195 amendments were considered.[51] Among those pushed to a vote was a Brownback (R-Kans.) amendment on fining broadcasters for indecency.

Most amendments are germane, and the sponsor's aim is to influence the substance of the bill. Individual senators do use nongermane amendments to pursue their personal agendas and to bring to the floor issues the leadership might like to avoid. Thus, during his long Senate career stretching from 1973 to 2003, Senator Jesse Helms forced innumerable votes in every Congress on hot-button issues such as abortion, pornography, and school prayer. At the other end of the ideological spectrum, Paul Wellstone became adept at the same strategy. In spring of 1999, for example, Wellstone, a strong opponent of the 1996 welfare reform legislation, offered and forced to a roll-call vote an amendment to the defense authorization bill requiring the Department of Health and Human Services to report on former welfare recipients' ability to achieve self-sufficiency—a nongermane amendment he had offered to other bills before.

The Senate Majority Leader's inability to limit amendments greatly reduces the majority party's control of the floor. When, in March 2004, Republicans brought to the floor legislation to shield the firearms industry from lawsuits, the bill had over sixty supporters and seemed assured of passing. The House had considered the bill under a rule that barred most amendments and had passed it easily. In the Senate, however, an amendment sponsored by Dianne Feinstein (D-Calif.), John W. Warner (R-Va.), and Chuck Schumer (D-N.Y.) passed on a 52 to 47 vote. The amendment extended for ten years the ban on nineteen types of military-style, semiautomatic assault weapons, which was set to expire in September. Minutes later, the Senate approved by 53 to 46 a proposal by John McCain (R-Ariz.) and Jack Reed (D-R.I.) to require criminal background checks for purchases from unlicensed as well as licensed dealers at gun shows, closing a loophole in current law that has been blamed by gun-control advocates for sales of weapons to criminals and terrorists. After the National Rifle Association (NRA) let him know that from their perspective the amended bill was worse than no bill, Larry E. Craig (R-Idaho), the bill's chief sponsor, took the Senate floor to say the bill had been "so dramatically wounded it should not pass," and the bill was defeated by 90 to 8.[52] Thus Republicans were unable to deliver on legislation of top priority to the NRA, a core Republican constituency, even though they had the votes.

The aggressive use of the Senate's permissive amending rules, often in combination with extended debate, has become a key minority party strategy. In the Senate, unlike the House, the minority party can bring its agenda to the floor via amendments. In the 108th Congress, for example, Democrats used nongermane amendments to force consideration—often repeatedly—of an increase in the minimum wage, the extension of unemployment benefits, and the blocking of Bush Administration regulations changing eligibility for overtime.

The majority party has employed a variety of strategies to counter such minority party offensives. As Majority Leader in the late 1990s, Lott often responded with hardball procedural tactics. He filed for cloture on a bill immediately, then pulled the bill from the floor until the cloture vote was due. If cloture succeeded, he had barred all nongermane amendments, since Senate rules require that all amendments after cloture is invoked be germane. If cloture failed, he did not bring up the bill. He sometimes used the tactic of "filling the amendment tree"; that is, he used the Majority Leader's prerogative of first recognition to offer amendments in all the parliamentarily permissible slots, thus preventing Democrats from offering their amendments. Outraged Democrats reacted by maintaining high cohesion on cloture votes, thus denying the majority the sixty votes it needs to make the tactics work. Consequently, when the majority employed these tactics, the result was most often gridlock, with no legislative work accomplished on the Senate floor until an accommodation was reached. As the Republican Policy Committee chair explained, "Inevitably, anybody who wants to get a vote on the floor of the United States Senate will get it if they're persistent."[53] After Bush became president, Lott had to change his approach so as to avoid gridlock on Bush's program. Hence he did not even attempt to keep campaign finance reform legislation off the floor. John McCain and his Democratic allies had threatened to add the bill as a nongermane amendment to every bill Lott did bring to the floor.

Tom Daschle and Bill Frist, the succeeding majority leaders, largely kept the Senate floor process open, allowing fuller and more unfettered debate. Daschle in the 107th Congress and Frist in the 108th had the narrowest of margins—only fifty-one votes. Having a Republican in the White House gave Frist a powerful ally but also put pressure on him to pass the president's ambitious agenda. In the political context of the early 2000s, hardball strategies by Senate majorities were most likely to result in stalemate.

Nevertheless, Frist was under pressure from his members to pursue partisan advantage and to protect them from politically damaging votes. In the 108th Congress he sometimes tried, though without much success, to use cloture to avoid votes on nongermane Democratic amendments. For example, he attempted to block a vote on the Democratic amendment raising the minimum wage that Senator Ted Kennedy was prepared to offer to the bill reauthorizing the welfare program. Frist wanted to protect his members from having to take a tough vote, and he feared he could not defeat the amendment, so he filed for cloture. But Democrats stuck together and defeated the cloture motion 51–47. Frist then pulled the bill from the floor. That prevented a vote on the minimum wage amendment but at the expense of the welfare bill—a bill with sufficient votes to pass but one that Republicans wanted considerably more than Democrats did. Nor did that bury the minimum wage amendment for the Congress. Kennedy could offer it to other legislation and was quite prepared to do so.

A bill to overhaul class action lawsuits became a victim of problems with nongermane amendments even though, by the time it came up, Frist had agreed to a vote on the minimum wage. Frist had negotiated changes in the bill that gave him the sixty votes to close off a filibuster. However, Frist tried to bar all nongermane (nonrelevant) amendments except the minimum wage amendment. Democrats and some Republicans as well had amendments they wanted to offer, and this bill seemed likely to be one of the last vehicles during the 108th Congress. To bar nonrelevant amendments, Frist filled the amendment tree and then filed for cloture.

Democrats were outraged. Daschle responded: "Let's understand what we are doing. This is a sham. This is a sham. The majority leader, for some reason, wants to deny his own caucus and the minority the right to offer legitimate amendments in the Senate. This may be the first time this majority leader has acquiesced to pressures within his caucus to do this, and that is unfortunate. . . . For us now to find ourselves in this situation seems a little bit to me like deja vu all over again. We have tried this, and it is going to backfire on this majority and this majority leader, just as it has in past circumstances."[54] Even Democrats who were party to the compromise on the bill itself were not willing to vote for cloture under those circumstances. Cloture failed and Frist pulled the bill.

A corporate tax bill passed by the Senate in May 2004 illustrates some of the strategies the parties have available and how they use them. The impetus for the bill was a European Union decision to impose higher tariffs on some U.S. goods because of a U.S. tax provision that the World Trade Organization had declared an illegal subsidy. Pressure to pass legislation fixing the problem was intense but did not result in an easy road to enactment.

The Finance Committee reported a bill in October 2003 on a bipartisan 19–2 vote, with the support of all the committee's Democrats. The end-of-session legislative crush, which included the Medicare/prescription drugs bill, precluded immediate consideration. Frist and Grassley aimed to bring the corporate tax bill to the floor about March 1. The party leaders could not, however, reach an agreement to limit either debate or amendments. Democrats wanted to use the floor debate to showcase their priorities; Republicans wanted to avoid votes on popular but, in their view, ill-advised policy proposals, especially in an election year.

Frist brought the bill to the floor on March 3 without a UCA. Tom Harkin (D-Iowa) offered an amendment to block the Labor Department from changing overtime pay rules. This was one of the Democratic amendments Republicans most wanted to avoid. It was popular, it had already passed the Senate once, and the administration was adamantly opposed to it. By the end of the week, more than 111 amendments had been filed. Republicans managed to delay a vote on the Harkin amendment, and after two days of debate, Frist pulled the bill to go on to the budget resolution. Frist announced that when the Senate returned to the bill he would attempt to impose cloture.

When Frist brought the bill back to the floor on March 22, the Republican leadership moved to recommit the bill to the Finance Committee with instructions and filed a cloture petition to cut off debate on that motion. This forestalled a vote on the Harkin amendment, and were cloture to be invoked, the Harkin amendment and any other nongermane amendments would then be out of order. Grassley meanwhile had been working on amendments to the bill that would serve as sweeteners and, he hoped, induce Democrats to desert Harkin and their leadership. The strategy failed; on March 24, cloture was defeated on a 51–47 vote with only one Democrat joining the Republicans.

The leaders had made attempts to reach agreement behind the scenes. The day before the failed cloture vote, Democrats presented Republicans with a list of thirteen amendments they wanted to offer, but Republicans rejected that as too much. A

Senate Republican leadership aide explained, "If they don't bring us a reasonable list of amendments, if they can't get Cantwell and Durbin and Schumer to back down, why should we give them anything?"[55]

After one more unsuccessful try at invoking cloture, Majority Leader Bill Frist capitulated and reached an informal agreement with Minority Leader Thomas A. Daschle. It provided that eighty amendments to the bill could be offered, fifty from Republicans and thirty from Democrats.[56] Further negotiations resulted in the whittling down of the list, but the most contentious amendments remained. Republicans offered their own milder amendment on overtime pay rules, hoping to draw off support from the Harkin amendment. The Gregg amendment passed 99 to 0, but then the Harkin amendment was adopted by 52 to 47. The Cantwell amendment extending unemployment insurance benefits fell on a 59–40 vote; it required sixty votes to waive the Budget Act. The bill passed on May 11 on a 90 to 5 vote.

The Senate majority's most powerful weapon is the budget process. The Budget Act protects both budget resolutions and reconciliation bills from filibusters in the Senate, so passing them requires only a majority in the Senate—not sixty votes. The Budget Act also makes amending the budget resolution and the reconciliation bill implementing it more difficult than usual Senate procedure; amendments must be germane and deficit-neutral, and waiving these Budget Act requirements takes sixty votes.[57]

All of the big, ambitious economic plans since Ronald Reagan's in 1981 have been considered under this special procedure. Most would have had little chance of passing in the Senate without that special protection from filibusters.

The majority party has an enormous incentive to do as much legislating as it can get away with in the reconciliation bill because of this protection from filibusters. During the 103rd

Congress (1993–94), Senate Democratic leaders and President Clinton discussed including the administration's health care program in the reconciliation bill. However, the Byrd Rule, instituted in 1985, limits what can be included in reconciliation bills by requiring that reconciliation provisions must reduce the deficit and that waiving the rule takes sixty votes. The Byrd Rule's purpose was to make it difficult to include extraneous matter in reconciliation bills, and while determining what is extraneous is not always clear-cut, the rule has largely had the effect intended. Hence although the budget process does provide a relatively cohesive majority party with a valuable tool, it is no panacea for the difficulties that beset the majority party in the Senate.

Resolving Interchamber Differences

High partisan polarization makes resolving interchamber differences on major legislation difficult when different parties control the two chambers. During the period of split partisan control of the House and Senate from June of 2001 through the end of 2002, major legislation such as the patients' bill of rights and an energy bill died at the conference stage because the differences between the Democratic Senate bill and the Republican House bill were irreconcilable. But even when the two chambers are controlled by the same party, the Senate's supermajority requirement can complicate the process. Although decisions in conference can be made by a simple majority of each chamber's conference delegation, conference reports can be filibustered in the Senate. To get an agreement that assures passage in the Senate requires that House Republicans satisfy not only the Republican majority in the Senate but some Democrats as well.

Yet Republicans are increasingly responding to the problems that the Senate's supermajority requirement creates for them in passing legislation in the Senate initially by using conferences to recoup losses suffered in the Senate. "If you can get a bill to conference," Republican Whip Mitch McConnell explained, "you have wide latitude to produce a bill the majority is comfortable with and the president is comfortable with."[58]

Despite their narrow margins of control, Republicans have taken to excluding most Democrats from conference negotiations altogether. When Democrats complained about being excluded from the negotiations on the budget resolution in April 2001, Senate Budget Committee Chair Pete Domenici (R-N.M.) baldly replied: "We don't expect you to sign [the conference report], so we don't expect you to be needed."[59] In 2003, no Democrats were allowed to participate in the energy bill conference, and only two Senate Democrats who were considered accommodating were admitted to the negotiations on the Medicare/prescription drugs bill. Republicans gambled that Senate moderates of both parties would be loath to vote against bills on such important issues even if those bills were considerably further to the right than they preferred. On the Medicare/prescription drugs legislation, the wager paid off, at least in the short run, and the conference report passed the Senate. The energy bill, in contrast, was blocked by a filibuster.

In the Senate, the minority party usually has strategic options when it feels misused by the majority. The motions necessary to go to conference can be filibustered. "The three steps [necessary to go to conference] are usually bundled into a unanimous consent agreement and done within seconds," explained former Senate parliamentarian Robert B. Dove. "But if some senators do not want a conference to occur and if they are very determined, they can force three separate cloture votes to close debate, and that takes a lot of time. It basically stops the whole process of going to conference."[60] Democrats responded to their exclusion from conference committee decision making by blocking conferences.

In 2004, Democrats blocked all conferences until early April, when they allowed conferees to be appointed on the Coast Guard reauthorization bill.[61] Among the legislation stopped were bills on charitable giving and job training. Later in the spring, the massive highway bill was stopped. Explaining his objection to the Republican motions to go to conference, Democratic Whip Harry Reid said: "Maybe we can reflect back on what happened on the energy bill. . . . We not only were not allowed to go to conference, we did not even know where the conference meetings were being held."[62] In each case the Democrats' demand was a guarantee that they be included in the negotiations. In late May, Democrats did allow the highway bill to go to conference in return for a promise from Majority Leader Bill Frist. Daschle and Frist explained—and put on the record—the agreement through this floor colloquy:

> *Frist:* The transportation bill we passed this year was a model of bipartisan cooperation that was marked by good faith on both sides. That is the essence of the agreement I am proposing, a commitment from both sides that they will work in good faith in conference to get the best possible result. I have spoken to Senator Inhofe, who will chair the conference. He has agreed he will not pursue a conclusion to the conference, nor sign any conference report that would alter the text of S. 1072 in a way that undermines the bipartisan working relationship that has existed in the Senate.
>
> *Daschle:* I have discussed this with my colleagues and can commit wholeheartedly to the good-faith process he has proposed. Our side understands that changes will have to be made, and we are not entering this process demanding a specific outcome on any provision. Instead, we are asking any changes to S. 1072 be the result of the mutual agreement of the lead Senate conferees acting in good faith.
>
> By moving S. 1072 through the Senate, Senators Inhofe, Bond, Jeffords, and Reid have already demonstrated they can make that process work. If the process should break down due to disagreements over either transportation policy or extraneous provisions, then we understand he and I will not bring such a conference report to the floor.

> *Frist:* That is correct, so long as the Democratic conferees are acting in good faith, and I have every expectation they will. Our goal is to reach a conference agreement that reflects the balance and broad bipartisan consensus S. 1072 achieves. That will be the test of good faith for both sides. I think we can do that, and we will not bring a bill to the Senate floor if it does not reflect that commitment.[63]

THE DILEMMA OF LEGISLATING IN THE SENATE

Legislating successfully in the nonmajoritarian Senate is difficult; sixty votes are often necessary to prevail. Partisan polarization has made constructing the necessary deals considerably tougher; the two parties' notions of what constitutes good public policy often have little overlap. Yet, to get anything done in the narrowly divided Senate, except via the budget process, requires a coalition that includes at least some members of both parties. And keeping the Senate functioning as a legislature day in and day out requires broad accommodation; it dictates satisfying every senator to some extent.

Thus partisan polarization has made the already tough job of the Senate Majority Leader even more difficult. The Majority Leader must work closely with the Minority Leader and must often accommodate the minority to some extent. Yet the Senate leaders are party leaders, elected by their party members in the chamber, and are expected by those members to pursue partisan advantage. With the increase in partisan polarization, the narrow margins, and the shifts in partisan control of the chamber, senators' expectations that their leader promote their collective partisan interests have intensified. Republican senators want Frist to promote the Republican agenda by passing legislation and publicizing Republican positions and successes; they also want him to keep off the floor the Democrats' agenda, much of which consists of issues on which Democrats and the public agree, and thus puts Republicans in a tough position.

Recent Majority Leaders have all faced the same dilemma. When Senator Jim Jeffords left the Republican Party and thereby turned control of the Senate over to the Democrats, Lott was criticized by fellow Republicans for letting it happen, just as he had been criticized earlier for being too accommodating to moderate Republicans and Democrats. With Tom Daschle as Majority Leader, Democrats passed some of their top priorities in the Senate—a patients' bill of rights, for example; they tempered or blocked a number of Bush initiatives with which they disagreed—energy legislation, for instance. Yet, facing a partisan Republican House of Representatives and a determined conservative president, Senate Democrats could seldom enact legislation in a form they favored. And even when Republican filibusters prevented action as on the Homeland Security Department bill, Democrats collectively and Daschle specifically were excoriated for blocking legislation. Daschle's decision to hold tough on the Homeland Security Department bill may have cost Democrats their majority in the 2002 elections; yet many of his fellow Democrats would have been extremely upset had he been willing to give in to Bush.

Bill Frist became Majority Leader in 2003 in a more favorable political climate; his party had won a considerable victory in the 2002 elections, controlled the House, and had a popular and politically formidable president. Frist did lead Senate Republicans to some major policy successes, most notably the enactment of the Medicare/prescription drugs bill. Yet he too failed to get many Republican initiatives through the Senate and, in 2004, was unable to pass the budget resolution. The 2004 elections further improved the political context for Frist, returning Bush to the White House and increasing the Republican Senate membership to fifty-five. Yet Republicans were still far from the filibuster-proof majority of sixty, and the intense polarization reflected in the campaigns and the vote decreased Frist's chances of getting Democratic support for Republican initiatives on the cheap.

The pressure to pursue partisan advantage and avoid policy compromise is particularly great on contemporary Republican Senate leaders. A considerable part of the Republican Senate membership consists of junior conservatives, many of whom were schooled in the highly partisan House of Newt Gingrich and Tom DeLay. As I discussed earlier, leaders are frequently pressed to accede to the more conservative House position in conference committee, but then the resulting conference report can be hard to pass in the Senate. Further, Democrats see such behavior as "bait and switch"; it undermines any remaining trust they may have in Senate Republicans and their leaders and makes future cooperation less likely.

At the same time that Senate leaders have to deal with sometimes unmeetable expectations from their members for the aggressive pursuit of partisan advantage, they must also handle the individualism within their own party that can derail partisan and bipartisan strategies alike. In the House, members are increasingly constrained to participating through their parties. Senators have many more options and do not pay a high price for going off on their own. Senator Ted Kennedy, usually a party stalwart, decided on his own and against the wishes of Democratic leaders to work with Bush and Republicans on the Medicare/prescription drugs bill in 2003. Frist's first major embarrassment as Majority Leader came when several moderate Republicans held out against Bush's tax cut in 2003; to pass it, Frist and Finance Committee Chair Charles Grassley were forced to agree to a much smaller tax cut than they had promised House Republican leaders to deliver. Similarly, Frist was unable to work out a deal on the budget resolution conference report in 2004. Although he needed only a simple majority, he could not persuade any of the four moderate Senate Republicans to accept any deal to which House Republicans would agree. Senator John McCain made his name by bucking the Republican Party establishment on tobacco taxes and campaign finance reform, among other issues. In early 2004, McCain and Joseph Lieberman (D-Conn.) held hostage the temporary extension of the highway program. Speaker Hastert had refused to grant the independent commission studying the 9/11 terrorist attacks the two-month extension requested, an extension the president had reluctantly approved and the Senate had passed. Faced with a high-visibility shutdown of the Department of Transportation and a cutoff of funds for local projects members hold dear, Hastert capitulated.[64] Since it was assumed that Hastert was acting on behalf of and taking the heat for the Republican Party and the Republican president, who did not want a report near the election, McCain, by his actions, foiled his own party's electoral strategy.

Senators complain, sometimes bitterly, when their party colleagues use Senate prerogatives in ways that harm the party effort, and they express outrage when opposition party senators do so. Yet senators have not been able and seemingly are not willing to give their leaders more powers for running the Senate. Doing so would require changing basic Senate rules on extended debate and on the amending process and thereby drastically reducing their own individual prerogatives. Altering Senate rules in the traditional way requires a two-thirds vote. When in 1975 senators agreed to decrease to sixty the number of votes needed to invoke cloture on legislation, they maintained it at two-thirds for changing Senate rules. In a period of high partisan polarization, a Senate minority is not likely to provide the needed votes.

In the wake of the Estrada nomination filibuster in spring and summer of 2003, Frist threatened to change the rules for nominations through a highly controversial procedure that requires only a simple majority. The "nuclear option" would entail the Senate's presiding officer ruling that cutting off debate on nominations requires only a simple majority. Democrats would, of course, appeal the ruling, but only a simple majority is required to uphold a ruling of the chair. This strategy was dubbed nuclear because minority Democrats could be expected to "go nuclear" and block Senate business indefinitely if Republicans resorted to it.

Republicans almost certainly lacked the votes to make the strategy work before the 2004 elections, and Frist did not bring it to the floor during the 108th Congress. The strategy's success depended on a considerable number of Republicans, both moderates and "old bull" Senate traditionalists, casting a vote for something they oppose on grounds of both principle and personal power interest. The 2004 elections increased the number of Republicans in the Senate to fifty-five, with most of the new members being militant conservatives. Thus strengthened and under pressure from Christian conservative groups, Frist prepared to "pull the trigger" on the nuclear option in May 2005. Literally at the last moment a group of fourteen senators, half Republicans and half Democrats, working independently of the party leaders, came to an agreement to avert the showdown.[65] The Democrats promised not to support filibusters on judicial nomination barring "extraordinary" circumstances; the Republicans pledged not to support the nuclear option. Senate individualism trumped partisan pressures, but how long the agreement would hold remained very much in doubt.

The combination of partisan polarization and individualism that characterizes the contemporary Senate has shaped a legislative process that often seems near breakdown. And yet it has not reached that point—at least not quite. Must-pass legislation such as appropriations bills does, in fact, pass. Even a considerable amount of controversial legislation gets through the Senate.

Asked what keeps senators as individuals and as party teams from pushing their prerogatives over the limit and trapping the Senate in total gridlock, senators, staff, and informed observers uniformly responded that almost all senators want to "get something done" and that they are aware that many senators' exploiting their prerogatives to the limit would make this impossible. As one knowledgeable insider phrased it, "I like to think of the Senate as a bunch of armed nuclear nations. Each senator knows he can blow the place up, but most of them came here to do something, and if he does blow things up, if he does use his powers that way, then he won't be able to do anything." Using one's prerogatives aggressively entails concrete short-run costs, most argued. "If you do object [to a unanimous consent request], it's going to hurt someone and maybe more than one person," a senior staffer explained, "so the next time you want something, it may very well happen to you next time." Senators do not put holds on every bill or nomination they oppose, another experienced aide said, "because people will put a hold on their stuff then." In the Senate, individuals can exact retribution swiftly and often quite easily on those they believe have harmed them. The likelihood that some retaliation will be forthcoming forces the wise senator to be somewhat selective in the employment of prerogatives.

In its everyday functioning, the contemporary Senate exhibits a peculiar combination of conflict and cooperation, of aggressive exploitation of rules and of accommodation. The hottest partisan legislative battles are studded with unanimous consent agreements. And the more intense the partisan fight, the more frequently the Majority and Minority Leaders confer. On bills not at the center of partisan conflict, senators routinely cooperate across the partisan divide. As a senior aide expressed the consensus, "If you really want to move stuff, if it's not a big partisan matter, a big ideological issue, and you really want to move it, then you really have to be bipartisan. You've got to work out the difficulties, and you've got to work across the aisle."

Senate procedures can exert a strong pressure toward bipartisanship. Senators as individuals put holds on one another's bills, but they also often attempt to accommodate one another on an individual basis in ways that extend far beyond what occurs in the House. The reason is not norms of civility and reciprocity but the facts of life in the contemporary Senate. It is "because they need to accommodate you to move something," an aide explained. "They want to get something done. They want to get legislation, and to do that you have to take care of people's problems."

Yet Senate procedure does take a toll on legislation. The Senate is now the most frequent graveyard of major legislation, the stage in the legislative process where legislation is most likely to die, as I demonstrate in chapter 10. Combine nonmajoritarian rules with intense partisan polarization, and the probability of stalemate rises steeply. The impact of Senate procedure is not limited to major controversial bills. Senators who want their bills to receive floor consideration are under tremendous pressure to negotiate with those who "have problems" with the legislation. "Things that aren't a top priority for the Majority Leader, he wants you to work it out," a senior staffer explained. "If you go to him and say you want something brought to the floor, he'll say, 'You work it out. You find out who has holds on it. You work out whatever problems they have, and I'll schedule it when you've worked it out.'" Thus, simply to get to the floor, a measure must often command a substantial supermajority. If working out the problems is not possible without gutting the legislation or if time is tight, even majority-supported legislation may nevertheless die.

CHAPTER 7

THE PRESIDENT AND CONGRESS IN A POLARIZED ENVIRONMENT

WHAT HAS BEEN THE impact of partisan polarization on the relationship between president and Congress in the policy-making process? Assessing the impact of partisan polarization on the politics and process of lawmaking at the national level requires moving beyond Congress and bringing in other key actors. In this chapter I begin that task with an initial analysis of the relationship between the president and Congress.

THE CONTOURS OF PRESIDENTIAL-CONGRESSIONAL AGREEMENT

Weak parties and the resulting lack of party cohesion in Congress have conventionally been seen as *the* great barrier to effective presidential legislative leadership in the United States. If a lack of cohesion has often been a problem for presidents, is the current high cohesion a blessing?

Americans have come to expect the president to act as policy leader: to set the agenda and to engineer passage of legislation to deal with the country's major problems. Yet the Constitution establishes a relationship of mutual dependence between the president and Congress and, in terms of policy making, puts the president in the weaker position. As a result, the extent to which a president's policy preferences and those of the congressional majority coincide or conflict should be a key determinant of presidential legislative success.

To assess the impact of changes in party cohesion, I examine the extent to which the president and Congress agree or disagree on major legislation at various stages in the legislative process. I want to answer the question: Does the president do better or worse at getting bills in a form he likes from Congress when congressional partisanship is high or low? Using *Congressional Quarterly* accounts, I coded presidential support/agreement or opposition/disagreement (or an intermediate, mixed position) for every major measure at each stage of the process. In the vast majority of the cases, CQ explicitly discussed the president's views, and the coding was straightforward. Presidential opposition does not necessarily mean that he opposes any bill on the issue; this is infrequently the case. It simply means he opposes the bill in the form in which it emerged from that stage—the House committee, for example.

What has been the effect of increasing partisan polarization on whether the president and Congress agree? Since agreement should be higher when a president has a Congress controlled by his own party than when the opposition is in the majority, the relationship must be examined separately for divided and unified control. Table 7.1 divides the Congresses into three periods: the 91st and before (1970 and before, 87th, 89th, 91st), a period of relatively low polarization; the 94th through 97th (1975–82), an intermediate period; and the 100th and later (1987 and later, 100th, 101st, 103rd–105th), a period of higher and increasing polarization.[1]

From the low polarization to the intermediate period, agreement between the president and Congress decreased under both unified and divided control, but the decrease was much steeper under divided control. In effect, this means that Kennedy as well as Johnson did considerably better with the Democratic Congresses they faced than did Carter; the difference between the two periods

TABLE 7.1
Presidential Agreement with Congress
The Impact of Divided versus Unified Control
and of Increasing Partisan Polarization

		House			Senate		
Stage	Control	91st and before (%)	94th, 95th, and 97th (%)	100th and after (%)	91st and before (%)	94th, 95th, and 97th (%)	100th and after (%)
Committee	Unified	82	76	94	85	67	89
	Divided	57	30	19	44	28	23
Floor	Unified	74	66	94	88	76	83
	Divided	61	38	19	42	33	31

Source: Author's calculations based primarily on accounts in *Congressional Quarterly.*

Note: Numbers are the percentage of major measures the president supported out of all major measures reported out of committee or passed on the floor. Polarization was higher in each of the succeeding periods.

is much greater for the Republican presidents, all of whom had to deal with Democratic-controlled Congresses (Reagan with only a Democratic House). Nixon fared quite well compared with Ford and Reagan. Increasing polarization, the reforms, or both seem to have made the Congress less accommodating—not only but especially to presidents of the other party. From the intermediate period to the period of high polarization, agreement under unified control goes up to exceed agreement during the initial period, and the increase is considerable in the House. Agreement under divided control continues to decrease, with the result that the effect of partisan control becomes massive. The first Bush and Clinton after Republicans took control of Congress fared very poorly in terms of congressional committees reporting and the chambers passing bills in a form the president supported.

Most notable is that presidents lost considerably more under conditions of divided control than they gained under conditions of unified control. Considering the frequency of divided control in recent decades, that is of major consequence for presidential success.

Table 7.2 shows comparable figures for the 107th Congress (2001–2002), which is not included in table 7.1 because it does not fit neatly into either of the partisan control categories. When George W. Bush's first presidential term started, the Senate was split 50–50; Vice President Cheney gave Republicans nominal control, but the organizational deal the parties negotiated gave the parties equal numbers of members on all committees. Jim Jeffords's switch from the Republican Party to caucusing with the Democrats in June 2001 changed the ratio to 51–49, giving the Democrats control and a one-seat advantage on each committee. It did not, however, alter the Senate's membership. Table 7.2 essentially reinforces the generalizations drawn from table 7.1. In the Republican controlled House, Bush did well; to a large extent, the committees reported and the floor passed bills in a form he supported. Even before Jeffords switched control of the chamber, Bush did considerably less well in the 50–50 Senate committees than in the clearly Republican-controlled House committees. After the switch, the legislation Senate committees reported tended to be in a form Bush opposed.

Bush's high success on the Senate floor in the months before the Jeffords switch illustrates that even in the Senate, control does convey a considerable advantage. The organizational deal allowed the Majority Leader to bring legislation to the floor without committee approval and thus essentially to set the agenda when an evenly split committee was unable to report. Majority Leader Lott did exactly that with the budget resolution that carried Bush's tax cuts. Repeal of the ergonomics rules would not have had such an easy route to the floor had control been in Democratic

TABLE 7.2

Presidential Support for Bills in the 107th Congress, 2001–2002

	House (%)	Senate, Pre–Jeffords Switch (%)	Senate, Post–Jeffords Switch (%)
Committee			
supported	78	50	20
opposed	6	0	73
Floor			
supported	87	75	58
opposed	5	25	29

Source: Author's calculations based primarily on accounts in *Congressional Quarterly*.

Note: Numbers are the percentage of major legislation the president supported and opposed as it emerged from committee or as it passed the chamber. The Jeffords switch changed control of the Senate from Republican to Democratic.

hands. Once Republicans lost control and Democrat Tom Daschle became Majority Leader, Bush's success on the Senate floor decreased but not to the low level suffered by other recent presidents under divided control. Certainly the 9/11 afterglow accounts for part of Bush's greater success, but so does the very narrow margin of opposition control.

THE PRESIDENT AND THE CONGRESSIONAL PARTY

When control is unified, high cohesion by his party advantages the president. Congressional leaders of the president's party are likely to see presidential success as in their best interest; they must concern themselves with the party's image and are likely to be judged by their success in enacting his program. Speaker Rayburn's willingness to pack the Rules Committee after John Kennedy's election shows that this was so even when the parties were much less cohesive and polarized.

Contemporary House Speakers can give the president a great deal of assistance; the institutional and procedural advantages of control of the chamber as well as the Speaker's partisan resources can be put at the service of passing the president's program and stopping measures the president opposes. Because the political parties are now quite homogeneous ideologically, the president and the members of his party in the House are likely to have similar legislative preferences, so party leaders are usually promoting their members' preferences when they seek to pass the president's program; seldom will the Speaker be forced to choose between the president and his members. In fact, the president is likely to have adopted some of his agenda from that of his congressional party.

Throughout Bush's first term, Speaker Dennis Hastert repeatedly mobilized his slim majority to pass Bush's priorities: tax cuts, education reform, the faith-based initiative, the Patriot Act, Medicare/prescription drugs legislation, and use-of-force authorizations for Afghanistan and Iraq are only the most prominent instances. "In the first six months the president got pretty much everything done that he promised in the campaign," a former White House aide said with only a little exaggeration if the remark is applied specifically to the House. "And Hastert drove the train."[2] In a number of cases, Hastert had to rely almost completely on Republicans, and in some—the Medicare/prescription drugs bill, for example—he had to use all his procedural and party resources to pull out a victory.

Just as valuable to a president is the House majority leadership's willingness to use its control over the floor agenda to block legislation he opposes. "[Hastert] made it clear that they would not allow bills that would be vetoed to reach the president's desk," according to Nick Calio, former head of White House liaison for Bush.[3]

To be sure, the relationship between the president and Congress is never without tensions, even when both are controlled by the same party and the party is ideologically homogeneous by American standards. The constitutional design assures that the president and members of Congress face somewhat different electoral circumstances and that ideological homogeneity within Congress and across the branches is never absolute. The interbranch conflict on the massive transportation reauthorization bill in 2004 illustrates how electoral incentives can lead to friction. For members of Congress, including many conservative Republicans, the bill not only promised an overall economic stimulus but offered the kind of local projects that could boost their reelection chances as well. Bush, facing sharp criticism in an election year for the enormous deficits, saw the bill as an opportunity to show fiscal discipline and vowed to veto a "budget busting" bill. Intent on sending the president a bill he could sign and one that satisfied his members to the extent possible, Hastert exploded when the White House seemed to be sending him conflicting signals about how high the president would go.[4] Nevertheless after this rare public disagreement—aimed at the White House chief of staff not at the president himself—Hastert went back to work on producing a bill that satisfied both the president and his members. When that proved to be impossible, no bill was sent to the president; the task of reauthorizing transportation programs was postponed until the next Congress.

The Medicare/prescription drugs bill exposed rifts in the Republican Party along both electoral and ideological lines. A number of the most conservative Republicans in the House opposed the bill on philosophical grounds; other Republicans including the president saw it as a major electoral coup. In the end, Speaker Hastert persuaded enough conservative Republicans to go along to pass the bill; not handing your president a major defeat was a key argument. In 2005, many Republicans were hesitant to offer strong support for Bush's attempt to restructure social security. Bush could be courageous and grasp the dangerous "third rail of politics," they grumbled; he would never have to face the voters again, but they would. The House Republican leadership tried to keep their members from open opposition while at the same time urging Bush to go slow. However, when Bush suggested he might be willing to talk about raising the earnings cap on which the social security tax is levied, Hastert and DeLay immediately and publicly shot back their adamant opposition. Raising taxes would be impossible in the House and politically destructive for the Republican Party, they believed.

The most recent instance of unified Democratic control—1993–94—also saw both regular cooperation and occasional tension between the president and the congressional party. In 1994, for example, electoral imperatives and policy differences split a Democratic president from the majority of House Democrats on the North American Free Trade Agreement (NAFTA). Members from the rust belt, where jobs in heavy manufacturing have been on the decline, fear that free trade will result in more jobs being exported to low-wage countries; members from the fast-growing sunbelt and from areas with a concentration of high-technology or export-oriented industries tend to see free trade as an opportunity. Although present in both parties, the split is much more intense among Democrats; they represent a greater proportion of rust belt districts, and organized labor, a key supporter of the party, tends toward protectionism. However, the expert consensus in favor of free trade is so overwhelming that a Democratic presidential candidate is under great pressure to adopt that position, and Clinton had endorsed NAFTA during the 1992 campaign. This fight even split the House Democratic leadership, with the Speaker supporting NAFTA and the Majority Leader and whip opposed. The eventual winning coalition was made up of more Republicans than Democrats. Yet on every other presidential legislative priority in the 103rd Congress, the House Democratic leadership and the president worked together. And, with the major exception of health care reform, the House leadership and the Democratic membership delivered for the president.

In this era of high partisan polarization, having the House controlled by his fellow partisans, even if it is by a narrow margin, is an enormous advantage for the president. However, legislation must pass both chambers, and in the Senate a simple majority is seldom enough. Barring a huge partisan majority, presidential priorities need minority party votes to pass, and high partisan polarization makes them much harder to get. As I show in chapter 6, the Senate is a barrier to positive legislative achievements under unified as well as divided control.

If, as I argued earlier, partisan polarization in Congress has constituency roots, then the policy differences between Democratic and Republican voters and the greater differences between the party activists are, in part, what account for presidents getting high support from members of their own party and much lower support from opposition party members. One might expect, however, that when a president is popular, even Congress members of the opposition party would feel some constituent pressure to support him.[5] In fact, something important has happened to citizens' evaluations of presidents; presidential approval is much more strongly related to a citizen's party identification than it used to be. That is, presidential approval has polarized along partisan lines—and this is among ordinary citizens. For the presidents from Eisenhower through Carter, the highest average difference between Democratic and Republican approval was 41 percentage points—very substantial; for as long as we have had them, polls have shown that people have approved of presidents of their own party significantly more than of presidents of the other; a good job is in the eye of the beholder to some considerable extent. That gap nevertheless increased enormously for Reagan to an average of 53 points and to 55 for Clinton.[6]

For most members of Congress, following constituent opinion—especially the opinion of those constituents who regularly vote for them—now means supporting a president of their own party *and* opposing a president of the other. Unless a president is incredibly popular, chances are that if you are a member of the opposition party in Congress, most of the people you count on for getting reelected do not like the president much. A huge event like 9/11 can change that, but even then the change was temporary.

Thus, in summer 2003, Bush's approval rating stood at about 60 percent, making him a clearly popular president.[7] Republicans loved him; 94 percent approved of the job he was doing. Among Democrats the story was different; only 29 percent approved, for a gargantuan gap of 65 points. In a July 2004 poll, when Bush's approval-disapproval rating stood at 45–48 overall, 84 percent of Republicans approved of the job he was doing and 9 percent disapproved; 16 percent of Democrats approved and 78 percent disapproved.[8] Even after winning reelection, Bush did not benefit from any sort of honeymoon among Democrats. An ABC Poll conducted in late January 2005 right around the inaugural found that while 87 percent of Republicans approved of his job performance and 11 percent disapproved, only 14 percent of Democrats approved and 83 percent disapproved.[9] These folks are hardly likely to be pressuring their representatives to support the president's legislative proposals.

This gulf in presidential approval between Democrats and Republicans should not be surprising when we compare the presidents, especially the Republican ones, of the last several decades with their predecessors. Compared to Eisenhower, Nixon, and Ford, Ronald Reagan and George W. Bush are a great deal further to the right. Judged by their legislative programs, their administrative regulations, their cabinet and subcabinet appointments, and their judicial nominations, Reagan and George W. Bush are ideological movement conservatives, while Eisenhower, Nixon, and Ford were moderately conservative pragmatists. The most liberal member of the current Supreme Court is a Ford appointee. Nixon signed the initial Clean Air Act; true, it was stronger than what he wanted, but he still signed it and took credit for it. Reagan's presidential victory was the first major triumph of the resurgent right, and he played an important role in cementing the hold of ideological conservatives on the Republican Party. George W. Bush can be seen as reflecting how complete that hold has become. During the 2000 campaign, Bush projected a benign and nonthreatening persona; a "Gingrich type" was clearly unelectable. But Bush's proposals, evident to those who listen with any care, were clearly conservative. As Representative Jim DeMint (R-S.C.) said soon after the 2000 election, "Bush has set a conservative agenda, moderated not so much in philosophy as in tone."[10]

STRATEGIC RESPONSES TO THE TRANSFORMED ENVIRONMENT: AN INTRODUCTION

The political environment in which the president and members of Congress operate has changed enormously in the last several decades. Partisan polarization has made legislative leadership more difficult for a president facing a Congress controlled by the other party; a president whose party controls both chambers of Congress may have an easier time in the House but now confronts a far more complicated situation in the Senate. For members of the opposition congressional party, high partisan polarization has also transformed the context in which they pursue their goals. And polarization is not the only major change. As I have shown earlier, both chambers have undergone considerable internal change. Interest groups have exploded in numbers and become much more diverse and active. And as I discuss more fully in chapter 9, the role of the media in the political process has changed as well.

The president and members of Congress are purposive actors; that is, they have fairly clear goals and they act in a way aimed at meeting their goals. One would therefore expect them to react to changes in their environment strategically—to adjust their behavior so as to try to take advantage of any new opportunities the altered environment presents and to cope with any problems it throws up.

The strategic responses of the congressional parties are the subject of the next chapter. Here I examine two increasingly prominent presidential strategies: veto bargaining, the use by the president of veto threats to extract policy concessions from hostile congressional majorities, and "going public," promoting his policies by appeals to the American public.

VETO THREATS AS A BARGAINING STRATEGY

A president facing a recalcitrant Congress has one real legislative power provided by the Constitution—the veto. It supplies a way to stop legislation the president dislikes. Getting two-thirds in both chambers to override has always been hard, and in this period of partisan polarization it is nearly impossible. George H. W. Bush and Clinton were each overridden once and neither was shy about using the veto; Bush vetoed forty-four bills and Clinton thirty-seven.[11] Very little legislation that the president absolutely abhors becomes law or even gets far in the process. By my calculation, only about eight bills, or 2 percent, of the major legislation enacted during the twelve Congresses for which I have data were bills the president unequivocally opposed.

Congress can and occasionally does override the president's veto, but interestingly, the eight bills are not all cases of presidential vetoes that were overridden. Sometimes the congressional opposition party can make a veto too expensive politically for a president and so force him to accept legislation he strongly dislikes. The purpose of a media campaign on plant closing that Democrats orchestrated in the late 1980s was to pressure President Reagan not to veto the bill requiring that workers be given advance notice of plant closings. By raising the visibility of this popular legislation, Democrats also raised the political price Republicans would pay for a veto. As a result, Reagan allowed the bill to become law without his signature. Similarly, George W. Bush declined to veto the campaign finance reform bill that came to him in 2002, although it did not at all meet the criteria he had specified and House Republicans strongly urged a veto. Given the issue's high visibility and the enormous publicity a veto would get, Bush knew that a veto would be extremely costly politically. In fact, by the time the bill got to the president's desk, Bush had backed so far away from opposition that one might even argue against categorizing the bill as one the president clearly opposed.

Nevertheless, the veto is clearly a very effective negative tool. In most cases, however, the president wants a bill; it is the current form of the bill that is problematical. Can and does the president use the veto under such circumstances? Veto bargaining has become an important presidential strategy for influencing legislation. When control is divided, a president threatens to veto legislation unless it is changed to conform more closely to presidential preferences. Opposition party members know they cannot muster the two-thirds vote needed to override a presidential veto and so often do make at least some alterations. Table 7.3 shows the increase in veto threats on major measures in selected Congresses between 1961 and 1998. When the president's party has controlled both houses of Congress, presidents have seldom issued veto threats. However, the frequency under conditions of divided control has gone up enormously; since the late 1980s, veto threats are the rule rather than the exception on major measures, varying from almost half in Reagan's last Congress to over two-thirds in 1997–98.

Do veto threats work? Do they, in fact, move legislation toward the president's position? The evidence indicates that the strategy is effective.[12] To test whether veto threats influence legislation, I

TABLE 7.3
Frequency of Veto Threats

Congress	Years	Major Measures Subject to Veto Threat (%)
87th	1961–62	0
89th	1965–66	0
91st	1969–70	**15**
94th	1975–76	**40**
95th	1977–78	18
97th	1981–82	**25**
100th	1987–88	**48**
101st	1989–90	**55**
103rd	1993–94	4
104th	1995–96	**60**
105th	1997–98	**78**

Source: Author's calculations.

Note: Divided-control Congresses are in bold. Only measures subject to a veto are included.

looked at how bills change over the course of their congressional consideration—that is, from the committee and the floor in each house to the president's desk. A variable that indexes presidential support for or opposition to legislation at a number of stages in the process is used to gauge whether a bill changed *in terms of presidential support* between, for example, when it was reported from the House committee and its final form. If the president opposed the House committee bill but supported the final bill, that would be considered a change in the bill in the president's direction. If the president supported the House committee bill and supported the final bill, that would be considered no change. If the president had a mixed response to the House

TABLE 7.4
The Impact of Veto Threats

Initial Stage		House Committee	House Floor	Senate Committee	Senate Floor
% that changed vis-à-vis pres. position	No veto threat	24	23	23	19
	Veto threat	59	47	52	38
% that changed to pro-pres. position	No veto threat	69	81	64	63
	Veto threat	84	89	84	78

Source: Author's calculations based primarily on accounts in *Congressional Quarterly*.

Note: The change in presidential support for a bill from earlier stages to final bill is taken as an index of change in the bill toward or away from the president's preferences. Only major bills that became law are included.

committee bill and opposed the final bill, that would be a change away from the president's position. Only bills that were enacted are analyzed. I found that the direction of movement in legislation tends to be disproportionately toward (rather than away from) the president's position whether or not the president has issued a veto threat (after all, everyone knows presidential acceptance is required), but the movement is always more toward the president's position when a veto threat has been issued than when it has not (see table 7.4).

After the Republicans won control of Congress, President Clinton showed himself to be particularly adept at using veto threats and vetoes to force spending increases for his priorities in appropriations bills. In 1999, for example, by a strategic use of vetoes and veto threats, he extracted from reluctant Republicans $5 billion in add-ons in the fiscal year 2000 omnibus spending bill. In 1998 Clinton's veto bargaining yielded $3 billion more for the Labor, Health and Human Services and Education bill, the full $18 billion he had requested for the International Monetary Fund, and $1.2 billion toward his plan to hire a hundred thousand teachers.[13] Before the mid-1990s, the consensus was that presidents could force reductions but not additions in spending by veto threats, because the default option was no spending (or spending at the previous year's rate, which was almost always lower than that proposed by either the president or Congress). However, after the government shutdown over Christmas 1995 for which they were blamed, Republicans feared another such showdown with Clinton, which gave him a strong bargaining advantage on appropriations bills.

Because partisan control switched during the course of it, the 107th Congress, Bush's first, was not included in the figures given. During 2001–2002, Bush threatened to veto six bills—14 percent of the major measures. Two bills central to the Senate Democrats' agenda received veto threats: the patients' bill of rights legislation allowing state suits against HMOs and their Homeland Security Department bill protecting workers' rights. However, the Democrats' difficulty in getting legislation Bush opposed through the Senate as well as Speaker Hastert's determination to protect Bush and the Republican Party from the consequences of a veto of popular legislation meant that Bush simply did not need to use the veto threat often. The Homeland Security bill Congress sent Bush after the 2002 elections contained the language he wanted; the amendment that had prompted Bush's veto threat was removed from the Trade Promotion Authority legislation in conference; patients' bill of rights legislation never reached Bush. Except for that bill, all Bush's veto threats moved the legislation at issue in his direction. Bush did not cast a single veto during the 107th Congress.

Although Republicans controlled both chambers of Congress in the 108th Congress, Bush actually used veto threats more than he had in the previous Congress. He threatened at least eighteen relatively major bills with vetoes.[14] Those threats, by and large, were directed at specific provisions—often appropriations riders—and may well have been intended to give the Republican leadership ammunition against majority-supported provisions that the president opposed. Thus the targets of veto threats—in some cases repeated threats—were attempts to overturn new Federal Communications Commission media ownership rules, to lift the ban on travel to Cuba, to prevent the administration from revising overtime rules in such a way as to deprive of overtime pay some of those currently eligible, to delay military base closings, to allow concurrent receipts for veterans, and to block the administration's efforts to outsource federal jobs to private companies. In some cases, Bush was forced to compromise, but again in every instance the veto threat moved the bill toward his position, and Bush did not veto a single bill in the 108th Congress.

In sum, presidents are able to use veto threats strategically to move legislation toward their preferred position, and in a period of high partisan polarization, presidents who face opposition party control in one chamber or both need to use every tool available to them. Bush's actions suggest that even presidents who have a Congress controlled by their partisans can use veto threats to increase their influence over legislative outcomes. To be sure, some of his veto threats have created resentment among congressional Republicans. Republican majorities in both chambers supported a considerably more expensive transportation bill than Bush was willing to accept. He has asked Republicans to take some politically difficult votes to uphold his position; for example, his insistence that all of the reconstruction aid for Iraq be in the form of aid rather than loans presented members with a vote difficult to explain back home. Nevertheless, Bush's veto threats have not yet sparked a revolt. In the current highly partisan climate, members seem willing to support their president even if it hurts.

GOING PUBLIC

To promote their agendas and themselves, presidents have long used appeals to the public. The term *bully pulpit* comes from Theodore Roosevelt, president at the beginning of the twentieth century. Political scientist Sam Kernell coined the term *going public* for the strategy in its modern form. Going public consists, in Kernell's words, of "a class of activities that presidents engage in as they promote themselves and their policies before the American public," with the aim of enhancing their "chances of success in Washington."[15] Mike McCurry, President Clinton's press secretary, explained the rationale behind going public in 1997: "Campaigns are about framing choices for the American people. . . . When you are responsible for governing you have to use the same tools of public persuasion to advance your program, to build public support for the direction you are attempting to lead."[16] Interestingly, this comment was in response to reporters' questions about why Clinton continued to travel so much after having won reelection.

Sometimes the strategy is conceptualized as going over the heads of Congress directly to the American people in order to stimulate the public to pressure the Congress into supporting the president's initiatives. One can argue that Reagan did this successfully on his economic plan in 1981; he delivered three nationally televised speeches promoting his program, which resulted in a flood of constituent messages urging members of Congress to support the president's plan. Achieving this, however, is a highly ambitious goal that presidents can seldom hope to accomplish.[17] More frequently the president hopes not to bludgeon members of Congress into submission but to increase the saliency of an issue that benefits him and to frame the debate on the issue in such a way as to advantage his stance and so enhance his bargaining position.

Recent administrations have organized their communications operations in four White House units.[18] The Press Office handles daily press relations. The press secretary, who heads the office, briefs the White House press—approximately one hundred strong—twice daily. The Office of Communications is responsible for longer-range planning of communications strategy, including the events intended to convey the president's message. The Office of Media Affairs deals with the regional, local, and specialty (ethnic, for example) media. The Speechwriting unit prepares drafts of everything from the State of the Union address to casual presidential remarks. The Clinton White House employed thirty-nine people in these four units in 1998; the Bush White House had forty-three people in 2001.[19]

"A president can expect to answer the queries of reporters two or three times a week and to make public addresses and remarks, including a weekly radio address, on an average of more than once a day, six days a week," notes scholar Martha Kumar in summarizing her quantitative studies of recent presidential communications.[20] At least once a year with the State of the Union address, the president has the opportunity to speak to a large nationwide audience, and that speech is customarily used to unveil or sometimes to refocus attention on the president's agenda. However, given the political inattentiveness of the American public and the jealousy with which the TV networks guard their time, the vehicle presidents choose for going public is seldom the big prime time speech, and the audience they target is seldom the entire American public. Less grand speeches and other appearances targeted at carefully selected audiences are less costly in presidential resources. The increasing prominence of the cable networks since the mid-1990s has resulted in more television coverage of such events, though cable audiences tend to be small.

Presidents frequently choose to travel outside Washington for such appearances. "Beyond the beltway," a presidential visit is assured of ample local news coverage; local media are more likely to provide favorable coverage than are the national media;

the ideal audiences are often located outside the Capitol. In his first hundred days in office, President George W. Bush traveled to twenty-six states on twenty-four different days; he thus surpassed his nearest competitor Bill Clinton—who took domestic trips on twenty-two of his first hundred days, visiting fifteen states—and far surpassed his father, who visited fifteen states on as many days.[21] Carter and Reagan lag far behind, in the single digits.

Bush's travels were part of "a massive public relations campaign on behalf of his priority initiatives" that the administration launched upon entering the White House.[22] Each of the first four weeks was dedicated to one priority—the faith-based initiative, education, tax cuts, and defense. From the beginning and continuing throughout the Bush presidency, communications staff sent out talking points on a daily basis. Other White House staff, Republicans on Capitol Hill, and Republican opinion leaders in the Washington political and interest group community who receive the talking points were encouraged to carry the message in their contract with the media.

To pass its tax cut in 2003, the administration ran an extensive public relations campaign. In addition to Bush's own public advocacy through speeches and other appearances, cabinet officials were deployed around the country. During two weeks in mid-April, top officials appeared at eighty events in thirty states "from the Omaha Chamber of Commerce to the City Club of Cleveland."[23] As reported in the *Washington Post*, "Some of the appearances are to reward lawmakers who have stuck with Bush, others are to encourage those who might switch, and some are to punish those who appear determined to cut the size of his tax cut."[24] The *Post* story continues: "Commerce Secretary Donald L. Evans recorded customized state-by-state versions of the pitch that have been offered to 300 radio stations. The New Mexico version was translated into Navajo. Next week, he plans to phone into editorial board meetings to add heft to the in-person visits of Republican lawmakers."

Perhaps because of the intensely partisan environment and competition from the opposition party, the Bush Administration has pushed its PR tactics to the edge of legitimacy and perhaps beyond. The administration secretly paid several commentators to tout its "No Child Left Behind" education program—with government money. Tapes with stories that mimicked newscasts were sent to local TV stations; one of the stories purported to explain the Medicare/prescription drugs bill, but Democrats argued that it and the others were, in fact, propaganda.[25]

CHAPTER 8

FILIBUSTER STRATEGIES AND PR WARS

Strategic Responses to the Transformed Environment

THE CONGRESSIONAL PARTIES, I argue, have also reacted strategically to the transformed political environment; they have adjusted their behavior so as to try to take advantage of new opportunities the altered environment presents and so as to cope with problems it throws up. Strategic responses include a concerted effort by the congressional opposition party to compete with the president in agenda setting; more emphasis by the congressional parties on PR politics—that is, on attempts to influence the opinions of attentive publics and sometimes the broader public so as to advantage one's electoral and policy goals; and the use of Senate prerogatives by the minority party to try to seize floor agenda control from the majority, and their use by both the majority and minority, to make the Senate floor a forum for PR politics.

AGENDA SETTING

Americans expect their president to be the nation's premier agenda setter. Although the legislature and the executive are constitutionally separate, the president is expected to present Congress with a program, and Congress is expected to give the program priority consideration. That was not, however, always the expectation; it emerged from the presidency of Franklin Roosevelt. Since Roosevelt, the public and political elites alike have expected the president to be a policy leader and to play the central role in setting the congressional agenda. Television greatly accentuated the president's advantage over possible competitors in media access and thereby served to reinforce these expectations in the post–World War II period.

The initial development of this role conception took place during the 1930s and 1940s, a time when one party controlled both the presidency and Congress. After two decades of unified control (broken only by the 80th Congress, 1947–48), the 1954 elections brought in a Democratic Congress to serve with Republican President Dwight Eisenhower. Policy differences between moderate Democratic congressional majorities and the moderate Republican Eisenhower were not vast, however, and in the 1950s, most political actors considered divided control an anomaly.

By the 1980s, in contrast, divided control increasingly appeared to be the norm, and the parties had moved much further apart ideologically. As the seemingly permanent House majority party but seldom the presidential party, Democrats became more and more restive with presidential supremacy in agenda setting.[1] They fundamentally disagreed with Ronald Reagan's conservative agenda and realized that their only hope of competing with the president in agenda setting was through collective action.

The Development of Congressional Agenda Setting

House Democrats made some attempts to counter Ronald Reagan with their own agenda even during the first Congress of his presidency, when he was politically strongest.[2] In April 1981 Speaker O'Neill announced a Democratic economic program that had been drafted by a task force chaired by Dick Gephardt. During the first half of 1981, the political tide was running strongly in Reagan's favor, and this agenda setting attempt sank without a trace; it produced neither legislation nor good publicity. In 1982, however, House Democrats, aided by the developing recession, were a little more successful. A leadership-appointed task force chaired by Majority Leader Jim Wright drafted an economic program consisting mostly of various sorts of jobs programs, which did become an important part of the congressional agenda.

By the last Congress of Reagan's presidency, when conditions were much more favorable, the Democratic leadership was the single most prominent agenda setter. Speaker Jim Wright in 1987, at the beginning of the 100th Congress, proposed an agenda of issues broadly supported within the Democratic Party, such as clean water legislation, a highway bill, and aid to the homeless. He relentlessly kept the spotlight on those items and used leadership resources aggressively to facilitate their passage. By the end of the 100th Congress, all the items had become law and the Democratic Congress had gained considerable favorable publicity.

Thereafter Democrats expected their to leaders to engage in agenda-setting activities. When Speaker Tom Foley was less vigorous than Wright about doing so, members criticized him sharply. Yet Foley and his leadership team did engage in considerable agenda-setting activity. When Foley succeeded Wright in June 1989, he inherited an agenda consisting of minimum wage, child care, clean air, ethics reform, and campaign finance reform legislation—an agenda that, as Majority Leader, he had participated in formulating. Foley pursued that agenda, he gave added emphasis to a combined pay raise–ethics package, and he added medical and family leave legislation to the list of top priority items. The Democratic agenda that emerged early in the 102nd Congress encompassed energy policy, anti-recession programs including legislation promoting infrastructure renewal and unemployment insurance extension, health care reform, and again campaign finance reform and family leave legislation. In May 1991, the party leadership explicitly added a middle-class tax cut to the agenda.

The "Contract with America" is the best-known instance of congressional party agenda setting. Under Gingrich's leadership in 1994, House Republicans developed an ambitious legislative agenda that included big tax cuts, major changes in regulatory policy, welfare reform, a balanced budget constitutional amendment, the line-item veto, and term limits for members of Congress. When Republicans won control of the House in the 1994 elections, the Contract became their legislative agenda and they sought to pass every item. The House Republican leadership dominated the agenda in 1995 to nearly the same extent that presidents do at the beginning of their administrations and almost completely eclipsed the president.

The Contract was an innovation in that no congressional leader had previously made a policy agenda the centerpiece of a nationalized congressional campaign. Its mixed success has led the congressional parties to shy away from doing so in the same detailed, explicit fashion again—at least to date. However, the congressional parties now routinely develop agendas to guide legislative action, to enhance the credit their party can claim from legislative productivity, and to boost the party's image.

Constructing the Party Agenda

The process of constructing the party agendas is a participatory one, illustrating again the inclusive character of leadership in the contemporary Congress. Leaders gain allegiance through getting members involved in party tasks, not through giving orders from on high. The putting together of the Contract with America exemplifies the strategy.[3] In late 1993, Gingrich, who was then Republican whip, began to talk about constructing an agenda to use in the 1994 election campaign. At the House Republicans' annual retreat in February 1994, members held intensive discussions in small groups and took the first steps toward identifying the common principles and core beliefs that would guide the drafting of the Contract. Republican incumbents and challengers were surveyed about what should be included. When that had been decided, working groups of members and leadership staff put together the actual bills. Any member who wanted to could participate, but younger activists were more likely to do so than senior committee leaders. Still, a large number of members did have a hand in putting together the Contract and so felt some pride of authorship. "By the time things got to the conference, there was a great deal of buy-in already," reported Peter Hoekstra (R-Mich.), an activist member of the class of 1992. "The members involved in the drafting had a great sense of empowerment and that began to run through the conference."[4]

The party retreats held early each year are an important stage in the agenda-constructing process for all four party chamber groupings; members discuss issues, provide feedback, and refine proposals. The party leaders coordinate the process and influence it greatly, through their appointment powers but even more through their informal authority.

For the minority House Democrats, eighteen or so task forces set up under the auspices of the Caucus develop and draft policy proposals; any member who wants to can participate, and in recent years, well over half of the Democrats have signed up to do so.[5] From the mid-1990s through mid-2004, Democrats presented their agenda under the rubric "Families First." In late 2002, after the disappointing elections, House Democrats under their new Leader, Nancy Pelosi, drafted an economic recovery program that they unveiled on January 6, 2003, preempting the president and gaining considerable favorable press.

In 2004 Democrats discussed putting together their own version of a Contract. "It will be a clear message about where Democrats want to go, what we stand for and what we will do when we take back the House," one Democratic leadership aide explained. "It will be broad enough so that all Democrats can get behind it, but it will also show our differences from Republicans."[6] In September 2004, House Democrats gathered outside the Capitol and proclaimed their "New Partnership for

America's Future," a series of goals that include creating ten million new jobs, ensuring affordable health care for all Americans, stopping the spread of weapons of mass destruction, and providing strong national security.[7] In a December op-ed piece in *Roll Call*, Pelosi reiterated: "House Democrats are determined to strengthen the middle class that is the heart of our democracy, and in September we put that commitment in writing. Our plan, the New Partnership for America's Future, reaffirms the commitment of House Democrats to six core values for a strong and secure middle class: national security, prosperity, fairness, opportunity, community and accountability."[8]

Then in February 2005, Pelosi and other senior Democrats unveiled legislative proposals "to promote prosperity and job growth as part of the House Democrats' New Partnership for America's Future." Pelosi announced: "Today, House Democrats are putting forth specific steps to achieve a prosperity that includes all Americans in the economic success of our country. By creating millions of new jobs, spurring innovation, and investing in America, we will advance economic security for America's families."[9]

So long as Clinton was in the White House, majority House Republicans constructed specific agendas. The Policy Committee, especially through its subcommittees, and, of course, Republicans on the committees of jurisdiction were involved in the drafting of agenda items. In the 106th Congress (1999–2000), for example, House Republicans labeled their agenda "The Republican Common Sense Agenda," and Speaker J. Dennis Hastert reserved the first ten House bill numbers for the top Republican legislative priorities.

On the Senate side, the Policy Committees and the Party Conferences are involved. Senate Democrats put together a detailed agenda in every Congress; the Democratic Leader introduces the agenda early in the Congress. In the 108th Congress, the agenda included a prescription drugs bill, legislation expanding health care coverage, an education bill, and a minimum-wage increase. In the 109th Congress, S11 through S20 included bills that packaged a number of items under titles such as Standing with Our Troops (increasing troop strength by up to forty thousand by 2007; creating a Guard and Reserve Bill of Rights) and Expanding Economic Security (restoring overtime protection; increasing the minimum wage; creating jobs through the expansion of infrastructure programs).

Since the mid-1990s, Senate Republican Conference rules have specified that "the Conference shall adopt a 'Conference Legislative Agenda' for the coming Congress to outline the general legislative goals."[10] In the 106th Congress, when majority Republicans confronted a Democrat in the White House, Senate Republicans trumpeted an explicit agenda that they introduced as S1 to S5, as had become customary.

With Bush in the White House, congressional Republicans still develop agendas but they are somewhat more general, specifying aims rather than specific bills, and they track the president's program closely. The low-numbered bills are reserved for major presidential initiatives; in the 108th, HR1 and S1 were the Medicare/prescription drugs bills, and HR2 and S2 were the Jobs and Growth Act—that is, the tax cut. Early in the 109th, Senate Republicans introduced their agenda as S1 through S10, but a number were just placeholder bills. Thus S1 was entitled Social Security, but no text accompanied the title.

In agenda setting, the president still has a huge advantage. Both the American people's assumption that the president should dominate the process and his enormous advantage in media access work to the president's benefit. When the president's party controls Congress, the considerable ideological homogeneity of today's parties translates into quite high agreement by majority members of Congress with the presidential agenda. In fact, the president is likely to have borrowed quite a lot of it from them.

Even when the president faces a Congress controlled by the other party, his advantages of legitimacy and media access have to this point assured the president of agenda space.[11]

During the long period they controlled the Congress, Democratic party leaders strongly believed that Americans expected a new president to be given a chance and thought their party would be punished if they did not at least consider the president's program. Thus, even though he abhorred most of Reagan's program, Speaker Tip O'Neill in 1981 promised cooperation in assuring that the House considered it expeditiously. Congressional Democrats did not believe George H. W. Bush had any sort of mandate, but they still considered his admittedly meager program in 1989–90. (Whether the opposition party will give the presidential program as much deference the next time a president is elected with a Congress controlled by the opposition party is not clear.)

Nevertheless the president now faces organized competition for agenda control in a way that was not the case in the past. Especially if the opposition party controls one or both houses of Congress, and can thus attract considerable media attention as well as influence the legislative process, the president is in a trickier position than formerly. A cohesive congressional majority party with a clear agenda of its own can compel a president of the other party to deal with its issues; sometimes, when the public strongly supports its proposals, the party can even coerce the president into accepting legislation he dislikes. Thus, in the late 1980s and early 1990s, majority Democrats forced onto the agenda plant closing notification, a minimum-wage increase, and the reversing of the Grove City Supreme Court decision limiting civil rights law in education. Reagan reluctantly allowed plant closing notification legislation to become law without his signature; he vetoed the Grove City bill but was overridden. George H. W. Bush forced a scaling back of the Democrats' minimum-wage increase, but even there, Democrats believed they had won a PR victory. Majority Republicans repeatedly put tax cut legislation and bills outlawing "partial birth" abortion on President Bill Clinton's desk, forcing him into vetoes. On their third try, they got Clinton to accept a welfare reform bill that many of his core supporters strongly disliked.

PR POLITICS

The congressional parties now routinely use PR strategies to promote their agendas and themselves. The president no longer has the public arena to himself.

The Congressional Party Enters the PR Arena

Although certainly not the first president who regularly "went public," Ronald Reagan was a much more adept practitioner of the strategy than his immediate predecessors. Reagan skillfully used the strategy to promote a conservative agenda that most Democrats abhorred and to paint a highly negative image of the Democratic Party. Democrats saw Reagan endangering both their policy and their electoral goals and realized that competing with a media-savvy president as individuals was a losing strategy. They turned to their party leadership.

Congressional leaders have always had contact with the press and undoubtedly have always attempted to use those interactions to burnish their party's image. Thus Sam Rayburn as Speaker in the 1950s briefly answered questions from Capitol Hill reporters daily before House sessions. These Speaker's press conferences continued under Rayburn's successors as low-key affairs, focusing quite narrowly on the work of Congress.

When Reagan defeated Carter in the 1980 elections and the Republicans won control of the Senate, Speaker Tip O'Neill became the nation's highest-ranking Democrat, and the press came to him to speak for his party. The dramatic character of the battles of Reagan's first year as well as Republicans' attempts to make O'Neill the symbol of the Democratic Party ("big, fat, and out of control—just like the federal government") increased O'Neill's visibility and his media access. He received a great deal more attention on the nightly television news than his predecessors had, with more than a hundred appearances per Congress in the 1981–86 period.[12]

Given the political pressure they were under, House Democrats demanded that O'Neill use his high visibility spokesman role to defend them and their party. O'Neill significantly enhanced his media operation; when his highest-ranked leadership staffer retired, O'Neill replaced him with the media-savvy Chris Matthews; O'Neill began to appear on the television interview shows.[13] Since that time, all the top party leaders have perceived media relations as a key part of their job and have equipped themselves with multiple press aides.[14]

Since the early 1980s, congressional leaders' media access has varied with political circumstances. During the first half of 1995, Newt Gingrich and the House Republicans were *the* political story, and Gingrich had almost limitless media access. Gingrich appeared on the national evening TV newscasts almost three hundred times during the 104th Congress and made numerous appearances on the Sunday interview programs.[15] When the House completed action on the Contract with America, Gingrich asked for and was granted national television time to talk to the American people, an event unprecedented for a legislative leader. In contrast, the leaders of the minority party have to struggle to get any press attention. Still the congressional party leaders have continued to be seen as public spokespersons for their parties in a way that was not the case before O'Neill. In 2001, Democratic Senate Leader Tom Daschle and Republican Senate Leader Trent Lott appeared more frequently on the Sunday talk shows than any senator other than John McCain; the only House member of the sixteen most frequent congressional guests was Democratic Leader Dick Gephardt.[16]

Party Leaders and PR Politics

Members of Congress, then, have come to expect their party leaders to participate effectively in national political discourse, influencing the terms of the debate so as to further their members' immediate legislative goals and to protect and enhance the party's image. Even senators, who have considerably more media access as individuals than House members do, put a premium on their leaders' abilities as public spokespersons. Democrats' choice of George Mitchell as their leader in the late 1980s was widely interpreted as reflecting their desire to have a more effective public spokesman. When Senate Republicans selected a new leader in 2003, Bill Frist's presumed media skills were a major consideration. And early criticism of his performance focused on his not being an aggressive enough spokesman. "What we're looking for in the majority leader's position is a Republican Tom Daschle," a Republican explained. "Someone who will steer the debate in the direction we want it to go."[17]

The leaders have equipped themselves with resources to take on the task. All the leaders now employ multiple press aides—communications directors as well as press secretaries—and these are considered among the most important of a leader's hires. When Nancy Pelosi was elected Democratic House Leader, she called on several former Clinton press secretaries for advice about staffing her press operation, particularly about finding a senior communications strategist to "put together a communications plan and make it work," a plan that involved "reaching out to voters beyond the Beltway."[18] When she was campaigning for Leader, Pelosi made a promise to her Democratic colleagues: "I told them never again will Democrats go into a campaign where we don't have a message as to who we are and what we stand for, . . . and how we differ from Republicans. They liked that, and it's what I believe," she said. "So, we will have a national message."[19]

Much message activity is simply a part of leaders' routines, and their hope is to affect press coverage and thus opinion at the margins. Leaders regularly speak to reporters, often on a daily basis. Senate Majority Leader Frist, for example, meets with reporters in the Senate chamber before each day's session. House Democratic Leader Nancy Pelosi and Democratic Whip Steny Hoyer each hold weekly press briefings. Even House Majority Leader Tom DeLay, not known for his media-friendly style, has instituted a weekly House floor speech "in an attempt to set the tone on a newsworthy issue or provide the proscribed leadership perspective before a major vote."[20]

Some of party leaders' media efforts are aimed at "putting out fires." For example, when the chair of President Bush's Council of Economic Advisers called the transfer of U.S. service jobs overseas "just a new way to do international trade," Speaker Hastert responded immediately. "I understand that Mr. Mankiw is a brilliant economic theorist, but his theory fails a basic test of real economics," Hastert said. "We can't have a healthy economy unless we have more jobs here in America."[21] Considering the media attention the Mankiw statement was getting, damage control was essential; Hastert made it clear that House Republicans did not agree. Of course, sometimes the leaders themselves make mistakes. Deborah Pryce, Republican Conference chair, was livid when she learned that the congressional delegation in attendance when the president signed the partial birth abortion bill did not include one woman. The picture in the media of an all-male delegation did not convey the right message, she believed.

The party that controls the White House can count on the president, as their key spokesperson, to have ready access to the media. The party without the president has a harder time breaking through. Well-timed major speeches, especially if they criticize the president, may get significant news coverage by the national and Washington newspapers. Senate Democratic Leader Tom Daschle in early 2002 and 2003 delivered speeches excoriating Bush for his handling of the economy and laying out a Democratic alternative. In 2003, the day before the State of the Union address, Daschle and new House Democratic Leader Nancy Pelosi made a joint appearance at the National Press Club and laid out their claim of a credibility gap between Bush's words and his actions on dozens of domestic issues, a theme Democrats continued to emphasize.[22] Daschle and Pelosi again preempted the State of the Union address in 2004 with a speech critical of Bush's handling of domestic and foreign policy, especially Iraq.[23] Pelosi and new Senate Democratic Leader Harry Reid joined forces in early 2005 to deliver a "prebuttal" to Bush's State of the Union address, criticizing Bush on Social Security, Iraq, and the deficit. These speeches receive considerable coverage in newspapers like the *New York Times* and the *Washington Post* but much less attention on television news.

Nancy Pelosi has taken to coining alliterative slogans to make House Democrats' points more memorable and attractive to the media.[24] The Democrats' economic stimulus is "fair, fast-acting and fiscally sound"; the Republicans have abused their power through "removal, redistricting, recount and recall." "She wants it to be memorable for Members and the press so they know specifically what we stand for," an aide explained.

Leaders often combine their fund-raising outside Washington with message activities. In mid-2002, for example, Democratic House Leader Dick Gephardt coupled a Democratic Congressional Campaign Committee fund-raiser in Houston with a town hall meeting for former Enron employees on pension protection legislation.[25]

Both parties use polls and focus groups to test their messages. Before naming the items in their Contract with America, House Republicans had pollster Frank Lutz test the language used to name the bills; welfare reform became the "Personal Responsibility Act," and a cut in the capital gains tax and changes in the regulatory process aimed especially at weakening environmental regulations made up most of the "Job Creation and Wage Enhancement Act." Lutz continues to advise Hill Republicans, frequently reminding them of the importance of their choice of words. Democrats too have hired consultants to try out messages in focus groups.[26] Polling by congressional party entities has become commonplace. Reporting to his members on the results of a commissioned poll in the summer of 2003, Republican Conference Chair Rick Santorum wrote: "Our message has not been as favorably received as in the previous months, largely because we have become bogged down in day-to-day inside-the-Beltway issues. We have to keep our eyes on the broader message."[27] To bring that about, Republican leaders designated a different theme for each week during the August recess.

After their disappointing showing in the 2004 elections, House and Senate Democrats joined forces and "launched a major internal effort to craft a new party brand that will help them better connect with the electorate."[28] Reid and Pelosi, along with Senate Policy Committee Chair Byron Dorgan and House Steering Committee Chair George Miller, consulted experts to help them package the party's message more effectively. "These days it is not just about where you stand but it is also the words you use to describe where you stand and the impact those words have on people. Frankly, I think we have got some catching up to do in language," explained Dorgan. "We've got to get out there and frame the debate, and show that this is what Democrats stand for," a senior Democratic staffer added.

Sophisticated websites that carry the party message are now ubiquitous. The House Republican Conference maintains GOP.gov. House Democrats have HouseDemocrats.gov and their Senate counterparts are Republican.Senate.gov and Democrats.Senate.gov.

In addition to issue information, the sites guide the user to other party and leadership sites as well as to member sites. They allow visitors to sign up for e-mail messages that will update them on issues and politics—from the sponsoring party's point of view, of course.

Participation and PR Politics

Constructing and disseminating the party message are not tasks for the leaders alone. As in most congressional party endeavors, inclusion is both necessary and desired. Members want to participate and leaders need members' help. "We need to empower Republicans to sell the Republican message," said DeLay's spokesperson, explaining DeLay's decision to deliver a speech of the week. "In order for us to do that, you have to be part of the team. You have to get out there and have press conferences and go out there and sell the message."[29]

House Republicans particularly were chastened by Gingrich's fate as a media personality. Eager to play the role of national Republican spokesman, Gingrich welcomed the enormous media attention that accompanied the 1994 Republican triumph. He even allowed the Speaker's press conference, traditionally a pencil and paper affair, to be televised. He soon found, however, that he could not control the agenda and that reporters were using their access to question him about his ethics problems. By the end of the 104th Congress, Gingrich had become a symbol of the far-right "take no prisoners, make no compromises" House Republicans and was deeply unpopular. Even had they been otherwise inclined, Hastert, Armey, and DeLay realized that a lower profile was likely a matter of survival. However, efforts by all four party groupings to include members in spreading the party message long predate the Gingrich debacle.

In both chambers, task forces of various levels of permanence involve members in message activities. Under Gephardt, House

Democrats had a Message Group consisting of party leaders and particularly media-savvy members who met daily to agree upon a message of the day; a larger group of members was charged with disseminating the message, especially through the one-minute speeches that begin the legislative day in the House. Currently the Caucus task forces play an important role in publicly promoting the policy proposals they have developed. The House Republican "Theme Team" is charged with organizing and delivering the one-minute speeches; made up of about fifty members, the team is responsible for "communicating the majority party's legislative issues, plans and ideas . . . during speeches given on the House floor."[30] The one-minute speeches sometimes take on the character of set-piece battles with waves of well-trained troops from the two parties waging an often bitter rhetorical fight.

In 2003, when she became House Republican Conference Chair, Deborah Pryce created a "Message Action Team" of thirty members of varying seniority and expertise. "It's sort of an inner circle of people that are willing to meet and talk about the message and help develop it and deliver it," Pryce explained. "These are people who are good on camera and good on their feet."[31] In May 2004, the House Republican leadership assigned the task of running the special orders, the often lengthy floor speeches at the end of the day, to the committee chairs. The aim was to assure that the speeches would have coherence and thus do a better job of conveying the Republican message.[32]

Senate Democrats have worked through five message teams, each to deal with a specific issue.[33] Under the auspices of the Policy Committee, Senate Democrats hold hearings to get their message out. The hearings mimic the official Senate hearings that Democrats, in the minority again during the 108th Congress, could no longer call; thus they include experts and interest group representatives as well as senators. The sixteen hearings held during 2003 and 2004 ranged in subject matter from Bush's budget request to contract abuse in Iraq, the administration's overtime rules, and China's labor practices.[34] At the beginning of the 109th Congress, the Democratic Policy Committee explicitly focused its hearings on oversight of the administration. "The fact is, with one-party rule—the presidency and the House and Senate—there is no oversight on anything," explained Policy Committee Chair Byron Dorgan (N.D.). "The oversight function . . . is nonexistent."[35] The first hearings, in January and February 2005, on "the Bush Administration's plans to privatize Social Security" and on "waste, fraud and abuse in U.S. government contracting in Iraq" received considerable press attention.

Senate Republicans also use task forces to get senators with an interest in and expertise on a particular issue involved in honing and conveying the party message. In March 2004, Conference chair Rick Santorum (Pa.), Republican Conference vice chair Kay Bailey Hutchison (Tex.), and Republican Policy Committee chair Jon Kyl (Ariz.) distributed a memo at the Tuesday Republican policy lunch laying out an initiative calling for a renewed focus on six issues: the war on terror, jobs and the economy, health care, education, retirement security, and marriage. GOP leaders were concerned that Democrats had used the floor more effectively than they had in recent months to advance their agenda, according to participants. "Democrats are using all of the time they can to try and score political points," Kyl said. "We should not cede the floor to them." The memo proposed expanding and energizing six existing working groups charged with conveying the Republican position on these issues.[36] Republican senators were also told that the Policy Committee would be making additional research material on the issues available to them. "The purpose of this proactive effort," the memo stated, "is to provide Republican Senators with enhanced resources to more effectively communicate our message to the public and the media."[37]

Message-related debates and activities are always a major agenda item at the party groups' retreats. What the message should be, how to frame it most appealingly, and how to disseminate it effectively are the themes preoccupying members and leaders. The party that lost ground in the last election feels the most pressure to address such questions. "I believe that in the last election Americans voted out of fear on security and whether individual candidates shared their values," said Democratic Caucus chair Bob Menendez (N.J.), discussing the agenda for the 2005 House Democrats' retreat. Democrats needed to find ways "to reframe the issues in a way that meets [Americans'] values, and strikes a responsive chord with the electorate," he added.[38] High attendance at the retreat indicated that members agreed with their leaders and wanted to participate in the enterprise. House Republicans focused their 2005 retreat on Social Security and how to sell the president's program. As the *Washington Post* reported, "The congressional Republicans' confidential plan was developed with the advice of pollsters, marketing experts and communication consultants. . . . The blueprint urges lawmakers to promote the 'personalization' of Social Security, suggesting ownership and control, rather than 'privatization,' which 'connotes the total corporate takeover of Social Security.'" The plan "urges the GOP to 'talk in simple language,' 'keep the numbers small,' 'avoid percentages; your audience will try to calculate them in their head' and 'acknowledge risks,' because listeners 'know they can lose their investments.'"[39]

Over the course of the 1980s and 1990s a number of party entities—especially the Caucus/Conferences and the policy committees—greatly enhanced their ability to help members take part in the enterprise of communicating the party message. These party organs engage in extensive press contacts, sending out press releases, talking to reporters, holding press conferences. They also produce a great deal of information—everything from "the message of the day" to fat issue briefs—for dissemination to their membership. The Senate Democratic Policy Committee, for example, describes its mission as being "the research arm of

Senate Democrats. . . . The DPC serves as a centralized source of information for all Senate Democratic offices and helps promote Democratic policies through hearings, special events, publications and graphic services."[40] The House Democratic Caucus series "On the Issues" consists of a compact statement on each of the major issues on the House Democratic agenda; each generally begins with a critique of President Bush's performance on the issue. On Jobs and the Economy, Democrats argued that Bush had "the worst economic record in 40 years" and provided supporting data—and then proceeded to lay out the Democrats' proposals and to report the status of Democratic bills. The Republican House Policy Committee produces "Policy Perspectives" and "Special Reports," which do much the same thing from a Republican viewpoint as do the Senate Republican Policy Committee's Policy Papers.

The information these party organs disseminate to their members constitutes a service to them and is also an attempt to nudge them into "singing from the same hymn book." The message of the day is often prominently displayed, and the arguments most favorable to the party's position are emphasized, frequently in the form of talking points; the hope is that members will use these messages in their contacts with their local media. The talking points are usually short, pithy, and easy to remember and understand. The Republican talking points on the Iraq prison abuse scandal in May 2004 illustrate their character—and, in this case, the difference between the Republican parties in the two chambers. Senate Republicans were advised to say: "The actions of the soldiers in the photographs depicting detainee abuse are totally unacceptable and violate the law. They betrayed their comrades, who serve honorably every day, and they damaged the cause for which brave men and women are fighting and dying." House Republicans were told: "For every additional released picture of prisoner abuse, we should release pictures of Saddam's mass graves; pictures of children executed during Saddam's brutal dictatorship; pictures of the four Americans in Baghdad burned, mutilated and dismembered in public."[41]

Both parties in both chambers have developed the technological infrastructure to help their members communicate. The Senate Democratic Technology and Communications Committee, established by Daschle when he first became Leader, was instrumental in developing the Democrats' electronic communication operation. It was charged with coordinating "television, radio and Internet strategy for the Senate Democratic Caucus."[42] Although they were slower than Republicans in developing such capacities, Democrats now have a state-of-the-art television and radio studio that senators can use, with extensive video editing capabilities and facilities for satellite hookups with local television stations. Staff help senators organize media events by doing everything from contacting reporters and selling them the story to reserving the room.[43] The Senate Republican Conference provides similar services for its members. By helping their members communicate efficiently through the media, leaders hope to enhance those members' reelection prospects directly and to get their members' aid in promoting the party message, with the expectation that this will help all the members of the party.

Recess packets and other printed materials intended to make it as easy as possible for members to disseminate the party message when they are home in their districts have been a staple for several decades at least. To aid members to communicate to their constituents their party's accomplishments and the other's failures, the parties produce lists printed on cards sized to fit in the inside-suit pocket—and presumably a purse as well—and back these up with extensive documentation. The level of coordination and sophistication involved has risen sharply in recent years. For example, before the Memorial Day recess in 2002, in addition to the usual printed list of accomplishments with the usually backup issue briefs, House Republican leaders gave their members a video to explain the party position on legislation creating a prescription drugs benefit.[44] More significant than the use of such technology, however, is the extent of coordination across districts. The party now regularly decides on an issue emphasis, a theme, and a message that members are asked to convey to their constituents. Thus at least seventy-five House Democrats held town hall meetings criticizing House Republicans' Medicare/prescription drugs bill in mid-July 2003. "Democratic members are taking the prescription drug issue straight to seniors to explain what Democrats are fighting for, and the irresponsible plan that Republicans are trying to push through Congress," explained a spokeswoman for House minority whip Steny Hoyer (D-Md.).[45] "House lawmakers from both sides of the aisle headed back to their districts Friday with instructions to focus on Medicare and economic issues," *Roll Call* reported on April 5, 2004. Republicans, who had already held over 150 local educational workshops for their constituents on the Medicare bill, planned to hold more. In addition, to emphasize the party's record of tax cuts, Republicans planned to stage district events leading up to April 15. Democrats would focus on "the real needs of our seniors, veterans and minority communities," according to their recess packet.

Coordinating Washington and district activities around a particular theme has also become commonplace. In an attempt to shore up the GOP's image on education, House Republican leaders in 2002 instructed committee and subcommittee chairs to hold hearings dedicated to publicizing education initiatives and accomplishments. They also put out a memo entitled "Weekly Education District Action Items," providing their members with a variety of suggested activities: visit a class room once a week; read a story to elementary school students; give a civic lecture to older students; hold a meeting for parents and teachers, preferably in the school gym, to discuss education; present flags flown over the Capitol to schools for special events.[46] In late 2003, House and Senate Democrats coordinated on "Operation Home Front," a four-week offensive to highlight Republican failures on key domestic issues. One focus of the campaign was in Washington with leadership press events and floor speeches; the other prong was getting members to hold issue-based events in the districts.[47] In the spring of 2004, Democrats again put together a similar "message blitz," the theme being "Are you better off than you were four years ago?"[48] About the same time, House Republican Conference Chair Deborah Pryce advised her members to focus on the "human face of economic growth," the "selfless face of the war for freedom in Iraq," and "the compassionate face of the new Medicare law."[49] She further urged: "Take advantage of the local coverage in your area, and beat back the despair, disillusionment, disappointment and doubt so often peddled by the media elite."[50]

In response to Bush's proposal to restructure Social Security, the congressional parties mobilized in Washington and in the country. Immediately after officially proposing such restructuring in his State of the Union address, Bush himself undertook trips around the country to sell to the public the need for change. He concentrated especially on "red" states represented by Democratic senators. Buoyed by polling that showed public trepidation about partial privatization, Democrats went on the offensive. By late January, House Democratic leaders were already urging their members to hold district forums, send out a newsletter, and meet with their local press on the issue.[51] Social Security information packets that included talking points, sample editorials, and other materials on the topic were prepared and distributed to members. Democrats planned events at senior centers and at one hundred of the country's largest college campuses. Senate Democratic leaders unveiled a Social Security calculator on their website that "demonstrates to Americans what they could lose under the Bush Privatization Plan." Senator Reid declared: "As Democrats, we have been saying for weeks that we are concerned that the president's privatization plan will cut benefits. Now all Americans can log onto our website and find out how true this is."[52] Democrats targeted two Republican leaders up for reelection in 2006 by holding campaign-style rallies in opposition to Bush's plan in their states. Altogether Democrats held 235 town hall meetings during the 2005 President's Day recess.[53]

Republican congressional leaders armed their members with briefing books, videotapes, and PowerPoint presentations making Bush's case on Social Security. The White House sent top officials to Capitol Hill for a clinic to answer questions before members headed home for the recess.[54] At the final Conference meeting before the recess, Speaker Hastert urged all House Republicans to hold town hall meetings on Social Security. Senate Republicans were joined at their weekly lunch meeting by Vice President Dick Cheney and Republican National Committee chair Ken Mehlman, who showed a four-minute video of Bush describing his Social Security plan. The video was distributed to all House and Senate Republicans for them to show to their constituents. Because of constituents' concerns about the Bush proposal, not all congressional Republicans were willing to tout the plan. "The situation is fluid, but it has the potential to blow up," said Virginia Republican Thomas M. Davis. "I'm going to keep my mouth shut." Yet many Republicans believed they could sell the plan, and as part of "a coordinated political effort that involves the White House, the Republican National Committee and outside business groups, as well as congressional leaders," they were determined to do so.[55]

To garner press attention, both parties sometimes orchestrate media events to dramatize their message. In the late 1980s, House Democrats held "The Grate American Sleep Out," in which a number of members of Congress, including Whip Tony Coehlo joined the homeless to sleep outside—on a grate—to publicize their bill to aid the homeless. Democrats also staged a series of events around the issue of plant closing notification; because they would make good copy, sympathetic victims of sudden plant closures were prominently featured. Senate Republicans in 2002 brought a team of bloodhounds to Capitol Hill to dramatize their claim that majority Senate Democrats were nowhere to be found when it came to doing the nation's business. Earlier in the year, Daschle had had a load of mattresses delivered to the Senate side of the Capitol to symbolize his resolve to pass campaign finance reform legislation. If opponents tried to hold up final action on the legislation, all-night sessions would be held.

Floor agenda control provides majorities with strategic options for getting out their message. In the spring and summer of 2004, House Republicans used their floor control to implement a strategy aimed at several problems they faced. Democrats, they feared, were making headway with their criticisms of Republican economic policy; much of the legislation House Republicans had passed was stymied in the Senate, and the issue message that the legislation was intended to convey had dissipated. The House's light schedule was also coming under attack—the "drive-by Congress," Democratic Leader Nancy Pelosi was labeling the House for its two- and three-days-a-week schedule. Republicans decided to repass in slightly altered form bills that the House had previously passed, to bring them up in thematic clusters, and to package them into bigger bills. "We won't just be blunting the [Democratic] criticism. . . . We'll be establishing our command of these topics," an aide to Majority Leader Tom DeLay explained. "It's about reminding people we're on top of this."[56]

Thus one week was devoted to energy legislation, another to cutting bureaucratic red tape, still another to curbing litigation. Republicans argued that all these bills would create jobs and stimulate the economy. During the week focused on job training and retraining, two bills aimed at increasing the number of highly qualified teachers and one on creating "personal re-employment accounts," all of which had been considered before, were passed and then, in Republican staffers' terminology, "MIRVed," or bundled into a single bill. By writing a highly restrictive rule, Republicans prevented Democrats from offering an amendment extending unemployment insurance and thereby muddying the Republican message. Although obviously aimed primarily at sending a message, the strategy did result in considerable publicity for the Republican effort.[57] Senate Majority Leaders have much less total floor control but they can force issues to the floor and thus highlight them. Thus, Majority Leader Bill Frist brought a constitutional amendment barring gay marriage to the Senate floor shortly before the Democratic presidential nominating convention in 2004. He knew he was not even close to the two-thirds vote needed to approve a constitutional amendment; however, forcing consideration showed the GOP base that the Senate was dealing with an issue they cared about and might embarrass Democrats from culturally conservative states.

Congressional minority parties, especially House minority parties, lack the procedural tools the majority commands. In the 1980s and early 1990s, the Republican House minority used the special order speeches at the end of the day to communicate their message to the small but politically active C-SPAN audience. Both parties use special orders and the one-minute speeches that start the legislative day to the same purpose. Forcing majority party members to go on the record on hard issues has been a favorite minority party strategy since the reforms of the 1970s that allowed recorded votes in the Committee of the Whole, and even restrictive rules cannot completely thwart the strategy. Appropriations bill are by long-standing custom considered under open rules and provide an attractive target. In

October 2003, for example, Democrats proposed an amendment to the Iraq supplemental appropriations bill that would have made half the reconstruction aid a loan instead. Bush's request for an additional $87 billion for Iraq was unpopular and, to many citizens, providing reconstruction help to the oil-rich nation in the form of loans seemed only fair. Republicans supported Bush, who adamantly opposed loans, and defeated the amendment but were far from happy to have to go on the record on a vote so difficult to explain to their constituents.

The Democratic minority has become increasingly innovative and aggressive in using the minority's limited procedural arsenal. Motions to instruct conferees are nonbinding, but when forced to a recorded vote, which requires a request by only twenty-five members, they can put members on the spot on difficult issues. Democrats have repeatedly used the motion to instruct on such issues and have won in several instances. In mid-2003, for example, a motion to instruct the conferees to accept the Senate provisions on extending the expanded child tax credit to low-income families passed. Democrats, in fact, forced eighteen recorded votes on motions to instruct on that issue in the 108th Congress. In 2003 and again in 2004, Democrats prevailed on a motion to instruct concerning overturning the Bush Administration's overtime rules changes.

Another weapon Democrats have employed is the discharge petition, a procedure for getting a measure onto the House floor over the opposition of the majority party leadership. The signatures of a majority of the House membership—218—are required for a successful discharge, and the majority party considers signing a discharge petition a grave offense against the party and its leadership. Thus discharge petitions are almost never successful—the petition on campaign finance reform legislation in 2002 being the major recent exception. Yet, because discharge petitions are public, they too can be used to put pressure on members of the opposition party, and Democrats have made considerable use of them.

During the 108th Congress, Democrats filed sixteen discharge petitions on issues such as the AMBER alert, veterans' benefits, extending unemployment insurance, and prescription drug benefits. In at least half of these cases, most Democrats signed the petition.[58] In June 2003, Democrats defeated two bills brought up under suspension—which require a two-thirds vote—to protest inaction on their legislation on child tax credits for low-income families.[59] In July they continued their protest by calling repeated procedural votes. For example, they offered a motion to adjourn during debate on a rule for two trade bills.[60] The majority can easily defeat such motions, yet that takes time and complicates life for majority party leaders and members. If the minority's tactics succeed in generating media coverage, the consequences can be more unpleasant. Certainly House Republicans suffered considerable bad publicity on the low-income child credit issue. House Democrats also argue that by PR pressure they forced Republicans in May 2003 to bring up a bill extending unemployment insurance—although one the Democrats believed inadequate; Republicans, of course, claimed otherwise.[61]

The House minority can annoy and sometimes embarrass the House majority, but it can seldom prevail on legislation. And because House minorities have so little legislative clout within the chamber, they often have great difficulty attracting media attention. Newt Gingrich's inflammatory message of a corrupt, bungling, out-of-touch Democratic majority was sufficiently attractive to the media that he managed to break through in the 1980s and early 1990s. He was greatly aided by the explosive growth of talk radio in the 1980s and especially by the rise of Rush Limbaugh, who picked up Gingrich's message and spread it far more widely than any member of Congress could.[62] Movement conservatives in Congress soon found talk radio to be a forum tailor-made for their brand of politics. Under Tom DeLay the Republican Steering Committee, a group of ultraconservative members, systematically cultivated talk show hosts, regularly sending them "issue briefs listing GOP talking points on current issues and offering half a dozen House Republican legislators as guests."[63] House Republicans have maintained and elaborated the practice over their years in the majority. They have also extended it to placing members on cable TV talk shows. After they lost their majority, House Democrats realized how far behind the Republicans they were in this arena and have attempted to imitate them. When she served as assistant to the Democratic Leader, Rosa DeLauro headed the Democratic booking effort. After Pelosi replaced Gephardt, her office took over the task and now broadly coordinates the effort, while Caucus staff do much of the detailed work.[64] Democrats, however, are hampered by their lack of the inflammatory kind of message on which talk radio especially feeds.

The minority party's difficulty in breaking through to the public at large often leads to frustration. In an unusually public display of that frustration, Democratic House Whip Steny Hoyer blasted reporters for their failure even to mention Democratic alternatives. "It's one thing for the Republican leadership to marginalize" Democrats by not allowing their bills and alternatives to come to the floor, "but it's another if the press doesn't cover our alternative," Hoyer said. "We represent 140 million people," almost half the nation's population, he added.[65] Even the Senate minority party with its much greater procedural prerogatives and its members' greater visibility must often battle to be heard. After losing control of the Senate in the 2002 elections, Majority Leader Tom Daschle asked Hillary Clinton to chair the party's Steering and Coordination Committee. "We need more ammo . . . more firepower and a better system of delivery," a top Democratic source said. "Hillary is a strong catalyst for that."[66] When Reid became Leader, he too sought to enhance Senate Democrats' message operation, establishing a new Communications Center (aka "war room") "to serve as a rapid-response operation designed to counter the Republican message."[67]

FILIBUSTER AND AMENDMENT STRATEGIES IN PR POLITICS

Senate rules give minorities enormous advantages that House minorities lack. In chapter 6 I showed how the number of filibusters, which are, of course, used by minorities, shot up from the 1960s on. As the parties polarized, the minority using filibusters and other permissive Senate rules was most often the minority party. By the 1990s and early 2000s, about half of major legislation encountered a filibuster-related problem in the Senate. Passing anything controversial has come to require sixty votes.

The minority party not only uses the Senate's permissive rules to kill legislation and nominations that it strongly opposes and to extract concessions but also to try to seize agenda control from the majority—to get its issues to the floor, and sometimes even to pass its legislation over the majority's opposition.

Democrats as the minority party after 1994 refined the strategy of combining procedural prerogatives with a PR campaign to seize agenda control from the majority. The lack of a germaneness requirement for amendments to most bills severely weakens the Majority Leader's ability to control the floor agenda. If the Leader refuses to bring a bill to the floor, the bill's supporters can offer it as an amendment to most legislation the Leader does bring to the floor. The Majority Leader can make a motion to table the amendment, which is nondebatable. But this does require his members to vote on the issue, albeit in a procedural guise, and the Leader may want to avoid that. Often the issues on which the minority party uses the strategy are "damned if you do and damned if you don't" issues for at least some majority party members: issues on which their notions of good public policy conflict with the dictates of pleasing constituents. Furthermore, even after the minority's amendment has been tabled, the minority can continue to offer other amendments, including even individual parts of the original amendment, and can block a vote on the underlying bill the Majority Leader wants to pass. The Leader can file a cloture petition and try to shut off debate, but he needs sixty votes to do so. The minority party can use this tactic to bring its agenda to the floor and, if the effort is accompanied by a successful PR campaign, can gain favorable publicity and can sometimes pressure enough majority party members into supporting the bill to pass it.

The model of this partisan strategy at its most effective is the Democrats' successful drive to raise the minimum wage in 1996. After their enormous electoral victory in 1994, congressional Republicans totally dominated agenda setting. President Clinton advocated raising the minimum wage in his 1996 State of the Union address; but despite the proposal's popularity with the American public, strong Republican opposition was expected to assure that the proposal would be "dead on arrival" in Congress. House Majority Leader Dick Armey declared that a minimum-wage increase would pass over his dead body. Majority Republicans would not even allow consideration of the legislation—which was easy to do in the House but not so easy in the Senate.

To force the issue onto the agenda, Senate Democrats decided to offer the minimum-wage increase as an amendment to every piece of legislation the Majority Leader brought to the floor. Lacking the votes to kill the minimum wage or to impose cloture on legislation he did want to pass, Majority Leader Dole was forced to pull bill after bill off the floor, prompting news stories of Senate gridlock. House and Senate Democrats, the White House, and organized labor all worked to keep the issue in the news and to put pressure on moderate Republicans. That Dole was running for president and attempting to use his "can-do" reputation in the Senate to that end certainly helped ensure plenty of media attention. Public approval of a minimum-wage increase went up to 85 percent. With an election approaching, Senate and House Republicans capitulated, and both chambers passed legislation raising the minimum wage.

The combination of an elaborate and sophisticated public relations campaign and a carefully planned and orchestrated procedural strategy now characterizes such minority party efforts. Ideally the minority party would like to enact legislation and garner credit with the public for having done so. However, since it is the minority in an increasingly polarized legislature, actually passing legislation is often an unrealistic goal. If the PR campaign is successful, the minority party will at least have increased the visibility of an issue that benefits it, reinforced the party's identification with the popular issue, and made the majority party pay a price in bad publicity for blocking the legislation. Democratic efforts on tobacco regulation, managed care reform, gun control, and campaign finance reform in the late 1990s did not produce legislation, but they did take a toll on the Republican Party's image.

In 2001, campaign finance legislation did pass the Senate—and this was *before* the Democrats took control of the chamber. Republican John McCain and the Democrats had threatened to use the add-it-as-an-amendment-to-everything strategy, which would have wreaked havoc with the consideration of Bush's program. Campaign finance reform is an issue the media love, and they adore McCain because he makes such good copy; Lott knew that the cost of trying to stop campaign finance reform from being considered would include terrible publicity. So the Senate Republican leadership capitulated. (This case again shows that the Senate is still a superb platform for the maverick. Despite the partisan polarization, a senator like McCain can cross his party for fun and profit in the form of lots of publicity. And there is really nothing his party leader can do to him—especially when the margins are so narrow.)

When Republican conferees on Bush's 2003 tax cut bill dropped a Senate provision to extend the child tax credit to low-income families, they handed congressional Democrats a dream issue from a PR standpoint. Democrats, who had been the primary supporters of the provision and had been excluded from the conference, attacked Republicans for choosing the rich over poor children. They mobilized friendly advocacy groups such as the Children's Defense Fund and held a string of news conferences.[68] "How the administration and the House and Senate conferees reached their conclusion that eliminating 12 million children was good for American families, their children and our overall economy defies logic," Senator Hillary Clinton said.[69] The media found it an attractive story and carried the Democrats' message. After two weeks of unrelentingly negative publicity, the Senate capitulated. Knowing they could not prevent a vote in any case, Senate Republicans themselves offered the provision—combined with another that also increased the credit for high-income families. It passed on a 94–2 vote. *New York Times* reporter David Firestone described the scene: "The 47 Republican senators who voted on Thursday to increase the child tax credit for 6.5 million low-income families were not, for the most part, a happy band. . . . Trent Lott of Mississippi made a gagging sound as he joined 93 other senators in voting aye. Republicans made little effort to disguise the fact that they had essentially been dragged into the vote by two weeks of bad publicity and unending Democratic accusations that President Bush's new tax bill was heartless for denying the families the credit."[70]

Although President Bush called on the House to follow suit quickly, House Republican leaders had other ideas. How the drama played out is illustrative of the differences between the chambers. Representing more homogeneous—and homogeneously conservative—constituencies, most House Republicans did not feel the same pressure to get the issue off the front page that senators and the president did. Probably even more important, however, were the procedural advantages the House leadership commanded. If House Democrats could have gotten a straight up-or-down vote, they probably would have prevailed. Majority Leader Tom DeLay, who led the Republican opposition on the issue, made sure that they did not. The proposal brought to the floor was a much more expensive tax cut including numerous provisions that Republicans liked but Democrats opposed. House Democrats had hoped to defeat the rule, allowing the House then to consider the Senate version. But the House Rules Committee adopted an unusual procedure to make that impossible. Instead of having two votes, one on the rule and one on final passage, the rule was structured so that its passage would automatically trigger acceptance of the underlying bill. Republican leaders are "trying to drive a stake in the heart" of expanding the child tax credit, Minority Leader Nancy Pelosi charged.[71] Such a bill would have to go to conference, where Republicans could let it die. Despite Democratic protests, the rule passed on a largely party-line vote. House Democrats continued to press the issue as discussed earlier and, by their tactics, did force House Republicans to bear a considerable price in bad publicity, something potentially costly to the moderates.

Raising the minimum wage and stopping the administration's weakening of overtime rules were prominent among the other issues Senate Democrats promoted through the combined procedural/PR strategy during the 108th Congress. Democrats forced Senate votes several times on the overtime rule issue and won majorities. Administration veto threats stopped enactment but at a price in bad publicity for Republicans and Bush. Kennedy's minimum-wage amendment did not come to a vote but only because Frist pulled bill after bill from the floor.

The defense authorization bill in 2004 provided Senate Democrats an excellent vehicle for publicizing their criticism of Bush's Iraq policy. During the approximately four weeks it was on the Senate floor in June, Democrats offered amendment after amendment that, as *Roll Call* observed, "attract[ed] big headlines."[72] Senator Frank Lautenberg (D-N.J.), for example, forced a vote on his proposal to open up Dover Air Force Base to photojournalists who wanted snapshots of coffins of soldiers killed in Iraq or Afghanistan. An amendment by Senator Edward Kennedy (D-Mass.) would have required President Bush to supply Congress with a detailed exit strategy for Iraq.[73] When five Republicans joined all but one Democrat in support, Democrats succeeded with Pat Leahy's amendment "to establish in law the presumption that detainees whose Geneva Convention status is unclear are entitled to its protections and to require the Pentagon to provide Congress with numerous reports on prisoner issues."[74]

PR WARS

When the congressional parties and the president, often working with their interest group allies, pull out all the stops in their efforts to shape debate and frame an issue to their advantage, we have what I call a PR war. Such high-visibility showdowns between the president and the opposition party in Congress have become almost routine. Through media strategies and sometimes also grassroots (or "astroturf") campaigns, the sides are attempting to shape public opinion so as to improve their bargaining position or, at least, their reputation looking toward the next election.

During the 1981 fight over Ronald Reagan's economic program, the administration and its congressional and interest group allies waged an extremely effective PR campaign, and Democrats found themselves completely outclassed. Not only did Reagan make three nationally televised speeches on the budget and one on tax cuts; but the White House also orchestrated countless other media contacts and grassroots efforts. The Republican National Committee sent operatives to the South to stimulate grassroots pressure on House and Senate Democrats. Campaign donors—mostly southerners—who had given to both Reagan and a congressional Democrat were asked to call the member to urge support of the Reagan program. Each of Reagan's television addresses generated a flood of letters and phone calls. Polls showed strong support for Reagan himself but, more important, also for his program.[75] "Lawmakers believed their constituents supported that program and they were afraid that Mr. Reagan could galvanize that support through an adroit use of television and punish any dissidents at the polls," reporter Steve Roberts wrote, summing up Reagan's victories.[76]

Being on the receiving end of this well-oiled steamroller convinced Democrats that they had to develop ways to compete. And, as I discussed earlier, they did develop both organizational forms and processes to make that possible—and congressional Republicans did so as well.

Other things being equal, presidents, of course, have the advantage in a PR battle against congressional opponents. However, the character of the issue as well as the lineup of allies can shift the advantage. A review of a few of the PR wars in the last decade and a half illustrate how they proceed and suggest the factors that make the difference in who comes out on top.

Budget Battles and Hillary Care

In 1990, George H. W. Bush decided he needed to achieve real deficit reduction. Concerned about the economy and about legal provisions that were likely to force automatic spending cuts, and aware that normal processes were unlikely to bridge the big gap between the two parties' budgetary policy preferences, the president invited the congressional leaders to negotiate, to what has come to be called a "summit."

Summits—relatively formal negotiations between congressional leaders and high-ranking administration officials representing the president directly—are a recent phenomena. President and Congress have resorted to summits when normal processes are, for one reason or another, incapable of producing legislation and the costs of failing to reach an agreement are very high.[77] Partisan polarization combined with divided government has often made summits necessary on budget issues. Presidents who face a Congress controlled by the other party have a much harder time than they used to in peeling off enough majority party members to pass their priorities; they are thus forced to deal with the leadership of the opposition party, who can extract a greater price than individual members can.

Over a period of months in 1991, congressional leaders and high-ranking administration officials representing President Bush negotiated a budget deal. While the talks were taking place behind closed doors, the public campaign to define the issues and the parties' positions intensified. Since the beginning of the Reagan presidency, Republicans had painted Democrats as tax happy; Democrats had responded with a fairness argument, claiming that Republicans just wanted to cut taxes for the rich. By the late 1980s, many Republicans saw opposition to new taxes as the defining tenet of their party creed and their best election issue. During the 1988 campaign, Bush had vowed never to raise taxes, saying: "Read my lips, no new taxes." A serious deficit reduction plan would require new taxes, but Bush wanted the Democrats to propose them. Determined not to shoulder the blame by themselves, congressional Democrats refused to do so. As the price of talking and then of a deal, they forced Bush to agree that everything was on the table, including taxes, and then to issue a statement that tax revenue increases would be required. The reaction made it clear why Bush had resisted so long. The media played the statement as a huge story and stressed Bush's reneging on his campaign promise. Some editorials commended Bush for finally recognizing reality, but headlines, first paragraphs, and TV news stories emphasized that Bush had broken his promise. Editorial page editor Lynn Ashby of Bush's hometown paper the *Houston Post* asked: "Was he lying or did he just not understand the situation?"[78] Many of the stories asked the same question directly or by implication.

Democrats used Bush's continuing insistence on a capital gains tax cut to highlight the fairness argument, putting Bush further on the defensive. After more hard bargaining, the parties agreed to a package that did include taxes. House Republican Whip Newt Gingrich, although initially one of the negotiators, denounced the agreement and set out to defeat it. His opposition was based on his determination to protect the party's message that he had worked to shape; only by maintaining a sharp difference between the parties and preserving the Republicans' best issue—lower taxes—could the Republicans hope to win a congressional majority, Gingrich believed. A majority of the House Republican membership agreed with him and joined with liberal Democrats opposed to social program cuts to defeat the budget deal negotiated by President Bush and the bipartisan congressional leadership. Bush had gone on national television to make a plea for passage, but his appeal only increased opposition; calls to congressional offices were overwhelmingly negative.

Democrats then worked out another deal for which they could marshal a majority among Democrats. Although this was much less to his liking than the first agreement, Bush signed off on it. He really had little choice but to do so because Democrats had won the media war.

The administration lost control of the issue when Democrats forced Bush to admit that the package would have to include taxes. The media played this as a huge story, placing the emphasis on Bush's reneging on his election promise. The fervent opposition among many congressional Republicans to Bush's change made it an even bigger story. Once the question of whether taxes would be included in the package was settled, interest centered on who would be taxed, and on this issue, Democrats held the upper hand. Democrats' success in the media battle with the fairness issue convinced Republicans to drop the capital gains tax cut that Bush so much wanted. When the first package went down to defeat in the House, the president's inability to muster a majority of his members was a much bigger story than the Democratic leadership's failure, especially since Bush had made a television appeal for support. Going public backfired for him in this case. Although a significant deficit reduction package was enacted, Bush's only serious attempt at domestic policy leadership cost him dearly in public perceptions.[79]

Early in 1993, Republicans killed newly elected President Bill Clinton's stimulus program through a combination of procedural and PR strategies. Republicans not only used extended debate to block Senate passage of the bill but engaged in an aggressive campaign to portray the bill as a grotesquely pork-laden waste of money; stories about particularly hard-to-explain projects—"fish maps," for example—appeared in the news across the country. The White House, distracted by other issues and not yet fully geared up to wage PR war, never countered effectively. Republicans clearly won the PR battle, and as a result, they actually gained political advantage from killing legislation they opposed but that a majority of the House and Senate supported.

For Clinton's health care plan, the public opinion war was decisive. Early on the process appeared as if it were going to take a traditional course. Clinton's nationally televised speech on health care reform in the fall of 1993 was well received, and polls showed that his proposal was popular. Making policy changes of that magnitude is never easy in the American political system, so failure was always a real possibility. Yet key Republicans, most notably Senate Minority Leader Bob Dole, were indicating that they were open to some sort of compromise. Many Republicans, believing that health care was probably going to pass, wanted to take part in shaping the legislation and thereby garner some of the credit.

However, key Republicans on the hard right of their party, namely Senator Phil Gramm (Tex.) and, most important, Newt Gingrich, concluded that health care reform would be detrimental to their party's electoral and policy goals. Bill Kristol—the son of Irving, former chief of staff for Vice President Dan Quayle, and then at a conservative think tank—wrote a widely circulated memo arguing that congressional Republicans should "kill" the Clinton plan. "It will revive the reputation of the party that spends and regulates, the Democrats, as the generous protector of middle-class interests. And it will at the same time strike a punishing blow against Republican claims to defend the middle class by restraining government," he argued.[80] Gingrich, Gramm, and Kristol were the vanguard of what became a Republican consensus to go all out in opposing Clinton's health care reform. Republicans, opposition interest groups, and their allies in the media launched a campaign that turned public opinion around. The "Harry and Louise" TV ads, in which a middle-class couple voiced a litany of concerns about the Clinton plan, were the most visible part of a much larger operation. Through about $100 million worth of media and grassroots campaigning, opponents convinced the public that the Clinton plan might lower the standard of health care available to them, decrease their choice of doctors, and raise their costs. Again, the White House and its allies attempted to counter, but they had less money and not as single-minded a focus. In any case, opponents had the advantage in that they had only to raise doubts among the public, while proponents had to sell a complicated plan.

Opponents' success in the battle for public opinion translated into success in the legislative arena. Ideological opposition and interest group pressure were not the primary reasons Democrats were unable to put together majorities from their own numbers for any significant health care bill. Rather, starting in the winter of 1994 when Democrats went home to talk to their constituents, many found more and more uneasiness about the plan. The media campaign and grassroots efforts by groups such as the National Federation of Independent Business, a trade association of small businesses, had had a major effect. Members feared being blamed at election time for their failure to produce, but they feared voting for an unpopular plan even more.

Once the Republicans took control of Congress, they discovered that their strategies could be used against them. In 1995, the new Republican congressional majority attempted to make comprehensive policy change through the congressional budget process. Republicans managed to pass in both chambers a massive reconciliation bill that drastically curtailed the federal government's role by cutting domestic spending and restructuring a number of the biggest federal entitlement programs, including Medicare. But while Republicans were legislating, Democrats, largely excluded from the legislative process, concentrated on their media strategy and were increasingly successful in defining the package as extreme and a threat to Medicare.

For much of the year, Republicans had dismissed Clinton as irrelevant; they had the mandate, he was a repudiated and, they were sure, a lame-duck president. True he possessed the veto; but Republicans were convinced that Clinton would cave in under pressure. Using a traditional congressional strategy, Republicans had attached to appropriations bills provisions that they knew Clinton would veto if they came to him as free-standing legislation. Appropriations bills fund the government; if they do not become law by the beginning of the fiscal year, much of the government shuts down. Clinton vetoed the reconciliation bill as well as several appropriations bills and threatened to veto others.

The vetoes set the stage for a high-stakes confrontation that would determine the legislative fate of the 104th Congress; key scenes of the drama, as is now so often the case, were played out on the public stage, and audience reaction determined the outcome. The actors had long been positioning themselves for the showdown—congressional Republicans by passing the legislation that balanced the budget in seven years and by threatening to shut the government down if Clinton did not go along with their policy thrust; the Democrats by attacking the Republicans for cutting Medicare so as to pay for tax cuts for the rich; and Clinton by agreeing that the budget could and should be balanced within a set number of years but contending that it should be done in a less draconian and more equitable fashion.

Given the vast distance between the policy preference of the president and the congressional majority, only summit negotiations at the highest level offered any chance of reaching a compromise. After several weeks of off-and-on negotiations failed to produce an agreement, Republicans shut the government down, not once but several times and for much longer than had ever happened before. The press was full of articles about the harm the shutdown might cause—preparation of the next year's flu vaccine was being hindered, for example—and of the suffering of ordinary federal employees at Christmastime. Republicans were shocked when not only did Clinton not cave in to their demands, but the public blamed them and not Clinton for the unseemly spectacle. Although a considerable proportion of the ideologically committed Republican House freshmen wanted to persevere, the public's negative verdict decided the outcome. The Republicans' ambitious plan to make comprehensive policy change was dead.[81]

Judge Wars

During the George W. Bush presidency, with a very cohesive Republican Party controlling the House and Republicans commanding either a majority or a near-majority in the Senate, one might expect that PR wars would be so one-sided that they would not deserve that label. In fact, as discussed earlier, Democrats did often find themselves frustrated by their inability to command media attention. Yet circumstances sometimes shifted the balance of power. Although Bush and his partisan allies could usually best the Democrats in media exposure, coverage did not necessarily lead to attitude change among the public or to votes for Bush's proposals in Congress.

Bush and his congressional Republican allies were often unable to create sufficient public concern to pressure Senate Democrats to capitulate and allow up-or-down votes on Bush programs. The White House and congressional Republicans made a major effort on energy legislation. Allies even ran ads against specific Democratic senators in their home states, hoping to pressure them to support the Republican bill. After 9/11, Bush attempted to recast his energy program as a vital component of his national security strategy. Majority Leader Tom DeLay came close to accusing opponents of treason. When gas prices rose steeply in 2004, the energy program was touted as a remedy. The House repassed a number of energy bills in an attempt to increase the visibility of the issue. Yet no public groundswell demanding that Senate Democrats change their behavior emerged. In fact, at various points in the years-long battle, Democrats countered the Republican energy ads with ones of their own, excoriating potentially vulnerable Republicans for wanting to drill in the Arctic National Wildlife Refuge (ANWR). The legislation died in both the 107th and 108th Congresses.

Similarly, elaborate efforts to pressure Democrats on Bush's judicial nominations did not succeed in the 108th Congress. Again, despite a media campaign by an allied group set up for just that purpose, Republicans were unable to get the votes of enough Democrats to break the filibusters against nominees that Democrats claimed were too far to the right. Majority Leader Bill Frist hoped to ratchet up media attention and public pressure by a months-long floor consideration of the Estrada nomination in early 2003.

Even after he moved on to other business, he called one cloture vote after another. As noted in chapter 6, after seven failed cloture votes and no sign of weakening of the Democratic opposition, Estrada withdrew his nomination.

In the summer of 2003 in heavily Catholic areas, ads appeared showing a sign hanging from closed doors under the words "Judicial Chambers." The sign read: "Catholics need not apply."[82] The Committee for Justice—founded specifically to rally support for Bush's judicial nominees—and the Ave Maria List, a Catholic anti-abortion group, ran the ads, which essentially accused Democrats of being anti-Catholic in opposing William Pryor, an extremely conservative Bush nominee. "Some in the U.S. Senate are attacking Bill Pryor for having 'deeply held' Catholic beliefs to prevent him from becoming a federal judge," the ads said. "Don't they know the Constitution expressly prohibits religious tests for public office?" Jeff Sessions, a Republican member of the Senate Judiciary Committee, echoed the same charge in slightly less inflammatory tones. No Republican on the committee was willing to repudiate the attack.

Democrats were outraged. "A false and detestable smear," charged a spokesman for Pat Leahy (Vt.), ranking Democrat on the Senate Judiciary Committee. "The question in Mr. Pryor's case is not his religion, which in fact is shared by several members of the Judiciary Committee. It is whether he is capable of fairly and impartially applying the laws to everyone who comes into the courtroom, as he would be required to do as a federal judge," Leahy continued.[83]

By late 2003, the number of nominees stopped by Democrats had risen to six. Frist periodically called cloture votes on various of the blocked nominees, but in no case were the Republicans successful in getting the necessary sixty votes.

Frustrated by the Democrats' successful filibusters and by criticism from conservative groups of their own lack of a sufficiently strident countercampaign, Senate Republicans in November 2003 mounted a thirty-nine-hour, three-day and two-night talkathon to excoriate Democrats for blocking the nominees. Instigated by junior conservatives, the effort eventually included most Republican senators and became a major PR production. Taking off on the "justice for janitors" slogan of the Los Angeles labor organizing drive, they dubbed the effort the "Justice for Judges Marathon" and even had T-shirts made with the motto. Amid a media throng, Frist led the phalanx of Republican senators from his office to the floor at 6:00 P.M., the hour appointed for the debate to begin. Both parties set up twenty-four-hour communications rooms in the Capitol. Republicans held press conferences or rallies every hour with a different set of senators and outside interest groups, beginning at 10:00 P.M. on the first night and running until 9:00 A.M. two days later.[84] Conservative broadcasters were housed in "Talk Show Alley" in one of the Senate office buildings. Conservative groups bussed in members to attend the rallies and sit in the galleries. Democrats countered with their own PR effort, debating Republicans on the floor, holding a rally for activists, and appealing to the media.[85] The campaign changed no votes, and none of the nominees won approval.

In early 2004, President Bush appointed two of the blocked conservative nominees to the appellate courts using his power to make recess appointments. Senate Democrats took that as a declaration of war. When behind-the-scenes talks between Frist and Daschle led to no resolution, Democrats decided at a Caucus meeting to block all Bush nominees. "A group of us felt very strongly on the Judiciary Committee that the recess appointments were such a finger in the eye of the Constitution that we had to do something about it," explained Chuck Schumer (D-N.Y.). "We went to our caucus, and there was almost unanimous acceptance."[86] In his floor statement announcing the blockade, Daschle asserted that no president had "ever used a recess appointment to install a rejected nominee on to the federal bench," and then added:

"These actions not only poison the nomination process, but they strike at the heart of the principle of checks and balances that is one of the pillars of American society."[87]

Republicans responded that what Democrats were doing was an unprecedented abuse of Senate rules. "The Democrats should stop playing delay games and give all of the nominees the simple up-or-down vote the Constitution requires," said Judiciary Committee Chair Orrin Hatch. "It is the unprecedented filibusters by the Democrats that necessitated the recess appointments that the Democrats are now criticizing."[88] The Democrats' action was "blatant, partisan obstructionism," Frist charged.[89] The White House criticized the Democrats and refused to budge.

No public pressure on Democrats to back down emerged; they followed through on their threat and refused to allow even noncontroversial nominations to come to a vote. The White House capitulated. On May 18, Daschle and Frist announced an agreement: the White House would make no more recess judicial appointments, and the Democrats would allow votes on twenty-five noncontroversial judicial nominees—but not on those they had been blocking.

Why did these campaigns fail? Certainly part of the answer is that neither energy policy nor judicial nomination is the sort of highly salient issue that is likely to resonate with the public at large. They *are* the type of issues about which activists care deeply and on which the two parties' activists are deeply split. Most Democratic activists would have regarded support for the far-right judicial nominees or for drilling in the ANWR as a betrayal. Republicans would certainly have been pleased if their "reverse filibuster" on judicial nominees had resulted in a groundswell of public pressure on Democrats, but in fact it was aimed primarily at their own activists. Republican senators were acting like wimps, Republican activists believed; they yearned to see their senators take on the "evil" Democrats for their "nefarious" use of Senate rules; and elected officials always have an incentive to keep their activists satisfied.

Drug Wars

The Medicare/prescription drugs issue occasioned the hardest-fought domestic-policy PR war of Bush's first term. Health care had long been an issue favoring Democrats, and that party had advocated adding prescription drug coverage to Medicare since 1998. Attempting to preempt the issue, candidate Bush in 2000 had made giving seniors help with their prescription drug costs a part of his agenda. Serious differences between the two parties' approaches to the issue led to stalemate in the closely divided but Democratic-controlled Senate, and no legislation was enacted during the 107th Congress. The administration and Republican congressional leaders were determined to succeed in the 108th, in which they controlled the Senate, albeit narrowly.

That this would be a legislative battle with major policy and political ramifications was clear to all the participants. The fundamental policy difference between Republicans and Democrats concerned the role of the private sector in Medicare. Republicans wanted to inject a major component of private sector competition into Medicare, believing that doing so would hold down costs. Democrats believed that doing so would be the first step toward privatizing Medicare, the end result being a two-tiered health system in which the less well-off would suffer. Politically, both parties saw the battle as an attempt by Republicans to appropriate one of the Democrats' best issues and make it their own. The high stakes made it inevitable that a PR war would accompany the legislative battle. The big question was whether minority Democrats could, in fact, mount an effective legislative or PR campaign.

Assisted by House Republicans' decision to exclude them from decision making on the legislation, House Democrats maintained high unity in opposition to the Republican bill, which passed on June 27, 2003 on a 216–215 vote. In the Senate, however, Ted Kennedy, the Democrats' premier spokesman on health care, decided early on to work with the administration and the Republicans, figuring that by participating he could influence the process enough to produce a bill that was a good first step. Majority Leader Tom Daschle urged against that course, convinced it would not work, but as happens in the Senate, Kennedy persisted. The Senate did, in fact, produce a bill that many Democrats could live with, and it likewise passed on June 27, by a vote of 76 to 21, with eleven Democrats but also ten Republicans voting against it. The Republicans who opposed the bill were the most conservative members; they largely opposed any new entitlement and certainly this bill, which they contended had given far too much ground to Democrats.

The message that the legislative process to that point had sent to those who were paying attention was a murky one. House Democrats, strongly opposed to the House bill, nevertheless began a PR campaign to shape perceptions on the issue. In July, the Democratic leadership urged their members to begin organizing town hall meetings in their districts on the bill. "While we lost a vote on June 27, the fight continues," the leaders wrote in their "Dear Colleague" letter to their members. "It's our strong belief that Democrats must take this debate directly to our seniors. . . . The best way to do that is through the give-and-take of town hall meetings that individually generate favorable media coverage in your District and collectively generate a pro-active, positive message about House Democrats in the national media."[90] In July as well, the Democratic Congressional Campaign Committee (DCCC) ran TV ads in the districts of eight Republican House members "chosen because they were judged to be vulnerable by the party in the upcoming elections and had large numbers of older voters in their districts."[91] According to the DCCC e-mail newsletter:

> The ads inform voters in eight Republican-held Congressional districts that their Representatives recently voted in support of a bill that would "end Medicare as we know it." The bill they just passed:
>
> •Pushes seniors into HMOs;
>
> •Has huge gaps in [drug] coverage and provides no guaranteed coverage;
>
> •Shortchanges rural seniors; and,
>
> •Prevents Medicare from negotiating the best prices for prescription drugs.[92]

These would continue as the Democrats' talking points throughout the battle. According to DCCC Chair Robert Matsui, the ads were intended to put pressure on Republicans negotiating the final bill as well as to assure that Democrats did not lose the issue.

Republicans interpreted the Democratic response as a sign of weakness. "This is a big feather in our cap," said Carl Forti, communications director for the National Republican Congressional Committee. "And it is another kitchen-table issue like education that were Democratic strengths that we are taking away from them."[93]

Senate Democrats were concerned about what would happen to the bill in conference. In early July, Ted Kennedy drafted and twenty-nine Democrats, including Minority Leader Tom Daschle, signed off on a letter to President Bush stating their bottom line. "We will oppose a conference report that forces seniors to choose between giving up their doctor or facing higher premiums to stay in the current Medicare program," they wrote.[94] Daschle warned Republicans not to be fooled by the big passage margin. Both parties sent their House members home for the August recess with instructions to talk about the legislation.

Conference negotiations stretched into November, with most Democrats being excluded. Finally the Republican leaders came up with a compromise that jettisoned much of what the Democrats had won in the Senate but that the most conservative Republicans still found hard to swallow. After a roll call that was held open for almost three hours, the conference report passed the House on a 220–215 vote. Several days later, the Senate passed it 54–44, a considerably closer tally than on the initial passage vote; the number of Democrats supporting the bill had shrunk from thirty-five to eleven.

"With the theatrics of a campaign kickoff rally," said the *New York Times*, President Bush sighed the bill on December 8 at an elaborate celebratory ceremony.[95] "We show our respect for seniors by giving them more choices and more control over their decision-making," the president told an invited audience of about two thousand at the bill-signing ceremony at Daughters of the American Revolution Constitution Hall, one of the largest halls in Washington.[96] Bush was surrounded by more than a dozen members of Congress, almost all Republicans; over his head was a blue banner with a large "Rx" and the words "Keeping Our Promise to Seniors." In the audience, in addition to lobbyists, campaign donors, and politicians, were seniors flown in by the White House from around the country and seated in bleachers directly behind the president, in full view of the television cameras.[97]

The legislative battle may have been over, but the PR war continued for opponents as well. On the day Bush signed the bill, congressional Democrats including Ted Kennedy, now a strong opponent, lambasted the bill at a Capitol Hill rally. "We have only just begun to fight," Kennedy told a cheering crowd of several hundred retirees—some wearing T-shirts reading "Drug Companies Make Me Sick"—who jammed a large Senate hearing room to protest the bill's enactment.[98] Along with their labor, senior, and consumer group allies, Democrats continued to blast Bush and congressional Republicans for passing a bill that helps drug companies and the HMOs at expense of the elderly.

The administration meanwhile set in motion a $22 million campaign that it claimed was intended to educate seniors about the new law. Run through the Department of Health and Human

Services (HHS), it included a mass mailing to 41 million seniors and TV, radio, and print ads. "Same Medicare, more benefits" was the slogan and the message.

Democrats were outraged, claiming that this was propaganda illegally paid for by the government; the ads were at best vague and misleading. Congressional Democrats demanded an investigation by the Government Accountability Office (GAO, formerly the General Accounting Office).

House Republicans initiated a counteroffensive. Leadership staff worked out scripts for public service announcements (PSAs) on the bill that members were urged to tape for TV or radio broadcast in their district. PSAs are run free, a considerable advantage. A "toolkit" was developed explaining how to set up meetings for constituents with health care experts and HHS officials. Explaining the rationale for the effort, Republican Conference Chair Deborah Pryce said: "Democrats who failed to support the plan are scaring seniors with false information."[99]

CBS decided to stop running the administration's ads until the GAO reached a verdict on their legality. Republicans were furious.[100] Polls showed that the public had grave doubts about the bill and that the more they learned about it, the less they liked it. The press began asking if the bill would backfire on Republicans. Congressional Republicans, realizing they were not getting their message through, brought in consultants and pollsters to help shape the message.

Democrats continued to hammer away. At the behest of the House Democratic leadership, Charlie Rangel and John Dingell, very senior Democrats in age as well as service, went on the road to publicize the Democrats' objections to the bill. Beginning with events in their home states of New York and Michigan, they then proceeded to hold town hall meetings around the country. "We want to get local press coverage and local interest in the issue," a Pelosi spokesperson explained.[101] Another round of member forums on the bill was also set in motion. The leadership even prepared a special video for members to show their constituents.

The GAO report released in March determined that the administration had not violated the restrictions on the use of federal money for "publicity or propaganda purposes" but that the HHS materials were flawed by "omissions and other weaknesses." They "are not so purely partisan as to be unlawful," the report concluded.[102] This less than ringing endorsement of the administration's information campaign and the controversy about an administration official withholding bill cost estimates from Congress kept the controversy over the bill on the front pages.

Meanwhile Democrats' interest group allies stepped up their efforts, highlighting the bill's flaws in television advertising, mailings, and videotapes circulated to ten thousand senior centers and retirement communities. "Families USA distributed a videotape narrated by Walter Cronkite to communities with elderly populations around the country. MoveOn.org Voter Fund ran TV ads . . . asserting, 'Instead of standing up for seniors, George Bush sided with the drug companies who'd given him huge contributions.'"[103]

May 3, 2004, was the first day Medicare recipients could apply for the drug discount cards intended to help them until the full program went into effect in 2006, and both parties targeted that date as a media opportunity. Building on dozens of district gatherings they had held to familiarize their constituents with the Medicare measure, Republican members conducted district workshops centered around enrolling seniors in the new prescription drug plan. They planned to continue holding workshops through June 1, when the drug cards themselves would become available. The National Republican Congressional Committee booked members onto talk radio programs in targeted districts to discuss the cards in the several weeks leading up May 3 and planned to continue that as well.[104]

Democratic Leader Nancy Pelosi sent her members off with another fat packet of materials—"a sample editorial on the topic, a sample press release and a variety of 'rhetoric versus reality' fact sheets."[105] While Pelosi held a press conference in Washington, a number of Democrats held district workshops.

This is a PR war destined to continue until the public or at least the voters have rendered a decisive verdict on the program. It also served as a model for the even more elaborate PR war over Social Security restructuring.

WHY GO PUBLIC?

Going public—attempting to influence public opinion sufficiently to pressure other actors to move toward your position—is clearly not a strategy that the congressional parties or the president can count on to work every time. It is not a sure-fire strategy even for a president who seems to be politically strong.[106] During most of the 107th Congress, when the energy and judicial nominee battles started, Bush was very popular. In 2003–2004, he headed a unified Republican government. As Clinton learned when he tried to institute comprehensive health care reform, and Gingrich when he tried to revamp Medicare and other major governmental programs, the opponents of change have the advantage. Given a governmental system rife with veto points, opponents need only raise doubts about a proposed change on a high-visibility issue; on low-visibility issues, they do not even need to do that, so long as the proponents are unable to raise the issue's visibility *and* present so compelling a case as to pressure them into action.

If going public to effectuate policy change is a difficult strategy to carry out successfully, why is it so commonly used? Intense partisan and ideological polarization is part of the rationale. When the two parties' conceptions of what constitutes good public policy are as far apart as they have been in recent years, compromise is costly in the policy concessions that must be made and potentially in electoral terms as well. Certainly activists are likely to be unhappy with a split-the-difference compromise. Often there is no compromise that both parties consider better than the status quo. Going public offers a possible way of increasing one's bargaining resources by getting the support of at least some attentive publics, if not usually the broad general public. And actors know their opponents are likely to go public and are unwilling to risk yielding the public forum to them.

In sum, in concert with other changes in the political environment, partisan polarization has altered the relationship between Congress and the president in the policy-making process. Both the president and the congressional parties have responded strategically to the changed political environment and thereby have changed the politics of the policy-making process. Although key, the president and Congress are not the only important actors in the drama of policy making at the national level. In the next chapter I turn to interest groups, policy experts, and the media to examine how partisan polarization has affected their roles in the process.

CHAPTER 9

FROM FLUID COALITIONS TO ARMED CAMPS

The Polarization of the National Political Community

THE NATIONAL POLITICAL AND policy community that, coming out of the 1960s, could be characterized as one of fluid coalitions is now better described as two armed and hostile camps. Not only have elected politicians in Congress and the presidency, political activists, and to a considerable extent ordinary voters polarized along partisan lines, but so have other key political actors—though to varying extents. Interest groups are increasingly firmly aligned with one or the other of the major parties and, in many cases, are functioning as full-fledged members of one of the two party "teams." The policy experts on whom office-holders and the media rely are more and more those associated with the various Washington think tanks, and many of those think tanks have a much more ideological and partisan cast than those prominent in the past. Even the news media show similar tendencies, though here an old-style "objective" press contests with media newcomers that are blatantly ideological and partisan.

In this chapter I elaborate on these generalizations and delineate how these developments have altered the politics of the policy-making process.

INTEREST GROUPS AS TEAM PLAYERS

As the parties have polarized, so to a large extent have interest groups active in the Washington policy process, I argue; interest groups are increasingly being forced to align with one party or the other, to become a part of one of two durable coalitions, and this is true even of those groups that would prefer to play both sides of the fence. Staying neutral has become a progressively more untenable strategy for major interest groups. Polarization also affects the ways in which interest groups participate in the political and policy processes.

Why Interest Group Polarization?

The alignment of interest groups with parties is not, of course, a new phenomenon. Because the parties, even at their least ideological and distinct, still represented different ideological thrusts and tended to represent or at least be more responsive to different interests, broad-gauge and ideological interest groups have tended to align with one party or the other. Thus labor has been a reliable Democratic party ally, one might even say a component of the party, since the 1930s. Big business, especially the broad umbrella organizations like the U.S. Chamber of Commerce and the National Association of Manufacturers, swung Republican. At the same time, however, many business trade associations and individual businesses were thoroughly pragmatic and worked with and gave money to whomever was in power, which in Congress was usually the Democrats.[1] Even groups that we tend to think of as clearly ideological—such as environmental groups—worked both sides of the street and attempted to avoid too close an association with either party.

That has changed. The House Republicans' "K Street Project" (named for the Washington, D.C., street on which many of the big lobbying firms are located) has received a great deal of attention in Washington. In the aftermath of the Republicans' taking control of Congress, Tom DeLay, then Republican whip and now Majority Leader, undertook to "persuade" business to hire only Republicans as lobbyists and to stop giving campaign contributions to Democrats. DeLay's attempt to get the Electronics Industry Association to reverse its decision to hire Dave McCurdy, a former Democratic House member from Oklahoma, was an instance of the strategy that became public.[2] On the Senate side, then Majority Leader Trent Lott did much the same thing. Other Republicans in positions of influence, such as committee chairs, have followed suit. For example, in 2003 Mike Oxley, chair of the House Financial Services Committee, seems to have tried to get a Democratic-connected lobbyist for the Investment Company Institute fired and replaced by a Republican; as reported in the *Washington Post*, "senior Oxley staffers told a group of lobbyists . . . that Oxley's probe of the mutual fund industry was linked to [the Democratic lobbyist's] employment at the mutual fund trade group."[3] After the 2002 elections Trent Lott, while still Senate Republican Leader, held a meeting with lobbyists for interests that had supported Republicans—and refrained from supporting Democrats—at levels Lott considered appropriate. "He made it clear that the groups that were in the room had preformed politically effective operations," said Greg Casey, president and CEO of the Business-Industry Political Action Committee and a former Lott staffer. "At the same time he made clear he has his eye on the wayward . . . that he wasn't universally happy with everyone in the business community."[4] The meeting and the word of mouth (as well as coverage in the Hill press) that it generated, sent the "wayward" a message that they would not find a friendly hearing in the Senate Majority Leader's office unless they changed their ways. In early 2004, House Majority Leader Tom DeLay increased the pressure by letting it be known that he did not think Republican lobbyists were contributing enough to congressional Republicans. "There is a real effort by a lot of people other than DeLay to get people to step up to the plate and do what they should be doing," said one lobbyist close to DeLay.[5]

When the Motion Picture Association of America hired former Democratic House member Dan Glickman as its top lobbyist, congressional Republicans were sufficiently upset that the MPAA's decision was raised at a Senate leadership meeting. "[Republican Conference chair Rick] Santorum said that persuading lobbying organizations to hire more Republicans is key to ensuring that the GOP's message is well communicated. 'Its very important for us and our ability to communicate and to be persuasive to have people [on K Street] who are honest and not partisan,' he said. Republican aides familiar with last week's meeting said the movie industry can expect to face 'ramifications' for its decision to hire Glickman, but not necessarily 'consequences.'" Glickman "'will not have the opportunities to do some of the things that a Republican could have done,' said one Republican aide. 'It does nothing to help their interests on the Hill.'"[6]

Although in a weaker position because of their minority status, congressional Democrats have not hesitated to rebuke allies who have seemed insufficiently loyal. When the AARP, the largest organization of older people and usually a Democratic policy ally, worked with the congressional Republican leadership on the Medicare/prescription drugs bill and then endorsed the Republican version, congressional Democrats were livid. Democrats resigned their AARP membership en mass and accused the organization's president of selling out. In 2004, House Democrats let the AFL-CIO know "they will have limited tolerance for the federation's support of GOP candidates," even though labor gives almost all of its campaign contributions to Democrats.[7] A high-level aide explained, "We're trying to demonstrate to organized labor that at the end of the day Nancy Pelosi as Speaker is more important to organized labor than finding one, two or five moderate Republicans to support to say they are bipartisan. They need to be careful about who they decide to support."[8]

Undoubtedly such pressure has had some effect, particularly Republican pressure on business interests whose main objective is access; but pressure by the political parties is not the root cause of the polarization.

As the parties became more distinct ideologically and as their key constituent groups changed, more and more interest groups found that one of the parties simply was so uncongenial to their interests and concerns that they were driven into the arms of the other. Thus the prominence of the Christian Right in the Republican Party drove women's groups and gays firmly into the Democratic Party. (Of course, feminists contributed to politicizing fundamentalist Christians in the first place.) The Republican Party's move to the right on property rights issues and environmental regulation drove environmental groups into the Democratic Party. Trial lawyers have become a major source of funding for the Democratic Party in response to the more aggressive stance Republicans have taken on tort reform, and that is partly in response to the central role now played in the Republican Party by the National Federation of Independent Business (NFIB). As gun control became a more prominent issue within the Democratic Party, the National Rifle Association (NRA) moved decisively into the Republican camp. Even labor, long at the center of the Democratic coalition, has been driven even more firmly into the party's embrace by Republican policies perceived as virulently anti-union. From Ronald Reagan's firing of the air traffic controllers to the quashing of ergonomics regulations by congressional Republicans in 2001 and the changes in overtime regulations by the Bush Administration, labor believes itself under unrelenting attack by the Republican Party. Many businesses and industries, on the other hand, have found the strong anti-regulation stance—and often anti-union stance—of the contemporary Republican Party highly attractive.

Interest Groups as Team Players in the Policy Process

What does this mean for the policy process? Members of Congress and the president have long worked with interest groups, probably as long as such groups have been in existence. For example, on many issues on which they agreed, Democrats and labor lobbyists have for decades plotted strategy together and coordinated their coalition-building efforts. Individual members of Congress as well as committee and party leaders have worked with those groups that have an interest in a particular bill in ad hoc coalitions.[9] Thus, for example, when Representative Jim Wright was trying to pass synthetic fuels legislation in the late 1970s, he had his staff call every interest group they thought might or should be interested and talked them into participating. (The message: Hey, this is something that you should be interested in, that will benefit you. Get yourself down here and help us pass the bill!)

In the 1980s and especially the 1990s, the character of the cooperation changed. First congressional leaders put more emphasis on working with groups efficiently and routinizing the process. By the late 1980s, all the House Democratic party leaders had staff dedicated to interest group liaison. House Republicans' efforts in the 104th Congress, however, signaled a more fundamental change.

By the mid-1990s, the Christian Coalition, the NRA, and the NFIB were core Republican constituencies and had been instrumental to the party's success in the 1994 congressional elections. The Christian Coalition has from its inception been closely though informally linked to the Republican Party. It emerged from Pat Robertson's run for the Republican nomination in 1988; Ralph Reed, its first and most influential executive director, had been a Republican operative before his stint at the Coalition and would be again afterward.[10] The NRA, a gun rights organization of over three million members, became more and more closely attached to the Republican Party as gun control became defined as a Democratic issue.[11] The NFIB has existed since 1943 but became highly active and political on the national stage only in 1992 when Jack Faris took over as president.[12] A strongly ideological

Republican, Faris threw in his lot with the Republican Party, and the organization quickly became a major power in that party. Representative Charles W. Stenholm, a conservative Democrat who had traditionally had good relations with small business, has complained that the NFIB has "become a total arm of the Republican Party. The only way to score high with them is to take the Republican leadership game plan and vote for it." With six hundred thousand members and an active grassroots presence, the NFIB can and does mobilize quickly and effectively to support candidates and issues. As the *Washington Post* reported, "It doggedly delivers calls on key legislation and votes on Election Day, mobilizing small-business owners, including bakery owners and car dealers, in virtually every congressional district. Politicians from both parties are loath to cross a group representing such a constituency."[13]

At the beginning of the 104th Congress, the House Republican leadership created the Thursday Group, consisting of representatives of ideological groups closely allied with the party and lobbyists for business groups with a major stake in the enactment of the Republican agenda.[14] According to a knowledgeable source, lobbyists were included because of who they were—trusted former Republican staffers; and because of whom they represented—core Republican constituencies. The initial membership consisted of the NFIB, the Christian Coalition, the U.S. Chamber of Commerce, National Association of Wholesaler-Distributors, National Restaurant Association, National Association of Home Builders, Citizens for a Sound Economy (CSE), and Americans for Tax Reform.[15] CSE is a think tank and advocacy group that favors "lower taxes and less government."[16] Americans for Tax Reform is an antitax group headed by conservative activist Grover Norquist. The group met weekly with Republican Conference Chair John Boehner, who, with Whip Tom DeLay, worked to orchestrate these groups' lobbying efforts to best effect.[17] Senate Republican Policy Committee Chair Paul Coverdell of Georgia soon joined Boehner as codirector and thus made it a bicameral effort. To be included, the interest group participants had to agree to lobby for all of the Contract with America items, whether or not they had a direct interest in them. The Republican efforts to maintain a united front among these groups and to enlist them in lobbying for legislation not at the top of their own priority list were highly successful, especially during the Contract period.[18] Groups such as the Christian Coalition and NFIB have strong grass roots and were quite successful at mobilizing their members to communicate with members of Congress.

In one guise or another, the group has continued to function. Thus, in January 2004, Republican House Conference Chair Deborah Pryce and Majority Whip Roy Blunt met with top allied lobbyists to preview the upcoming legislative session, indicating the issues on which they expected to need the groups' help.[19] The meeting was a prelude to the coalition efforts on specific issues that Deputy Majority Whip Mike Rogers is charged with coordinating (see chapter 5). On the Senate side, Republican Conference chair Rick Santorum also meets regularly with Republican lobbyists. Top Senate Republican leadership aides have met with a small group of lobbyists nearly every Thursday morning since 2001; many of the participants represent the same groups in the original Thursday Group—the NFIB, National Association of Wholesaler-Distributors, and U.S. Chamber of Commerce. Also included are the National Association of Manufacturers and the Business Roundtable. Grover Norquist, president of Americans for Tax Reform, is a frequent participant, and many of the lobbyists have deep and long-standing Republican ties.[20]

For the lobbyists, an opportunity to meet regularly with the party leadership is, of course, invaluable. They gain information, access, and an opportunity to influence the agenda as well as outcomes. In return, however, they are expected to be team players, to help out even when an issue is not their top priority, and to refrain from causing trouble.

Democrats have endeavored to follow the Republicans' lead. Actually, several times in the latter 1980s and early 1990s, Democratic party leaders had put together efforts involving representatives of many Democratic constituencies to pass legislation such as budget bills, which a number of the groups would not have worked on their own. Doing so took some leaning on allied groups without a specific interest in the bills. More recently, Pelosi has set up a number of member task forces to communicate regularly with core Democratic constituency groups. She also significantly expanded the staff charged with outreach. Six aides, each assigned a set of issues and of groups, are responsible for working with their assigned groups when relevant legislation gets to the House floor and for keeping in touch and building relationships with local activists as well as their Washington representatives on an ongoing basis. Senate Democratic Leader Tom Daschle instituted weekly meetings of top leadership staff and core constituency representatives. Among those included were the executive director of the Leadership Conference on Civil Rights, a coalition of numerous civil rights groups; the political director of NARAL Pro-Choice America; the legislative director of the Center on Budget and Policy Priorities, a liberal think tank; the political director of EMILY's List; and the legislative director of the AFL-CIO.[21] The Senate Democratic Steering and Outreach Committee, chaired by Hillary Clinton during the 108th and 109th Congresses, maintains a dialogue and works with a broader range of groups.

Presidents, too, have long worked with interest groups. A key part of the job of the Office of Public Liaison, established at the beginning of the Ford Administration, is to mobilize groups supporting the president's position on a particular issue and to direct those groups' efforts so as to maximize their impact. And, of course, an administration more frequently works with friendly interest groups than with those that tend to favor the policy stances and the candidates of the other party. Yet the way presidents work with interest groups is changing.

Consider, for example, the Bush Administration's campaigns to pass the president's tax cuts in 2001 and 2003. Bush's 2001 tax package focused on tax cuts for individuals and did not include tax breaks for corporations. Nevertheless, business groups lobbied hard for the plan and did not press Congress to add corporate tax breaks. That did not just happen. With White House encouragement—if not direction—the U.S. Chamber of Commerce, National Association of Manufacturers, National Association of Wholesaler-Distributors, and NFIB formed the Tax Relief Coalition, which eventually included hundreds of businesses and trade associations. Reportedly Karl Rove, Bush's top political adviser, selected Dirk Van Dongen, head of the National Association of Wholesaler-Distributors, to head the coalition.[22] The coalition undertook extensive lobbying, meeting and coordinating strategy with the congressional Republican leadership. A number of the component groups also worked at the grass roots; the NFIB, for example, targeted twenty-three Democrats thought to be persuadable and urged its members to "flood" their fax machines and phones.[23] The Club for Growth, a conservative, low-tax group, ran TV ads in targeted congressional districts. When the securities, chemical, forest, and paper industries launched a coalition to advocate the addition of three provisions to the package, the White House successfully pressed them to cease their activities.[24] All these groups' self-restraint in pushing their favorite tax-break provisions reflected their desire to remain on good terms with the White House, to be perceived as a member of the team, not as a "problem." For the same reason and out of ideological conviction as well, the Christian Coalition and other conservative groups that emphasize social/cultural issues, such as the Family Research Council, also worked for Bush's bill.[25]

The opposition coalition was essentially a mirror image. It too included many groups who are regular Democratic allies but seemingly did not have a direct interest in this bill. Organized by Ralph Neas, director of People for the American Way and formerly head of the Leadership Conference on Civil Rights, it included the Sierra Club, Common Cause, and the NAACP as well as the AFL-CIO, more than five hundred groups in total.

The campaign on the 2003 tax cut is an even better example. The effort was more elaborate, the White House having become more adept in its strategy. And, tellingly, much of the business community was considerably less enthusiastic about the form of the bill, particularly about the central provision making dividends tax-free for the recipients. Yet once again, the administration managed to engineer a united front among the business interests. Those business executives and lobbyists who criticized the bill soon after it was unveiled received phone calls from the White House and Treasury, essentially telling them to shut up.[26] The Tax Relief Coalition was again activated, this time six thousand strong. Members who join the coalition are required to sign a pledge that they will support whatever plan the White House proposes. "When the president says he wants apple pie, we want apple pie. When he wants raisin cake, we want raisin cake," said Jade West, a former GOP Senate staffer who helps run the group from her post at the National Association of Wholesaler-Distributors. "We will support the president. That is a condition of membership."[27] West unabashedly labels the Tax Relief Coalition an "administration coalition" that exists to provide operational support to the White House on Capitol Hill. During the campaign, top members of the coalition began each day with a conference call that included senior officials from the White House and the Treasury and Commerce departments.

One of the regular meetings of coalition members was held in the White House.

In late February 2003, Citigroup and Salomon Smith Barney sent out almost five million letters to stockholders promoting the dividend tax cut and urging recipients to call their members of Congress and press them to support it also. General Motors and Verizon followed suit, Verizon including the political message with dividend checks.[28] The Business Roundtable placed ads in regional newspapers targeting wavering senators. And the Tax Relief Coalition itself bought radio ads.[29] "The whole game now is to get out of this town and start conversations with the American people about the benefits of this plan and put grass-roots pressure on the elected members," said R. Bruce Josten, chief lobbyist of the U.S. Chamber of Commerce. The chamber set up a tax-relief website to allow workers to send automated letters and faxes to their lawmakers. In Maine, the American Forest and Paper Association provided mill workers sample letters to the editor and urged them to go to Senator Olympia Snowe's town meetings to back the tax cut. Snowe, a moderate Republican, had expressed serious doubts about it. Plant managers were encouraged to visit the editorial boards of their local newspapers to try to enlist support.[30]

In early 2005, the National Association of Manufacturers (NAM), long reticent about too close an identification with controversial causes, announced that it would make confirmation of Bush's judicial nominees "a top priority for the first time—providing money and a recently honed ability to stir grass-roots action nationwide."[31] Former Michigan governor and longtime Republican activist John Engler, who had recently taken over NAM, spearheaded the change in strategy and thus brought together the president's business allies and the social/cultural conservatives behind a cause of premier importance both to the cultural conservatives and to Bush.

In the fight over Bush's Social Security restructuring, the business interest groups again played major and completely supportive roles. The Alliance for Worker Retirement Security (AWRS), formed by the National Association of Manufacturers in 1998, concentrated on directly lobbying Congress. The Coalition for the Modernization and Protection of America's Social Security (CoMPASS), set up by the Business Roundtable, focused on conducting a nationwide television and grassroots campaign.[32] Both of these coalitions included the major business trade associations—NAM, the Business Roundtable, U.S. Chamber of Commerce, and NFIB—plus many individual businesses. The executive director of AWRS also serves on the board of CoMPASS and is a former employee of the Cato Institute, a conservative think tank that has been advocating Social Security privatization since the early 1980s.

Wealthy interest groups have become much more involved in the PR wars, spending large sums to influence public perceptions. Given the increasingly close relationship between interest groups and parties, much of this benefits the party with which the group or coalition is allied. A study by the Annenberg Public Policy Center found that in 2001–2002, over $105 million were spent in the Washington area on broadcast and print legislative-issue advocacy. The single biggest spender—at over $8 million—was Americans for Balanced Energy Choices, a coalition of mining companies, coal transporters, and electricity producers, funded primarily by the coal industry. Altogether over $15 million were spent on issue advertisements related to the Bush energy bill, 94 percent by business and energy interests. Another big spender was Citizens for Better Medicare, a pharmaceutical industry group first set up to block Clinton's plan for drug benefits for seniors.[33] In the late 1990s when Clinton proposed a plan that would make possible the negotiation of discounts on prescription drugs, the pharmaceutical industry defeated it, running a $30 million ad campaign. The ads featured Flo, an arthritic bowler, saying, "I don't want big government in my medicine cabinet."[34]

The business and ideological groups supporting Bush's tort reform and Social Security agenda planned to spend "$200 million or more" on those battles over the course of the 109th Congress.[35] As experienced Washington reporter Jeff Birnbaum sums up, the U.S. Chamber of Commerce "is at the forefront of a quiet revolution in business lobbying. Corporate groups now raise big money to advance broad issues, largely to help the Republican president enact his fiscal agenda. That's a long step away from what trade associations traditionally did: concentrate on narrow concerns while shunning partisan spats."[36]

The Bush Administration, more than any before it, has pursued almost exclusively what political scientist Mark Peterson calls a "governing party" strategy vis-à-vis interest groups.[37] The purpose of its interactions with groups is programmatic—to pass its program—as opposed to representational. Outreach is exclusive, not inclusive—the administration includes the groups that supported it in the 2000 election; it does not attempt in a meaningful way to include groups that are not longtime supporters. As I have just shown, the administration also expects those groups to act as part of a party team, working not only on issues of specific and direct interest to the group but on those important to the party as a whole. And the administration has largely succeeded at getting groups to meet that expectation.

The almost exclusive use of the governing party strategy—and its form in terms of expectations of team play—depend, I contend, on the partisan polarization that has suffused our political life. Although one saw considerable use of the strategy in the Reagan Administration, the almost exclusive reliance on it that we now see requires polarization. Groups find it harder to play one party off against the other when the parties' issue stances are so far apart; a threat to defect is not credible. Conversely, the home party's threat to cut the group out of the action if it does not do its share is more credible.

The benefits of being a team player are high. The reason I have emphasized the Bush Administration's success in getting all its allied groups to work for the Bush tax proposals even when the package did not contain some allies' top priorities, and to refrain from freelancing to get more, is that this would have been quite extraordinary only a few years ago. Overall, however, the allied groups are reaping huge gains from the administration—not because the administration is selling out but primarily because Bush and his political appointees agree with their allied groups, as do most congressional Republicans. What we know about the Cheney task force indicates that the energy bill was written with enormous input from the industry, but does anyone believe it does not reflect Bush's and Cheney's views? Bush energy policy epitomizes the coincidence of views and interests between the industry and the administration. The administration's actions in the regulatory arena—in rolling back a plethora of Clinton-era environmental and labor regulations—are an even better example. And the Christian Right and other allied groups most interested in cultural issues have gotten favorable judicial nominations and administrative actions furthering faith-based groups.

Partisan and ideological polarization seem to have led the Bush team and most congressional Republicans to conclude that satisfying the base is much more important than reaching out to the unaffiliated in the middle of the spectrum. "There's a realization, having looked at the past few elections, that the party that motivates their base—that makes their base emotional and turn out—has a much higher likelihood of success on Election Day," said Matthew Dowd, a senior Bush political adviser, in an interview with the *New York Times*.[38] Republicans seem to perceive little downside to excluding all but their allies from the policy process.

In terms of strategies vis-à-vis interest groups, however, there is asymmetry between the parties. No matter the extent of partisan polarization, no Democratic administration will be able to rely on the governing party strategy as exclusively as Republicans can. Republicans can exclude environmental, civil rights, and women's groups and labor from the policy process; Democrats cannot exclude business. Thus dancing exclusively with the ones "who brung you" works for Republicans but not for Democrats.

Groups in the Electoral Process

Interest groups have long been involved in the electoral process, contributing to varying extents money, campaign workers, and endorsements. Issue polarization has led to shifts in the patterns of contributions by some groups. The NRA, for example, has shifted its contributions to candidates and its expenditures on behalf of candidates more and more toward Republicans and away from Democrats.[39] In 1992 the NRA gave 64 percent to Republicans; in 2000, 92 percent went to Republicans.[40] With Al Gore excoriating the drug companies for gouging seniors in the 2000 elections, the pharmaceutical industry gave heavily to congressional Republicans and to Bush, who supported a drug benefit set up in such a way that would make it impossible for the government to bargain for big discounts from the industry.

A notable change in contribution patterns of business political action committees occurred with the switch in party control of the House in the 1994 elections. From 1988 through 1994, corporate PACs gave an average of 53 percent of their House contributions to Democrats, almost all of that to incumbents. For the period 1996 through 2002, the proportion given to Democrats dropped to 34 percent. The pattern is similar for trade association PACs and also for giving to Senate campaigns.[41] Political scientist Gary Jacobson neatly sums up the switch: "Willing to make a marriage of convenience with Democrats so long as

Democrats were running the show, the PACs were now free to pursue a love match with the ideologically more compatible Republicans."[42]

Polarization and, in some cases, the switch in control influenced other interest group electoral decisions as well. In 2000, the NFIB endorsed not a single Democrat for federal office.[43] The U.S. Chamber of Commerce, exceedingly hesitant until recently to oppose incumbent members of Congress of either party, in 2004 launched a $40 million campaign to defeat its opponents and put Senate Democratic Leader Tom Daschle at the top of its list of targets.[44] Some liberal groups have also changed their behavior. Liberal organizations in recent years have shifted to being more forthrightly partisan, says Nina Miller, political director of Planned Parenthood, according to political scientist Richard Skinner.[45] Planned Parenthood changed its policy to allow endorsements in presidential elections.[46]

Although business or other interest groups giving to the candidates that support their positions and interests is hardly new, the kinds of ads some business groups have begun to run do represent a change. The pharmaceutical industry, as the *New York Times* reported, "bought $50 million in TV commercials and millions more in radio, newspaper and direct-mail ads [in 2000]. The ads assured voters that Republican lawmakers were fighting for a Medicare drug benefit. Drug makers also gave the United States Chamber of Commerce $10 million more to run ads under its name. Months before the election, House Republicans passed a bill along the industry's preferred lines."[47] In the 2002 election season, the drug industry contributed $26 million, again mostly to Republican candidates. And, more telling for my argument, it again spent millions on television ads in crucial districts around the country—again telling voters that Republican incumbents had been fighting to add prescription drugs to Medicare. "What they did, which was so clever, was run ads in

Republican districts saying, 'Thank Congressman X for coming up with a prescription drug program for seniors,'" said Arizona Senator John McCain, who voted against the 2003 Medicare bill, saying it favored drug makers while providing the elderly little relief. "They were helping these guys get re-elected who had done nothing."[48] Clearly the pharmaceutical industry was pursuing its own interests, but it was doing so as an adjunct of the Republican Party.

The beginning of the twenty-first century has also witnessed increasingly aggressive campaigns by big business trade groups to stimulate employer-to-employee political persuasion. In 1999 NAM and the Business-Industry Political Action Committee (BIPAC), which it funds, launched the Prosperity Project, the purpose of which is "provide tools that help companies and associations educate and motivate their employees regarding candidates, issues and elections."[49] By 2004, the project had eighty field organizers, and more than seven hundred companies and trade groups had joined.[50] The Chamber of Commerce and NFIB are engaged in similar voter education projects aimed at employees. Comparisons of the candidates on issues of importance to business feature prominently in all these education efforts. Unsurprisingly, Republican candidates fare well; Democratic candidates fare poorly. John Kerry flunked on every one of the eight issues in the 2004 NAM guide.

POLICY EXPERTS AND THINK TANKS

Over the past three decades, think tanks—independent, nonprofit organizations dedicated to carrying out and disseminating public policy research and analysis—have become bigger players in national politics and policy making; many have taken on overt policy-advocacy roles; and the ideological balance of the think tank community has moved sharply right. According to Andrew Rich and R. Kent Weaver, scholars who have written extensively on think tanks, more than three hundred think tanks were operating in American politics as of the mid-1990s; three decades earlier, the number was less than seventy.[51] Because it grows tricky at the margins to determine what constitutes a think tank—as opposed to an interest group, for example—various scholars' numbers differ; but all agree that the numbers increased greatly in the 1970s and 1980s. Diane Stone lists sixteen think tanks as having come into existence through 1940, with several of those being the result of mergers of others; between 1941 and 1969, nineteen think tanks were formed; from 1970 to 1979, forty-one were established; and from 1980 through 1995, another fifty-six came into existence.[52]

The early think tanks were a product of the Progressive movement and its faith in expertise. Convinced that social science could fruitfully be brought to bear on social, economic, and political problems, several philanthropists established privately funded research institutes.[53] Among this first generation of think tanks were the Russell Sage Foundation established in 1907, Carnegie Endowment for International Peace (1910), National Bureau of Economic Research (1920), and the Brookings Institution, formed in 1927 by merging the Institute of Government Research (1916), Institute of Economics (1922), and Robert Brookings Graduate School of Economics and Government (1924). The period between the end of World War II and the late 1960s saw the formation of several major think tanks that primarily perform contract research work for the government—most notably RAND (1948) and the Urban Institute (1968). Most of the first- and second-generation think tanks placed a strong emphasis on research that met accepted academic standards and prided themselves on performing "objective," ideologically neutral analysis.

The typical think tank established after 1970 displayed a very different thrust. That period of explosive growth is characterized by the proliferation of "advocacy" think tanks, which "combine a strong policy, partisan or ideological bent with aggressive salesmanship [in] an effort to influence current policy debates."[54] Less concerned about generating new ideas from original research and more interested in disseminating ideas and proposals to policy makers, opinion leaders, and the public, these think tanks focus on "synthesizing and repackaging" existing research; on producing concise, user-friendly reports rather than books; and on gaining exposure in the media and access to policy makers.[55]

The world of advocacy think tanks has a strong conservative bias. Several decades ago, a number of foundations and rich individuals on the far right decided to invest heavily in such think tanks. They believed they were losing the battle of ideas and that an organized effort to right the balance was needed.[56] In the 1970s the John M. Olin Foundation, Smith-Richardson Foundation, Scaife family, Joseph Coors, and a few others began to fund new and existing conservative organizations with the aim of changing public policy discourse. The original givers have been joined over time by a number of others with huge assets and a dedication to conservative causes. The National Committee for Responsive Philanthropy (NCRP) found that over the years 1999 to 2001, 79 conservative grant-making organizations funded 331 public policy nonprofits with policy-related grants that totaled more than $254 million.[57]

The Sarah Scaife Foundation with assets of $323 million and the Olin Foundation with assets of $71 million are still among the top five; the totals they awarded in conservative public policy grants over the period 1999–2001 were $44.8 million and $17.4 million respectively. The Bradley Foundation with assets in 2001 of over $585 million made conservative public policy grants that totaled $38.8 million from 1999 to 2001. The Shelby Cullom Davis Foundation with assets of $78 million and giving of $13 million and the Richard and Helen DeVos Foundation with assets $97 million and giving of $12 million round out the top five.[58] Three

Koch Family foundations with combined conservative public policy grants of over $20 million in 1999–2001 would rank in the top five if combined.

Twenty-five conservative nonprofit organizations received more than half of the total public policy grants made by the seventy-nine conservative grant-making organizations over these three years, a total of almost $140 million. The top recipient with $28.5 million in grants was the Heritage Foundation; the American Enterprise Institute (AEI) was third, with $7.6 million.[59] The Cato Institute, Citizens for a Sound Economy, Manhattan Institute, and National Center for Policy Analysis—all broad-focus national think tanks—are among the top twenty-five recipients, as are a few more narrowly focused organizations, including for example the National Right to Work Legal Defense and Education Fund.

Conservative grant makers have amplified the impact of their generous contributions by pursuing smart funding strategies. NCRP's studies conclude that by providing general operating support rather than project-specific grants and by doing so over the long term, "in some cases for two decades or more," the conservative grant makers have succeeded in building strong institutions. "This type of unrestricted grant gives their grantees the flexibility they need to build strong institutions, do innovative work without having to worry about attracting new donors, and respond in a timely manner to policy issues without having to wait for a project specific grant," explain Jeff Krehely and colleagues.[60] Such investments by conservative grant makers "in institutions and projects geared toward the marketing of conservative policy ideas" and their support for "the development of conservative public intellectuals and policy leaders" have paid off handsomely.[61]

The Heritage Foundation is the epitome of the successful conservative advocacy think tank. It has an multimillion-dollar operating budget ($34.6 million in 2003), a staff of over 180, and impressive multistory headquarters on Capitol Hill.[62] Heritage is unapologetic about its ideological mission: "We state up front what our beliefs are and admit we are combatants in the battle of ideas," explained Burt Pines, a Heritage vice president. "The staff uses its expertise to mobilize arguments. They are advocates. . . . We make it clear to them that they are not joining an academic organization but one committed to certain beliefs."[63] Pines has stated matters even more crisply: "We're not here to be some kind of Ph.D. committee giving equal time. Our role is to provide conservative public policymakers with arguments to bolster their side."[64]

In keeping with its clear ideological mission, Heritage gives the dissemination of its ideas top priority. "We certainly spend as much money on marketing our ideas as we do on research," said Phillip Turlock, another vice president. "Our aim is to change public policy—not just comment on it—so we have to give marketing a key role in our total mission."[65] And, as president Edwin Feulner explained, "our role is trying to influence the Washington policy community . . . most specifically the Hill, secondly the executive branch, thirdly the national news media."[66]

To achieve its purposes, Heritage emphasizes concise and timely reports on major policy issues aimed at policy makers—especially at members of Congress. The reports are often hand-delivered to members' offices. The foundation disseminates ideas to the press through an elaborate set of mechanisms. It has its own TV and radio studios; it syndicates op-ed pieces through the Knight-Ridder wire service; it puts out to the press a weekly "hot sheet"; and in 2003 it began "web memos," short papers "issued exclusively online to provide information or insights on breaking news, debates or major events."[67] Heritage maintains an extensive database of journalists organized by specialty and sends its studies along with an easily read synopsis to all who might be interested. Each study is turned into an op-ed piece as well.[68] The think tank's sophisticated website, as the Heritage 2003 Annual Report explains, "presents instantly—to policy-makers, the press and the world—the hundreds of research papers, analysis, commentaries, lectures and debates we produce each year."[69] The website lists Heritage's experts by name and by area of expertise, supplying a phone number and e-mail address for each for ease of contact. "Our experts are available 365 days a year," the website offers. "To arrange an interview, call the Media Hotline," which functions twenty-four hours a day. Heritage also maintains townhall.com, a website linking more than a hundred conservative organizations and publications.

"Since day one, Heritage's primary audience has been those who govern—those who make policy decisions in Congress and the executive branch," Heritage proclaims.[70] In 2003, according to its Annual Report, Heritage experts conducted over five hundred briefings for members of Congress, administration officials, and congressional staffers. In addition, more than a hundred members of Congress visited the Heritage offices for private briefings. Heritage regularly holds issue forums featuring members of Congress and administration officials along with its own experts. Its Government Relations department helps members and their staffs prepare for hearings by identifying appropriate Heritage experts as possible witnesses. An eight-month-long internship for congressional staffers now graduates two to three dozen students a year.

All this effort pays off in considerable visibility for Heritage. Heritage experts made 1,100 TV appearances in 2003, up from 688 the year before; during 2003, they logged 1,418 radio appearances, up from 1,144. The Heritage.org website recorded 3.6 million hits that year, and townhall.com had 25 million.[71]

Heritage is only one, if perhaps the most successful, of the conservative advocacy think tanks. Over the years 1999–2001, thirty public policy organizations received grants in the public policy area that totaled over $1 million from conservative foundations, the NCRP found.[72] And many such organizations have funding sources other than foundations.

The rise of the advocacy think tank was not purely a conservative phenomenon. A number of liberal think tanks also sprang up and continue in existence. Some are fairly specialized; the Joint Center for Political and Economic Studies, which is dedicated to the advancement of African Americans, was established in 1970; the Center for Women's Policy Studies, a feminist think tank, dates from 1972. In 1981 the Center on Budget and Policy Priorities (CBPP) joined the Institute for Policy Studies (IPS) as broad-gauge think tanks on the left. IPS was founded in 1963 and can be considered one of the earliest of the advocacy think tanks. In 1986 the labor-supported Economic Policy Institute (EPI) was created. One could add several others if one's definition of "left" were not too stringent: the Center for National Policy (originally the Center for Democratic Policy), founded in 1981, states its mission as to "engage national leaders with new policy options and innovative programs designed to advance progressive ideas in the interests of all Americans." Its board has consisted mostly of centrist Democrats and has included Republicans.[73] The Progressive Policy Institute, created in 1989, is affiliated with the centrist Democratic Leadership Council.

The advocacy think tanks on the left, like those on the right, attempt to influence the issue agenda and policy outcomes through influencing policy makers directly and via the media. However, they work under the disadvantage of much smaller budgets. Thus in 1996, when Heritage's budget was $24 million and AEI's $13 million, the CBPP, EPI, and IPS budgets combined amounted to only $8.2 million. According to the Center for Responsive Philanthropy, liberal foundations and other givers have followed much less effective funding strategies vis-à-vis think tanks, often providing only project-specific grants when they give to think tanks at all.

Conservatives argue that Brookings and the Urban Institute, both large and affluent think tanks, are on the left. But clearly these first- and second-generation think tanks interpret their mission differently from how the advocacy think tanks view theirs. The Brookings Institution and the Urban Institute pride themselves on doing high-quality, unbiased research; they do not see their mission as promoting an ideology and certainly not a political party. Brookings, in fact, has worked hard to increase its credibility with conservatives by adding Republicans to its staff.

The disparity in resources between advocacy think tanks on the left and the right does make a difference. A careful study by Rich and Weaver found that the best predictor of media visibility was the think tank's budget—rich think tanks (and those located in Washington, D.C.) were much more frequently cited in 1991–98 in the six national newspapers they examined than were the think tanks with fewer resources.[74] That translated, they discovered, to identifiably conservative think tanks gaining much greater visibility than did liberal ones. Rich and Weaver further found that those visible in the media were more likely to have their experts called to testify before congressional committees.[75]

Reporters work under time pressure, so they are most likely to use sources that make it easy for them. Think tanks, especially those located in Washington, fit the bill. They are easy to reach, and advocacy think tank scholars realize they need to provide concise, timely analyses that are sensitive to reporters' deadlines. Once a source has been used and has proven satisfactory, it is much easier for a reporter to keep going back than to search for new sources. Thus, although definitive data are not available, think tanks seem to make up an increasing share of the public policy "experts" cited by the media. Of course, the larger the think tank's budget, the more reporter-friendly it can make its operation; twenty-four-hour press hotlines and dozens of experts well trained in providing reporters pithy quotes without jargon do not come cheap.

Policy makers, especially members of Congress, face similar problems in their search for information. They are nonspecialists. They lack the time to read long, complex analyses of issues and policy proposals, and information is useful to them only if it is available at the right time in the legislative process. Think tanks and their scholars are more likely to be sensitive to these needs than other scholars are. Members of Congress do, to a considerable extent, pick their think tank sources by ideological compatibility. Tim Groseclose found that over the period January 1, 1993, to December 31, 2002, members of Congress cited think tanks as sources of information more than fifty thousand times on the floor of Congress; Republicans cited conservative think tanks 83.4 percent of the time; Democrats cited liberal think tanks 81.5 percent of the time. Of the nineteen think tanks most frequently cited, at least fourteen are clearly advocacy organizations; only Brookings and RAND are clearly think tanks from the first and second generations.[76] The single most cited think tank was Heritage. It appears, then, that the experts on whom members of Congress rely are now more likely to be ideological advocates.

To the extent that partisan wars are fought out with ideas in the public sphere, Democrats are at an organizational disadvantage. The affluent think tanks with something of a liberal bent—Brookings, for example—certainly do not see their mission as promoting the Democratic Party in the way that Heritage and AEI promote the Republican Party.[77] The smaller and far less affluent think tanks that are clearly on the left have often criticized Democrats. Even the Progressive Policy Institute (the Democratic Leadership Council's think tank and, as such, clearly affiliated with the Democratic Party) seems to go after Democrats at least as often as it goes after Republicans. Clinton Administration spokesperson Joe Lockhart expressed the party consensus: "Certainly right now the conservative right does a much better job of feeding the media beast facts and arguments that make its case."[78] To counter this deficit, the Center for American Progress (CAP) was launched in 2003, a Democratic think tank with "a muscular communications component," to quote Laura Nichols, senior vice president.[79] It is headed by John Podesta, former Clinton chief of staff; Nichols is a former Gephardt staffer. CAP's statement of objectives makes clear just how central communication is to its mission:

> Our policy and communications efforts are organized around four major objectives:
>
> - developing a long term vision of a progressive America,
> - providing a forum to generate new progressive ideas and policy proposals,
> - responding effectively and rapidly to conservative proposals and rhetoric with a thoughtful critique and clear alternatives, and
> - communicating progressive messages to the American public.[80]

RETURN OF THE PARTY PRESS?

No discussion of our changing politics can leave out the media: how they and their role in the politics of the policy process have changed. In chapter 6, I briefly discuss how TV coverage of national politics increased in the 1960s and how that affected politics. In more recent years, coverage of government and politics in the mainstream media has decreased. In their search for the biggest audiences possible, the TV networks and many newspapers have moved away from covering politics to more emphasis on "news you can use"—lifestyle topics, health news, and the like. A recent Council for Excellence in Government study looked at coverage of the national government for selected years from the early 1980s through 2001 (1981, 1993, 2001) on the three TV network evening news shows, in two national newspapers (*New York Times* and *Washington Post*), and in four well-regarded local newspapers.[81]

The study found a big drop in stories about the national government on TV news and in the local papers (on the order of 30 percent on TV and 40 percent in the local press); coverage when measured by the number of stories also dropped in the national papers (12 percent), but when measured by column inches it actually increased. Coverage of each of the institutions—the executive branch, Congress, and the judiciary—decreased. The Project for Excellence in Journalism, in an examination of the front pages (section one, metro, and lifestyle) of sixteen newspapers in 1977, 1987, 1997, and 2003, also found decreases: coverage of government dropped from 33 percent of stories to 27 percent and coverage of foreign affairs from 27 to 21 percent. In 2003, the network nightly news ran a considerably lower proportion of stories about government than the newspapers ran on the front pages of section one (16 percent vs. 26 percent) but actually ran a larger proportion of foreign affairs stories (25 percent vs. 18 percent). The network nightly news has been shrinking in length since 1988; it averaged just under nineteen minutes of news in the thirty-minute slot in 2003. People who get their news from network TV or from their local newspaper are exposed to much less coverage of national government news now than they were twenty years ago.

The mainstream news media are losing audience. The proportion of Americans who read a daily newspaper has been dropping since the late 1940s. Currently 54 percent say they read a newspaper during the week.[82] A Pew study found that in 2004 only 42 percent said they had read a newspaper yesterday, down from 50 percent in 1996. The young are least likely to be newspaper readers; only 23 percent of those under thirty said they read a newspaper on a typical day.[83] Furthermore, young peoples are not acquiring the newspaper habit as they grow older, the way their parents did. And in all groups except those over sixty-five, the rate of newspaper reading is going down.

Americans have long named television as their primary source for news. In 2003, 83 percent of Americans said they got most of their news from TV.[84] Yet viewership of the nightly network news shows is down; their ratings have declined by 34 percent over the past decade, 44 percent since the 1980s, and 59 percent from their peak in 1969.[85] Only about a third of Americans say they regularly watch the network news; a Pew survey found that 34 percent said they did in 2004, down from 42 percent in 1996. Furthermore, viewers of the nightly TV news, like newspaper readers, are getting older. Again, the young are not developing the habit.

Where are Americans going for their news? Some are not going anywhere; for those with little interest, avoiding the news altogether is considerably easier than it used to be. The range of alternatives available just on TV is now enormous.

For those who do want news, alternatives to newspapers and the network news are also more available than they used to be. Cable television offers plenty of news about government and politics. CNN, Fox News Network, MSNBC, and CNBC, not to mention C-SPAN and C-SPAN II for the incurable Congress junkie, make news available 24/7. Talk radio and the Internet are other readily accessible sources.

Cable news has become Americans' medium of choice for national and international news; since at least the mid-1990s, more people say they get such news from cable than from either network or local broadcast TV.[86] In seven surveys carried out between February 2001 and March 2003, Pew found that between 35 and 50 percent of those questioned chose "cable news networks such as CNN, MSNBC, and the Fox News Channel" as their primary source. Another study found that 38 percent of those questioned said they regularly viewed cable news channels, and another 33 percent said they sometimes did; both figures were higher than the comparable figures for the nightly TV news.[87] Cable viewership more than doubled from the mid-1990s to the early 2000s, but growth in the core audience has stalled in the last several years. The audiences for the primary evening cable newscasts are still quite small compared to those for broadcast network evening newscasts, so presumably people are tuning into cable at various times of the day. Its availability when one wants it may well be part of its attraction.

Almost everyone—94 percent—listens to radio. Radio has avoided a decline in listenership by proliferation in the number of stations, fragmenting the audience into finer and finer niche groups.[88] About 15 percent of Americans report that their primary radio station is a news/talk station. In a January 2003 Gallup poll, 22 percent reported that they relied on talk radio as their primary news source; another 22 percent cited National Public Radio (NPR) as their primary news source.

The Internet has also become an increasingly important news source; in mid-1995, only 2 percent of those surveyed said they got news online three or more days per week; clearly, Internet news was the province of "computer nerds." By 2004, 29 percent reported going on line for news at least three times a week.

For those who get their news from cable TV or from talk radio, much of what they encounter has a hard ideological edge and a rightward tilt. Talk radio is dominated by conservatives. Rush Limbaugh, G. Gordon Liddy, Oliver North, and Sean Hannity are among the best-known talk show hosts and have the highest listenership, but there are a great many more.[89] On the left, only Al Franken of the recently established Air America comes anywhere close in fame, and he is far behind in audience reach. According to an estimate by longtime conservative activist Paul Weyrich, there were seventeen hundred right-wing radio talk show hosts by 2003.[90] Limbaugh could be heard almost everywhere in the United States, often multiple times a day, and drew about 12 million listeners per day.[91] Talk radio feeds on outrage. Most of the talk show hosts are high-decibel ranters who are none too careful about their facts.[92] The "news" that listeners receive from talk radio is likely to be not only ideologically biased but often just plain wrong. "Commercial radio . . . has by now totally abandoned serious journalism," Lawrence Grossman, former head of PBS and NBC, has observed.[93]

The Fox News Network was established in 1996 with the specific purpose of countering what its creators claimed was a liberal bias in the news.[94] Rupert Murdoch, its owner, and Roger Ailes, whom Murdoch hired to run the channel, are well-known conservatives; Ailes is a former Republican strategist. The network, according to the studies that have been done, clearly tilts right. "The attentive viewer, over time, inevitably detects . . . an unmistakable conservative biosphere, and a tendency to launch dialogue from right-of-center assumptions that need sorting out before the discourse can begin," according to the *Columbia Journalism Review*.[95] Respected *New Yorker* media writer Ken Auletta spent four months watching Fox in 2003 and concluded: "I saw a network that was not, as advertised, free of bias and 'fair and balanced.' . . . The network proclaims 'we report, you decide.' But too often Fox both reports and decides. The anchors are opinionated throughout the day, not just in the evening hours with Bill O'Reilly or Sean Hannity. Too often, the commentators tilt to the right and don't present both sides."[96] Fairness and Accuracy in Reporting (FAIR), a media watchdog group, found a systematic partisan bias in the political guests interviewed on Brit Hume's daily news show; 50 of 56 were Republicans, compared to 36 of 67 during the same period on Wolf Blitzer's CNN program.[97] Bill O'Reilly's *The O'Reilly Factor* and Shawn Hannity's *Hannity and Colmes* are TV versions of right-wing talk radio shows in their lack of ideological balance, their high emotional content, and their tendency to play fast and loose with the facts. (Both O'Reilly and Hannity host talk radio shows as well.)

Fox is now the most highly rated of the cable news networks and is still gaining in the ratings. *The O'Reilly Factor* is the single highest-rated cable show.[98] Fox's fast pace, jazzy graphics, and appeal to the emotions rather than the intellect certainly account for some of its popularity. Fox is blurring the line between news and entertainment just as it blurs the line between facts and opinions. The "Foxification" of news has become a worry among more traditional journalists.

Even excluding Fox, movement conservatives can be found all over the TV dial. Often they are presented in a debatelike format, but also quite often, the "liberal" opponent is a journalist who feels some obligation toward objectivity. A huge contingent of "pundits"—William Kristol, David Brooks, Tucker Carlson, Fred Barnes, Charles Krauthammer, Paul Gigot, Ann Coulter, George Will, and Bob Novak, to name only a few—promote the message on TV and in print. Many of them have been nurtured by the conservative infrastructure: Heritage and the other conservative think tanks, and journals like *The Weekly Standard*, another Murdoch property. Not only are they promoting the conservative cause; to a very large extent they are promoting the Republican Party.

The existence of the conservative media has an impact on politics and policy. Members of Congress and their staffs named talk radio as the single most influential media source for their constituents during the health care debate in 1993–94, and many named Rush Limbaugh specifically.[99] Talk radio generally and Limbaugh in particular may well have been a significant source of constituents' growing uneasiness with the Clinton plan that many Democratic members perceived in 1994. A study by the Program on International Policy Attitudes (PIPA) found that even when one takes into account their differences in education and other such factors, people who watched Fox were much more likely than those who got their news from other sources to hold a variety of misperceptions about the Iraq situation—that weapons of mass destruction had been found or that Iraq was directly involved in the 9/11 attacks, for example.[100]

The right-wing media can have a major impact on the mainstream media by making a story so big, even if it is highly questionable factually, that the mainstream cannot ignore it. A story may get into the media bloodstream via a blogger or the Drudge Report; after it has circulated among the conservative bloggers and Drudge, talk radio may pick it up; from there it is likely to move to Fox and then to the other cable networks.[101] Once the conservative media spread a story enough for significant numbers of people to be talking about it, both commercial interests and journalistic values pressure the mainstream media to cover the story and so give it even more visibility. The claims made by the "Swiftboat Veterans for Truth" about Democratic presidential candidate John Kerry's Vietnam service are a textbook example of this phenomenon. This obscure 527 group made a small media buy in three battleground states in early August 2004.[102] Within two weeks, 57 percent of a national sample of Americans had either seen or heard about the ad.[103] Those who watched cable or listened to talk radio were most likely to have seen or heard about the ads. Conservative talk radio and cable TV played the ads, gave air time and a respectful hearing to John O'Neill, the head of the group, and endlessly discussed the charges, usually uncritically, to the point that the mainstream media could no longer ignore the story even though evidence to back it up was lacking. In the words of *Washington Post* media writer Howard Kurtz, "The media . . . picked up the issue and ran with it on a hundred cable finger-pointing shows—without having the slightest idea whether it was true. Without that echo-chamber effect, this dinky little ad would have sunk without a trace."[104] Eventually good reporting by several major newspapers debunked the charges, but whether the facts ever caught up with the story as played in the conservative media is unclear. Limbaugh and many of Fox's programs gave short shrift to the conclusions of the investigative reporting that disproved the claims.[105] As one would expect, Republicans and Bush supporters were likely to find the charges credible and Democrats and Bush opponents were likely to find them not believable, but 46 percent of persuadable voters and 34 percent of independents found them either very or somewhat believable.[106]

Despite the continued drumbeat from conservatives about the "liberal media," Democrats and liberals are at a substantial disadvantage in the battle to frame the political debate and define the limits of the acceptable. Democrats and liberals lack clearly ideological and partisan media with the reach of Fox or talk radio. Conservatives argue that the *New York Times*, *Washington Post*, NPR, and sometimes CBS News are the left-wing counterparts of the *Washington Times*, talk radio, and Fox. Even if one accepts that the two newspapers lean left in their editorial policy—and on many issues that is a questionable assumption about the *Post*—the problem for Democrats is that none of these media outlets sees its task as promoting the Democratic Party, even in its editorials. A recent study by the Shorenstein Center compared editorials in those two liberal papers with those in the *Wall Street Journal* and the *Washington Times*, both conservative papers.[107] The author compared ten instances in the Clinton and George W. Bush presidencies that were roughly similar—for example, the furor over secrecy by Hillary Clinton's health care task force and Dick Cheney's energy task force. The study found that the conservative papers were more partisan, often far more partisan, in terms of the intensity with which they criticized the other side; their language was sometimes extremely harsh. They were also a lot less willing to criticize a Republican administration than liberal papers were to criticize a Democratic administration. As the author concludes, "The conservative editorial pages are more likely to think of themselves as being 'on the team' as it were, supporting a Republican administration, while the liberal papers do strive for more independence."[108] Or, as influential movement conservative Grover Norquist has expressed it, "The conservative press is self-consciously conservative and self-consciously part of the team."[109] NPR does not run editorials, but studies of the sources it uses have been made. FAIR examined every partisan source cited by NPR on its new shows in June 2003—"government officials, party officials, campaign workers, and consultants"—and found that 61 percent were Republicans and 38 percent Democrats. Since unified Republican government prevailed at that time, a Republican advantage might be expected, but a similar study in 1993 when unified Democratic government prevailed found that 57 percent of the sources were Republican and 42 percent Democratic.[110] The claim of liberal bias—at least if that implies a Democratic bias—does not seem to hold up.

With the development of the conservative news media has come an ideological polarization of the news audience. Increasingly, conservatives and Republicans are watching Fox; Democrats and liberals are more likely to get their news from CNN, the nightly network news, and NPR. In 2004, more than half (52 percent) of regular Fox viewers described themselves as conservative, up from 40 percent in 2000. The regular CNN audience has become more Democratic (44 percent) than the public as a whole but is very similar in ideology. NPR's audience has become significantly more liberal (30 percent) than the population as a whole (18 percent.) Not surprisingly, Rush Limbaugh's audience is overwhelmingly conservative (77 percent), as is the viewership of the *O'Reilly Factor* (72 percent). Very few liberals or Democrats are "ditto heads" or O'Reilly regulars.[111] Viewing patterns for the 2004 national party conventions nicely illustrate this partisan polarization. People who watched the Democratic convention on TV—who would tend to be disproportionately Democrats—watched it on one of the three networks or on CNN. People who watched the Republican convention—mostly Republicans, presumably—were most likely to watch it on Fox.[112]

Evaluations of media credibility are also polarized along ideological and partisan lines. Fox is the most trusted news source among Republicans and is among the least trusted by Democrats. Republicans are generally more distrustful of the media than Democrats, and between 2000 and 2004, they became significantly less trustful still. Among Republicans, the credibility of CNN, the nightly network news, and even C-SPAN and the *Wall Street Journal* have declined.[113]

Thus not only do Republicans and Democrats, conservatives and liberals, get their news from different sources—the two sides do not trust the others' media of choice. Republicans do not believe much of what the mainstream media say. Consequently, even when Republicans and conservatives are exposed to the mainstream news media, what they hear is unlikely to affect their attitudes since they give it little credence.

The development of prominent conservative and often partisan media and the audience patterns they make possible have almost certainly amplified partisan polarization among the interested. The situation is becoming analogous to that characteristic of the nineteenth century, when people got their news from highly partisan newspapers, and of course people read the newspapers aligned with their own party, which then reinforced their partisanship. Like the man from Sugarland, Texas, who gets his news from Fox, the Drudge Report, townhall.com, and assorted other right-wing websites, you can come close to restricting your news sources to ones that agree with you.[114] "We have lost our conversational commons," argues communications scholar Thomas Hollihan. "Common news experiences are fundamental to the formation of a political community."[115]

CHAPTER 10

THE CONSEQUENCES OF PARTISAN POLARIZATION

The Bad, the Ugly, and—the Good?

A HALF CENTURY AGO, a group of eminent political scientists decried the then current state of affairs in which "either major party, when in power, is ill-equipped to organize its members in the legislative and executive branches into a government held together and guided by the party program."[1] In a report titled "Towards a More Responsible Two-Party System," they called for parties that "are able to bring forth programs to which they commit themselves and . . . [that] possess sufficient internal cohesion to carry out these programs."[2] Responsible parties, they argued, are the essence of a well-functioning democracy.

Political parties seem to meet the requirements of responsible parties as defined by these scholars to a greater extent today than at any time in the past half century. Yet the contemporary assessment of the parties and of the partisan polarization that characterizes them is far from sanguine. Partisan polarization evokes near-apocalyptic hand-wringing from most commentators and many scholars. The most frequent arguments made: Partisan polarization is debasing political debate, which has become an endless stream of partisan bickering. It has altered the character of election campaigns from the state legislative level all the way up to the presidency; candidates are now focusing their appeals on their partisan base and so make highly ideological, "red meat" appeals. Both the partisan bickering and the divisive ideological appeals turn off moderates and independents, who consequently are dropping out of the electorate. The policy process has been distorted, with deliberation and compromise replaced by a partisan steamroller. The policy result is often stalemate, and so pressing national problems are left unaddressed.

Are these claims accurate or are they exaggerated? Did the responsible-parties scholars go badly astray in their analyses and prescriptions? To what extent and in what ways should we worry about the consequences of partisan polarization, and is there anything we can do about them? Those are the questions I attempt to answer in this final chapter. To a much greater extent than in the previous chapters, I enter the normative realm; while I present evidence and arguments for my conclusions, my values enter as well. Readers may use the same evidence to come to quite different normative judgments.

THE CHARACTER OF DEBATE AND THE NATURE OF CAMPAIGNS

When commentators accuse politicians of partisan bickering, they are implying that nothing of importance is at issue. Certainly contemporary politicians sometimes argue about issues of peripheral interest to many voters, though we may well differ about what those unimportant issues are. However, the ideological distance between the parties does result in much political debate being about matters of real significance. The parties differ greatly about the appropriate role of government in the domestic sphere and, increasingly, about how the United States should conduct itself in the world. The battles over tax policy, Medicare, and energy policy that were so prominent during the 108th Congress (2003–2004) were not mere fights for partisan advantage; policies that would have a major impact on most Americans now and in the future were at issue. The stakes in the conflict over Social Security in the 109th Congress grew even higher. Republicans and Democrats now hold two starkly different views of the policies that would get us where we want to be, if not two starkly different visions of the good society. The contemporary political parties do stand for something and do offer citizens a choice, as responsible-parties advocates argue parties in a well-functioning democracy should do. If you agree that politics in a democracy should be about something real and important, then parties that are ideologically polarized are not altogether a bad thing.

The narrow margins in both houses of Congress and the almost evenly split presidential electorate combined with the sharp ideological polarization of the parties raise the stakes of politics. Each side really does see the other's policy and electoral success as disastrous for the country; and this sometimes generates a feeling that anything goes, anything is justified to avert such a catastrophe. This sometimes leads to really ugly politics. The dueling ads on Kerry's and Bush's military service during the Vietnam War in the 2004 presidential election campaign are probably the first examples that come to mind, but there are many examples below the presidential level as well. Republicans accused Senate Judiciary Committee Democrats of being anti-Catholic for opposing a Bush judicial nominee. Senate Republicans made and reiterated the charge, and a Republican group associated with the White House ran media ads to that effect. In my judgment, that was way over the line of civilized political discourse. I would say the same thing about Republican ads equating Tom Daschle with Saddam Hussein or questioning the patriotism of Senator Max Cleland, a veteran who left two legs and an arm in Vietnam. And certainly the Republicans are not the only offenders. When Democrat Pete Stark calls Nancy Johnson, his Republican colleague on the Ways and Means Committee, a "whore for the pharmaceutical companies," he is doing nothing to raise the quality of political discourse. Some Democrats are too quick to call Republicans racists. When the perpetrators and the targets of such charges are members of Congress, the consequences for comity and a good working relationship across party lines can be easily imagined.

Even leaving aside such egregious instances of ugly politics, debate is too often mendacious, if not downright dishonest, some would argue. President Bush charges Senator Kerry with opposing body armor for U.S. troops in Iraq and with supporting hundreds of tax increases; Senator Kerry accuses President Bush of "outsourcing jobs" and suggests he is complicit in the Enron scandal. Republicans in Congress accuse Democrats of attempting to raise taxes on the middle class and of putting the wishes of union bosses over the safety of the American people (e.g., in the debate over the Department of Homeland Security). Democrats charge that the Republican Medicare/prescription drugs bill is a giant giveaway to the drug companies and that Congress under Republican control has completely abdicated its responsibility to oversee the executive branch. Almost certainly you think that some—or possibly all—of these charges are misleading.

But was political debate more straightforward and honest in the days before partisan polarization? Did candidates and elected officials just "tell it like it is" and refrain from distorting their opponents' records and positions? If the answer to that question is not obvious, I can say that the evidence does not support the notion of a previous golden age. In a democracy, politicians attempt to persuade citizens; they are advocates, so expecting total objectivity in how they present their case is unrealistic. In fact, ugly politics is not a new phenomenon either, though it may be worse now, at least in Congress, than it has been during most of the post–World War II period.

Partisan bickering and ugly politics have driven appalled citizens away from the polls in droves, it is sometimes argued. Voting participation in the United States is atrocious when compared with that in other industrialized democracies, and turnout has decreased since the 1960s.[3] The evidence, however, does not support attributing the decline to partisan bickering and ugly politics, as I discuss later. And turnout was up in 2004 despite—or perhaps because of—extremely high partisan polarization.

What, then, about the impact of partisan polarization on the character of election campaigns? Are candidates now focusing their appeals much more on their partisan base rather than on the undecideds who are presumed to be in the middle of the ideological spectrum? Relevant comprehensive data do not exist, so my conclusion must be tentative.

Most elections for the House of Representatives are not competitive.[4] This is not a new situation. House districts are relatively small; people who live near one another are likely to be similarly situated economically and to share similar cultural values and thus are likely to have similar political inclinations. And incumbents, who usually fit their districts, can, by tending their districts, make themselves even more secure electorally than they would be based on district fit alone. It does seem to be the case, in at least some states, that redistricting after the 2000 census did produce more districts that are strongly skewed to one party or the other. This may well affect the character of the candidates who win primaries; it is much less clear that it results in highly ideological, "red meat" general election campaigns. The evidence we have indicates that safe incumbents tend to run issueless campaigns; they use appeals based on their character and their service to the district, not on issues. After all, by definition issues have two sides—why offend anyone when you do not have to? It is a competitive challenger who forces an incumbent to address issues.

And yet, the lesson both parties took from the 2002 midterm elections was that the name of the game is now getting the base out to vote. Seemingly, in the 2002 midterm elections, Republicans did not convert anyone, but they did a better job than the

Democrats of mobilizing their base, and they took back the Senate and picked up seats in the House.[5] Certainly in some of the Senate races, they did use "red meat" appeals; for example, by running TV ads in Georgia accusing Max Cleland of opposing protection of the homeland from terrorists. Some of the relatively small number of competitive House races saw fairly ugly personal attacks but, of necessity, stayed away from highly partisan appeals. Outside groups did sometimes make highly emotional ideological appeals, on abortion and guns, for example.[6]

In presidential elections, when turnout is considerably higher, the dominant strategy has been to go after the undecided voters, though without offending the base. That has meant moving toward the ideological center, where the swing or undecided voters are presumed to be. There is considerable evidence that the 2004 election strategy, especially that of the Republican Party, did emphasize getting out the base more than appealing to the undecided. To quote Matt Dowd, a senior Bush reelection operative, "There's a realization, having looked at the past few elections, that the party that motivates their base—that makes their base emotional and turn out—has a much higher likelihood of success on Election Day."[7] To be sure, both candidates did try to appeal to swing voters as well. Yet, as anyone who watched the presidential debates discovered, the differences between the candidates were vast. Because the candidates' positions generally reflected those of their parties, the candidates, by articulating their positions, were in fact appealing to their partisan base. Who would argue that voters of any persuasion were ill served by this clarity?

Much of the strategy of getting out the base focuses on the "ground war," the efforts to identify one's supporters, persuade them to vote, and then make sure they actually go to the polls. In the last few election cycles, much more effort and money have gone into the ground war than in earlier years.[8] The unions made major efforts on behalf of Democrats in the late 1990s and 2000 and turned out a much heavier proportion of union members. In 1992 union members constituted 19 percent of the electorate; by 2002, they were 26 percent.[9] Republicans responded in 2002 with their "72-hour program" to turn out their base; that effort is given much of the credit for Republican success in those elections. In 2003–2004, America Coming Together (ACT), a Democratic 527 organization, mounted a sophisticated voter registration and get-out-the-vote campaign (GOTV) in seventeen battleground states; the focus was, of course, on heavily Democratic areas in those states. In the summer of 2004, the Bush campaign sent a detailed set of instructions to volunteers who were members of conservative churches; they were asked to turn over church directories to the campaign, identify another conservative church that could be "organize[d] for Bush," distribute issue guides in their churches, and persuade their pastors to hold voter registration drives.[10] And this was only one part of the extensive Bush-Cheney ground war.

What can we conclude about the consequences for campaigns? A democrat cannot object to efforts to enhance turnout, even if each party focuses only on those likely to vote for it. Other candidate and party activities that are sometimes included under the rubric of ground war are more disturbing. Direct mail, push polls, and other techniques that allow very fine targeting of voters are open to abuse because activity can be conducted more or less sub rosa; only the targeted group receives the message, and often, if it becomes more widely known, the source of the message is not ascertainable.[11] Such messages often qualify as really ugly politics: fervid appeals to emotions based on untruths. (In 2004, mailings suggesting that Democrats would try to ban the Bible appeared in some southern states.) Whether partisan polarization has exacerbated this problem is a lot less clear.

When candidates appeal to their partisan and ideological base in their public campaigns, does this demobilize the middle? Are moderates who are otherwise attentive and engaged voters so turned off by such rhetoric that they withdraw from the active electorate? Probably not, or not exactly. Yet there are problems with demobilization that may well be exacerbated by the character of debate. Those I discuss after considering the consequences of partisan polarization for the policy process and policy outcomes.

POLARIZATION AND THE POLICY PROCESS

The consequences of partisan polarization for the policy process at the national level are discussed in earlier chapters. To evaluate those consequences, we need normative criteria; what is it that we expect of the policy process? Most of us would agree that we value a legislative process that fosters deliberation, that is open to public scrutiny, and that takes into account the interests and demands of all segments of society; but we also want a process that has the capacity to make decisions relatively expeditiously.

Current arrangements in the House of Representatives promote decisiveness more than deliberation or inclusiveness. Ideologically homogeneous parties and stronger, more centralized leadership in the House facilitate timely and definitive decision making; gridlock is seldom a problem *within* the House. Furthermore, the current process is relatively inclusive within the majority party; rank-and-file Republicans have opportunities to express their views, and committee and party leaders are obliged to pay attention.

One can argue, however, that Republican House leaders have employed their procedural powers so aggressively in recent years that the result is pathologies in the legislative process. More and more, the current process excludes the minority party and the interests and segments of society it represents. When committees do manage to work in a bipartisan fashion on major legislation, the party leaders override the committee if segments of the majority party are unhappy with the bill. To protect party legislation and to spare their members tough votes, highly restrictive rules are employed, frustrating the minority party's ability to make its case. Major legislation is rewritten at the conference stage, often without any minority party involvement.

Even the appropriations process, long the basis of House power in the policy-making system, is becoming distorted with a resort to omnibus appropriations bills. In recent years, the party leadership has regularly superintended a process in which many of the appropriations bills are rolled into one huge omnibus bill in conference, on which members are then forced to vote as a single package. Members are presented with these several-thousand-page bills with little time to examine the contents before they must vote. This process excludes most members—majority as well as minority—from the decision-making process, it makes a mockery of deliberation, and it invites stealth lawmaking.[12] Not only does the leadership routinely drop provisions that have been approved by majority vote in one chamber or both; it also adds provisions that lack majority support.[13]

The current legislative process in the House breeds severe disaffection among minority party members.[14] Deliberation is, at best, truncated, and legitimate interests and views are shut out of the legislative process. Highly partisan decision making can lead to extreme policy incapable of surviving the entire legislative process, especially the Senate, where a bare majority is seldom enough.

The House majority party and its leaders argue that their approach to legislating—routinely using the full clout of the majority and its leadership to enact legislation in a form the president and the majority party prefer—is necessary for Congress to function under current conditions of partisan polarization and narrow margins. Their duty, especially when Congress and the presidency are controlled by the same party, is to govern. Clearly, however, there are costs as well.

Because of the Senate's permissive rules, partisan polarization has a quite different impact on the policy process in that chamber. The habitual exploitation of extended debate by senators has a pervasive influence on the legislative process that extends far beyond its effect on specific legislation. By requiring a supermajority to pass legislation that is at all controversial, Senate rules make the process of coalition building much more difficult. Minority party members and the interests they represent cannot be excluded from the process, as they often are in the House. Timely decision making, however, is a major problem for the Senate and one that is exacerbated by partisan polarization. The minority using the Senate's permissive rules is now often the minority party, and given its size and cohesion, the contemporary minority party can block the Senate from decision making when it so chooses.

The policy-making process includes the president and the executive branch, of course. How has partisan polarization affected the president's role in the process? If one can generalize from the George W. Bush presidency, then Republican presidents operating in a highly polarized environment are likely to pursue a governing party strategy vis-à-vis interest groups, dealing with and relying on those that are firm supporters, "members of the team," and largely excluding opponents. Democratic presidents, as I argue in chapter 9, cannot pursue this strategy to the same extent as Republicans can, because they simply cannot exclude business interests from the process. In dealing with Congress when their party controls at least the House, presidents of both parties are likely to employ a partisan strategy. When the parties are so far apart, compromise is painful. The president does not want to pay the price unless it is essential, and partisan supporters within and outside Congress are likely to be even less willing to do so.

Presidents facing a Congress of the opposing party are likely to have a very difficult time. If either party is to get anything done, compromise is required. Given the costs of compromise, especially to the weaker actor, PR politics is likely to play an even greater role under conditions of divided control of government than under unified control. Whichever side is more successful in framing the debate and defining the issues to its own advantage goes into negotiations with a significant advantage.

Because partisan polarization raises the costs of compromise, all the key actors are likely to resort frequently to PR politics whether control of government is unified or divided. Even under unified government, it is unlikely that the majority party truly controls the Senate, which now requires sixty votes. Although PR politics may seem unedifying and the media are likely to label it grandstanding and to interpret it entirely as posturing for the next election, it is often directly focused on policy, and it has the virtue of involving the public—at least the attentive public—in the process. President Bush's attempts to sell his Social Security restructuring plan and Democrats' efforts to refute his claims involve ordinary Americans in making a key decision that will significantly affect their future.

Partisan polarization may have its most deleterious process effects on congressional oversight of the executive branch. Congress is expected to ensure that the administration executes the laws in a manner that is competent, fair, and in accordance with congressional intent. Judged by the way oversight has been practiced since the mid-1990s, partisan polarization leads to overly aggressive and abusive oversight under divided government and no real oversight under unified government. Congressional Republicans used investigations and finally impeachment to harass President Clinton in ways that had little to do with legitimate oversight. The endless Whitewater investigations, after all, dealt with a business deal that occurred years before Clinton was elected president. When a member of their own party became president, congressional Republicans largely abdicated their oversight responsibilities. When members of the congressional majority party and the president strongly perceive themselves as members of the same team in a high-stakes battle against an opposition team, the lack of serious oversight should come as no surprise. Ferreting out corruption or incompetence in the administration of their own team's leader is unlikely to strike majority party members as a winning strategy.

POLICY OUTCOMES

Process is important, but for many citizens the bottom line is outcomes. What is the impact of partisan polarization on policy outcomes? We have a system of government and a policy process that make policy change difficult. Has partisan polarization exacerbated or alleviated the system's tendency toward the status quo and even gridlock?

We can start by looking at what has happened to the likelihood of major legislation becoming law since the early 1960s (table 10.1). A number of caveats should be kept in mind when interpreting data such as these; probably most important is that all these major bills are by no means equal in significance (take the Civil Rights Act of 1964 and the highway–mass transit act of 1987, as examples). Still, there is a general though not linear decline over time in the rate at which major bills survive the legislative process. That becomes clearer when we look just at the first Congress of newly elected presidents; we expect more bills to become law in a president's first Congress because a new president comes in with a new agenda and usually with somewhat of a honeymoon. The rate of major measures becoming law is 82 percent in the 1960s and early 1970s, quite a high rate, and this is despite President Kennedy's problems with the conservative coalition and President Nixon's with a Democratic Congress. For the period from the late 1970s through the early 2000s (Carter through the second Bush), the rate drops to 67 percent.

Clearly diverse factors are at work; the problem in the late 1970s definitely was not high party polarization. We have to

TABLE 10.1
The Rate of Bills Becoming Law, 1961–2004

Congress	Years	% Enacted	
87th	1961–62	81	**81**
89th	1965–66	77	
91st	1969–70	82	**82**
94th	1975–76	58	
95th	1977–78	69	**69**
97th	1981–82	68	**68**
100th	1987–88	84	
101st	1989–90	64	**64**
103rd	1993–94	65	**65**
104th	1995–96	52	
105th	1997–98	50	
106th	1999–2000	44	
107th	2001–2002	67	**67**
108th	2003–2004	59	

Source: Author's calculations.

Note: The far right column lists the first Congress of a newly elected president. Only major legislation is considered.

look further to get a reading on the impact of partisanship; still, something worth investigating is going on. A second point worth noting is how, in the 1990s, control divided between the presidency and the Congress was a recipe for stalemate. From 1995 through 2000, with Clinton as president and a Republican Congress, on average less than half the major bills became law.

As I show in chapter 7, when control is divided in this period of high partisan polarization, presidents are much more likely than their predecessors to confront legislation emerging from committee and from floor consideration in a form they dislike.

TABLE 10.2

The President's Success with His Agenda

The Impact of Divided versus Unified Control and of Increasing Polarization, Selected Congresses, 1961–2002

	Control				
		Divided			Mixed
President	Unified	All	Pre-100th	100th–105th	107th
Won (% of measures)	63	39	54	33	57
Lost (% of measures)	31	43	30	49	40

Source: Author's calculations based primarily on accounts in *Congressional Quarterly.*

Note: The president's agenda consists of those measures mentioned in his State of the Union address, other major messages to Congress, and important presidential speeches. Polarization was higher in each of the succeeding periods.

In terms of support in Congress, party polarization has hurt presidents more when control is divided than it has helped them when control is unified, though it has done that as well. Presidents confronting a Congress controlled by the opposition party now have a harder time getting their program enacted into law (see table 10.2). George W. Bush, who experienced both unified and partially divided control during his first Congress, did relatively well at getting his agenda enacted into law in a basically acceptable form. Without the issues pushed onto his agenda by the 9/11 attacks—and very likely the atmosphere 9/11 created—Bush's rate of success would be lower.[15] For Bush, as for all the presidents examined here, losses overwhelmingly take the form of legislation failing enactment.

If more major bills fail to make it through the process, where are they stopped? The legislative process has often been called an obstacle course, but are some of the obstacles higher than

TABLE 10.3
Where Major Measures Failed

	Number of Failed Measures	
Action by Chamber	91st, 95th, and 97th Congresses	103rd, 104th, 105th, and 107th Congresses
Passed by neither House nor Senate	16	22
Passed by House but not by Senate	12	33
Passed by Senate but not by House	8	3
Passed by House and Senate	6	22
Total number of failed measures	42 (of 156 measures)	80 (of 192 measures)
Percentage of total measures that failed	27 percent	42 percent

Source: Author's calculations.

others and has this changed? Table 10.3 answers those questions. In the period preceding high partisan polarization, it is hard to point the finger; major legislation that failed most often did not pass either the House or the Senate. In the later period of high partisan polarization, the Senate is the culprit; a lot more bills pass the House and get stopped in the Senate than vice versa.

Those bills that passed both chambers but still did not become law ran into two types of problems: a presidential veto that could not be overridden, also more frequent in the partisan period than earlier; or a problem in resolving House-Senate differences or in getting the resolution accepted (e.g., the bankruptcy bill with the abortion language that House Republicans voted down in 2002). The frequency of House-Senate postpassage problems is

TABLE 10.4
Impact of a Partisan Committee Process on Passage and Enactment, 1961–1998

	House		Senate	
Committee Process	Passed Chamber	Enacted	Passed Chamber	Enacted
Partisan	83	60	71	51
Not partisan	90	74	88	76

Source: Author's calculations.

Note: Figures are percentages. The selected Congresses, from 1961 to 1998, are listed in table 10.1.

not any higher in the later than in the earlier period; but when "blame" could be assigned, it was considerably more likely to be the Senate than the House that "done it" in the partisan period.

To shed some light on the impact of partisanship on the likelihood of a bill becoming a law, consider table 10.4. I use what happened in committee (or in the prefloor legislative process if the committee was bypassed) as my indicator of whether the process was partisan; thus I am looking at what happened to bills on which the process started as partisan or as not partisan. Clearly, partisanship does depress the chances of a bill passing the chamber and becoming law. Increased partisan polarization does account for some of the decrease in the rate of bills becoming laws. Also note that partisanship has a much greater impact in the Senate than in the House. That is as we would expect, since minorities have much more clout to block legislation in the Senate.

We would therefore expect to find a relationship between a bill running into a filibuster problem in the Senate and its ultimate fate. Remember that a lot of filibusters, actual or threatened, are not intended to kill the targeted legislation; often the intent is to extract concessions on the matter or even on another matter entirely. That

TABLE 10.5
Impact of Filibuster Problems on Senate Passage and Enactment, 1961–1998

Filibuster Problem?	Yes	No
Passed Senate	72	83
Enacted	56	72

Source: Author's calculations.

Note: Figures are percentages. The selected Congresses from 1961 to 1998 are listed in table 10.1.

should weaken the relationship. Table 10.5 demonstrates that a bill encountering a filibuster problem is less likely to pass the Senate and less likely to become law. Furthermore, when partisan legislation encounters a filibuster problem, the impact is especially likely to be fatal. Of the bills that were partisan in the Senate committee and then encountered a filibuster problem, only 54 percent passed the Senate and only 39 percent became law. And that combination is much more frequent now than it was in the past.

So what do we make of this? Is less major legislation becoming law a bad thing? True gridlock would be a serious problem, but that is not a correct description of the current state of affairs. The U.S. government does function; it is not about to break down completely. Congress does pass legislation, both must-pass measures such as appropriations bills and quite a lot of other significant legislation. Even when government control was divided between Democratic President Bill Clinton and congressional Republicans, some legislation of major significance was passed, perhaps most notably the 1997 reconciliation bill that set the budget on a path toward balance and established a new health care program for children of the near-poor. George W. Bush and his Republican congressional allies have been thwarted on issues such as energy and malpractice reform but have enacted huge tax cuts and a major change in the Medicare program. Under some circumstances, particularly circumstances that allow the budget process to be employed, the current high cohesion of the Republican Party has made possible the passage of nonincremental legislation supported by at best a narrow majority of the Congress and the public.

In a system with such a strong status quo bias, analysts understandably tend to worry about the barriers to policy change. Certainly that was a central concern of the responsible-parties advocates. But perhaps we should also consider whether we really want our elected officials to make choices that may be irrevocable so long as voters are so narrowly divided.

WHAT IS TO BE DONE?

In a chapter billed as evaluating the impact of partisan polarization, I have answered few questions unequivocally. The answers to questions about whether the impact is "a bad thing" or "a good thing" depend upon one's values. Even beyond that, for many of us, the answers are far from clear-cut because we hold multiple values that cannot be maximized simultaneously. Thus the values of inclusiveness, deliberation, and decisiveness point in different directions when answering questions about the evaluation of a legislative process.

I provide no definitive answers here, not even ones based solely on my own values. I do evaluate some proposals to alter the legislative process. Then I offer my perspective on what I see as perhaps the most basic problem facing American democracy.

When proposing alterations in the legislative process to ameliorate problems caused by partisan polarization, one must remember that the extent of partisan polarization has varied greatly over time and that polarization is likely to decrease again, though I do not expect that to happen soon. So alterations should not create enormous problems when the parties are not polarized. Most "reforms" instituting significant supermajority requirements in the House would, I believe, produce much greater problems than they would solve. Whether the parties are polarized or not, some minority would certainly use such rules to hold up action so as to kill legislation or extract concessions from the majority. We do not need two Senates!

There are changes in rules and procedures that could promote more deliberation and greater participation by the minority without a major impact on the chamber's decision-making capacity, but they are not silver bullets. Minority members could be guaranteed adequate time to study draft legislation and to propose and debate amendments in committee and on the floor; currently, so-called "layover" requirements that provide time for members to examine legislation are routinely waived, and minority members' opportunities to offer amendments have been increasingly restricted. More drastically and in my view unwisely, floor consideration of legislation not first considered in committee and of bills changed in a major way after committee consideration could be disallowed. But why should we expect the majority party to institute such rules, to abide by them if instituted, and to treat them as other than an annoying formality if abided by? The fear of negative publicity restrains the majority to some extent, and the threat of greater media scrutiny might well act as an incentive to greater minority inclusion. However, because reforms such as strict abidance by layover requirements have little pizzazz, generating the great public pressure necessary to institute them would be a difficult, if not impossible, task.

What about the Senate? The combination of the Senate's permissive rules and partisan polarization certainly increase a status quo–oriented system's tendency toward gridlock. Supporters of the filibuster argue that it promotes deliberation; by slowing the legislative process, it provides an opportunity for second thoughts and perhaps for cooler heads to prevail. Furthermore, many argue, it gives extra weight to intensity in the process, allowing an intense minority to protect itself from a tyrannical majority.

In reply one can argue that, quite apart from extended debate in the Senate, the legislative process advantages intensity. For example, the committee assignment process (in which members' preferences are given substantial weight) and members' considerable freedom in both chambers to choose the issues to which they will devote their time result in those with the more intense preferences on an issue generally exercising greater influence.[16]

Deliberation is promoted by ensuring that minorities have time to attempt to raise public opposition to a proposal they believe to be unwise, it is argued. Furthermore, individuals and small groups of senators have frequently used the Senate's permissive amending rules in combination with extended debate to highlight neglected issues and policy proposals. The minority party now regularly uses this strategy to force onto the agenda issues the majority party would rather not consider. Thus a minority of whatever sort can raise an issue's visibility, compel wide-ranging debate, and perhaps even pass legislation. But one might argue that guaranteeing the minority an opportunity to publicize its views does not require such a difficult cloture procedure. If Rule 22 were altered so as absolutely to guarantee a minority significant floor debate time but were also to specify that the supermajority needed for cloture would decrease the longer a measure is debated on the floor, the minority would have the floor time to make its case but would not be able to block action on majority-supported legislation forever.[17] Republicans have proposed a somewhat similar rules change for judicial nominations but have threatened to institute it through the "nuclear option," a maneuver requiring only a simple majority vote and thus of doubtful legitimacy (see chapter 6).

Whatever one's judgment of the desirability of this rules change in the abstract, were majority Republicans to impose their rule on minority Democrats, the consequences for Senate functioning would likely be dire. Partisan rancor would be enormously exacerbated. The pressures toward bipartisanship that Senate rules now exert on legislation not at the center of the parties' agendas would certainly be overwhelmed. That would then pressure the majority party to use the nuclear option to get rid of extended debate altogether. And, so long as the House functions as a lean, mean partisan legislative machine, changing the Senate to resemble the House does not seem advisable.

If restructuring the legislative process is not likely to be possible, and doing so in a major way may not even be desirable, what then? We need to recognize that not everything we think is wrong with our politics is attributable to partisan polarization. I contend that much of what many people dislike about the character of debate and the nature of election campaigns is not primarily a consequence of partisan polarization and that the infirmities of our policy process would not be solved were we to rid ourselves of partisan polarization. And there are things that we can do to improve our politics, though not easy ones.

Ugly politics—politics descending to personal attacks that are inflammatory and untrue—predate the current period of high partisan polarization; if one looks at the politics of the one-party South, it becomes evident that the lack of partisan polarization and even of interparty competition does not do away with ugly politics. The intensity of highly polarized politics may encourage ugly politics, but so may the need of candidates to differentiate themselves when their parties differ little. When the parties do differ on the major issues of the day, political debate is more likely to be meaningful—not all of it, and not all the time, but enough for voters to become aware of the real choices they face. The 2004 presidential campaign featured inflammatory and untrue Swift Boat ads, misleading charges of flip-flopping and global vetoes, and exaggerated claims about how much had been spent on Iraq and how many job had been lost Yet voters who paid some attention could not help but perceive the stark differences between the candidates and the parties, and voters learned a considerable amount about the issue positions and approaches that differentiated them.

The proposition that partisan bickering and negative campaigning have led large numbers of Americans to withdraw from the active electorate in disgust is not supported by studies of voting behavior. Nor is the proposition that these nonvoters are thoughtful moderates turned off by the extremists nominated by the faithful in each party. Nonvoters tend to know little about politics and to express little interest; often they believe they can neither understand politics nor make a difference. When 55 percent of eligible citizens or fewer vote in presidential elections, our most visible elections, we do have a problem. How low must participation sink before we can no longer consider ourselves a real democracy? The problem is especially acute because nonvoting is rampant among the young, who do not seem to be acquiring the habit of voting as they grow older, as their parents and grandparents tended to do. Partisan polarization is not, however, the root of the problem.

Part of the problem is that people who are not particularly interested in politics can now almost completely avoid exposure and thus avoid learning enough to become at all interested. Take television as an example. Cable TV allows people many more choices about what to watch than was once the case. There are now cooking channels, fishing channels, not just general sports channels but a golf channel and a tennis channel, MTV, and so on and on. Marty Wattenberg argues that this sort of narrowcasting allows people to avoid public affairs news in a way that was not possible (at least for TV watchers) in the past.[18] Time was when major presidential speeches, presidential debates, and the national conventions were on all three networks, and at evening news time, the news was on all three channels. Now, if you do not want news or speeches, you do not even have to get up and do something else—you can just switch the channel. And, of course, there are many forms of entertainment competing against news and politics for people's attention.

Wattenberg further argues that today's young adults have grown up in an environment in which many of them experienced little inadvertent exposure to political news and that this accounts in good part for their low levels of interest in and knowledge about politics and their extremely low rates of voting.[19]

The result is bifurcation of the citizenry into an interested, knowledgeable, and partisan segment and a segment that is not interested, knows little, and tends to be unaligned, or at least not strongly aligned, with either party. The first segment votes; the second most often does not.[20] Most problematical from my perspective is that with generational change, the demobilized segment may grow significantly.

Is it possible to reverse this trend? Certainly, it is unrealistic to expect that most people can or should be transformed into political junkies.[21] Yet voting turnout is much higher in most of the other industrialized countries than in the United States. Getting previously uninterested and disengaged people involved in politics is hard work. The political mobilization of evangelicals in the 1980s and 1990s shows that it can happen in the modern United States. There are some recent positive signs. In the 1990s the AFL-CIO mounted an aggressive grassroots campaign to increase voting turnout among its members and, as already noted, increased the proportion of union members in the electorate significantly. Political scientists Donald Green and Alan Gerber have demonstrated that personal contacts with potential voters have a significant positive effect on turnout—a much greater effect than mail or other impersonal contacts have. And by the early 2000s, the "ground game" had become a central focus of campaigns.[22] Republicans are doing GOTV through party organs such as the Republican National Committee. Democrats are relying more heavily on organizations such as ACT, which is headed by former AFL-CIO political director Steve Rosenthal and EMILY's List founder Ellen Malcolm. ACT did intensive grassroots mobilizing, issue education, and GOTV in targeted states for the 2004 election. Christian Right organizations continue to mobilize their members through their dense network of personal contacts centered on the church. The sons of Senator Paul Wellstone have set up Wellstone Action to train political organizers. ACT is committed to a continuing presence as educator and mobilizer. The Dean campaign made innovative use of the Internet to mobilize the previously inactive, especially young people. Other campaigns learned from the Dean success, and the Kerry campaign raised unprecedented amounts of money in small contributions via the Internet.

The 2004 elections demonstrated that such intense ground-game mobilization does increase turnout. Turnout rose to 60.7 percent of the eligible electorate, the highest since 1968.[23] Almost 17 million more people voted in 2004 than in 2000. And, according to one estimate, a majority of eighteen- to twenty-nine-year-olds voted for the first time since people aged eighteen became eligible to vote. A more stringent test of the parties' mobilization strategies is continued and increased engagement. The 2004 turnout, while encouraging, is still fairly low; only 51.6 percent of the age group eighteen to twenty-nine showed up at the polls. There is plenty of room for improvement.

Certainly high political polarization contributed to the increased turnout. People perceived important issues at stake in the election. Yet some analysts believe that higher turnout would work against partisan polarization because those who do not vote tend to be only lightly attached to a party, if not completely unaffiliated, and they tend to describe themselves as moderates. I would argue that they and many of the other people who show up as "moderates" in polls are actually often people without an opinion on the issue in question. (If one has no opinion but feels an obligation to answer the pollster's question, one is likely to place oneself somewhere in the middle.) In some cases the issues asked about are simply of little intrinsic interest to many people. However, many are issues on which, with more information, most people would form an opinion. That opinion would not necessarily be moderate. And, in fact, many of these newly informed citizens might well also develop an attachment—even a strong attachment—to the party closest to them. If the result is continued partisan polarization, so be it. Partisan polarization that reflects the full citizenry is, I believe, quite different from partisan polarization that results from a large chunk of the eligible electorate not participating.

To sum up my argument: Partisan polarization cannot be blamed for many of the features of contemporary politics that we do not like, such as ugly politics. Furthermore, of the actual consequences of partisan polarization, some are negative in my view, but others are positive. Among the most serious negative effects is the increasing tendency to exclude the minority party and the interests it represents from the policy process at the national level, except in the Senate, where the rules make it impossible to do so. On the positive side, the contemporary parties do bring forth programs to which they commit themselves, they do give the voters a meaningful choice, and when one of the parties controls both Congress and the White House, shared policy preferences and the perception of a shared electoral fate do lead to high levels of interbranch cooperation and intrachamber cohesion. If the responsible-parties advocates failed to recognize the possible downside of responsible parties, they were certainly correct about the virtues.

Finally, what about policy outcomes? This is the most difficult area to evaluate without relying primarily on one's own policy preferences and basing one's judgment too heavily on recent events. Earlier I showed that partisan polarization does seem to decrease the proportion of major legislation that gets enacted but that it certainly does not literally lead to gridlock. When control is unified, strong parties can facilitate the passage of highly significant legislation, as the responsible-parties advocates argued. During the George W. Bush presidency, narrow but cohesive congressional majorities enacted legislation that genuinely embodied nonincremental policy change. Supporters of this policy thrust argue that this represents government responding quickly and effectively to pressing national problems; opponents counter that their cohesiveness, and the effective PR operation backing them, allowed the Republicans to enact major legislation that was at best favored by a narrow and lukewarm majority, and in some cases, not even that. The Senate can sometimes stop legislation supported by a congressional majority; and because large, organized minorities are most likely to be successful at using Senate rules to kill bills, major majority-supported legislation may more frequently be blocked when the parties are polarized. A number of times during the Bush presidency the Senate did kill legislation—and nominations—that had majority congressional support. Supporters of these measures argue that such use of Senate rules is an illegitimate exercise of minority power to thwart the will of the majority. Opponents counter that sometimes the enactment of major legislation supported by only a narrow majority of the public may not be good for the political system, that inaction may be preferable to the passage of legislation that addresses problems in a manner that a large minority of the citizenry considers wrong. Some further argue that Senate Democrats, in fact, represent a majority of the American people. Democracy, no matter how structured, cannot guarantee good policy outcomes, for any individual or for the polity as a whole, much less ones that we all find pleasing. It does allow us, if we are willing to take the time and make the effort, to exert some influence over those outcomes.

NOTES

PREFACE

1. This account is based on *Los Angeles Times*, July 19, 2003; *Congressional Quarterly Weekly*, July 19, 2003, p. 1822, and July 26, 2003, pp. 1885–88; *Roll Call*, July 18, 2003.

2. *Congressional Quarterly Weekly*, July 19, 2003, p. 1822.

CHAPTER 1

1. Quotes are from "It's Long Enough: The Decline of Popular Government under Forty Years of Single Party Control of the U.S. House of Representatives," white paper released by Republican Conference Chairman Dick Armey, Rep. Jennifer Dunn, and Rep. Christopher Shays, July 1994, p. 29.

2. Annenberg Public Policy Center, *Civility in the House of Representatives: The 105th Congress* (March 1999).

3. Subcommittee on Rules and Organization of the Committee on Rules, House of Representatives, hearings on Civility in the House of Representatives, April 29, 1999.

4. Scores are available at Keith Poole's website, http://voteview.com. See Keith T. Poole and Howard Rosenthal, *Congress: A Political-Economic History of Roll Call Voting* (New York: Oxford University Press, 1997). (There is a technical explanation for the name of the scores, but it is not relevant here.)

5. See Keith Poole's website.

6. Richard Fenno, *Congressmen in Committees* (Boston: Little, Brown, 1973).

7. Earl Black and Merle Black, *The Rise of Southern Republicans* (Cambridge, Mass.: Harvard University Press, 2002), pp. 87–91.

8. *Congress and the Nation*, vol. 1 (Washington, D.C.: CQ Press, 1965), p. 60.

9. Sean Theriault, "The Case of the Vanishing Moderates: Party Polarization in the Modern Congress," paper delivered at the Midwest Political Science Association meetings, Chicago, April 2003; Michael McDonald and Bernard Grofman, "Redistricting and the Polarization of the House of Representatives," paper delivered at the Western Political Science Association meetings, Seattle, Washington, March 25–27, 1999.

10. Norman Nie, Sidney Verba, and John Petrocik, *The Changing American Voter* (Cambridge, Mass.: Harvard University Press, 1979) p. 220.

11. Jeffery Stonecash, Mark Brewer, and Mack Mariani, *Diverging Parties* (Boulder, Colo.: Westview Press, 2003), p. 53.

12. Stanley Berard, *Southern Democrats in the U.S. House* (Norman: University of Oklahoma Press, 2001), p. 76; Black and Black, *Rise of Southern Republicans*.

13. Alan Abramowitz and Kyle Saunders, "Ideological Realignment in the U.S. Electorate," *Journal of Politics* 60 (August 1998): 641. Independent leaners are included as identifiers.

14. Ibid.

15. Gary Jacobson, "Party Polarization in National Politics: The Electoral Connection," in *Polarized Politics*, ed. Jon Bond and Richard Fleisher (Washington, D.C.: CQ Press, 2000), p. 25.

16. Berard, *Southern Democrats*, pp. 80–81.

17. Pew Research Center for the People and the Press, "Democratic Candidates Face Southern Voters," press release, January 30, 2004.

18. Barbara Sinclair, *Congressional Realignment* (Austin: University of Texas Press, 1982).

19. The post-2000 Census reapportionment and redistricting did not increase the number of majority minority districts.

20. Berard, *Southern Democrats*, p. 76.

21. Jacobson, "Party Polarization," p. 17; Richard Fleisher and Jon Bond, "Evidence of Increasing Polarization among Ordinary Citizens," in *American Political Parties: Decline or Resurgence*, ed. Jeffrey Cohen, Richard Fleisher, and Paul Kantor (Washington, D.C.: CQ Press, 2001), pp. 64, 71.

22. Herbert Weisberg, "The Party in the Electorate as a Basis for More Responsible Parties," in *Responsible Partisanship*, ed. John Green and Paul Herrnson (Lawrence: University of Kansas Press, 2002), p. 173; Fleisher and Bond, "Evidence of Increasing Polarization," p. 65.

23. Jacobson, "Party Polarization," p. 18.

24. Fleisher and Bond, "Evidence of Increasing Polarization."

25. Weisberg, "Party in the Electorate," p. 174.

26. Jacobson, "Party Polarization," p. 19.

27. David G. Lawrence, "On the Resurgence of Party Identification in the 1990s," in *American Political Parties: Decline or Resurgence*, ed. Jeffrey Cohen, Richard Fleisher, and Paul Kantor (Washington, D.C.: CQ Press, 2001), p. 33; Larry Bartels, "Partisanship and Voting Behavior, 1952–1996," *American Journal of Political Science* 44 (January 2000): 36–37.

28. Keiko Ono, "Polarization in Congress and Voter Turnout," paper delivered at the Western Political Science Association meetings, 2003; Martin Wattenberg, *Where Have All the Voters Gone?* (Cambridge, Mass.: Harvard University Press, 2002).

29. Bartels, "Partisanship and Voting Behavior," p. 37.

30. Herbert McClosky, Paul Hoffman, and Rosemary O'Hara, "Issue Conflict and Consensus among Party Leaders and Followers," *American Political Science Review* 54 (June 1960): 406–27; Warren Miller and M. Kent Jennings, *Parties in Transition* (New York: Russell Sage, 1986).

31. Scholars who argue that "extreme" elected officials are not faithfully representing their much more moderate constituents need to deal with this problem; to some extent, the people who appear in the center of the distribution are "fake" moderates.

32. Miller and Jennings, *Parties in Transition*, pp. 133–35.

33. Ibid., pp. 133–39, 148.

34. Walter Stone, Ronald Rapoport, and Alan Abramowitz, "Party Polarization: The Reagan Revolution and Beyond," in *The Parties Respond*, ed. L. Sandy Maisel, 2nd ed. (Boulder, Colo.: Westview Press, 1994).

35. Stone et al., "Party Polarization," p. 76.

36. Ibid., pp. 78–81.

37. Jacobson, "Party Polarization," p. 22.

38. Ibid., pp. 23–24.

39. Fleisher and Bond, "Evidence of Increasing Polarization," p. 58.

40. Richard Fenno, *Home Style* (Boston: Little, Brown, 1978).

41. Morris Fiorina with Samuel Abrams and Jeremy Pope, *Culture War? The Myth of a Polarized America* (New York: Pearson Longman, 2005); see also Paul DiMaggio, John Evans, and Bethany Bryson, "Have Americans' Social Attitudes Become More Polarized?" *American Journal of Sociology* 102, no. 3 (1996): 690–755.

42. Fiorina et al., *Culture War?* p. 49.

43. Alan Abramowitz and Brad Alexander, "Incumbency, Redistricting, and the Decline of Competition in Congressional Elections: Evidence from the 2002 Midterm Elections," paper delivered at the Western Political Science Association meetings, 2004.

44. Ibid., fig. 3, p. 29.

45. Ibid., p. 14.

46. McDonald and Grofman, in "Redistricting and the Polarization of the House of Representatives," argue that possibly one sixth of the polarization between the 1970s and the 1990s is due to changes in the partisan composition of House districts. See also Bruce Oppenheimer, "Deep Red and Blue Congressional Districts: The Causes and Consequences of Declining Party Competitiveness," in *Congress Reconsidered*, ed. Lawrence C. Dodd and Bruce I. Oppenheimer, 8th ed. (Washington, D.C.: CQ Press, 2005).

47. The aim is to pack opposition party voters into as few districts as possible and create the maximum number of winnable districts for one's own party; this does mean creating very safe districts for the opposition but only comfortably secure seats for one's own party.

48. Stonecash et al., *Diverging Parties*.

49. Nolan McCarty, Keith Poole, and Howard Rosenthal, "Political Polarization and Income," unpublished paper, 2002. Copy in possession of the author.

50. Oppenheimer, "Deep Red."

51. *Austin-American Statesman* website, "The Great Divide," http://www.statesman.com/specialreports/content/specialreports/greatdivide/index.html, accessed February 2005.

52. Abramowitz and Alexander, "Incumbency," table 6, p. 30.

53. See Jacobson, "Party Polarization." See also Marc Hetherington, "Resurgent Mass Partisanship: The Role of Elite Polarization," *American Political Science Review* 95, no. 3 (2001): 619–31.

CHAPTER 2

1. All the quotes are from Godfrey Hodgson, *The World Turned Right Side Up* (Boston: Houghton Mifflin, 1996), p. 104.

2. Peter Steinfels, *The Neoconservatives* (New York: Simon and Schuster, 1979), p. 6.

3. Ibid., p. 6, emphasis added.

4. See Steinfels, *Neoconservatives*; Hodgson, *World Turned*; Sidney Blumenthal, *The Rise of the Counter-Establishment* (New York: Times Books, 1986); E. J. Dionne, *Why Americans Hate Politics* (New York: Simon and Schuster, 1991).

5. One can make at least as good an argument that this is nonsense. See Robert Kuttner, *Everything for Sale: The Virtues and Limits of Markets* (Chicago: University of Chicago Press, 1996).

6. Hodgson, *World Turned*, p. 136.

7. Dionne, *Why Americans Hate Politics*, p. 60.

8. *New York Times*, January 19, 1995.

9. Hodgson, *World Turned*, p. 137.

10. Steinfels, *Neoconservatives*, p. 8.

11. Hodgson, *World Turned*, p. 137.

12. Quoted in Blumenthal, *Rise of the Counter-Establishment*, p. 180.

13. Quoted in Blumenthal, *Rise of the Counter-Establishment*, p. 181.

14. Quoted in Hodgson, *World Turned*, p. 195.

15. Blumenthal, *Rise of the Counter-Establishment*, pp. 182, 344.

16. Quoted in Blumenthal, *Rise of the Counter-Establishment*, p. 185.

17. Quoted in Blumenthal, *Rise of the Counter-Establishment*, p. 185.

18. Blumenthal, *Rise of the Counter-Establishment*, pp. 184–88, 218.

19. *Congressional Quarterly Almanac* 1978, p. H170, roll call #601.

20. See Blumenthal, *Rise of the Counter-Establishment*, chapter 7.

21. Quoted in Blumenthal, *Rise of the Counter-Establishment*, p. 203; see also pp. 186–203.

22. *Congressional Quarterly Almanac* 1980, p. 91.

23. Fundamentalists and evangelicals are not identical theologically; see Hodgson, *World Turned*, p. 160; but both are religiously and culturally conservative, which is what is relevant here. When I refer here to evangelicals or fundamentalists or to adherents of the Religious Right, I am referring to whites only.

24. Quoted in Geoffrey Layman, *The Great Divide: Religious and Cultural Conflict in American Party Politics* (New York: Columbia University Press, 2001), p. 10.

25. Hodgson, *World Turned*, p. 176.

26. Ibid., pp. 162, 166–68.

27. See N. A. Valentino and D. O. Sears, "Old Times There Are Not Forgotten: Race and Partisan Realignment in the Contemporary South," *American Journal of Political Science* 49 (2005): 672–88, and D. O. Sears and N. A. Valentino, "Is the Proof in the Pulpit? Race, Religion, and Party Realignment in the South," paper presented at the annual meeting of the American Political Science Association, Boston, August 29–September 1, 2002.

28. Quoted in Hodgson, *World Turned*, p. 162.

29. Layman, *Great Divide*, p. 44; also see Byron Shafer, *The Two Majorities: The Puzzle of Modern American Politics* (Lawrence: University of Kansas Press, 2003), p. 174.

30. Paul M. Weyrich, "Blue Collar or Blue Blood? The New Right Compared with the Old Right," in *New Right Papers*, ed. Robert W. Whitaker (New York: St Martin's Press, 1982), p. 51.
31. Ibid., p. 57, emphasis added.
32. Ibid., p. 62.
33. Ralph Reed, *Active Faith* (New York: Free Press, 1996), p. 107.
34. Quoted in Layman, *Great Divide*, p. 44.
35. Reed, *Active Faith*, pp. 108–109.
36. Shafer, *Two Majorities*, pp. 172–76.
37. Layman, *Great Divide*, pp. 170–85.
38. Hodgson, *World Turned*, p. 176.
39. Both quotes are taken from Layman, *Great Divide*, p. 116.
40. Ibid., pp. 116–17.
41. Ibid., p. 101.
42. Quoted in Hodgson, *World Turned*, p. 182, and Reed, *Active Faith*, p. 111.
43. Reed, *Active Faith*, p. 111.
44. Layman, *Great Divide*, p. 102.
45. Quoted in Reed, *Active Faith*, pp. 113–14.
46. Layman, *Great Divide*, p. 185
47. Dionne, *Why Americans Hate Politics*, p. 235.
48. Layman, *Great Divide*, pp. 170, 188.
49. *New York Times*/CBS News polls of delegates to the 2004 national conventions, August 29, 2004.
50. Layman, *Great Divide*, p. 185, for 1980 through 1996.
51. James Guth, Lyman Kellstedt, John Green, and Corwin Smidt, "A Distant Thunder?: Religious Mobilization in the 2000 Elections," in *Interest Group Politics*, 6th ed., ed. Allan Cigler and Burdett Loomis (Washington, D.C.: CQ Press, 2002), p. 177.
52. Pew study cited in *National Journal*, November 21, 2004.
53. Dan Blatz and Ronald Brownstein, *Storming the Gates: Protest Politics and the Republican Revival* (Boston: Little Brown, 1996), p. 308.
54. 1996 data from *New York Times* poll cited in Layman, *Great Divide*, p. 109; 2004 data from CBS/*New York Times* delegate poll.
55. Blatz and Brownstein, *Storming the Gates*, p. 314.
56. Kimberly Conger and John Green, "Spreading Out and Digging In: Christian Conservatives and State Republican Parties," *Campaigns and Elections*, February 2002.
57. Layman, *Great Divide*, pp. 180–83.
58. Ibid., p. 183.
59. Ibid., p. 191.
60. Hodgson, *World Turned*, p. 170.
61. Ibid., pp. 170–71.
62. Ibid., p. 171.
63. See Reed, *Active Faith*, and Hodgson, *World Turned*, pp. 176–78.
64. Hodgson, *World Turned*, pp. 176–77.
65. Ibid., pp. 172–74.
66. Quoted in Layman, *Great Divide*, p. 11.
67. Reed, *Active Faith*, p. 109.

68. Ibid., pp. 109–10.
69. Ibid., p. 110.
70. Blatz and Brownstein, *Storming the Gates*, pp. 309–12.
71. The following is mostly based on Reed, *Active Faith*, chapter 4.
72. Blatz and Brownstein, *Storming the Gates*, p. 311.
73. Scholars have found that pastors also were often unwilling to become so overtly political.
74. Reed, *Active Faith*, p. 122.
75. Guth et al., *Distant Thunder*, pp. 163–64.
76. Christian Coalition of America website, cc.org, accessed April 26, 2004.
77. Guth et al., *Distant Thunder*, pp. 174–81.
78. Reed, *Active Faith*, p. 120.
79. Guth et al., *Distant Thunder*, 162.
80. Quoted on the Focus on the Family website, http://www.family.org/welcome/, accessed spring 2005.
81. Quotes and information from www.traditionalvalues.org, accessed spring 2005.
82. Quotes from website www.cwfa.org, accessed spring 2005.
83. Steinfels, *Neoconservatives*, p. 11.
84. Blumenthal, *Rise of the Counter-Establishment*, p. 37.
85. Quoted in Eric Alterman, *What Liberal Media?* (New York: Basic Books, 2003), p. 82.
86. Quoted in Blumenthal, *Rise of the Counter-Establishment*, p. 49.
87. Ibid., pp. 47–50.
88. Alterman, *What Liberal Media?* pp. 84–85.
89. Blumenthal, *Rise of the Counter-Establishment*, pp. 34–35, and Andrew Rich, *Think Tanks, Public Policy and the Politics of Expertise* (Cambridge, U.K.: Cambridge University Press, 2004), p. 230.
90. Jack L. Walker, "The Origins and Maintenance of Interest Groups in America," *American Political Science Review* 77 (1983): 360–406; Jeffery M. Berry, *The Interest Group Society* (Boston: Little Brown, 1989).
91. David Brock, *The Republican Noise Machine* (New York: Crown, 2004), p. 40; John Micklethwait and Adrian Wooldridge, *The Right Nation* (New York: Penguin, 2004), pp. 77–78.
92. Brock, *Republican Noise Machine*, p. 40.
93. Blumenthal, *Rise of the Counter-Establishment*, p. 66.
94. Ibid., p. 194.
95. Quoted in Blumenthal, *Rise of the Counter-Establishment*, p. 148.
96. Ibid., p. 190.
97. Quoted in Blumenthal, *Rise of the Counter-Establishment*, p. 207.
98. Ibid., p. 294.
99. Ibid., pp. 294–96.
100. Quoted from the Collegiate Network website, www.isi.org/cn/, accessed spring 2005.
101. See the Young America's Foundation website at http://www.yaf.org/, accessed spring 2005.
102. See Blatz and Brownstein, *Storming the Gates*.
103. Ibid., p. 163.

104. Quoted in Dionne, *Why Americans Hate Politics*, p. 238.
105. Reed, *Active Faith*, p. 163.
106. Ibid., pp. 161–63.
107. The demise of the equal time requirement in the late 1980s spurred that development.
108. Blatz and Brownstein, *Storming the Gates*, p. 164.
109. Ibid., p. 168.
110. Quoted in Blatz and Brownstein, *Storming the Gates*, p. 170.
111. Alterman, *What Liberal Media?* p. 242.
112. See Sears and Valentino, "Is the Proof in the Pulpit?"

CHAPTER 3

1. There is some controversy over whether parties and leaders have an impact on how members behave and on what the House decides beyond passively channeling homogeneous preferences. Keith Krehbiel argues that members' preferences—not party—drive the vote and that what appears to be partisanship is actually "preferenceship." See Keith Krehbiel, *Information and Legislative Organization* (Ann Arbor: University of Michigan Press, 1991), and "Where's the Party?" *British Journal of Political Science* 23 (1993): 235–66. Proponents of the partisan model argue that the majority party and its leadership influence outcomes through structuring the legislative process and through directly influencing members' legislatively relevant behavior, especially when legislative preferences within each party are homogeneous and differences between the parties are substantial. See Joseph Cooper and David W. Brady, "Institutional Context and Leadership Style: The House from Cannon to Rayburn," *American Political Science Review* 75 (1981): 411–25; Gary Cox and Mathew McCubbins, *Legislative Leviathan: Party Government in the House* (Berkeley: University of California Press, 1993); and David Rohde, *Parties and Leaders in the Postreform House* (Chicago: University of Chicago Press: 1991). As my argument in this and the next chapter should make clear, I am a proponent of the partisan model.

2. Much of what follows is based on my research. All unattributed quotations are from interviews I conducted or meetings I observed.

3. See Richard Bolling, *House Out of Order* (New York: Dutton, 1965); Cooper and Brady, "Institutional Context and Leadership Style"; Richard Fenno, "The Internal Distribution of Influence: The House," in *The Congress and America's Future*, ed. David B. Truman (Englewood Cliffs, N.J.: Prentice-Hall, 1965), pp. 52–76.

4. Bolling, *House Out of Order*, p. 70.

5. Kenneth Kofmehl, "The Institutionalization of a Voting Bloc," *Western Political Quarterly* 17 (June 1964): 256–72.

6. Bruce Oppenheimer, "The Rules Committee: New Arm of Leadership in a Decentralized House," in *Congress Reconsidered*, ed. Lawrence C. Dodd and Bruce I. Oppenheimer (New York: Praeger, 1977), pp. 96–116.

7. Barbara Sinclair, *Majority Leadership in the U.S. House* (Baltimore: Johns Hopkins University Press, 1983), p. 7.

8. Burton Sheppard, *Rethinking Congressional Reform* (Cambridge, Mass.: Shenkman, 1985), p. 42.

9. Sheppard, *Rethinking Congressional Reform*, p. 65.

10. *Congressional Quarterly Almanac* 1970, p. 453.

11. *Congress and the Nation*, vol. 2 (Washington, D.C.: CQ Press, 1971), p. 906 passim.

12. See Sheppard, *Rethinking Congressional Reform.*

13. Norman Ornstein, Thomas Mann, and Michael Malbin, *Vital Statistics on Congress 2001–2002* (Washington, D.C.: AEI Press, 2002), pp. 130, 128.

14. Burdett Loomis, *The New American Politician* (New York: Basic Books, 1988).

15. Steven Smith, *Call to Order: Floor Politics in the House and Senate* (Washington, D.C.: Brookings Institution, 1989).

16. Sinclair, *Majority Leadership*, p. 167.

17. Quoted in Sidney Waldman, "Majority Party Leadership in the Contemporary House: The 94th and 95th Congresses," manuscript, 1978. Copy in possession of the author.

18. Smith, *Call to Order*, pp. 40–41.

19. See Fenno, *Congressmen in Committees.*

20. Ninety-fifth Congress (1977–78) *Congressional Quarterly* party unity scores, adjusted to disregard absences, are used; CQ party unity scores are also the basis of calculations for later Congresses discussed.

21. Sara Brandes Crook and John Hibbing, "Congressional Reform and Party Discipline," *British Journal of Political Science* 12 (April 1985): 217, 221-22.

22. *Congressional Quarterly Weekly*, January 24, 1987, p. 139.

23. *Congressional Quarterly Weekly*, December 8, 1990, p. 4059.

24. *Politics in America* 1986, p. 485.

25. *Politics in America* 1990, p. 587.

26. See Lawrence C. Dodd, "The Expanded Roles of the House Democratic Whip System: The 93rd and 94th Congresses," *Congressional Studies* 7 (Spring 1979): 27–56.

27. See Dodd, "Expanded Roles."

28. Randall Ripley, *Majority Party Leadership in Congress* (Boston: Little, Brown, 1969), p. 199.

29. David Price, *The Congressional Experience* (Boulder, Colo.: Westview Press, 1992), p. 80.

30. James C. Garand and Kathleen M. Clayton, "Socialization to Partisanship in the U.S. House: The Speaker's Task Force," *Legislative Studies Quarterly* 11 (August 1986): 409–28.

31. Barbara Sinclair, *Legislators, Leaders and Lawmaking* (Baltimore: Johns Hopkins University Press, 1995), p. 108.

32. In the 93rd, the number of days on which suspensions could be considered was increased from two to four, the procedure under which the Speaker could adjust the daily meeting times of the House was revised, and committee meetings were required to be open. In the 94th, the House Unamerican Activities Committee was abolished; the Budget Committee was increased in size, and sunshine reforms were extended to conference committees.

33. *Congressional Quarterly Almanac* 1979, p. H134.

34. When Republicans took the majority they abolished the rule, but later, when Bush became president, they reinstated it.

35. *Congressional Quarterly Almanac* 1983, pp. 596–97.

36. Ibid., p. 597.

CHAPTER 4

1. Barber B. Conable, Jr., *Congress and the Income Tax* (Norman: University of Oklahoma Press, 1989), p. 76.

2. John Pitney, "The Conservative Opportunity Society," manuscript, December 1988. Copy in possession of the author.

3. Identified by CQ as key players in the mid-1980s Conservative Opportunity Society, *Congressional Quarterly Almanac* 1984, p. 206; or by William Connelly and John Pitney, *Congress' Permanent Minority?: Republicans in the U.S. House* (Lanham, Md.: Rowman and Littlefield, 1994), as COS members.

4. *Politics in America* 1981, p. 284.

5. Sinclair, *Majority Leadership*, p. 48.

6. *Politics in America* 1981, p. 284.

7. Ibid.

8. Connelly and Pitney, *Congress' Permanent Minority?* p. 77.

9. *Congressional Quarterly Almanac* 1984, pp. 206–208.

10. Ibid., p. 208.

11. All quotations are from *Politics in America* 1986, p. 277.

12. *Congressional Quarterly Almanac* 1985, p. 29.

13. Ibid., p. 29.

14. Sinclair, *Legislators, Leaders*, pp. 250–51.

15. The twenty-four-hour layover requirement before a rule can be considered on the floor can be waived, but that necessitates a two-thirds vote—an impossibility given Republican opposition.

16. Connelly and Pitney, *Congress' Permanent Minority?* p. 83.

17. Ibid., p. 82.

18. Douglas L. Koopman, *Hostile Takeover: The House Republican Party 1980–1995* (Lanham, Md.: Rowman and Littlefield, 1996), p. 12.

19. Ibid., p. 13.

20. Quoted in Koopman, *Hostile Takeover*, p. 18.

21. Connelly and Pitney, *Congress' Permanent Minority?* p. 56.

22. *Congressional Quarterly Almanac* 1992, p. 16.

23. Connelly and Pitney, *Congress' Permanent Minority?* p. 55.

24. Quoted in Connelly and Pitney, *Congress' Permanent Minority?* p. 60.

25. Ibid., p. 57; Koopman, *Hostile Takeover*, p. 141.

26. Quoted in Connelly and Pitney, *Congress' Permanent Minority?* p. 23.

27. Blatz and Brownstein, *Storming the Gates*, pp. 144–46.

28. Koopman, *Hostile Takeover*, pp. 51–53.

29. Quoted in *Politics in America* 1994, p. 571.

30. Blatz and Brownstein, *Storming the Gates*, pp. 170–71.

31. *Congressional Quarterly Weekly*, November 12, 1994, pp. 3210–15; Barbara Sinclair, "Transformational Leader or Faithful Agent? Principal Agent Theory and House Majority Party Leadership in the 104th and 105th Congresses," *Legislative Studies Quarterly* 24 (August 1999): 421–50.

32. Republican Conference Rules, quoted from 100th Congress edition of the *Republican Conference Directory*.

33. Calculated from data in *Congressional Quarterly Weekly*, April 8, 1995, p. 1006.

34. Koopman, *Hostile Takeover*, pp. 142–47, and Daniel Stid, "Transformational Leadership in Congress?" paper presented at the annual meeting of the American

Political Science Association, San Francisco, August 29–September 1, 1996, pp. 6–8.

35. C. Lawrence Evans and Walter J. Oleszek, *Congress under Fire: Reform Politics and the Republican Majority* (Boston: Houghton Mifflin, 1997), pp. 132–33.

36. Newt Gingrich, "Leadership Task Forces: The 'Third Wave' Way to Consider Legislation," *Roll Call*, November 16, 1995, p. 5.

37. Unattributed quotes are from interviews I conducted.

38. *Congressional Quarterly Weekly*, March 29, 2003, p. 748.

39. As of this writing, the vacancy has not been filled.

40. House Democratic Caucus website, www.dems.gov, accessed fall 2004.

41. House Republican Conference rules, 108th Congress, House Republican Conference website, gop.gov, accessed spring 2004.

42. House Republican Policy Committee website, policy.house.gov, accessed spring 2004.

43. *The Hill*, January 15, 2003.

44. *Congressional Quarterly Weekly*, March 29, 2003, p. 751.

45. *Roll Call*, December 10, 2001.

46. *Congressional Quarterly Weekly*, December 9, 2000, p. 2796; January 6, 2001, p. 10.

47. *Congressional Quarterly Weekly*, January 11, 2003, p. 89.

48. *Roll Call*, March 26, 2003.

49. Ibid., January 10, 2005.

50. Emphasis in original.

51. *Congressional Quarterly Weekly*, November 16, 2002, p. 3015.

52. *Roll Call*, January 6, 2003.

53. Ibid., March 31, 2004.

54. Ibid., January 24, 2005

55. Ibid., January 5, 2005.

56. *Congressional Quarterly Weekly*, March 29, 2003, p. 749.

57. Donald Wolfensberger, "Suspended Partisanship in the House: How Most Laws Are Really Made," paper presented at the annual meeting of the American Political Science Association, Boston, August 29–September 1, 2002.

58. *Roll Call*, December 1, 2003.

59. Center for Responsive Politics website, www.opensecrets.org, accessed spring 2005.

60. Paul R. Brewer and Christopher J. Deering, "Musical Chairs: Interest Groups, Campaign Fundraising, and Selection of House Committee Chairs," in Paul S. Herrnson, Ronald G. Shaiko, and Clyde Wilcox, *The Interest Group Connection: Electioneering, Lobbying, and Policymaking in Washington* (Washington, D.C.: CQ Press, 2005): 141–63.

61. *Los Angeles Times*, June 12, 2004.

62. Center for Responsive Politics website, www.opensecrets.org.

63. *Roll Call*, April 5, 2004; January 24, 2005.

CHAPTER 5

1. *National Journal's CongressDaily*, June 11, 2003.

2. Data are from *National Journal's CongressDaily* Markup Reports.

3. *National Journal's CongressDaily*, June 25, 2003.

4. Ibid.

5. *Los Angeles Times*, June 28, 2003.

6. For more detail see Barbara Sinclair, *Unorthodox Lawmaking*, 2nd ed. (Washington, D.C.: CQ Press, 2000).

7. Richard Fenno, *The Power of the Purse* (Boston: Little Brown, 1966); John Manley, *The Politics of Finance* (Boston: Little Brown, 1970).

8. J. Dennis Hastert, "Reflections on the Role of the Speaker of the Modern Day House of Representatives," address delivered on November 12, 2003, accessed at speaker.house.gov, December 2003.

9. *Congressional Quarterly Weekly*, July 12, 2003, p. 1727.

10. Hastert address.

11. Major measures are those that *Congressional Quarterly* identified as such plus those measures on which a key vote occurred, again as identified by CQ. This definition yields approximately forty to fifty measures per Congress. Sinclair, *Unorthodox Lawmaking*, p. 91.

12. *Congressional Quarterly Weekly*, March 18, 1995, p. 815.

13. Ibid., March 18, 1995, p. 787.

14. Ibid., October 13, 2001, p. 2399.

15. Ibid., June 29, 2002, p. 1726.

16. See Sinclair, *Unorthodox Lawmaking*, chapter 8.

17. *Congressional Quarterly Weekly*, August 4, 2001, p. 1904.

18. Ibid., June 22, 2002, p. 1651.

19. Sinclair, *Unorthodox Lawmaking*, p. 91.

20. Entitlement programs funded by trust funds,—social security, for example—are not funded by annual appropriations.

21. Fenno, *Power of the Purse*.

22. David Maraniss and Michael Weisskopf, *Tell Newt to Shut Up!* (New York: Simon and Schuster, 1996), p. 88.

23. *Congressional Quarterly Weekly*, September 21, 2002, pp. 2432–38, and November 16, 2002, pp. 3014–16; *Roll Call*, September 26, 2002; *Congressional Quarterly Weekly*, February 15, 2003, p. 385.

24. *Congressional Quarterly Weekly*, November 20, 2004, p. 2767; November 27, 2004, p. 2778.

25. See the Rules Committee website, www.house.gov/rules, accessed spring 2005.

26. After the 105th Congress, the data compiled by Donald Wolfensberger no longer distinguish between open and modified open rules.

27. Wolfensberger's data.

28. *Washington Post*, May 8, 2003.

29. *Congressional Quarterly Weekly*, August 2, 1990, p. 2517.

30. *The Hill*, January 15, 2003.

31. *Roll Call*, July 7, 2003.

32. *Congressional Quarterly Weekly*, April 8, 1995, pp. 1010–14.

33. Barbara Sinclair, "Do Parties Matter?" in *Party, Process, and Political Change in Congress*, ed. David Brady and Matthew McCubbins (Stanford, Calif.: Stanford University Press, 2002).

34. Republicans no longer designate any of their whips "regional" whips, but region is still an important basis for the assignment of names.

35. *Congressional Quarterly Weekly*, December 11, 2004, p. 2907.
36. Ibid., March 29, 2003, p. 750.
37. Ibid., p. 751.
38. Ibid., p. 750.
39. *Los Angeles Times*, November 23, 2003.
40. *Congressional Quarterly Weekly*, April 3, 2004, p. 796.
41. *Roll Call*, May 14, 2003.
42. *Los Angeles Times*, December 7, 2001.
43. *Congressional Quarterly Weekly*, March 29, 2003, p. 751.
44. *Los Angeles Times*, December 7, 2001.
45. *Washington Post*, November 22, 2003.
46. Quote from *Congressional Quarterly Weekly*, November 29, 2003, p. 2962; account also based on *Congressional Quarterly Weekly*, November 22, 2003, pp. 2879–82, and November 29, 2003, pp. 2956–63; *Washington Post*, November 22, 2003; *Roll Call*, November 19, 2003; *Los Angeles Times*, November 23, 2003.
47. *Los Angeles Times*, November 23, 2003.
48. *Congressional Quarterly Weekly*, April 3, 2004, p. 795.
49. Ibid., April 3, 2004, p. 797.
50. *Roll Call*, June 4, 2003.
51. Ibid., June 23, 2004.
52. Ibid., June 4, 2003.
53. David Price, *The Congressional Experience*, 3rd ed. (Boulder, Colo.: Westview Press, 2004), p. 195.
54. *Roll Call*, June 4, 2003; November 6, 2004.
55. All quotes from *Roll Call*, November 19, 2003.
56. *Washington Post*, November 21, 2003.
57. *Congressional Quarterly Weekly*, November 22, 2003, p. 2881.
58. Ibid., November 29, 2003, p. 2959.
59. *New York Times*, November 28, 2003.
60. *Congressional Quarterly Weekly*, March 29, 2003, p. 742.
61. *New York Times*, December 6, 2003.
62. Quoted in *Los Angeles Times*, November 22, 2004.
63. Hastert address.
64. See Price, *Congressional Experience*, 3rd ed., pp. 203–10.

CHAPTER 6

1. Sinclair, *Unorthodox Lawmaking* (Washington, D.C.: CQ Press, 1997; 2nd ed. 2000); Sarah Binder and Steven S. Smith, *Politics or Principle? Filibustering in the United States Senate* (Washington, D.C.: Brookings Institution, 1997).
2. Donald E. Matthews, *U.S. Senators and Their World* (New York: Vintage Books, 1960).
3. Ralph Huitt, "The Internal Distribution of Influence: The Senate," in *The Congress and America's Future*, ed. David Truman (Englewood Cliffs, N.J.: Prentice Hall, 1965); Barbara Sinclair, *The Transformation of the U.S. Senate* (Baltimore: Johns Hopkins University Press, 1989).
4. Bruce Oppenheimer, "Changing Time Constraints on Congress: Historical Perspectives on the Use of Cloture," in *Congress Reconsidered*, ed. Lawrence C. Dodd and Bruce I. Oppenheimer, 3rd ed.(Washington, D.C.: CQ Press, 1985).

5. Sinclair, *Transformation;* Michael Foley, *The New Senate* (New Haven, Conn.: Yale University Press, 1980); David Rohde, Norman Ornstein, and Robert Peabody, "Political Change and Legislative Norms in the U.S. Senate, 1957–1974," in *Studies of Congress,* ed. Glenn Parker (Washington, D.C.: Congressional Quarterly Press, 1985).

6. Kay Lehman Scholzman and John T. Tierney, *Organized Interests and American Democracy* (New York: Harper and Row, 1986).

7. Sinclair, *Transformation,* p. 64 ff.

8. Ibid., p. 73. The top four committees, recognized in the rules of the Senate parties, are Finance, Appropriations, Foreign Relations, and Armed Services.

9. Ornstein et al., *Vital Statistics,* tables 5-2, 5-5, p. 128.

10. Sinclair, *Transformation,* p. 115.

11. To be sure, the data must be regarded with some caution. When lengthy debate becomes a filibuster is, in part, a matter of judgment. Nevertheless experts and participants agree that the frequency of obstructionism has increased, as the table indicates. Sources are given in the note to table 6.1. The Democratic Study Group publication relies on data supplied by Congressional Research Service experts; these experts' judgments about what constitutes a filibuster are not limited to instances in which cloture was sought. For the 103rd through the 108th Congresses, instances in which cloture was sought are used as the basis of the filibuster estimate. One can argue that this produces an overestimate because in some cases cloture was sought for reasons other than a fear of extended debate (a test vote or to impose germaneness); however, one can also argue that it produces an underestimate because those cases in which cloture was not sought—perhaps because it was known to be out of reach—are not counted. For an estimate based on a different methodology, see table 6.3.

12. Gerald Gamm and Steven Smith, "Emergence of Senate Party Leadership," manuscript, 2003. Copy in possession of the author.

13. Patrick J. Sellers, "Winning Media Coverage in the U.S. Congress," in *U.S. Senate Exceptionalism,* ed. Bruce Oppenheimer (Columbus, Ohio: Ohio State University Press, 2002); Donald Baumer, "Senate Democratic Leadership in the 100th Congress," in *The Atomistic Congress,* ed. Ronald Peters and Allen Herzke (Armonk, N.Y.: M. E. Sharpe, 1992); Steven S. Smith, "Forces of Change in Senate Party Leadership and Organization," in *Congress Reconsidered,* ed. Lawrence C. Dodd and Bruce I. Oppenheimer, 5th ed. (Washington, D.C.: CQ Press, 1993); *Roll Call,* March 9, 1995.

14. *Roll Call,* January 8, 2001.

15. Quoted in *Washington Post,* November 15, 2004.

16. Dan Gilgoff, "The Dobson Way: An Evangelical Leader Steps Squarely into the Political Ring," *U.S. News and World Report,* January 17, 2005.

17. *New York Times,* November 15, 2004.

18. *Congressional Quarterly Weekly,* November 20, 2004, p. 2731.

19. Conference Rules, 108th Congress, Senate Republican Conference website, src.senate.gov, accessed spring 2004.

20. *Roll Call,* June 28, 2004.

21. *Congressional Quarterly Weekly,* November 20, 2004, p. 2733

22. Ibid., January 4, 2003, p. 17.

23. *Politics in America* 2004, p. 616.

24. *Congressional Quarterly Weekly*, May 15, 2004, p. 1130.
25. Ibid., p. 1131.
26. Ibid., June 5, 2004, pp. 13423–25.
27. Ibid., November 20, 2004, p. 2726.
28. Ibid., April 19, 2003, p. 944 ff.
29. Ibid., October 13, 2001, p. 2408; December 8, 2001, p. 2907.
30. Senate Rules and Administration Committee, hearings, June 2003.
31. Ibid.
32. *National Journal's CongressDaily*, Wednesday, July 2, 2003.
33. *Congressional Record*, August 2, 1996, S9465.
34. C. Lawrence Evans and Daniel Lipinski, "Obstruction and Leadership in the U.S. Senate," in *Congress Reconsidered*, ed. Lawrence C. Dodd and Bruce I. Oppenheimer, 8th ed. (Washington, D.C.: CQ Press, 2005).
35. *Congressional Record*, February 10, 2000, S582.
36. Senate Rules and Administration Committee, hearings, June 2003, Opening Statement.
37. *Congressional Record*, August 2, 1996, S9465.
38. Ibid., October 31, 2001, S11273-4.
39. Tom Daschle, *Like No Other Time* (New York: Crown Publishers, 2003), p. 208.
40. See, for example, *Congressional Digest*, May 7,2003.
41. *Roll Call*, June 15, 2004.
42. *Congressional Quarterly Weekly*, November 15, 2003, p. 2815.
43. *Roll Call*, February 7, 2005.
44. Holds and threats to filibuster as well as actual extended-debate-related delay on the floor were coded as filibuster problems. The definition of major legislation used here—those measures in lists of major legislation published in CQ *Almanacs* and the CQ *Weekly* plus those measures on which key votes occurred, again according to *Congressional Quarterly*—yields forty to sixty measures per Congress. Thus, although truly minor legislation is excluded, the listing is not restricted only to the most contentious and highly salient issues.
45. *Roll Call*, April 6, 2004.
46. *National Journal's CongressDaily PM*, June 24, 2004.
47. Sheldon Goldman, "The Senate and Judicial Nominations," *Extensions* (Journal of the Carl Albert Congressional Research and Studies Center), Spring 2004, pp. 8–9.
48. *Congressional Record*, March 6, 2003, S3216.
49. *Congressional Quarterly Weekly*, July 24, 2004, p. 1785.
50. Author's calculations; selected Congresses.
51. *Congressional Quarterly Weekly*, June 26, 2004, pp. 1568, 1575.
52. *Washington Post*, March 3, 2004.
53. *Roll Call*, July 5, 1999.
54. *Congressional Record*, July 7, 2004, p. S5838.
55. *Congressional Quarterly Weekly*, March 26, 2004, p. 741.
56. *Washington Post*, April 12, 2004.
57. Walter Oleszek, *Congressional Procedures and the Policy Process*, 6th ed. (Washington, D.C.: CQ Press, 2004), chapter 2.
58. *New York Times*, August 2, 2003.

59. *Congressional Quarterly Weekly*, April 28, 2000, p. 904.
60. *Roll Call*, May 3, 2004.
61. *Roll Call*, April 6, 2004.
62. *Congressional Quarterly Weekly*, May 8, 2004, p. 1080.
63. *Congressional Record*, May 19, 2004, S5838.
64. *Washington Post*, February 28, 2004.
65. *Roll Call*, May 23, 2005; *Washington Post*, May 24, 2005.

CHAPTER 7

1. The breaks also coincide with the prereform period; the period of adjustment to the reforms; and the period of growing party leadership strength, especially in the House. See Rohde, *Parties and Leaders;* Sinclair, *Legislators, Leaders*.
2. *Roll Call*, December 15, 2003.
3. *Roll Call*, December 15, 2003.
4. *Roll Call*, March 14, 2004.
5. See discussion in George C. Edwards III, *At the Margins: Presidential Leadership of Congress* (New Haven, Conn.: Yale University Press, 1989).
6. Gary Jacobson, "Partisan Polarization in Presidential Support: The Electoral Connection," *Congress and the Presidency* 30 (Spring 2003): 26–27.
7. CNN/*USA Today*/Gallup poll, cited in *Los Angeles Times*, July 14, 2003.
8. CBS/*New York Times* poll conducted July 11–15, 2004.
9. ABC poll conducted January 26–31, 2005.
10. *Congressional Quarterly Weekly*, December 16, 2000, p. 2853.
11. Ibid., January 20, 2001, p. 175.
12. See also See C. Cameron, *Veto Bargaining* (New York: Cambridge University Press, 2000).
13. *Congressional Quarterly Weekly*, January 20, 2001, pp. 175–77.
14. Relatively major means mentioned in CQ but including appropriations bills as well as major measures as defined earlier.
15. Samuel Kernell, *Going Public: New Strategies of Presidential Leadership*, 3rd ed. (Washington, D.C.: CQ Press, 1997), p. ix.
16. Quoted in Kernell, *Going Public*, p. 34.
17. George Edwards, "Riding High at the Polls: George W. Bush and Public Opinion," paper presented at the conference on "The Presidency, Congress and the War on Terrorism: Scholarly Perspectives," University of Florida, Gainesville, February 7, 2003, table 8.
18. This account based on Martha Joynt Kumar, "News Organizations as a Presidential Resource in Governing: Media Opportunities and White House Organization," in *New Challenges for the American Presidency*, ed. George Edwards and Philip John Davies (New York: Pearson Longman, 2004).
19. Kumar, "News Organizations," p. 78.
20. Ibid., pp. 65–66.
21. Data are from a table in the *Los Angeles Times*, April 29, 2001. The data are attributed to the White House.
22. George Edwards, "George W. Bush's Strategic Presidency," in Edwards and Davies, *New Challenges*, p. 25.
23. *Washington Post*, April 21, 2003.

24. Ibid.
25. *Los Angeles Times*, January 8, 2005.

CHAPTER 8

1. Sinclair, *Legislators, Leaders*.
2. See Sinclair, *Legislators, Leaders*, chapter 11, and Douglas Harris, "The Rise of the Public Speakership," *Political Science Quarterly* 113 (Summer 1998): 193–212.
3. Koopman, *Hostile Takeover*, pp. 142–47, and Stid, "Transformational Leadership in Congress?"
4. Quoted in Stid, "Transformational Leadership," p. 7.
5. *Roll Call*, May 19, 2003.
6. Ibid.s, June 6, 2004.
7. *Washington Times*, September 23, 2005
8. *Roll Call*, December 6, 2004.
9. Pelosi Press Release, February 16, 2005.
10. Senate Republican Conference website, src.senate.gov, accessed spring 2005.
11. George Edwards and Andrew Barrett, "Presidential Agenda Setting in Congress," in *Polarized Politics*, ed. Jon Bond and Richard Fleisher (Washington, D.C.: CQ Press, 2000).
12. Douglas Harris, "Media Leadership in the House of Representatives and Theories of Legislative Leadership," paper presented at the Midwest Political Science Association, Chicago, 1998, fig. 1.
13. John A. Farrell, *Tip O'Neill and the Democratic Century* (Boston: Little Brown, 2001), chapter 24.
14. Harris, "Media Leadership," fig. 3.
15. Ibid., figs. 1 and 2.
16. *Roll Call*, January 10, 2002.
17. *Congressional Quarterly Weekly*, August 30, 2003, p. 2066.
18. *Roll Call*, January 13, 2003.
19. Ibid., May 14, 2003.
20. Ibid., January 29, 2003.
21. *Washington Post*, February 12, 2004.
22. *New York Times*, March 3, 2003.
23. *Roll Call*, January 5, 2004.
24. Ibid., October 15, 2003.
25. Ibid., May 17, 2002.
26. Ibid., September 8, 2003.
27. Ibid., July 30, 2003.
28. Ibid., February 17, 2005.
29. Ibid., January 29, 2003.
30. House Republican Conference website, gop.gov, accessed spring 2003.
31. *Roll Call*, April 21, 2003.
32. Ibid., May 18, 2004.
33. *New York Times*, March 3, 2003.
34. Senate Democratic Policy Committee website, senate.gov/~dpc, accessed December 2004.
35. *Roll Call*, December 13, 2004.
36. Ibid., April 2, 2004.

37. Ibid.
38. Ibid., February 3, 2005.
39. *Washington Post*, January 31, 2005.
40. Senate Democratic Policy Committee website, senate.gov/~dpc.
41. *CQ Today*, April 20, 2004.
42. *National Journal*, July 17, 2004, pp. 2266–67.
43. Sellers, "Winning Media Coverage."
44. *National Journal*, July 3, 2004, p. 2099.
45. *Roll Call*, July 21, 2003.
46. Ibid., May 6, 2002.
47. Ibid., October 22, 2003.
48. Ibid., May 18, 2004.
49. *The Hill*, June 9, 2004.
50. Ibid.
51. *Roll Call*, January 27, 2005.
52. Senate Democrats Press Release, Democrats.Senate.gov, accessed spring 2005.
53. *Roll Call*, February 22, 2005.
54. *Washington Post*, February 17, 2005; *Roll Call*, February 22, 2005.
55. *Washington Post*, February 17, 2005.
56. *Roll Call*, April 5, 2004.
57. *Congressional Quarterly Weekly*, June 5, 2004, pp. 1347–48. MIRV stands for multiple independently targeted reentry vehicles and refers to nuclear bombs with multiple warheads.
58. Office of the Clerk of the House website, Clerk.House.gov, accessed December 2004.
59. *Congressional Quarterly Weekly*, June 14, 2003, p. 1450.
60. *CQ Today, July 23, 2003.*
61. *Roll Call*, May 22, 2003.
62. Blatz and Brownstein, *Storming the Gates*, p. 164–71
63. Ibid., p. 167.
64. *Roll Call*, November 5, 2003.
65. Ibid., May 13, 2003.
66. Ibid., November 18, 2002.
67. Ibid., December 13, 2004.
68. *Congressional Quarterly Weekly*, June 7, 2003, p. 1372.
69. *New York Times*, June 4, 2003.
70. Ibid., June 8, 2003.
71. *Roll Call*, June 12, 2003.
72. Ibid., June 22, 2004.
73. Ibid., June 24, 2004; *Congressional Quarterly Weekly*, June 26, 2004, pp. 1575–77.
74. *Congressional Quarterly Weekly*, June 26, 2004, pp. 1567, 1576.
75. Kernell, *Going Public*, 143–51.
76. Quoted in Kernell, *Going Public*, 151.
77. John B. Gilmour, *Reconcilable Differences?* (Berkeley: University of California Press, 1990); Sinclair, *Legislators, Leaders*.
78. *Houston Post*, June 29, 1990.
79. For more detail see Barbara Sinclair, "Governing Unheroicly (and Sometimes Unappetizingly): Bush and the 101st Congress," in *The Bush Presidency:*

First Appraisals, ed. Colin Campbell and Bert Rockman (Chatham, N.J.: Chatham House, 1991).

80. Haynes Johnson and David Broder, *The System* (Boston: Little, Brown, 1996), p. 234. For more detail, see Barbara Sinclair, "Trying to Govern Positively in a Negative Era: Clinton and the 103rd Congress," in *The Clinton Presidency: First Appraisals*, ed. Colin Campbell and Bert Rockman (Chatham, N.J.: Chatham House, 1996).

81. Sinclair, "Transformational Leader or Faithful Agent?"

82. *New York Times*, July 22, 2003.

83. Ibid.

84. *Roll Call*, November 12, 2003.

85. *Congressional Quarterly Weekly*, November 15, 2003, pp. 2817–21.

86. *New York Times*, March 27, 2004.

87. Ibid.

88. Ibid.

89. *Roll Call*, March 29, 2004.

90. Ibid., July 9, 2003.

91. *New York Times*, July 12, 2003.

92. DCCC E-Mail Newsletter, July 14, 2003.

93. *New York Times*, July 12, 2003.

94. *Roll Call*, July 8, 2003.

95. *New York Times*, December 9, 2003.

96. *Washington Times*, December 9, 2003.

97. *New York Times*, December 9, 2003.

98. *Washington Post*, December 8, 2003.

99. *Roll Call*, February 10, 2004.

100. *Los Angeles Times*, February 14, 2004.

101. *Roll Call*, February 26, 2004.

102. *New York Times*, March 11, 2004.

103. *New York Times*, March 17, 2004.

104. *Roll Call*, May 3, 2004.

105. Ibid.

106. See Edwards, "Riding High."

CHAPTER 9

1. Gary Jacobson, *The Politics of Congressional Elections*, 6th ed. (New York: Pearson Longman, 2004), pp. 59–79; Richard Skinner, "Interest Groups and the Party Networks: Views from Inside the Beltway," paper presented at the annual meeting of the Southern Political Science Association, New Orleans, Louisiana, January 8–11, 2003.

2. *Roll Call*, March 5, 2003.

3. Quoted in *Roll Call*, March 5, 2003.

4. Ibid., December 2, 2002.

5. Ibid., February 11, 2004.

6. Ibid., July 21, 2004.

7. Ibid., March 8, 2004.

8. Ibid.

9. See Raymond Bauer, Ithiel de Sola Pool, Lewis Anthony Dexter, *American Business and Public Policy* (New York: Atherton, 1963); John Wright, *Interest Groups and Congress* (New York: Longman, 2003); Sinclair, *Majority Leadership*.

10. Blatz and Brownstein, *Storming the Gates*, p. 318.

11. Kelly Patterson, "Political Firepower: The National Rifle Association," in *After the Revolution: PACs, Lobbies, and the Republican Congress*, ed. Robert Biersack, Paul Herrnson, and Clyde Wilcox (Boston: Allyn and Bacon, 1999).

12. Ronald Shaiko and Marc Wallace, "From Wall St. to Main St.: The NFIB and the New Republican Majority," in Biersack et al., *After the Revolution*, p. 25.

13. Both quotes are from *Washington Post*, May 16, 2002.

14. The NRA was not part of the Thursday Group. For members, see Shaiko and Wallace, "From Wall St. to Main St.," p. 35.

15. Ibid.

16. Citizens for a Sound Economy website, cse.org, accessed spring 2005.

17. *Congressional Quarterly Weekly*, January 28, 1995, pp. 261–62; Blatz and Brownstein, *Storming the Gates*, pp. 198–99.

18. Republicans do seem to have given affected interest groups a considerably greater role in drafting legislation than the Democrats ever did. See Elizabeth Drew, *Showdown: The Struggle between the Gingrich Congress and the Clinton White House* (New York: Simon and Schuster, 1996), pp. 116–17.

19. *Roll Call*, January 21, 2004.

20. Ibid., June 9, 2004.

21. Ibid., February 13, 2003.

22. Ibid., March 10, 2003.

23. *Congressional Quarterly Weekly*, March 10, 2001, p. 503.

24. Ibid., March 3, 2001, p. 474.

25. *Christian Science Monitor*, March 6, 2001; *Washington Post*, March 11, 2001.

26. *Roll Call*, March 10, 2003.

27. Ibid., May 7, 2003.

28. Ibid., March 10, 2003.

29. Ibid., March 13, 2003.

30. *Washington Post*, April 21, 2003.

31. *Los Angeles Times*, January 6, 2005.

32. *Washington Post*, February 13, 2005; website of the Alliance for Worker Retirement Security, www.retiresecure.org, accessed spring 2005.

33. Annenberg Public Policy Center press release, June 19, 2003.

34. *New York Times*, September 5, 2003.

35. *Washington Post*, February 13, 2005.

36. Ibid., February 5, 2005.

37. Mark Peterson, "Bush and Interest Groups: A Government of Chums," in *The George W. Bush Presidency: Appraisals and Prospects*, ed. Colin Campbell and Bert Rockman (Washington, D.C.: CQ Press, 2004).

38. *New York Times*, September 1, 2003.

39. Kelly Patterson and Matthew Singer, "The National Rifle Association in the Face of the Clinton Challenge," in *Interest Group Politics*, ed. Allan Cigler and Burdett Loomis, 6th ed. (Washington, D.C.: CQ Press, 2002) pp. 68–69.

40. Skinner, "Interest Groups," p. 12.

41. Jacobson, *Politics of Congressional Elections*, p. 72; also see 63–67.
42. Ibid., p. 72.
43. Skinner, "Interest Groups," p. 10.
44. *Roll Call*, February 2, 2004.
45. Skinner, "Interest Groups," p. 12.
46. *Roll Call*, July 28, 2003.
47. *New York Times*, September 5, 2003.
48. Quoted from *New York Times*, September 5, 2003.
49. National Association of Manufacturers website, www.nam.org, accessed spring 2005.
50. *Los Angeles Times*, October 29, 2004.
51. Andrew Rich and R. Kent Weaver, "Think Tanks in the U.S. Media," *Press/Politics* 5, no. 4 (2000): 82.
52. Compiled from Diane Stone, *Capturing the Political Imagination* (London: Frank Cass 1996), pp. xiii–xviii. Remarkably few in any period went out of existence; one in each of the four periods.
53. Donald E. Abelson, *Do Think Tanks Matter?* (Montreal: McGill–Queen's University Press, 2002), pp. 22–23.
54. Weaver, quoted in Abelson, *Do Think Tanks Matter?* p. 10.
55. Stone, *Capturing the Political Imagination*, p. 23.
56. See Mark A. Smith, "Advocacy Groups, Think Tanks and the Economic Programs of Liberals and Conservatives," paper presented at the Midwest Political Science Association meetings, Chicago, 2004.
57. Jeff Krehely, Meaghan House, and Emily Kernan, *Axis of Ideology: Conservative Foundations and Public Policy* (Washington, D.C.: National Committee for Responsive Philanthropy, March 2004).
58. Ibid., appendix A, p. 44.
59. Ibid., table 7, p. 35.
60. Ibid., p. 16.
61. Ibid., executive summary, p. 1.
62. See heritage.org website, accessed September 17, 2004 for staff; also see Heritage Foundation Annual Report, 2003, available on the website.
63. Quoted in James Allen Smith, *The Idea Brokers* (New York: Free Press, 1991), pp. 205–206.
64. Quoted in Alterman, *What Liberal Media?* p. 83.
65. Quoted in Abelson, *Do Think Tanks Matter?* p. 40.
66. Ibid.
67. Heritage Foundation Annual Report, 2003, p. 24.
68. Alterman, *What Liberal Media?* p. 83.
69. Annual Report, p. 24.
70. Ibid.
71. Ibid.
72. Krehely et al., *Axis of Ideology*, appendix B.
73. From the website cnponline.org, accessed spring 2005.
74. Rich and Weaver, "Think Tanks." See also Rich, *Think Tanks, Public Policy*.
75. Cited in Abelson, *Do Think Tanks Matter?* p. 89.
76. Tim Groseclose and Jeff Milyo, "A Measure of Media Bias," manuscript, September 2003. Copy in possession of the author. The authors start with the two

hundred organizations listed on the website www.wheretodoresearch.com, which they consider a list "of the most prominent think tanks in the U.S." (p. 5); some of these are not what most scholars would identify as think tanks—Amnesty International and the AARP, for example. In counting advocacy organizations, I did count Amnesty International as an advocacy organization but not AARP or Common Cause, because the ideological thrust of the latter two is not as clearly defined. See tables 1 and 4.

77. Tax law requires that all these think tanks remain nominally nonpartisan. The 2003 annual report of the Heritage Foundation is one indicator that this is, in fact, only nominal in the case of Heritage. President Bush and Vice President Cheney chose Heritage as the site of major speeches in 2003; pictures of them and of Attorney General John Ashcroft are prominently featured in the report.

78. *The Hill*, June 1, 2003.

79. Ibid., June 4, 2003; NPR October 13, 2003.

80. Center for American Progress website, www.americanprogress.org, accessed spring 2005.

81. Council for Excellence in Government, Center for Media and Public Affairs, "Government: In and Out of the News," July 2003, www.excelgov.org, accessed sping 2004.

82. Project for Excellence in Journalism, "The State of the News Media 2004," An Annual Report on American Journalism, journalism.org, accessed spring 2005.

83. Pew Research Center for the People and the Press, "News Audiences Increasingly Polarized," press release on Pew Research Center Biennial News Consumption Survey, June 8, 2004.

84. Multiple replies were possible; 42 percent said newspapers. "State of the News Media," citing Pew.

85. "State of the News Media."

86. "State of the News Media," citing Pew data.

87. Pew press release.

88. "State of the News Media."

89. Eric Alterman, *What Liberal Media?* chapter 5.

90. Brock, *Republican Noise Machine*, p. 273.

91. Ibid., Brock quoting *Mediaweek*, a magazine that provides news and analysis of the media industry.

92. See Alterman, *What Liberal Media?* and Brock, *Republican Noise Machine*.

93. "State of the News Media."

94. Brock, *Republican Noise Machine*, p. 313.

95. Quoted in Brock, *Republican Noise Machine*, p. 317.

96. Quoted in Brock, *Republican Noise Machine*, pp. 324–25.

97. Brock, *Republican Noise Machine*, p. 324.

98. "State of the News Media."

99. Kaiser Family Foundation survey referenced in Brock, *Republican Noise Machine*, pp. 284–85.

100. Program on International Policy Attitudes, e-mail news release, October 3, 2003.

101. The Drudge Report is a well-known blog that sometimes carries unsubstantiated rumor with a right-wing slant.

102. "A 527 is a non-profit organization formed under Section 527 of the Internal Revenue Code, which grants tax-exempt status to political Committees. . . . [IRS rulings allow] these groups to gain political committee status under tax law, while avoiding regulation under federal election law." Thus they can raise and expend soft (that is, unregulated) money. "On the federal level, 527s cannot coordinate with or contribute to a federal candidate in any way. They also may not expressly advocate for the election or defeat of a specific federal candidate, although 527s are quite free to portray federal candidates in such a way that there is little doubt as to the message." publicintegrity.org, accessed July 11, 2005.

103. National Annenberg Election Study Survey, press release, August 20, 2004 (survey conducted August 9–16).

104. *Washington Post*, August 24, 2004.

105. *Los Angeles Times*, August 24, 2004.

106. Annenberg press release.

107. Michael Tomasky, "Whispers and Screams: The Partisan Nature of Editorial Pages," Research paper R25, Joan Shorenstein Center on Press, Politics and Public Policy, July 2003.

108. Tomasky, "Whispers and Screams," p. 54.

109. Quoted in Alterman, *What Liberal Media?* p. 29.

110. FAIR, "How Public Is Public Radio?" June 2004.

111. All from PEW study, released June 8, 2004.

112. *New York Times*, September 2, 2004.

113. All from PEW study, released June 8, 2004.

114. *Washington Post* profile, April 26, 2004.

115. Comments at University of Southern California Conference, "The 2004 Election: What Does It Mean for Campaigns and Governance?" October 8, 2004.

CHAPTER 10

1. APSA Committee on Political Parties, "Towards a More Responsible Two-Party System: A Report of the Committee on Political Parties," *American Political Science Review* 44 (September 1950): v.

2. Ibid., p. 1.

3. Wattenberg, *Where Have All The Voters Gone?*

4. Gary Jacobson, *Politics of Congressional Elections*, chapter 3.

5. David B. Magleby and J. Quin Monson, *The Last Hurrah? Soft Money and Issue Advocacy in the 2002 Congressional Elections* (Provo, Utah: Brigham Young University, Center for the Study of Elections and Democracy, 2003).

6. See case studies in Magleby and Monson, *Last Hurrah?*

7. *New York Times*, September 1, 2003; see also *Los Angeles Times*, August 22, 2004.

8. Magleby and Monson, *Last Hurrah?* pp. 22–25.

9. BusinessWeek online, March 22, 2004, www.businessweek.com.

10. *Washington Post*, July 1, 2004; *New York Times*, July 2, 2004.

11. Push polls are "polls" intended not to gather information but to change peoples' votes, often by spreading untruthful information about one of the candidates.

12. Scott Lilly, "When Congress Acts in the Dark of Night, Everyone Loses," *Roll Call*, December 6, 2004.

13. *Congressional Quarterly Weekly*, November 20, 2004, pp. 2724–28.

14. House Rules Committee Minority Office, "Broken Promises: The Death of Deliberative Democracy," released by Democratic Leader Nancy Pelosi and Rules Ranking Minority Member Louise Slaughter, March 8, 2005, accessed at www.democraticleader.house.gov/press.

15. This is still higher than the average for the 100th through 105th Congresses. Almost certainly this is because he controlled the House. Also only one Congress (101st) that was the initial one of a newly elected president (the first Bush, in that case) is included in the span from the 100th through 105th.

16. Kenneth Shepsle, *The Giant Jigsaw Puzzle: Democratic Committee Assignments in the Modern House* (Chicago: University of Chicago Press, 1978); Richard Hall, *Participation in Congress* (New Haven: Yale University Press, 1996).

17. A number of people have made this suggestion, including Smith and Binder and Norman Ornstein. See, for example, Binder and Smith, *Politics or Principle?*

18. Wattenberg, *Where Have All the Voters Gone?* chapter 3.

19. Ibid., chapter 4.

20. Ibid., pp. 65, 89.

21. See Fiorina et al., *Culture War?*

22. Donald P. Green and Alan Gerber, "The Effects of Personal Canvassing, Telephone Calls, and Direct Mail on Voter Turnout: A Field Experiment," *American Political Science Review* 94 (September 2000): 653–64.

23. Committee for the Study of the American Electorate, press release, January 14, 2005.

INDEX